REDISCOVERING GANDHI

VOLUME I : Hind Swaraj: Gandhi's Challenge to Modern Civilization

Rediscovering Gandhi Series

General Editors: ***Prof. R.P. Misra***

Vol. I: Hind Swaraj: Gandhi's Challenge to Modern Civilization

—R.P. Misra

Forthcoming

Ahimsa: The Way to Peace

—Jonathan K. Crane, Jordi August Panareda

Truth is God: Gandhi's Search for Religion of Religions

—Jai Narain Sharma

Law of Love: Gandhi's Concept of State and Power

—Ashu Pasricha

Satyagraha: Gandhian Approach to Conflict Resolution

—Ashu Pasricha

About the Author

Prof. R.P. Misra, a former Vice-Chancellor of the University of Allahabad and Chief Technical Advisor of the United Nations, is a well-known development planner and Gandhian scholar. He founded the Institute of Development Studies, University of Mysore in 1971 and remained its director until 1979. He was the vice-director of the UN Centre for Regional Development, Japan (1979-84). Most recently (2002-04), he was Mahatma Gandhi National Fellow of Gandhi Smriti & Darshan Samiti, New Delhi. He began his academic life as a social geographer; then he moved to the field of Development Planning and finally arrived at Gandhian Studies. Editor of *Anasakti Darshan,* an international journal of non-violence-in-action. He has authored and edited over fifty seminal books.

Gandhian Studies and Peace Research Series-29

REDISCOVERING GANDHI

General Editor
Prof. R.P. Misra

Volume I

HIND SWARAJ

Gandhi's Challenge to Modern Civilization

Prof. R.P. Misra

in Colaboration with

GANDHI SMRITI & DARSHAN SAMITI, NEW DELHI

Published by

CONCEPT PUBLISHING COMPANY, NEW DELHI

ISBN : 978-81-8069-374-8 (Series)
ISBN : 978-81-8069-375-5 (Vol. I)

First Published 2007
Reprinted 2016

Published and Printed by

Concept
Since 1974

Concept Publishing Company Pvt. Ltd.
A/15-16, Commercial Block, Mohan Garden
New Delhi-110059 (India)
T: 25351460, 25351794, *F*: 091-11-25357109
E: publishing@conceptpub.com, W: www.conceptpub.com
Editorial Office: H-13, Bali Nagar, New Delhi-110 015, India.

Cataloging in Publication Data--Courtesy: D.K. Agencies (P) Ltd. <docinfo@dkagencies.com>

Misra, R.P.
Hind swaraj : Gandhi's challenge to modern civilization/ R.P. Misra.
p. cm. — (Gandhian studies and peace research series ; 29
(Rediscovering Gandhi ; v. 1)
Includes bibliographical references (p.)
Includes index.
ISBN : 9788180693748 (Series)
ISBN : 9788180693755 (Vol. 1)

1. Gandhi, Mahatma, 1869-1948. Hinda Svaraja. 2. India—Politics and government—1919-1947. 3. Nationalism—India. I. Title. II. Series: Gandhian studies and peace research series ; 29. III. Series: Rediscovering Gandhi ; v. 1.

DDC 320.954 22

Preface

Hind Swaraj is the first and the most fundamental book written by Gandhi. It has been the subject matter of several seminars, symposia, articles, Ph.D. theses and books. It has been hailed as Magna-Carta of a new world order as also the work of a cranky who wants to take the world back to the stone-age. However, it is a book, which cannot be ignored in any discussion and debate on human progress and socio-economic development. It goes deep into the question of human destiny and draws a road map to reach.

Hind Swaraj was written when Gandhi was in South Africa fighting the British administration to secure legitimate human rights of the indentured labourers. Back home in India, there was stirring, even if subdued, to secure self-government within the British Empire. But Gandhi's vision was different and higher and his goals far beyond political freedom. For him real freedom was 'Swaraj', rule over one's senses and real progress was spiritual, not material. Once a person gained 'Swaraj', nothing could chain him, no power on earth could defeat him. All other freedoms – political, economic, social and cultural – were subsumed in Swaraj and could be easily attained once one moved on the road to Swaraj.

Gandhi outlined the method of gaining Swaraj and thereby the political and economic independence from Britain. How and why India became a colony of Britain and how it could become free again by aspiring to achieve Swaraj and working for it, is what this little book with great ideas is all about.

As the new economic policy of globalization moves on to make the world a global village, new challenges and problems have emerged before humanity. The belief that all emergent problems – ecological, social, economic, political and moral – could be resolved by scientific discoveries and technological innovations persists, failures in the past notwithstanding. What is happening today is in line with what Gandhi almost predicted in Hind Swaraj as he prepared its manuscript in 1908. There is, therefore, a need to have yet another look at it and to see what guidelines it can offer to us. ICGSR Series on Rediscovering Gandhi is a modest attempt in this direction.

'Hind Swaraj—Gandhi's Challenge to Modern Civilisation' is the first volume of the series. It looks at Hind Swaraj in the backdrop of the emerging problems of violence, moral decay, poverty, social disintegration and environmental degradation and shows the direction in which humanity must move now to save itself from impending catastrophe. Apart from introductory chapter, it has sixteen other chapters grouped into five parts.

Chapter 1: 'Introduction' gives the aims, objectives and organization of the book. Part I has three chapters (2 to 4), which gives the essence of Hind Swaraj and place it in a class of books that are seminal in character and have lasting implications for humanity in general and India in particular.

Part II discusses factors and forces, which influenced Gandhi and prompted him to write the book almost non-stop aboard a ship while returning from London to South Africa in 1908. It has six chapters (5 to 10). Gandhi's own experiences, especially during the first forty years of his life, are discussed in Chapter 5. It covers the period from early childhood to his education in England and the struggles he had to go through in South Africa. Chapter 6 looks at Gandhi's view of history written by Western historians and the way it was distorted to give an impression that only wars and conflicts shaped human destiny; and that the West was progressive and a paragon of virtues while the rest of the world was retrogressive and primitive. Indian Renaissance of the nineteenth century produced a number of men and women of eminence practically in all walks of life. Some of them struggled hard in their own ways to free India from the yoke of British imperialism. Then, there were several writers and poets who left an indelible imprint on Gandhi's life and thinking. Hind Swaraj owes much to these personages. The immediate provocation for writing the book came from his interaction with the London based young revolutionaries. The life and works of some of these persons form Chapters 7 and 8. Chapter 9 highlights Gandhi's exposure to Western thought, and Chapter 10 looks at his understanding of science and technology and its impact on his thinking.

Part III has five chapters (11 to 15). Chapter 11 looks at the comments on Hind Swaraj made before First World War and, the next chapter reviews comments published after First World War. The *Aryan Path Symposium* in 1938 and books and journals devoted to Hind Swaraj published and written during the last fifty years are also included in this review. Chapters 13 and 14 are devoted to the review of books published after the Second World War, which at least partially support the views expressed by Gandhi in Hind Swaraj. The review of these books proves that what Gandhi said in the early part of the twentieth century, has become a post-modern theme of scientific analysis. Among the books reviewed and discussed are: *The Ages of Gaia* by James Lovelock; *The Turning Point* by Fritjof Capra; *Entropy: A New Worldview* by Jeremy Refkin; *Human Destiny* by Le Compte du Nouy, *Clash of Civilisations* by S.P. Huntington; *The Third Wave* by Elwin and Heidi Toffler; *De-schooling Society* by Evan Ellich and *Mega Trends* by John Naisbitt. Chapter 15 is devoted to a quick review of the Message of Hind Swaraj.

Part IV discusses the agenda for action to realise the goals of Hind Swaraj. It has two chapters (16 and 17). It suggests action at both international and national levels to shift from modern to Truly-modern (as Gandhi would have liked to say) cultural transformation. The global agenda for action is discussed in Chapter 16 and the national, including local, agenda in Chapter 17. The role of India as a catalytic agent and the rationale for India going to its roots, instead of blindly following the West also forms part of this Chapter.

It would be useful to say a few words about the history of this series of books. The idea that there was a need for a series on *Rediscovering Gandhi* with original contributions was conceived and planned when I was associated with Gandhi Bhawan, Delhi University, as its director and later as chairman (1990-1997). It could, however, take a concrete shape only in 2001 when I joined the International Centre for Gandhian Studies and Research, Gandhi Smriti and Darshan Samiti, Rajghat, New Delhi as Mahatma Gandhi National Fellow. I discussed the matter with a number of Gandhian scholars. They liked the idea and agreed to write thematic volumes within a period of 1-3 years. A meeting of the potential authors was held in 2001 to finalize the project. This is how the series on "Rediscovering Gandhi" came into being. This is the first and inaugural volume of the series.

I am grateful to the International Centre for Gandhian Studies and Research (ICGSR), Gandhi Smriti & Darshan Samiti for offering the necessary facilities and conducive environment to edit the series.

I would like to put on record our profound thanks to Dr. Savita Singh, Director of the GS & DS for giving all the support needed in this venture. Discussions with Professor K.D. Gangrade, Dr. Y.P. Anand and authors of other volumes of the series sharpened my own thoughts on Hind Swaraj.

While planning the project I benefited from the discussions with a number of colleagues. Prof. N. Radhakrishnan, former Director, Gandhi Smriti & Darshan Samiti and several others made very valuable suggestions. Among the associates who helped in the project are Dr. (Mrs.) Sita Ojha, Dr. Anil Dutta Mishra and Dr. Suresh Misra.

I appreciate Shri Ashok Kumar Mittal, Concept Publishing Company for taking up the publication of the series. Leaving aside Gandhian Organisations like Navjivan Trust, Concept Publishing Company is now a forerunner in the publication of books on Gandhi and his thoughts.

October 2, 2005 **R.P. Misra**

Contents

Preface v

Editorial xi

1. Introduction 1

PART I: ESSENCE OF HIND SWARAJ

2. Western Civilization is Not Modern 27
3. Gandhi's Outline of a Truly Modern Civilization 56
4. Development Means Spiritual Progress 84

PART II: BUILDING BLOCKS OF HIND SWARAJ

5. Gandhi's Own Experiences and Experiments 101
6. Gandhi's Interpretation of Indian History 122
7. Contemporary Political Thinkers and Activists 152
8. Contemporary Social Reforms and Intellectuals 169
9. Gandhi's Exposure to Western Thought 189
10. Gandhi's Valuation of Modern Science and Technology 211

PART III: RELEVANCE OF HIND SWARAJ

11. Pre-Independence Assessment 237
12. Post-Independence Assessment 257
13. Hind Swaraj in the Light of Recent Scientific Studies 271
14. Hind Swaraj in the Light of Recent Future Studies 288
15. The Message of Hind Swaraj 315

PART IV: REALIZING HIND SWARAJ

16. Global Agenda for Action 343

17. National Agenda for Action 354

Appendix A: Notable Events in Gandhi's Life During 1869-1914 384

Appendix B: Glossary of Terms Used in *Hind Swaraj* 407

Index 422

Editorial

'Rediscovering Gandhi' constitutes a series of books, which look at the relevance of Mahatma Gandhi in the new millennium. Two concurrent and contrasting tendencies have emerged in recent times. With the globalization process penetrating every department of life, Gandhi has become a global icon. The Gandhian wave, like the Yoga wave, is spreading fast cutting across political, religious, cultural, social and economic boundaries. In a world torn by conflicts, Gandhian way appears to be the only way for human survival and development.

Then there is an opposite trend too. Gandhi is being ridiculed as a moral philosopher who advocates localism in a world that is globalizing fast and exploring the other planets of the outer space. He is being torn into pieces and seen not as one integrated whole which he was but in pieces as a politician, economist, religious leader and so on. He is being painted in different colours to suit the tastes, needs and requirements of the painters and thereby bringing him down to our way of doing things and perceiving problems. This type of analysis finds Gandhi a poor specimen of a politician, economist, sociologist or religious leader. The very fact that a fanatic Hindu assassinated him indicates that many Hindus do not consider him a good Hindu. He was not accepted by other religionists – Islamic and Christian – either. It's quite another thing that he considered all religions noble even if not final and that he tried to bring them together on a common platform. Some of his closest friends and associates were Muslims and Christians; he called himself a *sanatani* Hindu.

Gandhi was not a good economist or politician either for his point of departure in both thought and action was different from that of the modern academic disciplines. To him science and scientific disciplines could not be value neutral. Only that which put man on a higher pedestal of consciousness and made him a better human being was good and therefore all human pursuits – intellectual, material and social – must not digress from the path of morality.

Gandhi was not a specialist who saw the reality from only one perspective. He was a practical philosopher who transcended all disciplinary limitations and barriers. Gandhi considered the roots of the problems we face today in the twists and turns of our evolutionary journey. We emerged from the animal existence to become Homo sapiens not very long ago, just a few million years back. We are in the transitional stage and tend to oscillate between our animal origin, that we have not yet forgotten, and the enlightened future of intellectual and spiritual awakening that flickers unsustainably. Our history of the last five millennia is witness to these oscillations. There were men and women among us who scaled great spiritual heights and set the course of human evolution in right direction. And then there was a relapses caused by the inherent tendencies to return to the animal in man. The evolutionary journey of man is marked with fits and starts; it has not been continuous to be self-sustaining.

At this stage, it would be pertinent to emphasize that all that is associated with animals is not un-human. The love that animals bestow on their offspring till they stand on their own feet and become self-reliant is worthy of emulation by humans too. Animals do not kill other animals except to satisfy their hunger. Man is equipped with huge brain to think, remember and recall millions of bits of information and convert them into knowledge and through practice into wisdom. He must therefore be far above the animal, which works by instinct rather than by logic and feeling. But in the real world of today what many humans do would put even the animals to shame.

I received an electronic mail from one of my sons, which tells so vividly the paradox humanity faces today. I reproduce it hoping that its father, whosoever he is, would forgive me for doing so without his formal permission.

THE PARADOX

The paradox of our time in history is that we
have taller buildings, but shorter tempers;
wider freeways, but narrower viewpoints;
we spend more, but save less;
we buy more, but enjoy it less.

We have bigger houses and smaller families;
more conveniences, but less time;
we have more degrees, but less sense;

more knowledge, but less judgment;
more experts, but more problems;
more medicine, but less wellness.

We have multiplied our possessions, but reduced our values,
we talk too much, love too seldom, and hate too often.
We've learned how to make a living, but not a life;
We've added years to life, not life to years.
We've been all the way to the moon and back,
but have trouble crossing the street to meet the new neighbor.

We've conquered outer space, but not inner space;
We've cleaned up the air, but polluted the soul;
We've split the atom, but not our prejudice;
We have higher incomes, but lower morals;
We've become long on quantity, but short on quality.

These are the times of tall men, and short character;
steep profits, and shallow relationships.
These are the times of world peace, but domestic warfare;
more leisure, but less fun;
more kinds of food, but less nutrition.

These are days of two incomes, but more divorce;
of fancier houses, but broken homes.
It is a time when there is much in the show window
and nothing in the stockroom;
a time when technology can bring this letter to you, and a time
when you can choose either to make a difference, or to just hit
delete.

I hope I have been able to convey the message I wanted to. It is this paradox that made Gandhi change his course of life and living and thereby to change the course of human history, and thus the human evolution too. A number of men and women like Gandhi emerged on the scene to show the path of real progress, not material but spiritual. Gandhi was such a one in the twentieth century. He brought himself down to the level of a commoner and showed a unique path of self-realization – a path that brought spirituality down to the real life situation: to the world of action. He tried to make each individual a pathfinder – his own teacher. He saw the solution of human problems not in terms of Marxist analysis of thesis, antithesis and synthesis but in terms of synthesis and from synthesis to synergy and symbiosis. Thesis and antithesis in his way of thinking and doing things merged into a common whole through love (nonviolence). Symbiosis is born out of Love for all that exists, especially the things living. It is through Love that one can reach the Truth i.e. God. Thus pursuing the path of Love, humans can move forward on the path of self-realization and become super-conscious human being.

He crossed all boundaries of space, time, academic disciplines, religions and cultures to represent humanity in the truest sense. That is why he is one of the most written on and read leaders of the world. There is no aspect of life on which Gandhi did not write, speak and act upon. For him, reaching the Truth was the ultimate goal of human life and one cannot reach the Truth without service and sacrifice. It is amazing how this frail man busy for practically the whole of his life in freeing India from the shackles of colonial rule, remained steadfast on the path of Truth. Rationality, for him, was the foundation for Truth and it must inform all departments of life. Things that fail to pass the test of logic must be discarded. This applies to even religious writings and edicts. But his concept of rationality was not the same as that of science; it was soaked in spirituality. His rationality was soaked in Love; he did not see it within the framework of self-interest, and self-aggrandizement, which takes man closer to the animal in him. Rationality that hurts others is not true rationality. True rationality would always lead to Truth and Nonviolence, said Gandhi.

Hundred volumes of the *Collected Works of Gandhi* published by the Publications Division of the Government of India testify his wide-ranging interests and steadfast adherence to Truth and Nonviolence. There are other series of books such as the one by D.G. Tendulkar (*Mahatma: Life of Mohandas Karamchand Gandhi*) and hundreds of books published by Navjiwan Trust, Ahmedabad, which bring out his multifaceted life, mission and vision and continued relevance. Each year scores of books come out on him or his philosophy. He has remained a perennial subject matter of study because the aspects of human life he probed and the social, economic, ecological, and political problems he tried to solve continue to plague humanity and are likely to plague it for centuries or even millenniums to come. He was a traveller whose destination was known but not within reach in his lifetime or for that matter in the lifetime of any individual. Each milestone one covers takes man closer to the destination but not to the destination. And the destination is self-realization. He is one of the most quoted pathfinders for the perplexed world in search of peace and harmony.

If proper justice is to be done to Gandhian philosophy, it must be considered in its entirety and in its proper setting of Indian conditions of the time and the problems he encountered. Time and place specific responses must be set aside to uncover the fountain of practical wisdom that the Mahatma was. The relations of the parts with whole scheme of his thoughts must be unearthed. His political thoughts, for example, cannot be separated from his economic, social, religious or ecological thoughts without doing injustice to him. If there are gaps in his system of thinking, it is because the situation in which he worked demanded doing too many things at the same time.

Why Yet Another Series?

'Rediscovering Gandhi' is a modest attempt to unravel the man who swam against the current and made a difference to the world he lived and the world in which we live. He treaded a path of sanity (truth and nonviolence) and tried all through his life to lay down the principles and practices, which would ensure the survival of humanity and take it to its ultimate goal of super-consciousness. Each volume looks at one aspect of Gandhi's life and thoughts in the context of the twenty first century. This makes the task of respective authors very challenging. Our disciplinary training and specialization come in the way of proper understanding of Gandhi, his philosophy, and life. Secondly, Gandhi was highly dynamic. Being an experimenter with Truth, he changed his views and strategies in response to his new findings and changing situations. To take what was written or done by him during the first half of the twentieth century as a guiding principle in the twenty first century may not, therefore, Gandhian in approach. One has to explore deeply his personality and philosophy to separate temporal from eternal and principles from strategies to find solutions for the myriad problems we face today.

It is easy to be wise once the event is over; very few are wise enough to foresee the consequences in advance. Gandhi belonged to the latter category. He laid certain principles, which were derived from the experiments he carried out and endorsed the postulation that:

'Politics without Principles
Pleasure without Conscience,
Wealth without Work,
Knowledge without Character,
Business without Morality,
Science without Humanity and
Worship without Sacrifice.'

would ruin humanity, for it prompts man to transgress the Cosmic Law, is as true today as it was in his time. Principles derived from basic human values would remain principles. They cannot be violated. But how the principled were to be acted upon and what strategies, policies and progrmmes were to be adopted to put the principles into practice would vary with time and place. Had Gandhi been alive today, what would have done to root out corruption that pervades all walks of life in India? What strategies would he have adopted to curb violence, especially terrorism which has acquired global dimensions? What would he have done to put Indian democracy on the rails again? What would he have done to save the environment? Would he have changed the definition of Swadeshi in the context of the globalization process? These and many others are the questions that must be answered even if tentatively to understand the Mahatma.

The reader may legitimately ask: would a new series of books find a final answer to the question: Is Gandhi relevant today? No, it would not. Each generation has to interpret Gandhi in its own contexts for the problems humanity faces change through time even if the roots thereof are the same and find appropriate strategies, policies and programmes to solve them. In the present context of globalization, there is a need to look at Gandhian thought afresh to find solutions to the problems we face today.

Those conversant with Gandhi's life and philosophy know that his personality was a complex one even though it was so simple and straightforward. There was logic in what he said and did yet he was beyond logic for logic too has its limitations. He was scientific in approach but was above science. He fell back on the call of his inner voice whenever his scientific approach failed to provide him answers to the problems he encountered. For him logic was only the first step in the understanding of the reality. Beyond the logic derived as it is from the experiences gained by senses, there is a vast vista, which can take man from visible reality to the one that is felt and perceived but not sensed.

To depend on the felt reality or truth one has to be a traveller on the road to self-realization. Gandhi was indeed such a traveller. He titled his autobiography as '*My Experiments with Truth*'. He was not infallible and suffered from all the weaknesses normal human being suffered from. But he developed capabilities to rise above them all. No wonder then, many a thinker in recent years have pointed to apparent weaknesses and inconsistencies in him that led to serious implications for freedom movement as well as the ethical principles he advocated. Gandhi continues to be enigmatic for all those who fail to see consistency in his words and actions and who believe that science, as it is conceived today, has answers to all the ills humanity faces today. Einstein, the greatest scientist of the twentieth century had rightly exclaimed that generations to come would not believe that such a one treaded on this earth in flesh and blood.

As stated earlier, Gandhian philosophy is not a product of intellectual exercise alone. It is borne out of Gandhi's deep understanding of cultural traditions of both east and west, especially the Indian civilization, and equally deep understanding of the social, political, and economic realities of his time. Above all, it is a product of his thinking on the innate nature and ultimate future of man – a future, which is hidden in the debris of sensual urges and desires rooted in the unpleasant memories of the past and the fear of the unknown future. Gandhi is often referred to as a practical visionary, for what he thought, said, and did was the product of his deep contemplation on the purpose of the purpose of human life on the one hand and the real life situations with which he had to content with on the other.

Gandhi was convinced that man's evolutionary journey did not stop when some animal was transformed into a new species of Homo sapiens. Then one began his spiritual journey from sub-consciousness to super-consciousness. Gandhi's genius lay in linking man's forward movement on the road to his ultimate destiny with the progress he makes in mundane affairs of life and living – politics, economics, social organization and self-realization of the individual. Like the prophets of the hoary past he too sought the salvation of the individual through spiritual progress but unlike them he applied those very spiritual means on a mass scale to solve the problems that came in the way of spiritual progress. Gandhi brought spirituality down to the ground and applied it to find lasting solution to the problems of conflicts and wars, which man inherited from his animal beginnings.

Let us be very clear at the very outset that Gandhiji never attempted to construct a system of thought. "There is no such thing as Gandhism and 'I do not want to leave any sect after me'. I do not claim to have originated any new principle or doctrine." said he. Elsewhere, he clarified, "I am not built for academic writings. Action is my domain." To him, action is the source of knowledge. To understand Gandhi and his thoughts we too have to be *Karmyogis*, which very few of us are for all that we do is linked to self-interest directly or indirectly.

Gandhi in disclaiming originality was only working in consonance with the genius of Indian *rishis* who never claimed originality for themselves. All their thoughts, they said, could be traced back to the old, time-honoured and recognjzed authorities. Often, the names of those who put forward new ideas remain buried under the debris of time. Indian genius has generally worked impersonally and anonymously. Given this situation, it is for us to distil ideas, ideals, theories and concepts revealed by his life, writings, and above all by his actions. His philosophy is more a way of life that is borne out of total integration of thoughts, words and deeds rather than a set of structured ideas.

We can see Gandhian thought from two perspectives: (1) eternal and universal, and (2) time and place specific. Truth and nonviolence and all that he derived from them constitute his eternal and universal values. It is quite akin to what the great religions of the world have proclaimed. There is a Cosmic Law that governs everything visible or invisible; it governs the universe as it governs the life of each human being and each cell that constitute the building block of various life forms. The myriad problems man faces emanate from his animal origin and his incapacity to throw out what is selfish in him. Gandhi perceived that the future of man did not lie in any further physical evolution that Darwin explained so vividly; it lies in his spiritual journey towards ever ascending levels of consciousness.

The second strand of his thought emanates from the empirical realities: the real life situation as it prevailed in his time. It was the era of colonialism in which nations preyed on nations; races on races, societies on societies; and individuals on individuals. Gandhi suffered many indignities only because he was a non-white as also because he was a citizen of a slave country. Gandhi set upon to change this Darwinian social process of survival of the fittest. He was convinced that unless man evolved spiritually to reach still higher levels of consciousness, he would render the earth unlivable; he may become the cause of his own extinction. The political, social and economic systems must therefore emancipate the individuals and communities from the conflicts and wars, instead of rendering them sick both physically and mentally.

Man has been struggling hard to live in peace so that he could move forward on the road to enlightenment; to reach a stage of evolution where there is no hatred, no greed and no self-aggrandizement and therefore, no conflict and war. He knew that man would never reach his evolutionary destination unless he was free from fear and miseries perpetrated by the institutions created for managing the society.

He, therefore, embarked on reforming such institutions whether economic, political, social or cultural. He moved against the current carrying the people with him. He had the backing of the people because what he was trying to do consciously was there in the sub-conscious mind of each and every individual. He could feel the pulse of the people. He knew that his task was difficult. Many a times he said that he knew that he would not be able to achieve much in his lifetime. His joy lay in travelling, and each milestone he crossed was a step in the long and ever lengthening journey he set upon. Gandhi's originality lay in the application of the time honoured eternal values like truth and nonviolence to the real life of not only individuals but also of the groups, communities, nations and societies. Thus he not only traced the road for spiritual evolution of man but also a peaceful and harmonious social, economic and political development.

Gandhi has written a lot on the specific issues and problems he encountered; each experiment with truth revealed new truths, which he communicated to his innumerable correspondents, followers, and adversaries through letters, speeches and books. Gandhi's philosophy, therefore, emerged from what he did. As such his thoughts as revealed in his writings are not coherent to those who try to reach him in bits. In fact he has not bothered even to be consistent for his views changed with time.

There is no department of life, which is left untouched by Gandhi. What is unique is, however, not the breadth of coverage but the common thread that binds all that he thought, said and did. Satyagraha, Sarvodaya, Swaraj, Swadeshi, and Swadharma are different terms but they come out of the same source. And thus what is temporal in Gandhi cannot be separated from what is eternal in him. When translated into policies, strategies, tactics, programmes and project, they differ from place to place and time to time but they all have a common denominator: Truth and Nonviolence. Truth is the end and nonviolence the means to reach that end.

The greatest book that the Mahatma wrote was his own life so that he could say boldly 'my life is my message'. His thoughts emanated from a vision that transcended the differences that separated man from man, man from nature, man from himself, nation from nation, society from society, and discipline from discipline. He was a thinker, synthesizer, creative genius, and *Karmayogi* in the true sense of the term. He has written a lot on spirituality, religion, *dharma*, ethics, unity of means and ends. In fact his interests range from cosmology to cleanliness. The purpose of his writings was to guide the individual to find his own path of self-actualization, which alone can lead to a higher level of consciousness. Much of it was related to the mundane problems; how to solve those problems using the right means was the mission of his life.

Since Gandhi saw the salvation for humanity in the ever ascending levels of consciousness while living and working in the real world – a world which is ever changing, and full of contradictions, he has to be reevaluated from time to time for each stage of human progress throws new challenges before the eternal values and principles he discovered through meditation and experimentation. It is for this reason that the series on 'Rediscovering Gandhi' has been produced. The spirit behind it is to tell the reader that Gandhi remains relevant, nay, indispensable in the twenty first century too as he was in twentieth century not so much because he led India to political freedom, because he showed the way to become more human.

Irrespective of the subject matter of his writings or speeches, Gandhi's ideas were off the beaten path; they were not new but they were original; they did not appear earth-shaking but they were undoubtedly revolutionary. They arose out of the creative mind of an individual to whose reforming zeal, the social situation and the difficulties of those times were a great challenge. He gained knowledge from direct contact with life and the practical experience it offered. It is the aim of the series to present his apparently mundane ideas and ideals in a form and language that the educated youth of the first quarter of the twenty first century trained in modern methods of acquiring knowledge understands.

Gandhi lived and died for peace and harmony in the world, the twin crucial needs and aspirations of the society today. He swam against the currents of his time and showed to the world that only dead fish swim with the current. He redefined progress much before the latest definition of development was even conceived. Since progress is an eternal process, Gandhi's relevance is eternal. Each generation of men and women have to interpret and reinterpret Gandhi in the light of the new problems it faces. He tackled the problems of his time, successfully because he could convince the people that a peaceful and harmonious world order could be brought about by being more human. He was unsuccessful on many fronts and many a times for what he tried to do was much ahead of the time. His failure was not because the path he treaded was wrong but because the people were not prepared to go along with him all the way. For an experimenter with truth, failure too is a step forward – a revelation of new truth. It is for the new generation of men and women to continue the experiments he left incomplete or untouched.

Gandhi was fully aware that he would never achieve his goal of reforming humanity in his lifetime but he stubbornly followed his inner voice derived as it was from the Law of Love to die for the principles he discovered and the causes he set upon to fight for. His was a never-ending fight for it aimed at a never-ending destination, i.e. transforming Homo sapiens into human being. He was a pilgrim on the way to self-realization. While doing so he was trying to ennoble all those who came in touch with him directly or indirectly. Millions who followed him worked for the solution of myriad of social, economic and political problems through the means, which were pure, i.e. based on truth and nonviolence.

Gandhi integrated the spiritual and the mundane into a common whole; like Kabir he proclaimed that life of a commoner could become as pure as that of a spiritually enlightened soul. He redefined sin as something, which man knowingly and deliberately perpetrates on his surroundings including his own fellow beings by being so individualistic and self-centred as to deprive others of their rights. He did not despise politics, pleasure, wealth, knowledge, business, science and worship, In fact, his whole life was full of these, but he never deviated from Law of Love.

With the passage of time and especially with the advent of the twenty first century, the problems that humanity faced emerged in new forms. While globalization process has set new standards for political, economic and social development in the world, violence too in different forms has become a global phenomenon. No individual or nation is safe. The possibility of a global war on conventional lines can now be discounted; even the use of atomic weapons is no longer a distinct possibility. It does not, however, herald the coming of a world without conflicts and wars. There is a possibility of war in every village, city, home, and street. Terrorism has spread like a wild fire. There are people prepared to die in order to kill others for causes that range from religious bigotry to money or even personal enmity. So the war is now decentralized globally.

Gandhian principles of Truth and Nonviolence have now acquired greater importance than ever before. The world community cannot face the escalating violence in myriad forms by the conventional means for the weapons of war are no longer the sole monopoly of the select few. There is a terrorist within. The only way to ensure a secure future for humans is to make him more human. And this to happen, the World has to move from the fear of mutual destruction to mutual symbiosis engendered by truth and nonviolence. All great religions of the world proclaim humans to be potentially divine. Gandhi too had a great and abiding faith in the divinity in man.

The aim of the series 'Rediscovering Gandhi' is thus to reinterpret Gandhi in the light of the newly emerging realities of life and to see how he can help us guide our life and living. Let us not forget that conflict is built in man for he continues to be guided by senses as do their ancestors – the animals. The large brain that he is endowed with and the mind that has evolved through time when interacting with the cosmic energy that unites all that is living leads to self-realization which in turn leads to super-consciousness. How to reduce and finally, eliminate differences, which lead to conflicts and which are so ingrained in man with love was the real concern of Gandhi. It called for a different approach to life and living, which emanated from thinking different from the one we are accustomed to.

About the Present Volume

This volume is the first of the twenty volumes slated for publication in the next couple of years. 'Hind Swaraj: The Indian Home Rule' is the first book written by Gandhi. Its origin lies in a series of articles he published in *Indian Opinion*. He then put these articles together into chapters and after appropriate editing published in a book form in Gujarati, his mother tongue. It was later translated into English.

While revisiting Hind Swaraj, almost after a century (it was written in 1908 and published in 1909), I thought of two alternative titles:

Hind Swaraj: Gandhi's Magna Carta for Peace and Progress; and Hind Swaraj: Gandhi's Challenge to Modern Civilization.

Other titles suggested by my friends did not register in my mind as appropriate and befitting to the import and purpose of the book. I finally chose the second title because it takes our attention immediately to Gandhi's views on our craze for modernity and modern civilization. We are so proud of modern civilization that all that is old and traditional is dumped as archaic, irrelevant and unworthy of sympathetic and unbiased consideration.

Hind Swaraj: Gandhi's Challenge to Modern Civilization traces the factors, forces and circumstances which prompted Gandhi to write the book. Important among these were: his early life upbringing, South African sojourn, his assessment of Indian history written by foreigners, and the work, life and vision of the leading figures of Indian Renaissance of the first half of the twentieth century.

The book then explains how Hind Swaraj marks a paradigm shift in human progress; quite different from economic progress that later came to be known as development. It is being increasingly realized that development as conceived in the West and then extended to the whole world is not likely to bring a peaceful world order. Nor would it ever be able to remove poverty and hunger from the face of the earth. What would ensure human survival and development is spiritual progress backed by economic development of all, social equity and nonviolent ways to resolve conflicts. In Gandhian praxis economic development is a means, not the end. The end is progressive movement of man on the way to super-consciousness.

Gandhi was highly critical of modern civilization as conceived in the west and felt that Indian civilization in its original form was, in many respects, more modern than the so-called modern civilization. His outline of what he considered to be a truly modern civilization is discussed next.

How Hind Swaraj was received by different sectors of the society soon after its publication is presented next. Some dismissed it as the work of a crank; some considered it irrelevant. A few treated it as a seminal work. To bring out its significance, the book is compared with many the recently published books that call far rethinking on civilization and development. The idea is to bring home the fact that Hind Swaraj continues to be a book far ahead of many of those published during the last twenty five years.

The last section of the book presents an agenda of action to promote Gandhian philosophy. It also suggests the policies and strategies, which can make India rise again – culturally, socially and economically; which can show to the world a paradigm of development wherein people matter; and which can present a model of civilization that takes man to a higher level of consciousness. It would be pertinent to remind the reader the special meaning Gandhi attached to the word 'Swaraj'. It means self-control; rise above the senses that generate greed, lust and hatred. For the Mahatma, Hind Swaraj did not mean mere political independence of India; it meant a national renaissance; it meant a nation full of vigour and self-respect; a nation whose citizens are truthful, nonviolent, and proud of the values enshrined in their culture. Hind Swaraj calls upon the people of India to work towards a future that is full of honesty and courage at the personal level, and peace and prosperity at the national level. Gandhi warned in Hind Swaraj that pursuit of economic growth without simultaneously pursuing the goal of equal access for all to the seven basic human needs – food, clothing, shelter, health, education, security and self-esteem, is a dangerous proposition. It will further widen the gap between rich and poor. He called for Sarvodaya, the rise of all.

Concluding Remarks

Rediscovering Gandhi is not series that presents a fresh look at Gandhian praxis in the context of the twenty first century. It is an attempt to present new perspectives on Gandhian thought and its continued relevance for human progress. Given the present over-emphasis on economic growth, globalization and bringing peace through violent means, the series deserves to find a place in all libraries of the world. Let it reach to all those who are engaged in shaping the world of tomorrow; it must reach every individual for human destiny rests on what individuals are and what they do in their day-to-day life.

The series is a reminder to all those who call themselves Gandhians. They must redouble their efforts to propagate and act upon what Gandhi thought, said and did. They must join hands to launch a new movement to carry Gandhi to each school, college, university, village community and city. This series aims at providing the intellectual impetus for this movement.

R.P. Misra

1

Introduction

Hind Swaraj is a manifesto for a new world order based on morality. Progress in the West means material advancement: material welfare is the overriding aim of life; anything that can enhance it must be treated as desirable and anything that comes in the way, morality included, must be undesirable. If the religions of the world are reflective of the values of our ancestors, man has been steadily moving from instinct driven animal existence to self-managing humane living; from physical security as the goal of life to achieving a far higher purpose of life; from self-centrism to universalism; and from trampling the rights of others to performing one's duties towards others. This universal trend continued with ups and downs until the advent of the Industrial Era.

A new thinking has now begun and the worldview that governed the industrial era is being challenge by the one emanating from the information age. According to Elvin Toffler and Heidi Toffler, the Third Wave is breaking down the values and structures of the industrial age (Second Wave) in the same way as the latter forced the reversal of values and structures of the agricultural era (First Wave) that brought about domestication of crops and animals and necessitated settlement of permanent villages and towns some 10,000 years ago. Gandhi challenged the values of the Second Wave three-quarters of a century ahead of Toffler. The solutions he offered were integrated in a new worldview. But Gandhi's Third Wave was different from that of Toffler.

Gandhi put forward the idea of a post-industrial or post-modern Third Wave rooted in morality as early as 1909. Toffler's Third Wave is essentially a special case and extension of the Second Wave, although his claims are taller. Gandhian paradigm is not an extension or special case of the Second Wave. It heralds the reversal of the values of the Second Wave. We have attempted a comparative study of the Third Waves of Gandhi and Toffler in chapter 15. Here suffice it to say that Gandhi's Third Wave marks a paradigm shift while that of Toffler only the reformulation and extension of the Second Wave.

How did Gandhi hit upon a new paradigm at a time when industrial revolution as far as Europe was concerned was at its peak, is a fascinating story. Part I of the book is devoted to the Making of *Hind Swaraj*. It has seven chapters. The beauty of Gandhi's paradigm lies not so much in the heuristic model that he proposed but in its practical demonstration. He proved that his was a feasible proposition and that one could put it into practice adhering to the basic tenets of his own civilisation.

Fearlessness is the first quality of a cultured person, said Gandhi. One should not fear even death and should be prepared to sacrifice one's life for others and for a right cause. One should have full control over one's senses. Only a morally strong person can be fearless. Gandhi renounced everything material except the barest necessities of life for he knew that there was no other way to become fearless. No wonder then that he was lovingly and reverentially called Mahatma Gandhi.

Gandhi basing his thesis on the basic tenets of Indian civilisation and various religious traditions of the world brought out the fallacy of the Western paradigm. He propounded a new paradigm, which takes humanity to super-consciousness and thus forward on the road to divinity. Humans do not live by bread alone even though for a hungry man bread is God. Humans can progress towards their destiny only if they are imbued with *Swaraj* or self-control; when they are ready to care for and share with others. So long as people individually or collectively have the pressing desire to accumulate, to own, to possess and to deny others the same privileges they enjoy, they cannot advance towards human destiny and thus cannot enjoy peace. And they would get into the habit of sharing and caring only if they have real *Swaraj*. When applied to a country it means self-rule or freedom from desire to deny others the resources of the earth, the freedom to live according to their own choices but of course without directly or indirectly harming others. The book was tailored specifically to the needs of India partly because Gandhi was concerned about the problems posed by British colonialism in India, and partly because Indian soil was more fertile for the ideas he propounded to take root, germinate, grow and spread around. He, therefore, named it *Hind Swaraj* and the language he used was that of the common people of India.

The questions that *Hind Swaraj* raises are not amenable to pure intellectual analysis. There can be no answers to questions: Why should we be truthful? Why should we be non-violent? Why should we be compassionate and loving? If man is guided by self-interest, greed and jealousy alone, why should he be truthful and nonviolent? Man has achieved great heights in the physical spheres. He has reached the moon and the time is not far off when he would land on some other planets too. He has gone to the ocean deeps and has penetrated the interior of the atom. He knows that electrons and neutrons circle the core of the atom but he does not know why? They take the behaviour of the electrons and neutrons as given and proceed further to utilise the power of the Atom. According to Gandhi, there is a Cosmic Law that regulates everything from atom to universe. Science does not recognize any such law, for it does not recognize any invisible superpower. Darwin suggested that it was the natural selection that governed the evolutionary process. But is it so? If we reverse the order and say that the whole evolutionary process was designed to give rise to human beings with Ego and then on to a superconscious human beings with muted Ego, it would be branded as an unscientific proposition.

What is life and where does it come from? Are the humans and other life forms just organic phenomena without any higher purpose? These questions take us to spiritual and metaphysical spheres beyond the scope of modern science. The best answer would be: we do not know. But such an answer has not satisfied humanity so far. People from times immemorial have speculated about the origin and working of the universe, about the origin and purpose of life, and about the ideal, which human beings should pursue for their survival and development. These speculations and models gave rise to various cultures and civilisations. Gandhi took the toolbox of several of these civilisations, both dead and alive, and chiseled a new civilisation with its starting point in India. This model civilisation answered all the questions that humanity had been seeking for the last several millennia.

The merit of the book lies in its capacity to make us think different from what the general run of thinking is. After reading it, we start asking ourselves: how far have we travelled at least mentally with Gandhi and with what results? In the process of assessing ourselves, we hope to understand more clearly that Gandhi conceived of a paradigm at a time when the West was enjoying the full glory of the Second Wave Revolution and when Indians in general were trying to imitate, some positively while others negatively, to catch up with the West.

Hind Swaraj was reviewed and examined by many a thinker in the past although it never got the attention it deserved. In India, it was generally ignored as a book on moral philosophy and hence outside the realm of scientific discourse. Science is amoral, so goes the modern thinking. Many considered it backward looking. While those who have a firm faith in science and technology as panacea for all the ills of the world, debunk it as utopian. Until very recently, Marxist treated it as a product of a reactionary mind; perhaps they do so even today. Gandhi's political heirs have consigned it to the dustbin of the history of freedom struggle. Most of them have neither read nor even seen the book. Those who consider it seminal and a Magna Carta for the liberation of humanity; of bringing peace in the world; and of ushering in a really modern civilisation are, however, not lacking. *Hind Swaraj* still represents the voice of the common people of India, nay the common people of the whole world.

Hind Swaraj is written in a style that is too mundane for those accustomed to linguistic complexity and finish. Its profundity is nevertheless deep and elevating. It is path breaking in the sense that it transcends the prevailing worldview and gives a new meaning to human life, living and civilisation. It declares modern industrial civilisation a systemic disease, which could be eradicated only by a systemic change in human life. It proceeds along two converging paths: self-realization (*moksha*) and self-preservation (*suraksha*). Neither is possible so long as humans remain chained in the shackles of *Kam*, *Krodh*, *Mad* and *Lobha* (desire, anger, arrogance, and greed). Both *Moksha* and *Suraksha* come from inner strength, from self-sacrifice, from truth and non-violence, from love and compassion, and from voluntary poverty. They do not come from more consumer goods and more arms and ammunitions.

The model of the new civilisation Gandhi presented in *Hind Swaraj* is not utopian. Whatever it contains has been empirically demonstrated not only by Gandhi in South Africa and then in India but also by several of his followers and fellow travellers in the USA, South Africa, Poland, and several other countries both before and after Gandhi even if only partially.

UNDERSTANDING HIND SWARAJ

Gandhi spent about seven months in prison during 1908-09. This gave him an opportunity to read and reread Hindu scriptures like

Upanishads, *Bhagawat Geeta*, *Ramayana*, *Mahabharata*, *Patanjali Yogadarshana*, *Sandhyani Gutika*, *Ahnika Prakasha*, and *Manusmriti*; other religious books like *Bible* and *Koran* and philosophical writings of Plato, Tolstoy, Ruskin and many others. He read and meditated on the ideas contained in these books and wrote a number of serials for *Indian Opinion* published in South Africa. The serials were later put together as a book. The serials that constitute the book were written aboard S.S. Kildonan Castle between November 13 and 22, 1908 while returning from London to Durban. It was written in Gujarati, Gandhi's mother-tongue. The book is a record of what transpired between Gandhi and the London based Indian anarchists who were devotedly engaged in freeing India from British colonialism by violent means. Gandhi tried to dissuade the revolutionaries from the path of violence because lasting peace could come only through non-violence. Apparently, he was not successful in his efforts. Realising that the message of peaceful resolution of conflicts that he gave to the revolutionaries should reach a larger audience particularly in India and South Africa, he decided to serialise it in *Indian Opinion*.

It came down heavily on violence because:

(1) Violence is inhuman;
(2) Violence breeds more violence and hence it cannot bring peace;
(3) It is the weapon of those who lack courage;
(4) Indian civilisation does not permit the use of violence;
(5) India should use nonviolent means to fight the British; and
(6) Hence the young men of India should not use violence to win freedom.

Hind Swaraj continues to attract attention both in and outside India. The issues it had raised continue to be live and germane and the ideas and ideals it propounded are no longer dismissed as 'reactionary' except in the fast shrinking circle of Marxists; or utopian except in 'ultramodern' circles 'corrupted by the violence prone Western civilisation'. So far as the silent majority is concerned, it still pins its hopes in the concepts of 'civilisation', 'progress', 'freedom' and '*Swaraj*' as put forward by Gandhi in *Hind Swaraj*.

Hind Swaraj is not only a book on how to win political freedom for India. More importantly, it is a Magna Carta for the freedom of mind and the evolution of human species from conscious and material beings to super-conscious and moral beings. Since the book deals with human destiny, it would remain relevant as long as man's journey into the unknown future remains unfinished. And since the journey is eternal, at least in human reckonings of time, its relevance too must remain eternal.

Meaning

Hind Swaraj literally means Indian Self-Government. That is why the full title of the book is *Hind Swaraj* or Indian Home Rule. The title of the book is indicative of author's growing disintachment with colonial rule in India and the consequent denigration of Indians in South Africa where he lived at the time of writing the book. Unless India was a free nation, Indians could not get the respect they deserved as human beings anywhere in the world, realised Gandhi. How could a small island nation colonise a subcontinental India, asked Gandhi? The answer he found was not only unusual and unconventional but also of far reaching significance for the whole world, Britain included. Unlike many of his contemporaries who attributed the enslavement of India to medieval feudalism, lack of industrial development, poor technological base, and incompetence of its ruling classes, Gandhi transcended all these and looked within to conclude that no power on earth could enslave a people unless they were willing to concede the right of the slave-master to keep them in bondage. India could not become and remain a British colony, had the people of India refused to recognize the British as their rulers. It was, however, possible only if the people were imbued with the spirit of *Swaraj*: they were spiritually so advanced that no material allurement could prompt them to barter their freedom. They would die but would not suffer enslavement.

Gandhi declared: "British occupied India not because they were a superior force; we Indians invited them to rule over us because we were prepared to barter our freedom with their money. We abandoned our culture of simple living and high thinking and developed a taste for material goods and slavery. A slave can remain a slave only so long as he recognises the slave driver as his master. To regain freedom, India must return to its cultural moorings once again." It must refuse to accept the British as their rulers and face death in doing so.

The beauty of the book lies in its capacity to present a very scientific and philosophical discourse in the most ordinary language. It could be read and understood by any literate Indian. Saint Tulsidas wrote

Ramcharit Manas popularly known as *Ramayana*, some 400 years ago, which is perhaps the most widely read literary and spiritual book in India. Gandhi was highly inspired by *Ramayana*. Tulsidas wanted to restore Ram in the hearts of the people, the Ram who set a code of conduct for a civilised behaviour. Gandhi tried to restore the character of Ram (truth, non-violence, love and compassion) in the minds and hearts of the people of India. Tulsidas liberated the common man of India from frustration and hopelessness; Gandhi tried to liberate them from social and political bondage on the one hand and cultural degeneration on the other. He tried to show the path of getting rid of both inner and outer bondage with the help of soul force, not brute force.

What does Gandhi say in this little book? First, he tells that India should use the means sanctioned by its own culture to win independence from the British: it should neither copy the West as the anarchist revolutionaries were doing, nor should it confine itself to petitioning and prostrating before the British as liberal moderates were doing. It should create a nonviolent political force to fight back if the petitions do not work. Such a force can be created only if Indians understand the meaning of *Swaraj*, a special gift of Indian civilisation. True *Swaraj* would come when India organises its public life per our ancient civilisation.

The British government was opposed to *Swaraj* because they as well as British people were captives of a civilisation, which was satanic: it was immoral. So long as they were captive of that civilisation, they could not behave otherwise. Thus the real enemy was Western civilisation. It had a hold on India too through five great evils: railways (which made people move fast), courts and lawyers (which made people fight each other), hospitals and doctors (which engendered ill-health), English education (which alienated people from their civilisation) and modern technology (which made people less human).

D.G. Tendulkar in volume 1 of his series of books entitled *Mahatma* (p.108) refers to a letter Gandhi wrote to a friend wherein he summarised *Hind Swaraj* in following words:

(1) "There is no impossible barrier between East and West.

(2) There is no such thing as Western or European civilisation, but there is a modern civilisation, which is purely material.

(3) The people of Europe before they were touched by modern civilisation, had much in common with the people of the East; anyhow the people of India, and even today the Europeans

who are not touched by modern civilisation, are far better able to mix with Indians than the offspring of that civilisation.

(4) It is not the British people who are ruling India, but it is modern civilisation, through its railways, telegraph, telephone, and almost every invention, which has been claimed to be a triumph of modern civilisation.

(5) Bombay, Calcutta and other chief cities of India are the real plague-spots.

(6) If British rule were replaced by Indian rule based on modern methods, India would be no better, except that she would be able to retain some of the money that drained away to England; but then India would only become a second or fifth nation of Europe or America.

(7) East and West can really meet when the West has thrown overboard modern civilisation almost in its entirety. They can also seemingly meet when East has also adopted modern civilisation, but that meeting would be an armed truce, even as it is between, say, Germany and England, both of which nations are living in the Hall of Death in order to avoid being devoured, the one by the other.

(8) It is impertinence for any man or any body of men to begin or to contemplate reform of the whole world. To attempt to do so by means of highly artificial and speedy locomotion, is to attempt the impossible.

(9) Increase of material comforts, it may be generally laid down, does not in any way whatsoever conduce to moral growth.

(10) Medical science is concentrated essence of black magic. Quackery is infinitely preferable to what passes for high medical skill as such.

(11) Hospitals are the instruments that the Devil has been using for his own purpose in order to keep his hold on his kingdom. They perpetuate vice, misery and degradation, and real slavery. I was entirely off the track when I considered that I should receive a medical training. It would be sinful for me in any way whatsoever to take part in the abominations that go in the hospitals. If there were no hospitals for venereal diseases, or even for consumptives, we would have less consumption, and less sexual vice amongst us.

(12) India's salvation consists in unlearning what she has learnt during the last fifty years or so. The railways, telegraph, hospitals, lawyers, doctors, and such like have all to go, and so called upper classes have to learn to live conscienously and religiously and deliberately the simple life of a peasant knowing it to be a life giving true happiness.

(13) India should wear no machine-made clothing whether it comes out of European mills or Indian mills.

(14) England can help India to do this and then she would have justified her hold on India. There seems to be many in England today who think likewise.

(15) There was true wisdom in the sages of the old having so regulated society as to limit the material conditions of the people: "the rude plough of perhaps five thousand years ago is the plough of the husbandman today. Therein lies salvation. People live long under such conditions, in comparative peace much greater than Europe has enjoyed after having taken up modern activity, and I feel that every enlightened man, certainly every Englishman, may, if he chooses, learn this truth and act according to it."

"It is the true spirit of passive resistance that has brought me to the above almost definite conclusions. As a passive resister, I am unconcerned whether such a gigantic reformation, should I call it so, can be brought about among people who find their satisfaction in the present mad rush. If I realise the truth of it, I should rejoice in following it and, therefore, I could not wait until the whole body of people had commence doing so. All of us who think likewise have to take the necessary step, and the rest, if we are in the right, must follow."

In 1921, twelve years after the book was first published, Gandhi wrote 'A Word of Explanation' which deserves to be reproduced here to remove some of the doubts people have about its contents and its theses. It shows that the book was not received so enthusiastically and a number of people were highly critical of it on one ground or the other:

"It is certainly my good fortune that this booklet of mine is receiving wide attention. The original is in Gujarati. It has chequered career. It was first published in the columns of *Indian Opinion* of South Africa. It was written in 1908 during my return voyage from London to South Africa in answer to the Indian school of violence and its prototype in

South Africa. I came in contact with every known Indian anarchist in London. Their bravery impressed me but I felt that their zeal was misguided. I felt that violence was no remedy for India's ills and that her civilisation required the use of a different and higher weapon for self-protection. The *satyagraha* of South Africa was still an infant hardly two years old. But it had developed sufficiently to permit me to write of it with some degree of confidence. What I wrote was so much appreciated that it was published as a booklet. It attracted some attention in India. The Bombay Government prohibited its circulation. I though it was due to my English friends that they should know its contents.

"In my opinion it is a book, which can be put into the hands of a child. It teaches the gospel of love in place of that of hate. It replaces violence with self-sacrifice. It puts soul force against brute force. It has gone through several editions and I commend it to those who would care to read it. I withdraw nothing except one word of it, and that in deference of a lady friend.

"The booklet is a severe condemnation of 'modern civilisation'. It was written in 1908. My conviction is deeper today than ever. I feel that if India will discard 'modern civilisation', she can only gain by doing so.

"But I would warn the reader against thinking that I am today aiming at the *Swaraj* described therein. I know that India is not ripe for it. It may seem impertinent to say so. But such is my conviction. I am individually working for the self-rule pictured therein. But today my corporate activity is undoubtedly devoted to the attainment of Parliamentary *Swaraj* in accordance with the wishes of the people of India. I am not aiming at destroying railways or hospitals though I would certainly welcome their natural destruction. Neither railways nor hospitals are test of a high and pure civilisation. At best they are a necessary evil. Neither adds one inch to the moral stature of a nation. Nor am I aiming at permanent destruction of law courts, much as I regard it as a 'consummation devoutly to be wished.' Still less am I trying to destroy all machinery and mills. I require a higher simplicity and renunciation than the people are prepared today.

"The only part of the programme, which is now being carried out is that of nonviolence. But I regret to have to confess that even that is not being carried out in the spirit of the book. If it were, India would establish *Swaraj* in a day. If India adopted the doctrine of love as an active part of her religion and introduced it in her politics, *Swaraj* would descend upon India from heaven. But I am painfully aware that that event is far off as yet.

"I offer these comments because I observe that much is being quoted from the booklet to discredit the present movement. I have even seen writings suggesting that I am playing a deep game, that I am using the present turmoil to foist my fads on India, and I am making religious experiments at India's expenses. I can only answer that *Satyagraha* is made of sterner stuff. There is nothing reserved and nothing secret in it. A portion of the whole theory of life described in *Hind Swaraj* is undoubtedly being carried into practice. There is no danger attendant upon the whole of it being practiced. But it is not right to scare away people by reproducing from writings passages that are irrelevant to the issue before the country."

Contents and Format

The book contains 20 chapters capsuled in just 96 pages or 30,000 words. The opening chapters 1-3 deal with the Indian National Congress and the Indian awakening. Chapter 4 explains the true meaning of *Swaraj*. A critique of modern industrial civilisation is presented in chapters 5-6. The pitiable condition of India is elaborated in chapters 7-12. Why Gandhi considered the Indian civilisation to be superior to modern civilisation is given in chapter 13. The potency of *satyagraha* or passive resistance is explained in chapters 14-17. Chapters 18-19 discuss the problems associated with modern education and technology. The last chapter (20) gives conclusions.

It is written in question-answer format; the question were put by a reader and the answers were given by the editor of *Indian Opinion* published in South Africa, *i.e.* M.K. Gandhi as he was known then. When he wrote the book, he was already well known in South Africa, India and England as a leader who as fighting for the emancipation of Indians in South Africa using a unique means, that is, non-violence.

To understand post-1909 Gandhi, one must read this book first, for the genes of all that Gandhi spoke, wrote and did in his life are present there. Many books and articles have been written on and about *Hind Swaraj*, appreciative as well as depreciative, both in India and abroad. But the book has proved to be so seminal that there is always a scope for looking at it afresh. It challenges the very basis on which the edifice of what we call modern civilisation stands. And since rapid change is the basic tenet of modern civilisation, it throws up newer problems that confound humanity faster than ever before. One is forced to look at Gandhi and the panacea he has presented in

Hind Swaraj, which is accessible to all equally, individuals or groups, rich or poor, slaves or masters and from which there is no escape even if it is difficult to acquire and use.

Purpose and Objectives

Gandhi had three main purposes in writing *Hind Swaraj*. After deep contemplation, extensive reading and experimentation, he concluded that humanity had strayed away from the path of its destiny and it was treading a course that would lead it to disaster. Man is the ultimate in the evolution of species, but he has yet to abandon his animal instincts and urges. This he could see and experience more vividly in South Africa where human behaviour was at times worse that even animal behaviour. Animals kill each other to satisfy their hunger but humans kill and maim each other to satisfy their anger and ego.

He traced the source of the malady to modern industrial civilisation, which he often referred to as western civilisation or just modern civilisation. The immediate provocation for writing the book was to expose the inadequacies of the industrial civilisation, which was branded as modern. He called it regressive, satanic, *Kali Yugi*, a disease and an intoxicant. All those who come in its grip are so intoxicated that they fall into the death trap of the ecstasy of pleasure. Having done that, he put forward a new paradigm of progress that would bring humanity back to a path of sanity and lead it to its destiny of super-conscious being.

The path he tried to trace passed through *Swaraj*, which in common parlance meant self-rule or independence or freedom. But *Swaraj* to him connoted a far broader and deeper meaning than political independence. It meant self-control over baser aspects of life by the individuals groups and societies, which in essence meant service of all that is living. As an individual, one should have control over his senses and the instincts related thereto. Duties should precede the rights for the latter is protected if the former is honestly performed. A community, society and nation in a like manner must be imbued with service motivation: service of and sacrifice for all living things especially the fellow human beings.

Thus, Gandhi enlarged the meaning of freedom from mere political independence to freedom from baser elements of life. A person who is free, will be fearless. He will not fear even death and will be prepared to sacrifice all that he has for the sake of truth. And the one who is fearless cannot be made a slave for his soul can never be made captive.

As regards the immediate objectives of writing *Hind Swaraj*, two of them appear to have been uppermost in Gandhi's mind. He wanted to secure political freedom for India and to resque the Indian civilisation from the bondage of western civilisation. He felt that the tendencies of Indian civilisation took man towards moral, growth while that of western civilisation took him to material growth and hence India's political freedom would release inherent latent energy that would spread all over Asia, Africa and Latin America to liberate the millions groaning under the colonial exploitation of European countries. In fact, he thought and, rightly so, that it would help the Europeans too in getting out of the yoke of industrialism and move towards real *Swaraj*. Thus Gandhi fought for India's political independence with two objectives: one to free India and second to show the right path for the rest of the subjugated people of the world to gain their independence.

Gandhi was, however, not the only one fighting for political independence. All societies have tales of bravery displayed by freedom loving people. The number of people who sacrificed themselves at the altar of political freedom was a legend. They inspired the younger generations to follow suit. If Gandhi has fought just to free India from bondage, he too would have joined the queue of freedom fighters and would have not been known as Mahatma Gandhi. The uniqueness or, one should I say, the greatness of Gandhi lies in the fact that he totally deviated from the path trodden by his predecessors, and discovered a path that not only gave political freedom but more importantly liberated man from what is animal in him and directed him to move towards his ultimate destiny – super-consciousness.

What that path was? It was the path of Nonviolence. Humans have fought each other like animals for millennia but they have failed to solve their problems. They have been engaged in developing more powerful and lethal weapons to kill each other without realizing that 'violence breeds violence'. He has used his brainpower not to distance himself from animal but to move closer to become far more destructive than a animal. Gandhi wanted man to get back to sanity and adopt nonviolence, soul force in stead of brute force, in resolving the conflicts that must arise in a society that consists of individuals who, even though of the same species, are so different from each other.

Non-violence is a weapon that is accessible to all: strong or week. And hence it has inbuilt socialism. Gandhi tried to kill (save!) two birds with one stone. He wanted to secure political freedom for India and wanted to demonstrate a weapon accessible to all to fight against oppression and injustice without harming the adversary. Thus, he extracted from the garbage of industrialism a new paradigm of thinking: a new worldview which when used on a mass scale can usher in permanent peace in the world. It would herald a world without wars.

Underlying Philosophy

According to Gandhi, all human problems have a common source, *i.e.* deviation from the path that would ensure continued evolution of man from animal to super conscious human beings (*Maha Manav*); they appear in different garbs and shades at different times in different circumstances. It is rare that people go to the root cause. The general tendency is to mistake symptoms as causes. Let us take the case of our health. When a disease attacks, people tend to rush to doctor who on the basis of the symptoms prescribes certain medicines. The symptom may be fever, which might have been caused because of overeating, over-indulgence in pleasure, or violation of the biological laws governing human body. The medicines may give relief but the basic problem that caused the fever remained unattended. Soon, it may come back as another bout of fever or some other symptom.

Humans have been in unconscious search of peace ever since they branched off as Homo sapiens and this search has become conscious when he became human about 10,000 years ago. Despite innumerable regional and local wars in ancient and medieval times and two global wars of the twentieth century, conflicts have multiplied in form as well as an intensity. No country or individual is in peace. Wars are waged to bring peace; people are killed to save people and cultures are destroyed to save cultures. The Taliban of Afghanistan killed thousands of their co-religionists to save Islam and destroyed their cultural heritage enshrined in the Bameyani Buddha. But where is peace. Talibans are gone but Afghanistan and its people are still suffering. Each war unleashes new wars and each killing leads to far more killings. Except for Asoka's Kalinga war in BC 320, no war has so far brought peace.

Each war is fought ostensibly for 'a just cause' without realising that war is an unjust means even for a just cause. No goal, objective or cause howsoever laudable and pure it may be can justify wrong means, said Gandhi, for means and ends are inseparable; they are interchangeable. What is 'means' for one becomes 'end' for another and what is 'end' for one becomes 'means' for the others. There is no country, which is not on some sort of war with some other country:

in fact no individual is at peace. The dangers of nuclear annihilation and chemical and biological weapons of mass destruction and global climatic changes threaten the very existence of life on the earth. The ever-growing problems of ill health, illiteracy and poverty have assumed epidemic proportions. None of these are being tackled satisfactorily and speedily because our mindset does not take us to the root cause. We behave like modern doctors trained to deal with symptoms, not the root cause. We get rid of one symptom to face many others, more serious and more complex.

The germs of war lie in the mind of man; the key to peace therefore lies in the mind of individual human beings. No amount of economic prosperity, political power, and weaponry can bring peace.

The views expressed in *Hind Swaraj* are that of Gandhi, "I have but endeavoured to humbly to follow Tolstoy, Ruskin, Thoreau, Emerson and other writers besides the masters of Indian philosophy. Tolstoy has been one of my teachers for a number of years."

MAIN PILLARS

Gandhi put forward four main goals before humanity so as to move towards its destiny. These are: *Swaraj*, *Non-violence*, *Swadeshi* and *Sarvodaya*. These are the main pillars of the thesis he has propounded in *Hind Swaraj*.

Swaraj

"We measure the universe by our own miserable foot-rule. When we are slaves, we think that the whole universe is enslaved. We are so much intoxicated by Western civilisation that we cannot appreciate our own." Said Gandhi. Citing the example of forced Austrian withdrawal from Italy during the First World War, Gandhi remarked: 'what substantial gain did Italy obtain after the withdrawal of the Austrian troops? The gain was only nominal. The reforms for the sake of which the war was supposed to have been undertaken have not yet been granted. The condition of the people in general still remains the same. I am sure you do not wish to reproduce such a condition in India. I believe that you want the millions of Indians to be happy, not that you want the reigns of government in your hands. If that be so, we have to consider only one thing: how can the millions obtain self-rule? You will admit that people under several Indian princes are being ground down. The latter mercilessly crush them. Their tyranny is greater than that of the English, and if you want such tyranny in India, then we shall never agree. My patriotism does not teach me that I am to allow people to be crushed under the heel of Indian princes if only the English retire. If I have the power, I should resist the tyranny of Indian princes just as much as that of the English. By patriotism I mean the welfare of the whole people.... (*Hind Swaraj*, p. 59)

Gandhi gave a detailed picture of what he meant by *Swaraj*. As discussed in this volume elsewhere also, *Swaraj* did not convey just political independence; it conveyed the meaning of self-control. Self control comes from self-realization, which in turn comes from firm faith in God which is Truth; respect for human dignity; willingness to sacrifice for others; and belief in *Vasudhaiva Kutumbakam* (whole earth constitutes a family). None of the above qualities can come unless one has self-control, i.e. one is not swayed by selfishness, sensual urges and instincts; and desire to accumulate wealth and power.

Swaraj is therefore, a difficult proposition and cannot be achieved instantaneously. People and societies have to work for it continuously and consistently for a long time. It would never be achieved if we do not start moving in that direction. So walking on the path of *Swaraj* brings man nearer to it. As such moving in the direction of *Swaraj* is itself an achievement. The most potent means to set on the path of *Swaraj* is the observance of non-violence.

"It is *Swaraj* when we learn to rule ourselves. ...*Swaraj* that we wish to picture is such that, after we have once realized it, we shall endeavour to the end of our lifetime to persuade others to do likewise. But *Swaraj* has to be experienced by each one for himself. One drowning man will never save another. Slaves ourselves, it would be a mere pretention to think of freeing others."

Political *Swaraj* does not mean expulsion of the British. It means people's Raj in accordance with the norms set by Indian culture. It means that foreign rules must be ended. That should be our immediate goal. But the method that we apply in removing the foreign rule must not be that of the foreigners. British came to India by brute force; India should not expel them by brute force. Arming India to fight the British amounts to the acceptance of foreign civilisation but rejection of foreign rule. "Then her (India's) condition will be as pitiable as that of Europe." To indulge in killings and assassinations to get independence would be un-Indian. What we need to do is to use our time tested method of nonviolence to throw the British out. If they use brute force, we should be prepared to sacrifice ourselves. The very thought of killing others, is cowardly. Assassinations do not bring *Swaraj*. Nor our people want such things to happen. "Those who are intoxicated by the wretched modern civilisation think these things. Those who rise to power by murder will certainly not make the nation happy."

The British could rule over India because we were enamoured of British goods, British ideas and ideals, British literature, British history and British culture. The day we become enamoured of Indian goods, Indian ideas and ideals, Indian literature, Indian history and Indian culture, we will not tolerate British rule in India and will be prepared to sacrifice ourselves rather than remain under its shadow.

Swaraj cannot be given; it has to be taken and won. Only those who are brave can secure it. We need men and women who defy death; who would sacrifice themselves for it. "One who is free from hatred requires no sword." A petition backed by force is a petition from an equal and he transmits his demand in the form of petition, it testifies to his nobility. Two kinds of forces can back petitions. 'We shall hurt you if you do not give this' is one kind of force; it is the force of arms whose evil results we have already examined. The second kind of force can thus be stated: "If you cannot concede our demand, we shall no longer be your petitioners. You can govern us only so long as we remain the governed; we shall no longer have any dealings with you." The force implied in this may be described as Love Force, Soul Force or more popularly but less precisely passive resistance which Gandhi renamed as *Satyagraha*. The force of arms is powerless when matched against the force of love or soul.

"A coward would never disobey a law he did not like; he feigned to obey it but broke it stealthily. The extremists advocated brute force and hence they would come to power, they would enforce on us their laws and rules. Even a man weak in physical power could practice passive resistance. Those who believe that India has gained by Dhingra's act and other similar acts in India, make a serious mistake. He gave his body in a wrong way; its ultimate result can only be mischievous for "those who take sword would perish by the sword."

Even when India becomes politically free and has a parliamentary form of government, there will be occasions when people would oppose the government. Since democracy means government by majority, it is presumed that whatever the majority view, it must be right. This may, however not be so. "It is a superstition and ungodly thing to believe that an act of a majority binds a minority. ...All reforms owe their origin to the initiation of minorities in opposition to majorities. If among a band of robbers knowledge of robbing is obligatory, is a pious man to accept the obligation? So long as the superstition that man should obey unjust laws exists, so long will there slavery exist. And a passive resistance alone can remove such a superstition."

As such the minority must have a weapon to fight the majority and to convince them that they are wrong. In the armory of the modern civilisation, there is no remedy except armed rebellion or terrorism. A small group of people who considers itself to be right takes up arms and forces the majority to accept its views. The disease becomes contagious and many more aggrieved groups with imaginary or real grievances against the majority emerge and kill people just to terrorize the government to accept their demands. Nonviolence is a weapon that not only gives lasting results but also transforms the opposite party into a friend.

Right type of Education is a must for gaining *Swaraj*. Modern education, however, prepared the youth for self-indulgence. "Our ancient school system is enough. Character building has the first place in it and that is primary education. A building erected on that foundation will last. Unfortunately, this basic function of education is lost today."

"If education is only an instrument, it may be well used or abused. ...We daily observe that many men abuse it and very few make very good use of it; and if this is a correct statement, we have proved that more harm has been done by it than good." Education, as it is imparted today, is not an instrument of gaining *Swaraj*.

"Ordinary meaning of education is knowledge of letters. To teach boys reading, writing, and arithmetic is called primary education. A peasant earns his bread honestly. He has ordinary knowledge of the world. He knows fairly well how he should behave towards his parents, his wife, his children, and his fellow villagers. He understands and observes the rules of morality. But he cannot write his own name. What do you propose to do by giving him knowledge of letters? Will you add an inch to his happiness? Do you wish to make him discontented with his cottage or his lot? And even if you want to do that, he will not need such an education."

Gandhi advised the professionals (lawyers, doctors, educationists, and politicians) who served the people to acquire the wisdom to promote *Swaraj*. But this could happen only if they possess enviable character. Logically then right kind of education as imparted by the parents, family members, community members, and schools etc., was the very foundation of *Swaraj*.

Gandhi lamented the fact that knowledge gained through modern education was being used to perpetuate foreign rule. Lawyers tightened the English grip; they misused their knowledge to proliferate litigation. The doctors harmed the society more than they served. "Carried away by the flood of western thought, we came to the conclusion without weighing pros and cons that we should give this kind of education to the people."

Soul Force (Non-violence)

"Those that take the sword shall perish by the sword. ...The fact that there are so many men still alive in the world shows that it is based not on the force of arms but on the force of truth or love. Therefore, the greatest and the most unimpeachable evidence of the success of this force is to be found in the fact that, in spite of the wars of the world, it still lives on."

"Thousands, indeed tens of thousands, depend for their existence on the very active working of this force. Little quarrels of millions of families in their daily life disappear before the exercise of this force. Hundreds of nations live in peace. For history does not and cannot take note of this fact. History is really a record of every interruption of the even working of the force of love or of the soul.

"Everyone admits that sacrifice of self is infinitely superior to sacrifice of others. Moreover, if this kind force is used in a cause that is unjust, only the person using it suffers. He does not make others suffer for his mistakes."

Swadeshi

"Swadeshi is that spirit in us which restricts us to the use and service of our immediate surroundings to the exclusion of more remote.... Much of deep poverty of the masses is due to the ruinous departure from Swadeshi in the economic and industrial life. If not an article of commerce had been brought from outside India, she would be today a land flowing with milk and honey.... Then every village of India would almost be self-supporting and self-contained unit, exchanging only such necessary commodities with other villages as are not locally producible.... I would urge that Swadeshi is the only doctrine consistent with the law of humility and love."

Swadeshi does not necessarily mean rejecting foreign goods merely because they are of foreign origin. It would be waste of time and resources to produce goods for which a country, region, or locality is not fit to produce. A true votary of Swadeshi would never harbour any ill will towards foreigners, says Gandhi.

Sarvodaya

Let us go a little deeper. Pursuit of self-interest is the core around which modern civilisation is build. Darwin's concept of survival of the fittest has been successfully applied to all walks of life, including economic. The goal of life being material welfare, each individual tries to acquire as much wealth and goods as possible. The rich want to become richer or at least to protect what they have, and the poor want to become rich as early as possible by hook or crook. According to John Locke, man is not born in heaven, he has to preserve himself by acquiring and protecting all that he needs for the purpose. Devotion, morality and other spiritual pursuits cannot be his primary concerns.

The problem with Locke's analysis is that it considers that man would be happier by acquiring material goods. More goods he has happier would he be. While it is true that man cannot be happy if his basic needs of food, clothing, housing, education, health, security and self-expression are not met satisfactorily, these are only physical needs which enable man to achieve his higher goals. Even after these needs are met, man does not become happy. If he does not have any higher goals, then he must get satisfaction in having more of those goods and services. Then a stage comes when he gets satisfaction by preventing others from possessing those goods and services because he does not want to be inferior or even equal to anyone else.

The pursuit of self-interest gives rise to violence because there is no way to acquire and possess infinitely without depriving others of their basic needs. If nature had provided unlimited resources, this would have not become a problem. Unfortunately nature is niggardly and permits man to use its resources only within its carrying capacity. So one can become rich only if his neighbours are poor. This is what Gandhi calls 'self-corroding competition'. The emerging inequity leads to deprivation, exploitation, domination, slavery, jealousy, and violence. Colonialism was a part of it. Modern civilisation, says Gandhi, "does not respect all life and, and in its progress onward, it has not hesitated to resort to wholesale destruction of even human life." (*Collected Works*, Vol. IV, p.243)

The pursuit of material welfare and self-interest leads to ceaseless activity to possess more goods and services. There is growing tendency to subdue nature and other peoples. New scientific and technological innovations are made to reduce time and space. All these in turn further strengthen humans in conquering nature and man. His desire to possess more increases further. This is not to suggest that scientific and technological developments are *per se* undesirable. This is to suggest that the motive for these developments are ulterior and hence the consequences thereof are not salutary.

The civil society has to step in to regulate the behaviour of people so that peace and harmony is maintained. But the very people who are entrusted with the task of regulation, are bitten by the same bug. Instead of safeguarding and promoting the interests of all, they become sectional representatives and 'hypocritical and selfish. Each thinks of his own interest.' Gandhi called the House of Commons (the Mother of Parliament) as a 'sterile prostitute... Members vote for their party without thought.' This amply demonstrated by recent decision of the House of Commons to permit the British government to invade Iraq. What Gandhi said about House of Commons in 1908 is far truer today for the Lok Sabha of India. Members cross the floor to serve their ulterior immediate goals; they fight pitched battles on the floor of the House, abuse each other and the following day praise each other. To get elected, some of them use the foulest means one can think of. No wonder then, our parliament and state legislators are full of criminals and anti-social elements.

CONTEMPORARY RELEVANCE OF HIND SWARAJ

What is the relevance of *Hind Swaraj* to the contemporary world of the twenty-first century. This is a question that often forms the central theme of seminars and conferences on Gandhi and his philosophy. I think the question has to be phrased differently. One should ask: how relevant the present day world is to the thesis advanced by Gandhi? We tend to take the world as it is as given. There are wars, conflicts, poverty, ignorance, etc. etc. We also see that the Gandhian way of governance has not been adopted by even the country which is his *Karma Bhoomi* (land where he demonstrated his theses), *i.e.* India. We naively conclude that Gandhi is no longer relevant.

This thinking suffers from two fallacies. First, all that is not practiced is not irrelevant. Is Christ's compassion irrelevant? Is Buddha's *Ahimsa* irrelevant? Is Mohammad's stress on human dignity and equality irrelevant? I am not trying to put Gandhi in the category of these *avtars,* messengers and *paigambars*. I do, however, stress that these are eternal truths that make man human and these truths are always relevant. They are the needles of the compass that tells the mariner the direction in which he should take the ship to reach the destination. We tend to misread the compass or care not to do so and go on making round and round of the treacherous sea. It is not the fault of the compass and its needle. Our mindset detracts us from the right route.

Second, Gandhi not only presented a thesis but also demonstrated its practicability. He used it to throw the British out of India. True, the British would have gone out even if India had chosen a violent path. Britain was too weak a country to contain the fire of freedom. But under the leadership of Gandhi, the struggle remained peaceful even if the end was full of bloodshed. It was, however, not because of Gandhi but in spite of him for the very forces, which he fought against (western civilisation), albeit nonviolently, appeared in communal garb to divide the people.

Gandhian method has been successfully used elsewhere in the world after his death. The Civil Rights movement in the USA, freedom struggle in South Africa, Poland, and several other countries and places prove the relevance of Gandhi in today's world. Let us not forget that the non-governmental organisations are using Gandhian methodology all over the world in one form or the other to secure the rights of individuals and communities in distress. And the day is not far off when Gandhi's *Hind Swaraj*, will become Global *Swaraj.*

TO SUM UP

Hind Swaraj is basically a critique of modern industrial civilisation. And the critique is based on a paradigm of progress, which is unique and, off the main currents of modern thinking. Let it be clear at the very outset that Gandhi did not equate Western as it existed prior to industrial revolution with modern civilisation. People do not make a distinction between the two because industrial civilisation took birth in the West. Real Western civilisation was rooted in Greek and Roman thought, which had close affinity with Indian and Chinese civilisations. The superimposition of Christianity did not alter the paradigm of Western thinking because Christianity too was born in the East and hence was quite close to Eastern religions. A civilisation, which is related to the teachings of Jesus Christ, whose love and compassion had no bounds, could not be considered to be satanic. Gandhi applied the Law of Love to win over his detractors in South Africa and India to liberate the people from bondage. Real Christians would not produce Atom Bomb and drop it on Hiroshima and Nagasaki in Japan for the ostensible purpose of frightening the Japanese by killing thousands and maiming still more of innocent men, women and children who had nothing to do with war. They would not kill thousands of unsuspecting and unprotected innocents in Bhopal, India by releasing deadly chemicals; nor would they poison the environment of the world and threaten the very survival of life on planet earth. A real Christian civilisation would not be witness to global wars.

Before we discuss the main elements of a truely modern civilisation as outlined in *Hind Swaraj*, let us be clear about Gandhi's point of departure—the vantage point from which he defined real civilisation. His point of departure was spiritual development of humans and hence his analysis was quite often devoid of rigour a social scientist would expect. A first look at the expressions he uses to drive his points home appear subjective. The import of *Hind Swaraj* can thus be grasped only if the analyst has sensitivity. We consider Gandhi's industrial civilisation to be modern because in our scheme of things development means material advancement. Modern civilisation must appear modern especially to the West because it has enjoyed unprecedented material prosperity. But if we look at it from the point of view of the rest of the world, it must be called most un-modern and satanic to use Gandhi's terminology.

Gandhi considers western civilisation to be "a civilisation only in name. Under it the nations of Europe are becoming degraded and ruined day by day.... A great English writer (Carpenter) has written a work called *Civilisation: Its Cause and Cure*. People are unable to understand it because, busy as they are in day-to-day life, they do not go deep into its real nature and long run problems it poses to humanity. Further, it is sensual in the sense that it pleases the senses, and hence it is highly attractive. "A man whilst he is dreaming, believes in his dream; he is undeceived only when he is awakened from his sleep. A man labouring under the bane of civilisation is like a dreaming man. What we usually read is the work of defenders of modern civilisation, which undoubtedly claims among its votaries very brilliant and some very good men. Their writings hypnotize us. So one by one we are drawn into the vortex."

Modern industrial civilisation promotes material development and does not even consider moral development as one of its focal concerns. *Hind Swaraj* is a moral response to the votaries of material advancement. Gandhi wrote *Hind Swaraj* in response to the votaries of violence in India and South Africa. "I came in contact with every known Indian anarchist in London. Their bravery impressed me, but I felt that their zeal was misguided. I feel that violence was no remedy for India's ills, and that her civilisation required the use of a different and higher weapon for self-protection."

PART I

ESSENCE OF HIND SWARAJ

2

Western Civilization is Not Modern

Gandhian Modernism

It was the hey day of modernism when Gandhi wrote *Hind Swaraj*. Western civilisation was approaching its zenith. The sun did not set in the British Empire; Industrial Revolution had sucked even the European colonies of Asia, Africa and Latin America into its orbit and made them paupers to the hilt. The elites of the colonies were so educated that they believed in the superiority of the Western (Industrial) Civilisation; so much so that it was branded as modern civilisation, an improvement over the pre-modern civilisation, which still prevailed in the colonies. The 'non-western civilisations were un-modern and behind the time; they were to be modernized so that they could also progress, become rational and scientific and participate in industrialization even if as raw material producers of European industries. Only those who were imbued with Protestant Ethics could progress. Non-western civilisations had no chance of modernizing themselves without being the white man's burden, perhaps perpetually.

Gandhi made a frontal attack on Western civilisation; he called it un-modern, regressive, a disease, intoxicant, satanic, and Black Age. "This civilisation is such that one has only to be patient and it will be self destroyed." Among the characteristics of modern civilisation as it prevailed in the first decade of the twentieth century, Gandhi took note of the following in *Hind Swaraj*:

(1) It equates human body with machine consisting of interconnected limbs, tissues and cells. Life emerged as a matter of chance and has no other significance. It has firm faith in Darwin's theory of evolution of species and does

not brook any intervention by any supernatural power to intervene in the evolution and functioning of the universe.

(2) It makes body welfare (material development) the object of life at the utter neglect of moral progress. Having better houses to live, better clothes to wear, better weapons to fight, better implements to cultivate land, faster means of transportation to move around and improved mechanical devices to dispense with manual work.

(3) It is irreligious in the sense that it is devoid of morality and universal human values. If moral progress is real progress of human society, then the so-called modern civilisation is regressive.

(4) Its claim of being democratic is false and illusory. Democracy can prosper only if people are free to make choices, if they are fearless and they know their rights and responsibilities. Modern civilisation is marked with inequality; it divides society in high and low, haves and have-nots, rich and poor, white and black, Christians and non-Christians, Western and Eastern, and so on.

(5) Money is the God of modern civilisation. The West has inflicted incalculable harm to other societies. It has made millions of people captive and slave and destroyed their economic base and socio-cultural heritage just for making money and getting materially rich.

(6) It promotes violence. Conflict is the essence of modern civilisation. Two World Wars in the twentieth century took away millions of lives and destroyed cities and villages, factories and farms. It divides, fragments and isolates thing, living or non-living that comes anywhere near it.

(7) It is competitive, not cooperative. It pitches man against nature, man against man, and man against himself. As such conflict is inbuilt in modern civilisation. There can be no peace and harmony so long as this civilisation rules over the world.

(8) It organizes the society hierarchically into a pyramid with wide base and narrow top. At the base are the commoners and the top the elites. The commoners have to bear the burden of the elites. Modern civilisation thus is unmindful of the welfare of the poor, women, peasants, artisans and other

marginalised people. Similarly, it cares for large cities but ignores villages and robs the latter of their wherewithal because urbanisation and urban development promotes economic growth.

(9) Its truth is derived from scientific research and rational thinking. Both science and rationality have their own limitations. In order that science that can uncover the secrets of the material world does not take man astray, it must be tempered by spirituality. Since spirituality is outside the sphere of modern civilisation, the results derived from science could not be final.

(10) Institutions created by modern civilisation to promote truth, justice and human welfare are counterproductive. Hospitals, which are supposed to promote good health, spread diseases; courts, which are supposed to deliver justice, promote litigation; and educational institutions, which are supposed to turn out morally strong, knowledgeable and skilled human beings, produce elites who conform to the norms of the modern western civilisation.

Gandhi debunked western (industrial) civilisation as a caricature of modern civilisation and declared that a truly modern civilisation was still in the womb of time. Civilized people, according to him, were those who were morally strong; who were prepared to die rather than abandon the path of Truth (which is God). Civilisation was the sum total of thoughts, life styles, actions and hopes and aspirations that enriched human life, that respected the dignity of individuals, that advanced human freedom, that maintained peace and harmony, and that ensured a better future for humankind. Those who worked against these values were mal-civilized, if not uncivilized.

As stated earlier, *Hind Swaraj* in essence is designed to counter the generally held view that modern industrial civilisation marks a quantum jump in human progress. Gandhi debunked this civilisation as Satanic; people all over the world like it because they have developed a materialistic bent of mind. He gave the outline of a truly modern civilisation that would ensure happiness for man and take him forward on the path of his destiny.

Gandhi gave primacy to spiritual development of man. By spiritual development he meant moral and ethical progress. Gandhi indicts modern civilisation as immoral and therefore anti-developmental. Gandhi was critical of modern industrial civilisation on several counts; he branded it satanic; elsewhere he labelled it as a disease requiring urgent cure. He even called it "a civilisation only in name. Under it the nations of Europe are becoming degraded and ruined day by day.... Several English writers refuse to call that civilisation which passes under that name. Many books have been written upon that subject. Societies have been formed to cure the nation of the evils of civilisation. A great English writer has written a work called *Civilisation: Its Causes and Cure*. Therein he has called it a disease."

In this context it would be pertinent to warn the reader that Gandhi was not against the original European civilisation imbued with Christian values. He was a follower of Christ and hence there was no question of his advocating anything against a civilisation based on Christian philosophy. In fact, Gandhi's contention was that western civilisation as it was practiced in his time was non-Christian in its broad contours as well as details.

When Gandhi condemned the western civilisation, he was referring to modern industrial civilisation, which took birth in the west sometimes in the sixteenth-seventeenth centuries. It spread its tentacles so that by the turn of the seventeenth century it brought practically the whole of Europe under its sway. The Christian values and ethical standards were lost and a new set of values that sidetracked morality and ethics were propagated and put into practice. It was no longer a civilisation that aimed at taking humanity to peace and harmony and individuals to the higher reaches of psychic evolution. In fact, it became a caricature of civilisation for it promoted whatever was animal in man. It used the power of knowledge not to make this earth a better place to live but to develop various mechanical means for enslaving people and making this earth unfit for life. Great civilisations and nations were colonized, impoverished and emasculated. He considered it un-modern because it took humanity back to the animal behaviour.

Gandhi was critical of the industrial civilisation, not the original European civilisation, which was based on the remnants of Greek, Roman and Judaic civilisations on the one hand and Christian values on the other, even if in distorted forms. He criticized this civilisation on four main counts:

(1) It sidetracked morality and ethics as the basis for human survival and development;

(2) It focused on material progress and body welfare;
(3) It promoted violence and war as the means to out-compete others; and
(4) It emphasized growth and expansion unmindful of its implications for systems functioning.

Gandhi's measuring rod for human progress was morality. A civilisation that promoted morality was true and the one that promoted immorality was false. Since the core concern of the modern industrial civilisation was economic well-being unmindful of the means used to earn money, Gandhi considered it regressive.

Gandhi considered western civilisation immoral because it subordinated morality and ethics to the lust for power and money. Success was measured in terms of how much political, economic and military power one had, not on how the moral and spiritual a person was. It mattered little how the power was secured. "This civilisation takes note neither of morality nor of religion. Its votaries calmly state that that their business is not to teach religion. Some even consider it a superstitious growth. Others put on the clock of religion, and prate about morality. But after twenty years experience, I have come to the conclusion that immorality is often taught in the name of morality. Even a child can understand that in all I have described above, there can be no inducement to morality. Civilisation seeks to induce bodily comfort and it fails miserably even in doing so."

In Gandhian praxis all humans are born to achieve self-realisation and this was possible only if they followed a moral and ethical path. The ends and means of modern civilisation are just the opposite. It mattered little what means were used; all that mattered was the end and the end was the accumulation of power to subdue others. Gandhi stood and worked for a world, which was founded on morality, on love and sacrifice, not on power and money. And that is the reason why he branded modern civilization immoral and irreligious. "This civilisation is irreligious, and it has taken such a hold on the people in Europe that those who are in it appear to be half mad. They lack real physical strength or courage.... For the sake of pittance half a million women in England alone are labouring under trying circumstances in factories or similar institutions." And this situation in England changed only when more people in Asia, Africa and Latin America were put under more trying conditions.

CHARACTERISTICS OF MODERN CIVILIZATION

A number of characteristics combine to make modern civilisation immoral. Gandhi identified five of these characteristics:

(1) it transgresses the Cosmic Law,
(2) it is irreligious,
(3) it engenders mechanical mentality,
(4) it promotes violence, and
(5) it aims at material welfare alone.

It Transgresses the Cosmic Law

The whole universe and each element of it has been functioning efficiently for so many billions of years by dint of a force, which keeps it in balance. It follows a set pattern of development and does not allow anything to go astray. There are disturbances, sometimes major ones, but they are not allowed to get the whole system derailed. Gandhi called this force the Cosmic Law. He did not consider it necessary to bring in any super power into the picture although all religions do try to explain this force in terms of Almighty God.

Gandhi appears to have a sort of systems theory in the back of his mind. He could see that all natural systems from the universe to minute cell in human body are self-contained, self-reliant, self-regulating. They are at the same time interdependent. They are thus marked by maximum autonomy with maximum interdependence. The force that keeps the whole system and every sub-system of it on a path that neither violates their autonomy nor disturbs their interdependence, was referred to as Cosmic Force. It was Cosmic because it kept the whole cosmos in order. 'The universe would disappear without the existence of that force.'

Thus Gandhi perceived a symbiotic relationship among all physical and biological phenomena. Everything is geared to function in harmony with everything else. We have discussed the essential elements of the Cosmic Law in chapter 7. Here we propose to look into some aspects, which prove that modern civilisation is a dangerous proposition and unless man unhinges himself from it, he would land himself in a suicidal whirlpool.

These are:

(1) universe is marked by interdependence and symbiosis;
(2) rights and duties go together;
(3) growth is subordinate to efficient functioning;
(4) births and deaths are not discrete phenomena; they form a continuity; and
(5) change is the law of nature but organic change alone can ensure continuity of life.

The universe is marked with interdependence and symbiosis. Interdependence forces each element of it to cooperate with each other while symbiosis forces it to help each other. The mode of functioning is more important for biological phenomena; no part of a plant, animal or human being can change without affecting the whole body, mind and soul; not even a cell. Each of the billions of cells is interlinked with each other and supportive of each other. It has its assigned roles, which it performed without any interruption.

Humans are the most highly evolved species of life forms. They have three different levels of intelligence: sub-conscious, conscious and super-conscious, while the animals and the plants are governed by only one fully developed intelligence, *i.e.* sub-conscious. As such the factors of interdependence and symbiosis are more fully developed in them. No wonder then that all religions talk of human brotherhood, love, compassion, nonviolence, self-sacrifice, etc. Hinduism goes still further and treated all life to be part of a single family: *Vasudhaiva Kutumbakam.*

Modern civilisation, however, cares a hoot for the above-mentioned qualities. Its *mantra* is competition not cooperation; survival of the fittest, not symbiosis; specialized knowledge, not all-embracing wisdom; analysis, not synthesis; individual achievement, not community development; violence, not nonviolence; complexity, not simplicity and greed not need.

In nature nothing is marked with growth without development. Anything that grows alone must burst because there is always a limit to growth without its horizontal spread. Growth must be governed by the requirements of a functioning system: when growth outweighs functioning, the system suffers from malignancy or explosion. Modern civilisation is however gripped by what we may call growth mania. Everything grows and grows: economy grows, population grows, wants grow, desires grow, and diseases grow. Everything appears to go upwards linearly. This leads to mal-functioning of all social, economic and other systems despite innumerable control measures contrived and put in place.

Gandhi was not against growth as such. Even human body grows to become adult. But its growth is part of the overall development: the mind, the organs, the tissues, and the cells grow in harmony with each other. Growth in nature takes place within the limits set by it. If our technological, economic and social systems also follow the laws of nature, most of the problems we face today would not be there. If economic growth were tempered by the requirements of ecology and environment and the basic needs of the people, we would have more happiness and peace in the world. The poverty that maims billions of people (one third of humanity) would become a phenomenon of the past.

Gandhi contended that the solution lay in bringing physical and material developments within a circle formed by the Moral Law. Material growth and body welfare should be determined by the needs of the humanity as a whole. This means that each person must follow a moral code of conduct prescribed by his or her own culture. That is the only way to solve the problems humanity faces today. Very few of us realize that the moral laws are derived from the natural laws and rationally derived human values. If we follow the moral laws, the social, economic and other problems we are facing would start unhinging.

It is Irreligious

Gandhi was a religious man but he was against the institutionalization of religion. He felt that bureaucratized religious institutions corrupted the very purpose for which they were created. He considered religion to be a purely private affair of individuals; the state and government should have nothing to do with it. Morality and ethics, which form the bedrocks of religion must, however, find their legitimate place in the duties of the government. And since all religions were meant to promote morality and ethics, they all deserved equal respect.

For Gandhi, religions were different paths to achieve self-realization. Each individual should interpret the religious approaches to this goal through his own studies, experiments, and experiences. There can be no set rules. To deny human beings the right to choose their own paths of self-realization amounted to denial of human dignity and the potentials of man to scale spiritual heights he aspired to reach. As such there must be as many religions as individuals.

Religion to Gandhi was not set of rituals as many people tend to believe; it was a code of ethics and morality which was to be practiced in thought, words and deeds (*mansa, vacha, karmana*). It was a belief in God (*Parmatma*), a ray of which was the *Self* within (*Atma*). And since Truth is God, and ultimate Truth could be found only through moral and ethical conduct, religious man is one who practices ethical code of conduct. Thus in Gandhian praxis, a person who practices ethical and moral laws would be called religious.

Gandhi was a religious man. He saw God in everything that existed, particularly in living things. His thoughts, words and deeds were directed to realize the Self within. He considered various religions as different paths to achieve this great and final purpose of life. That is the reason why he considered conversion from one religion to another as irrational and uncalled for.

Institutionalization of religion is one of the potent factors in creating conditions for modern civilisation to take shape. So long as religion remains a private affair, it remains rooted in morality. Once it is institutionalized, it brings a hierarchy of priests between the individual and the God. Religion then is not what individuals feel, experience and live but a set of rules as enunciated by the religious mediator. Institutionalization of religion means snapping of individual's direct communion with God.

Gandhi did not consider any religion to be perfect. Nor did he consider any of the religious books like *Geeta*, *Bible*, and *Koran* so sacrosanct that all that they contained must be followed without revaluation. Even if they were inspired by God, they had the imprint of the progress man had made at the time of the revelation. Since no human being can be perfect, the transcription of even such messages or revelations must be imperfect. To deny human beings the opportunity to improve upon what religious books contained amounted to denying human dignity.

The problem with institutionalized religions is that they deny the individuals to experience God directly without a mediator and to find their own path of self-realization. More institutionalized a religion is, greater the chances of its being rigid in rituals and against the freedom man must have to experiment. They go by the book literally, not contextually and in relation to the moral and ethical principles underlying the text. How else, morality and ethics have often become the casualty in inter-religious feuds. Great fights among the followers of Judaism, Christianity and Islam took millions of lives. This is also perhaps the reason why religions remain divided not on the basis of how to achieve self-realization but on the interpretation of the words used in the books to suit the intents of the political power.

This brings us to yet another major drawback of over institutionalized religion. It tends to ally itself with the political power of the day. And in this process, it gets impregnated with all those defects, which afflict power politics. The religious wars, which have been fought all over the world, were rooted in this tendency. European religions have thus willy-nilly encouraged modern civilisation to take roots and spread all over the world. The Cross had accompanied trade and raid in Latin America, Australia and Africa. It had been so in Asia the birth place of great religions like Hinduism, Buddhism, and Jainism. The Moslem invaders descended on India in the name of Islam. The number of the sons of Allah they butchered to please their creator (Allah) was unprecedented in the annals of history. There were rivalries and may be even fights even among India-based religions, which adhere to nonviolence. The fights between Shaivaits and Vaisnavaits and between Hindus and Buddhists were not uncommon.

Institutionalized religion has been a good ally of modern civilisation. So long as such religions continue to have a hold on the minds of the people, modern civilisation would continue to prosper at the cost of morality and ethics. In this connection, it would not be out of place to mention that the number of people who have been killed in the wars of religions is not less than that killed in wars of nations. Let us not forget that whole races and civilisations have been wiped out in Latin America and Australia, all in the name of Religion.

It Engenders Mechanical Mentality

Mechanization is a major characteristic of modern civilisation. Machines have always been there and they will continue to be there in future, too. But when development of machines overrides the development of human beings, as is the case with the modern industrial civilisation, then we get into a problem. Should we have machines to save labour? Yes, we should have, if we are short of labour. But the machines should not be used to destroy nature and rob the people of their livelihood.

In Gandhian praxis, mindless mechanization symbolizes a mechanical worldview, which sets modern civilisation apart from what

Gandhi considered to be the real civilisation. He epposed machines for machines sake because they rise to machine mentality and a mechanical worldview. Mechanical worldview sees the whole universe as a grand machine with innumerable parts and nuts and bolts. It runs like a machine. It can be repaired and rectified if something goes wrong. This applies to the universe as well as its parts both physical and biological, including human beings. But we know that the universe does not function like a machine, nor its various elements do so. It is more so with the biological systems. Our body, for example, is a machine but it is a live machine. It is not an assemblage of limbs, tissues and cells. It is a highly integrated live system in which each of the billions of cells is in vertical as well as horizontal communication with each other. Each is dependent on the other. A live system exhibits perfect symbiosis. No part of it can stand separately. It is functional only so long as it is a part of the whole. Machines are run by the energy supplied from outside. Energy for the living systems is generated within. As such the living systems cannot be compared with machines. It is more so with human beings and the social systems they form because man is not only a living system but also the most advanced life form on the surface of the earth.

Gandhi, as a matter of principle, was against mechanization for mechanization's sake. "Machinery represents a great sin. I cannot recall a single good point in connection with machinery", said he. Where machines grow man decays, felt he. He was pained to see the pitiable condition of workers in Bombay cloth mills. "If machinery craze grows in our country it will be an unhappy land. It may be considered a hearsay but I am bound to say that it were better for us to send money to Manchester and to use flimsy Manchester cloth than to multiply mills in India. By using Manchester cloth we only waste our money; but by reproducing Manchester in India, we shall keep our money at the price of our blood, because our very moral being will be sapped, and I call in support of my statement the very mill hands as witnesses."

Gandhi did not subscribe to the view that Indians in the past did not encourage mechanization because they were interested only in other worldly things. Indians knew how to invent machinery from time immemorial but they deliberately refrained from doing so because they knew that "if we set our hearts after such things, we would become slaves and lose our moral fibre. They therefore after due deliberations decided that we should do only what we could with our hands and feet. They saw that our real happiness and health consisted in a proper use of our hands and feet."

Gandhi was aware that machines were essential; so he repeatedly said that he was not against machines as such. He considered human body to be a sort of biological machine. What he objected to was not the machine but the machine mentality and the use of the machine to dominate others or to deprive others of their right to live. When to use the machine and when not to use it, he said "if the thought is sound, we shall always find out what we can give up and gradually cease to use them. What a few may do, others will copy: the movement will grow like the Author of the mathematical problem." We should prefer things, which are hand made and home made.

Mechanization leads to mass production. Gandhi was a votary of decentralized production so as to provide adequate employment in creative activities to all. He was an advocate of a system wherein large industries contracted thousands of small producers for manufacturing parts needed by them to produce final goods. "If they (industrialists of India) would be good, they would gradually contract their businesses. They can establish in thousands of households the ancient and sacred handlooms and they can buy out the cloth that may be thus woven."

Mechanization has helped man move at great speed and to change things fast. But high speed without moral reawakening can prove dangerous to human survival and development, says Gandhi. "....but for railways, English could not have such a hold on India as they have. The railways too have spread bubonic plague. Without them the masses could not move from place to place. They are the careers of plague germs. Formerly, we had natural segregation. Railways have also increased the frequency of famines because owing the facilities of means of locomotion, people sell out their grains and it is sent to the dearest market.... Railways accentuate the evil nature of man. Bad men fulfil their evil designs with greater rapidity. The holy places of India have become unholy. Formerly, people went to these places with very great difficulty. Generally therefore only the real devotees visited such places. Now-a-days rogues visit them in order to practice their roguery."

And he adds, "good travels at snails pace—it can, therefore, have little to do with the railways. Those who want to do good are not selfish; they are not in hurry; they know that to impregnate people with good requires a long time. But evil has wings.... It may be debatable matter whether railways spread famines, but it is beyond dispute that they propagate evil."

The points that Gandhi raises are valid. Many of the problems we face today are rooted in speed. The wide disparities in levels of living, opportunities for earning livelihood, and expressing one's talent or skills, and standard of living are the main causes for the movement of the people from place to place. If these disparities are eliminated or at least reduced to a tolerable level, the necessity for movement will also come down.

High speed is related to the nature of economic and social system we have created. A global economy definitely needs high-speed transport system. In the context of the Gandhian economy, frequency of long distance travels will be very much reduced for much of the needs of the people would be met locally and regionally. Further, the ill effects of speed and mass scale movement of people and goods can be substantially reduced by building institutions, which bind people together at the grassroots level.

It Promotes Violence

Nonviolence is the basic creed of civilized societies. "The fact that there are so many men still alive in the world shows that it is based not on the force of arms but on the force of Truth or Love." The power of Love binds the world into one family. Everything is linked to everything else. So long as the law of Love remains intact, the whole world moves smoothly. Once it gets weakened or fractured, everything falls apart.

"The force of Love is the same as the force of the Soul or Truth. We have evidence of its working at every step. The universe would disappear without the existence of that force.... Thousands, indeed tens of thousands depend for their existence on a very active working of this force.... Soul Force being natural is not noted in history."

The power of Love can be used to resolve all conflicts: interpersonal or international. A true civilisation will use only the power of Love, which is soul force. The power of arms or brute force will be non-existent in it. Gandhi called this power of Love in conflict resolution Passive Resistance. Later, he improved upon this term and called it *Satyagraha*.

If the Force used in conflict resolution is taken as a criterion to judge human progress, our present civilisation is the worst. We nevertheless call it modern. Today we have the weapons of mass destruction. We have atom bomb, hydrogen bomb, chemical weapons and biological weapons, which can wipe out all life from planet earth in no time. And there are countries in the world which are still in search of more devastating weapons based on laser technology. These weapons can be mounted on the moon or mars or in the outer space and beamed on any country to destroy it. Gandhi would have used far stronger term than satanic for this civilisation, had he been alive.

The weapons we use are the products of science and technology that we teach our youth in schools and colleges. What we teach our children is knowledge of letter. When they grow up we train them as physicists, chemical engineers, biologists, historians etc. it is these young men and women who give shape and content to our civilisation. Civilisation is the product of accumulated experience of the past and contemporary education seen in its broader perspectives to include family education, informal education and formal education. The most important task of education, says Gandhi, is character building. No nation can become great unless its people are morally strong. Knowledge of letters is only an instrument; it is not education. "The same instrument that can be used to cure a patient, may be used to take his life, and so may a knowledge of letters. We daily observe that many men abuse it and very few make good use of it; and if this is a correct statement, we have proved that more harm has been done by it." Thus it is not fault of weapons, it is the fault of our mechanical and violence-prone mentality, which is at fault. This mentality can change only through education.

When the British came to India they introduced English education, which was meant to serve the British interests and promote their brand of civilisation. Since, in the new civilisation system morality and ethics did not occupy the central place, Gandhi wanted the education system of free India to be different. In his scheme of things it should be multi-dimensional and multi-functional. Its first and basic function should be character building. "Religion that is ethical education will occupy the first place." Then it should impart knowledge of humanities, physical and biological sciences, mathematics and applied fields like engineering, architecture, technologies etc. And, finally, it should train each and every child in productive activities to enable him to earn his livelihood. In fact, the character building, knowledge acquisition and training in skills should go side by side. This is possible in something like Ashramite schools of Indian's hoary past with a strong input of modern educational processes. A combination of austere living, home and skill building is the answer. Gandhi tried this through *Nai Talim* (basic education) institutions. So long as its basic functions and methodologies remain archaic, education would continue to play its destructive role.

It Aims at Material Welfare Alone

Man is not body and mind alone. He has the soul too, says Gandhi. The body is a biological machine; the mind reasons and gives it unity so that its parts cannot function outside it. The soul gives it meaning, purpose, and goal of existence; it links it to its Creator. Modern civilisation serves the body and mind alone. Apart from meeting the basic needs so that the body is not in any ways disabled to keep man in active state, it also lures him to go for comforts and luxuries some of which are highly injurious to both body and mind. It is, however, neglectful of the soul, firstly, because it cannot see the soul and secondly, and more importantly, because it does not concern itself with anything that is outside the physical existence of man. It is not concerned with morality and ethics; love and compassion; or truth and nonviolence. It aims at material welfare of man. Anything that comes in the way of this great task, must not be taken note of. Modern civilisation does not care for the means so long as the ends are good. Earn money and wealth by any means, is the hidden motto.

The values that make man human are outside the scope of modern development theory and practice. In this connection it would be important to note that Gandhi was not against material advancement so long as it aimed at serving the people. As stated earlier, the highest goal of human life, in Gandhian praxis, is *Swaraj* or self-control, which leads to self-realization. Man has to advance towards a higher level of consciousness where body, mind and soul could work in unison. This level of consciousness could not be achieved by all and at the same time. It is the task of civilisation and its institutions to help man move in that direction.

Gandhian economics, therefore, prescribes minimisation of wants. Modern economic theory suggests that, the more goods and services man has access to the happier he is. In other words, the more of his material needs are satisfied, the more happy he is. Since there is no end to wants (because newer wants crop up as old one's are satisfied) there is no possibility of man ever being happy and satisfied. Gandhi, therefore, suggested minimising the wants. Lesser the wants, lesser the pains caused by them. And lesser the physical needs, lesser the man's demand on nature and fellow human beings. Thus the cruelty man inflicts on both nature and fellow human beings would be lessened by reducing the wants. That is why he advocated simple living and high thinking. High thinking comes from spiritual awakening, which boils down to love and compassion towards all. In practical terms, it means having enough to satisfy one's basic material needs, and aiming at spiritual attainment while living in this world of good and evil and working to build a civilisation of peace and harmony.

What Gandhi said was not a utopia. It is not something that cannot be achieved in the long run. Gandhi wanted it to be the goal of life and living even if it was impossible to achieve in one's own lifetime. An individual is a link in the chain of what we call human evolution. Each one contributes to the civilisation man creates and lives in. The civilisation should help man reach the goal of self-realization. This can happen only if he does not deviate from the path of righteousness; the path of love and compassion, the path of truth and nonviolence; and the path of voluntary poverty.

WHAT HAS MODERN CIVILISATION ACHIEVED?

It Has Fractured the World

One of the major achievements of modern civilisation lies in the division of the world into rich and poor. The growing disparity in earning capacities, incomes and living conditions among individuals, groups of people, regions and nations has fractured and shattered the world into pieces. Some countries, regions, and individuals have become richer while many others have become poorer than before. The widening gap between the rich and poor is one of the main characteristics of modern civilisation. Those who are left behind in the mad race for economic prosperity are branded as unfit, illiterate, ignorant, blacks, scheduled castes and tribes or just uncultured. The fact that the very process of modern economics produces pockets of affluence and poverty is ignored. The rich are considered civilised while the poor uncivilised.

This anomalous situation is covered up by much publicised new policies to eradicate poverty, illiteracy, ignorance, inequality, etc. International agencies like World Bank offer loans at concessional rates for these purposes. Behind these policies lies a desire to postpone the deepening crisis rather than to solve it. Further, all these projects bring new benefits to the haves, the politicians, bureaucrats, technocrats and contractors. Poverty eradication programmes in the developing countries have served as showpieces only, they have failed to make any dent in the depth and breadth of poverty.

Each crisis in the economic system brings in new policies and programmes to keep the system going. The latest policy fad is 'globalization, liberalization and privatization'. It has been brought in place by the West ostensibly to bridge the development gap but in reality it is designed to maintain the superiority of the West in all spheres. 'Industrialization' and 'Socialism', the old fads have been replaced by the new ones: 'Information Technology' and 'Privatization'. The new policy would certainly make countries like India and China grow faster; the feel good factor would not dim so long it is in the interest of rich nations. Since their interest lies in incorporating the potentially great nations like India in the League of the Rich Nations. None of these would work so long as the fundamentals of the global economy do not change in favour of the poor. According to some projections more people will be poor after ten years than today.

Gandhi offered a new model of modernity, a model, which can tone down, if not stop, the mad race for economic growth, technological advancement, accumulation of wealth, pilferage of nature and exploitation of the weaker sections of the society and which can ensure basic needs of all at substantially high level and also promote corporate development of nations, regions and communities without adverse effects on ecology. The true test of an economic system lies not in how many billionaires are there in a country but in how many people are still there with pot bellies and empty pockets.

It Has Perfected the Creed of Violence

Over-emphasis on acquisition of money and wealth by hook or crook has created an atmosphere of violence all over the world. There is violence in the minds of individuals; among groups of people; and among the nations. People are prepared to sacrifice everything for money and material welfare. At the global level, the efforts of the United Nations to maintain peace remains fractured. There is no country of the world, which does not have disputes with its neighbours. Killing, kidnapping and looting at the individual level is on the increase. And to top this all is the rise of terrorism. People are motivated to kill innocent men, women and children in order that their 'legitimate' or 'ill-legitimate' demands are accepted. Some of them are prepared even to become human bombs to indulge in mass killing. What is painful is that many of these killing 5 are done in the name of religion, race or ethnicity or tribe.

One of the major pre-occupations of the people in modern times is to get rich as fast as possible. Finding no legitimate shortcuts, they prey on each other. And this is done in the name of competition, a necessary ingredient of modern economics.

It Has Landed the World in Ecological Crisis

Ecological and environmental decay is another major contribution of modern civilisation. Over and wasteful use of natural resources and the goods and services produced on farms and factories on the one hand and increased use of chemicals specially the petroleum and its products on the other, is the major cause of ecological destruction. The situation is highly explosive. Unless corrective steps are taken soon the very survival of life on planet may be put in jeopardy.

The other day I went to the *Sangam* (the confluence of Ganga, Yamuna and mythical Saraswati) in Allahabad. I saw lakhs of people taking bath in a water that was not only muddy but highly polluted. There was a time when the water at the Sangam was pure and clean and one could easily see the line along which the Ganga and Yamuna waters met. One was white and the other blue. Now those days are gone. The water at the Sangam is no longer suitable for human use. It has been polluted by sewage of large cities like Kanpur. Much of the water of the two rivers is diverted to canals for irrigation. So the capacity of the rivers to cleans themselves up has drastically declined. Further, the fish, the tortoises and other animals, which cleaned up the biological contaminations have been caught and exported. The river is left half dry and devoid of life to fend for itself. It is now choked with dirt released by 'great cities,' Gandhi could see this impending crisis even in 1909; well before anyone else could see and forewarn.

It Has Destroyed the Moral Base of the Society

Another major consequence of the undue emphasis on material goods and services is the moral decline of man. Today morality does not find a place in our educational system; it has no place in our economics, politics, science and technology. Man has started preying on man; he is prepared to sell himself for money. Humanity has drifted away from spiritualism to reach the apex of materialism.

Hind Swaraj calls for a return to spirituality, morality and ethical behaviour. Things that downgrade morality and actions that are patently immoral, must be shunned. In the postmodern civilisation too there will be science and technology but they would not be used for the advantage of a few and the disadvantage of the many as has been the case in modern civilisation.

It has Promoted Growth without Development

Today the most important preoccupation of man both in rich and poor countries is economic development. In Gandhi's time it was known as 'progress'. The West was progressed and progressive. The rest of the world was backward and primitive; it started progressing after it came under the spell of the West.

The twentieth century witnessed the emergence of freedom movements in European colonies of Asia and Africa. Most of the colonies became free countries by 1980s and tried to catch up with their former masters in economic and technological fields. Economic historians told the newly emerging nations that they could also become economically and technologically advanced if they followed the path laid down by the Europeans. They forgot their own cultural moorings and followed the West. They decided to jump on the bandwagon of Industrial Revolution, which, in its classical form at least, was already on the decline. The nature was tamed and the other life forms were exploited to meet the increasing human wants and greed triggered off by the new economic policy. Even human beings were re-designated as human resources to be used for enhancing material prosperity.

Gandhi was appalled by the digression Western civilisation forced upon humanity. He was not impressed by the economic progress of Europe for, as he put it, it did not represent 'real progress'. Progress that de-humanized man; that increased distance between man and nature and between man and man; that increased avarice and greed at the cost of love and compassion; and that enriched some and impoverished many was not real progress, declared he. Progress should not be measured by the physical goods one possessed; or by the destructive power one commanded; it should be measured by the moral strength one possessed and creativity one exhibited in day to day life; by the sacrifices one made for others and the privileges one denied for himself so that the needs of others were better served. He felt rather strongly that Industrial Revolution improved the material well being of Europeans but weakened their moral fabric. The other continents suffered doubly. They were impoverished materially as well as morally.

Gandhi challenged the contemporary theories of progress, be they economic, social or biological. He considered industrial civilisation a deviation from the eternal journey of man with Ego to become a 'super-conscious' man without Ego. Sooner it ended, better it was. To achieve lasting progress humans must discard the ruling paradigm of progress; they must endeavour to upgrade their ethical and moral standards: through service, sacrifice and selflessness. Material progress with moral degeneration would lead to nowhere. A civilisation that ignored moral progress would destroy itself and, maybe, it would destroy the whole living earth. *Hind Swaraj* is a *Magna Carta* of a truly humane civilisation.

In Gandhi's scheme of things, no country is developed: some are underdeveloped while others are mal-developed. In the latter category, fall the countries which parade themselves as developed (European countries). These countries constitute the greatest stumbling block in the real development of man, and hence they are mal-developed. And the countries (like India and China), which are declared by the Europeans as backward, are underdeveloped because they have failed to unearth their own cultural potentials; they try to copy the former and lose their moorings.

As we enter the twenty-first century, we realize the mess – moral, ecological, economic and social—we have created. We have come to a pass that even a single rogue could destroy the whole world. What happened on September 11, 2001 in New York is just a sample of what is in store for us if we do not change our ways. A great tragedy was providentially averted on December 13, 2001 when Indian parliament was attacked by the terrorists. Not one but many Osamas, big and small, are roaming the streets all over the world to destroy the great edifices, visible as well invisible, of modern civilisation. In fact, these sick people are the products of a sick mind that the western civilisation is deft in creating. They can be punished and done to death. But that is not the end of it. More of them will emerge, for modern civilisation is a hospitable host for the survival, reproduction and growth of the viruses that disorient humans and lead them to blind alleys.

Osama-bin-Laden is only a new *Avatar* of Hitler. The *Avatars* of such destructive forces are in-built in modern civilisation. The war unleashed by America on Iraq is not an isolated event. It is part of a chain that is unending. It is not the first time that humans have faced such crises. Many civilisations disappeared in the past, as they could not cope with their own monstrosities. They were, however, localized and regional in character. The present industrial civilisation is global and, therefore, impacts all humans; it impacts the whole world. If it is allowed to reach its logical conclusions, it may amount to the end of all life on planet earth.

But there is hope. While the capacity of humans to destroy has increased many fold, their capacity to create and preserve and recognise the mistakes has also increased. If Hitler and his ilk are reborn to attempt the annihilation of the world, Rama, Krishna, Buddha, Mahavir, Zoroaster, David, Jusus, Mohammad, Emerson, Tolstoy, Vivekananda, Gandhi and many others may return to this earth in new Avatars to show the alternative paths of sanity. The forces of destruction appear to be counterbalanced by the forces of creation. Gandhi was the twentieth century *Avatar* of the creative forces.

Hind Swaraj was written in response to the violent method adopted by some of the angry young men of India who wanted to dislodge the British from Indian soil by brute force. They were logically right. Did the Bolshevik Revolution in Russia not take place in response to that logic? Those who are tormentors must be tormented. How many wars and conflicts had humanity suffered just to avoid the next war? But each war has given rise to another and often time bigger wars. India's occupation by the British was also a war against a nation. Throwing the British out violently would not have heralded the end of more violent conflicts in India and the rest of the world. If violence produced violence, then the very logic that it would bring *Swaraj* for India was false. Those who kill the foreigners would not hesitate to kill their own countrymen once they assumed power. *Swaraj* without truth and nonviolence is not real *Swaraj*, argued Gandhi.

But why do people opt for violence? Gandhi's answer is twofold. One, modern industrial civilisation is founded on violence; its central organizing principle is violence. As long as it continues to shape human destiny, there would be no peace in the world, not even in the minds of the people. There is no aspect of life, which is not touched by it and hence there is no scope for short-term and part solutions, which a mechanistic view of the world is prone to attempt. Its remedy, according to him, lies in total transformation of its value systems, premises and directions. That is why Gandhi's condemnation of modern civilisation is total. And two, Gandhi did not consider the situation beyond retrieval. There is something very special that distinguished India from the rest of the world. Indian civilisation has always given supremacy to moral and ethical values. That is not to say that there were no deviations from the main tendencies and that other civilisations were necessarily more violent. If we look at the central theme of Indian civilisation, we find it to be hovering around moral development. Since those tendencies had not disappeared altogether, it was possible to built around it a new global civilisation of peace and harmony.

Postmodernism is only the First Step

Postmodernism is a paradigm that pervaded art, literature, history, sociology and political science during the second half of the twentieth century in the West. It emerged as a reaction to modernism, a product of the industrial civilisation that emerged in the West during the nineteenth and first half of the twentieth centuries. Gandhi was highly critical of modern civilisation for, in his opinion, it was un-modern and retrogressive. A progressive civilisation was one, which advanced man further on the path of evolution. It was still in the womb of time. Gandhi gave the basics of such a civilisation in *Hind Swaraj*. Thus, the modernism of the West was un-modernism of Gandhi and postmodernism of the West would, at best, signify an aspect of modernism of Gandhi and the last phase of the modernism of the West.

In this section, we propose to compare Gandhi's modernism with that of West. To do this, let us first look at the meaning of pre-modernism, modernism and post-modernism as understood in the West. In the premodern times, all aspects of life were governed by the authority of social institutions like joint family, Catholicism, feudal lords, kings, etc. and the life of the individual was governed by traditions carried forward and strengthened from generation to generations. One of the main characteristics of pre-modern societies was the captivating presence of grand narratives (often religious) that gave meaning to life and living. These narratives not only moulded the life of people but also offered models for behaviour within the given institutional and traditional constraints.

European Renaissance and Reformation in the nineteenth century gave rise to a new paradigm, which came to be known as modernism.

It rejected tradition and authority in favour of reason and scientism. Individual was recognised as autonomous who alone could find the truth by reasoning and scientific study of nature. Time was conceived as linear and so was progress. Man was no longer treated as a creature of nature; he became the master of nature. Modernism in art and architecture meant the rejection of the tradition in favour of creativity for no other purpose than novelty. Art for art's sake allowed the artist to explore possibilities and perpetually search for uniqueness and individuality.

Modernity stood for rationality and order and for universality of Western culture as the guiding star for human progress. Creating order out of chaos, discontinuities and fragmentation was its main signpost. Anything that came in the way of the order must be removed or subdued. The logic ran something like this: more rational a society was, more ordered it was; and more ordered it was, more progressive it was. Modern societies, therefore, tried to remove or subdue disorders. The non-whites, non-males, non-hygienic, non-rational, etc. were considered elements of disorder.

To sum up, modernism was based on the premises that:

(1) There is a conscious, stable, rational, autonomous and universal self, which knows itself and the world around through reason, or rationality.
(2) The mode of knowing is 'science' which provides universal truths about the world, regardless of the status of individual knower; science is neutral and objective.
(3) The knowledge produced by science is 'truth' and is eternal; it can be used to analyze and improve things to utilize nature and human beings for social progress, which is none other than economic progress.
(4) Knowledge will always lead to progress and perfection; it can be used to harness the resources of nature.
(5) Freedom lies in obedience to the laws that conform to the knowledge discovered by reason and utilizing it to produce more goods and services.
(6) Material goods give happiness to people; material development is, therefore, real development.
(7) In a world governed by reason, truth *(satyam)* will always be the same as the good *(shivam)* and the right *(sundaram)*.

There can be no conflict between what is true, good and right.

(8) Language and mode of expression to represent the truth must be precise and exact and hence mathematics is the best vehicle for it.

The Second World War had a de-stabilizing effect on the minds of the people. The faith in the grand designs was shattered and so was the rationality of man. The universality of western values was questioned. If modernism produced wars after wars and more devastating weapons of mass destruction, if it chained millions of people of Asia, Africa and Latin America in the name of grand narratives of the West, and if it created economic, social and technological disparities unmindful of human values, then there was something fundamentally wrong with it. And thus was laid the foundation of post-modernism in the West.

The term 'post-modernism' was first used in 1947 in reference to architectural expressions. Literary critics started using the term in 1960s and it entered the public debate on social and political issues in the 1970s. The linchpin of modernism was art's autonomy (art for art's sake) from the sordid daily concerns of a bourgeois commercial culture. Post-modernism signifies a sort of revolt against rules and regulations that kept the artist away from ordinary life. The new art form was branded as unrealistic.

Post-modernism rejected the concept of sovereign autonomous individual. Early post-modernists wanted to integrate the classical tradition with the modern utilitarian realities. Later the traditions were left behind. The distinctions of high and low forms were dissolved, subjects and objects were merged, and gap between 'we' and 'others' was narrowed. This led to a combination of innumerable traditional styles and patterns to form what we may call the collage. Thus from universal standards, multidimensionality, complexity and co-existence, became the normative principles. The post-modernist art form was thus aligned to the emerging post-industrial or post-modern culture of the second half of twentieth century.

Post-modernism exhorted people to 'Cross the border and close the gap' (Fedler) and pulled the artist back to the maelstrom of daily life. Art started expressing the social ethos and values as it came closer to the society. To suggest that the artist could maintain his autonomy was, therefore, unrealistic. As against the liberal's emphasis on legally guaranteed equality and Marxist's formula of everything being determined by the class relations, the post-modernists, insisted that the language, education, media etc. had built-in biases against the poor, the women, the gay, the lesbians, etc.

In post-modern societies, knowledge is no longer acquired for knowledge's sake, it is acquired for functional purposes; 'you learn things to use them' and so the emphasis on skills and training, rather than on vague humanist ideals of education to 'know thyself'. Knowledge becomes information; it is utilitarian and stored and processed electronically in computers. In the new age of information technology, opposite of knowledge is not ignorance; it is noise.

Thus the main ingredients of post-modernism are:

(1) It does not believe in the rationality of human action and challenges the emancipatory vision of Western science;
(2) It rejects the grand- or meta-narratives. The search for universal truths and laws gives way to search for differences, diversity, variety and plurality.
(3) It asserts that the prevailing system produces exploitation of poor by rich, females by males, core by periphery and weak by powerful; it champions the cause of the marginalized.
(4) It rejects the traditional view of development as structural transformation in the economy to the transmogrification of the society, from linear economic growth moving up in Rostowian stages to human development and from modernization or westernization to cultural transformation. It also rejects development as a top-down process; it is participatory, culture specific and bottom up process.
(5) It lays emphasis on behavioural, experiential and participatory approaches to knowing the truth rather than statistical and positivistic approaches.
(6) It lays stress on micro rather than macro; specific rather than general; and detailed case studies than uncovering of the universal forces underlying the social changes.

Gandhi's Vision of Post-modernism

Gandhi did not consider western Industrial Civilisation modern. When asked as to what he thought about it, he said 'it is a good idea'. As far as he was concerned, modern civilisation was an idea to be put into practice in future, not a fact. Elsewhere he branded it as a reverse of civilisation. Gandhi did not consider the pre-industrial civilisation of Europe primitive although he did recognize many defects in it. For that matter, all civilisations had good and bad aspects, much depended on who was looking at them, where and when. Nor did Gandhi believe in the linear changes in civilisation. He was a votary of spiral growth that emerged from the integration of linear and cyclic changes. Further, for Gandhi, it was not the body welfare and accumulation of wealth, even at the cost of morality and ethics, that signified progress or development. A true civilisation aimed at moral development of man; it promoted the evolution of individuals who led a dignified life, who were fearless, who were loving and compassionate, and who were truthful and nonviolent. All societal developments—social, political, and economic—supported and promoted moral development.

For Gandhi, the industrial civilisation, otherwise known as modern civilisation, marked an interruption in the dynamic changes through which all civilisations must pass to become human. Had Gandhi been alive, he would have treated post-modernism as only a special case of modern industrial civilisation and hence his criticism of the post-modernism would have not been different from that of modernism. The post-modernism of Gandhi was thus not the same as that of the West. He advocated a paradigm shift, an about turn in the path of progress to move in the direction of human destiny as perceived by him. Human destiny, thought Gandhi, lay in self-realization, in knowing one self and developing the potentials inherent in each individual. Moral ascent alone could take man to his destiny. For Gandhi, the measuring rod for progress was morality, not money or consumer goods.

Thus the social situation prevailing in 2005 AD cannot be called post-modernistic; it is modernistic in its new incarnation for the premises on which modernity was based have stood the ground; they continue to hold their sway. Gandhi, therefore, equated what is known as post-modernism with the modern industrial civilisation of the West. So, whenever he talks of true civilisation or real civilisation, he was referring to post-modern civilisation as conceived and perceived by him. That civilisation was not there in his time nor it is there in our times.

The main ingredients of Gandhi's post-modernism are listed below for ready reference:

(1) 'Civilisation is that mode of conduct, which points out to man the path of duty. Performance of duty and observance of morality are convertible terms. To observe morality is to attain mastery over our mind and our passions.' Thus *Swaraj*, self-control and civilisation are coterminous. Post-modern civilisation must conform to this golden rule.

(2) Post-modern civilisation would be based on morality and ethics, not on money, wealth and consumer goods. It will elevate man into a moral being.

(3) It would protect human dignity. Human being can do wonders; don't question their dignity. No individual would, therefore, be poor and dependent on others for basic human needs. The economic system would ensure equity in matters basic needs: food, clothing, shelter, education, health, security and self-esteem.

(4) Everyone will engage in manual work. Production and consumption would not be separate functions and activities. Only producers would be consumers. Manual work would keep people healthy; it would also engender a sense of equality.

(5) The post-modern civilisation would be nonviolent. It would value sacrifice rather than accumulation of wealth. There would be no world wars nor would there be perpetual social tensions and violence, as they are in the post-modern civilisation of the West. Patriotism would mean welfare of all.

(6) In the new civilisation, conflicts, as and when they arise, would be resolved by dialogue and soul force, not by guns and brute force. Both the means and ends would be pure and duties would get priority over rights.

(7) The real post-modernism will be based on democratic principles. It will not be rule of the majority because majority is not always right. Many great positive changes in the past have been initiated by the minority, not by the majority. It would be a democracy by consensus in which the opinion of each and every member would be important and respected.

(8) Nature would be part of life. In the pre-industrial civilisation, man lived in and with nature; in the modern industrial civilisation, he has become the master of nature; in the post-modern civilisation, nature would be part of man. Nature

would be protected and conserved so that life on planet earth continues to prosper. Simple living and high thinking together with high standard of life would be the norm.

(9) Education, in the post-modern civilisation, would be the chief vehicle to promote healthy style of life, morality in thought, words and deeds; equality among religions; linguistic and ethnic groups; love and compassion among fellow human beings; to develop skills to earn livelihood through creative work; and to acquire knowledge to understand the world around and wisdom to know the Creator. Education is that, which liberates.

(10) The post-modern civilisation would not discard science and technology but neither of them would control the man. Science would help know the nature and its laws. The knowledge of the laws of nature would be used to further enrich the nature and human life. Machinery would be used for constructive and creative purposes only. It would not be used to throw people out of their work.

The above are some of the ingredients of Gandhi's post-modernism of the future. Naturally, it is different from the post-modernism of the West, which we are experiencing today. As for as life of the people is concerned, modernism has not disappeared from the scene. All that has happened is that the classical industries have lost their supremacy as sources of income, employment and exploitation. Information technology has acquired unexpected importance. Globalization is likely to become another means of colonial exploitation unless humanity forges global solidarity to change its course. What else has changed? The moral foundations of man are being secularly subverted. True, there is freedom in poetry and prose, painting and music and in philosophic outlook. None of these have, however, percolated down to the common man. Inequalities reign supreme; exploitation of the marginalized people continues; rape of the earth has become a permanent feature. Where is post-modernism then? It is still in the womb of time, as Gandhi said.

GANDHI'S WARNINGS

Let me quote a few passages from *Hind Swaraj* to substantiate what I have written in this chapter.

"This civilisation is such that one has only to be patient and it will be self-destroyed. According to the teachings of Mohammad, this would be considered a Satanic civilisation. Hinduism calls it the Black Age (*Kaliyuga*).... It is eating into the vitals of the English nation.... Civilisation is not an incurable disease but it should never be forgotten that the English people are at present afflicted by it." (p. 34)

"Those who will rise to power by murder will certainly not make the nation happy." (p. 62) Those that take the sword shall perish by the sword. With us the problem is that professional swimmers will find a watery grave." (p. 70)

Gandhi believed that unless the leadership of the country follows the truth and shows the way to the people, there is no possibility of the true civilisation taking roots. "What the leaders do, the populace will gladly do in turn. The matter is neither complicated nor difficult. You and I need not wait until we can carry others with us. Those will be losers who will not do it, and those who will not do it, although they appreciated the truth, will deserve to be called cowards." (p. 84)

Making a clear distinction between modern industrial civilisation and Indian civilisation, Gandhi asserts that "the former relies on money and machines while the latter on morality and human labour; the former seeks the rights of individuals, the latter prescribes duties towards others; the former has the power of the weapons while the latter has the power of love."

"Some Englishmen state that they took and they hold India by sword. Both these statements are wrong. The sword is entirely useless for holding India. We alone keep them. Napoleon is said to have described the English as a nation of shopkeepers. It is a fitting description. They hold whatever dominions they have for the sake of their commerce. Their army and navy are intended to protect it.... they wish to convert the whole world into a vast market for their goods. That they cannot do so is true; but the blame not be theirs. They will leave no stone unturned to reach the goal."

3

Gandhi's Outline of a Truly Modern Civilization

MORALITY IS THE SHEET ANCHOR

Gandhi on Morality

Before we proceed further, let us be clear about what did Gandhi means by morality? While serializing *Ethical Religion* by William MacIntyre Salter in Indian Opinion in its issues from January 5 to February 23, 1907, Gandhi wrote:

"Hypocrisy has now-a-days increased in the world. Whatever a man's religion, he thinks only of its outward form and falls in his real duty. In our crazy pursuit of wealth, we seldom think of the harm we cause or are likely to cause, to others. Women in Europe do not hesitate in the least to wear soft (kid) gloves even though these are made by killing young and tender animals. It is known the world over now that Mr. Rockefeller, said to be the richest man in the world, violated many rules of morality in amassing his fortune. It is because such conditions prevail around them that many people in Europe and America have turned against religion. They argue that, if any religion worth the name existed in the inordinate wickedness that is rampant all round would not be there. This is a mistaken view."

"It is the moral nature of man by which he rises to good and noble thoughts. The different sciences show us the world as it is. Ethics tells us what it ought to be. It enables man to know how he should act.... It is necessary to know about the evil effects of injustice, wickedness, vanity and the like and the disaster they spell where the three are found together. And mere knowledge is not enough; it should be followed by appropriate action.... There are some who believe that moral principles are not intended to be practised in this world.... A great thinker has said: "If you wish to attain perfection, you must begin from this very day to live according to the laws of morality."

"In the path of morality there is no such thing as reward for moral behaviour. If a man does some good deed, he does not do it to win applause; he does it because he must. For him doing good is a higher kind of food, if one may compare food and goodness. And if some gave him an opportunity to do a good deed, he would feel grateful just as a starving man would be grateful to the giver of food and bless him."

Any particular act is moral or immoral would be judged from the intensions behind the act. Most of our actions are neither moral nor immoral. They are non-moral acts performed mechanically following the prevailing conventions. When we perform a moral act deliberately because we feel it is right to do and not because it is beneficial in one way or the other to us, then and then alone it can be categorized as moral act. Further a moral action must be free from fear or compulsion.

ETHICS CENTRED ECONOMICS

Morality and ethics occupy a central place in Gandhian economics. "True economics never militates against the highest ethical standard, just as all true ethics to be worth its name must at; the same time be also good economics. An economics that inculcates Mammon worship and enables the strong to amass wealth at the expense of the weak, is a false and dismal science. It spells death. True economics, on the other hand, stands for social justice, it promotes the good of all, equally including the weakest, and is indispensable for decent life." (*Harijan* 9-10-37, p. 292). That economic is untrue which ignores or disregards moral values. The extension of the law of nonviolence in the domain of economics means nothing less than the introduction of moral values as a factor to be considered in regulating international commerce." (*Young India*, 26-12-24, p. 421)

Gandhi was fully acquainted with Adam Smith's Wealth of Nations, which points to certain disturbing factors, which prevent economic laws having free play. Chief among these is the human factor, *i.e.* human selfishness. Unless this factor is taken care of, the economic principles based on the premise of free competition would not work. This factor can be taken care of only if man follows the moral and ethical principles.

In Gandhian economics, the supreme consideration is the human being. Everyman has the right to live indignity and therefore to find work to meet his basic needs of food, clothing, shelter, education, health and self-esteem. 'These should be freely available to all as God's air and water are ought to be. They should not be made a vehicle of traffic for exploitation of others. Their monopolization by any country, nation or group of persons would be unjust. The neglect of this simple principle is the cause of the destitution that we witness today not only in this unhappy land but other parts of the world too.' (*Young India*, 15-11-28, p. 381)

We must utilize all human labour before we entertain the idea of employing mechanical power. 'Real planning' according to Gandhi, 'consists in the best utilization of the whole man power of India and the distribution of the raw products of India in her numerous villages instead of sending them outside and re-buying finished articles at fabulous prices.' (*Harijan* 23-3-47)

Let us examine this concept of Gandhi in the light of the emerging global economic scenario. The world leaders gathered in Rome in 1996 announced their determination to halve world poverty in the next two decades (by 2015). In the next 50 years, world population is likely to touch 9 billion, marking a 50 per cent increase. In the mean time the world food requirements would go up by 100 per cent. Scientists feel that biotechnology offers a solution. They always come out with one solution or the other but such solutions either do not work in the long run or produce unforeseen adverse effects. It appeared that the Green Revolution solved our food problem for ever. It did not and the level of poverty and destitution did not change much.

Now the emerging scenario is grim again and scientists are looking for another short-term solution to postpone the problems for future generations to take care. Biotechnology is the new weapon. The Director General of the International Food Policy Research Institute (IFPRI) cites three main reasons for the looming crisis: natural disasters, military conflicts and unequal economic development. He prescribes green revolution for Africa and some poorer countries of Asia and the application of biotechnologically developed new variety of crops for other parts of the world. The need for bio-safety is acknowledged even if grudgingly but advises that the new crops be introduced forthwith to solve the problem of hunger and malnutrition.

We are however not sure of the long-term effects of newly created plants and animals on productivity and human health. Further, those engaged in finding the new solutions to the problems of food scarcity etc. take for granted the existing paradigm of development. They do not question this paradigm and transgress its shortcomings in the mad rush for new solutions. Gandhi took the problems of humanity head on and traced the source to the development paradigm of the industrial civilisation. It is apparent that our scientists refuse to see beyond their own noses. They are not concerned about the possibility of bio-disasters these newly developed crops can lead to. They refuse to see the problem of hunger in a holistic frame of reference. It is not only the problems of production and productivity but also of distribution, consumption and waste. It is also the question of the type of economy we are trying to build and for whom?

Gandhi comes to our aid here. We must bring our desires and wants down and concentrate more on moral development. Our real needs can be met by organic farming, adequately educated and independent small farmers, and by small scale entrepreneurs. Let development be seen more in terms of human development and less in terms of more goods to consume. Let production be shifted back from high cost cities to low cost villages; from mass production to production by masses and better distribution of means as well as the fruits of the productive systems.

We would return to these issues in other sections of the book.

Muir Central College Speech

Speaking at the Muir Central College Economic Society, Allahabad on December 22, 1916, Gandhi said:

"Frankly and truly, I know little of economics, as you naturally understand them. Only the other day, sitting at an evening meal, a civilian friend deluged me with a series of questions on my crankisms. As he proceeded in his cross-examination, I being a willing victim, he found no difficulty in discovering my gross ignorance of the matter. I appeared to him to be handling with cocksureness worthy only of a man who knows not that he knows not. To his horror and even indignation, I suppose, that he found that I had not even read books on economics by such well known authorities as Mill, Marshall and Adam Smith, and a host of such other authors. In despair, he ended by advising me to read these books before experimenting in matters economic at the expense of trusting friends. For there comes to us moments in life when about some things we need no proof from without. A little voice within us tells us, 'You are on the right track. Turn neither to your left nor right, but keep to the straight and narrow way.' With such help, we march forward, slowly indeed, but surely and steadily. That is my position."

"Before I take to the field of my experience and experiments it is perhaps best to have a mutual understanding about the title of this evening's address: Does Economic Progress Clash with Real Progress? By economic progress we mean material advancement without limit, and by real progress we mean moral progress, which again, is the same thing as progress of the permanent elements in us. The subject may, therefore, be stated thus: does not moral progress increase in the same proportion as material progress. I know that this is wider proposition than the one before us. But I venture to think that we always mean the larger one even when we lay down the smaller. For we know enough of science to realize that there is no such thing as perfect rest or repose in this visible universe of ours. If, therefore, material progress does clash with moral progress it must necessarily advance the latter. Nor can we be satisfied with the clumsy way in which sometimes those who cannot defend the larger proposition put their case. They seem to be obsessed with thirty millions of India, stated by the late sir William Wilson Hunter, living on one meal per day. They say that before we can think or talk of their moral welfare we must satisfy their daily wants. With them, they say material progress spells moral progress. And then is taken a sudden jump. What is true of thirty million is true of the universe. They forget that hard cases make bad laws, I need hardly say to you how ludicrously this deduction would be. No one has ever suggested that grinding pauperism can lead to anything else than moral degradation.

"Every human being has a right to live and, therefore, to find the wherewithal to feed himself and where necessary to clothe and house himself. But for this very simple performance we need no assistance from economics and their laws. 'Take no thought for the morrow' is an injunction, which finds an echo in almost all the religious scriptures of the world. In well-ordered society the securing of one's livelihood should be and is found to be the easiest thing in the world. In deed the test of orderliness in a country is not number of millionaires it owns but of absence of starvation among its masses. The only statement that has to be examined is, whether it can be laid down as a law of universal application that material advancement means moral advancement."

Gandhi then gives the examples of ancient civilisations of Rome, Egypt etc., which suffered a moral fall when they attained high material influence. He also referred to his South African experiences: 'I observed almost invariably that greater the possession of riches, the greater was their moral turpitude.... I venture to think that the scriptures of the world are far safer and sounder treatises on laws of economics than many modern text books.' Gandhi considered Jesus as the greatest economist of the world. He concluded that 'in so far as we have made the modern materialistic craze our goal, in so far are we going downhill in the path of progress. Hence the ancient ideal has been limitation of activities promoting wealth. This does not put an end to all material ambition. We should still have, as we have had, in our midst people who make the pursuit of wealth their aim in life. But we have always recognized that it is a fall from the ideal. It is a beautiful thing to know that the wealthiest among us often know that to have remained voluntarily poor would have been a higher state for them.'

"We cannot serve God and Mammon is an economic truth of the highest value. We have to make our choice. Western nations are groaning under the heels of the monster – God of materialism. Their moral growth has become stunted. They today measure their progress in pounds, shillings and pence. American wealth has become the standard. She is the envy of other nations. I have heard many of our countrymen say that we will gain American wealth but avoid its methods. I venture to suggest that such an attempt, if it were made, is foredoomed to failure. We cannot be wise, temperate and furious in a moment. I would have our leaders to teach us to be morally supreme in the world.

"This land of ours was once, we are told, the abode of the gods. It is not possible to conceive gods inhabiting a land which is made hideous by the smoke and the din of mill chimneys and whose roadways are traversed by screeching and puffing engines. Dragging numerous cars loaded with men most of whom know not what they are after, who are often absent minded, and whose tempers do no improve by using uncomfortably packed like sardines in boxes and finding themselves in the midst of utter strangers, who would oust them if they could and whom they would, in their turn, oust similarly.

"I refer to these things because they are held to be symbolical of material progress. But they add not an atom to our happiness. Here is what Wallace, the great scientist, has said as his deliberate judgment: 'In the earlier records which have come down to us from the past, we find ample indications that general ethical conceptions, the accepted standard of morality, and the conduct resulting from these were in no degree inferior to those which prevail today.' In a series of chapters he then proceeds to examine the position of the English nation under the advance in wealth it has made. He says, 'This rapid growth this wealth and increase of our power over nature put too great a strain upon our crude civilisation and our superficial Christianity, and it was accompanied by various forms of social immorality almost as amazing and unprecedented.'

'He then shows how factories have risen on the corpses of men, women and children, how as the country has rapidly advanced in riches, it has gone down in morality. He shows this by dealing in sanitation, life destroying trades, adulteration, bribery and gambling. He shows how the advance in wealth, justice has become immoral, how deaths from alcoholism, and suicide have increased, how the average of premature births and congenital defects have increased, and how prostitution has become an institution. He concludes his examination by these pregnant remarks: 'The proceedings of the divorce courts show other aspects of the results of wealth and leisure ... both in country houses and in London, various kinds of orgies were occasionally to be met, which would hardly have surpassed in the Rome of the most dissolute emperors. Of war, too, I need say nothing. It has always been more or less chronic since the rise of the Roman Empire. But there is now undoubtedly a disinclination for war among all civilized peoples. Yet the vast burden of armaments taken together with the most pious declarations in favour of peace, must be held to show an almost total absence of morality as a guiding principle among the governing classes.'

"Under the British aegis we have learnt much, but it is my firm belief, that if we are not careful, we shall introduce all the vices that she has been a prey to owing to the disease of materialism. We can profit by that connection only if we keep our civilisation and our morals straight, that is if instead of boasting of the glorious past we express the ancient moral glory in our own lives and let our lives bear witness to our past. Then we shall benefit her and ourselves. If we copy her because she provides us with rulers, both they and we shall suffer degradation.

"We need not be afraid of ideals or of reducing them to practice even to the uttermost. Ours will only then be a truly spiritual nation when we shall show more truth than gold, greater fearlessness than pomp of power and wealth, greater charity than love of self. If we will but clean our house, our palaces and temples of the attributes of wealth and show in them the attributes of morality, one can offer battle to any combination of hostile forces, without having to carry the burden of a heavy militia. Let us first seek the Kingdom of God and His righteousness, and the irrevocable promise is that everything will be added unto us. These are real economics. May you and I treasure them and enforce them in our daily life."

BHU Foundation Day Speech

It would be interesting to read the speech Gandhi delivered at the foundation ceremony of Banaras Hindu University wherein he lambasted the Maharajas and Zamindars for having bedecked themselves with costly jewellry while millions of Indians did not have enough food to eat. He made this speech on February 4, 1916 a few months before he spoke at Muir Central College, Allahabad.

"Friends, under the influence of the matchless eloquence of Mrs. Besant who had just sat down, pray, do not believe that our university has become a finished product, and that all young men who are to come to the university, that has yet to rise and come into existence, have also come and returned from it finished citizens of a great empire. Do not go away with any such impression, and if you, the student world to which many remarks are supposed to be addressed this evening, consider for one moment that the spiritual life, for which this country is noted and for which this country has no rival, can be transmitted through the lip, pray, believe me, you are wrong. You will never be able merely through the lip to give the message that India, I hope will one day deliver to the world. I myself have been fed up with speeches and lectures. I except the lectures that have been delivered here during the last two days from this category, because they are necessary. But I do venture to suggest to you that we have now reached almost the end of our resources in speech making. And it is not enough that our ears are feasted, but it is necessary that our hearts have got to be touched and that our hands and feet have got to be moved."

Gandhi first pleads for the adoption of mother tongue as the medium of teaching and speaking and then complaints about the conditions in which the whole city of Banaras was, particularly the precincts of Kashi Vishwanath temple. He asks people to change their lifestyle and live clean and keep the environment around them clean. He considered both to be important for winning *Swaraj* for the country. 'We do not know the elementary laws of cleanliness.' And then he introduces another scene.

"His Highness the Maharaja who presided yesterday over our deliberations spoke about poverty of India. Other speakers laid great stress upon it. But what did we witness in the great *pandal* in which the foundation ceremony was performed by the Viceroy? Certainly, a most gorgeous show, an exhibition of jewellery, which made splendid feast for the eyes of the greatest jeweller who chose to come from Paris. I compare with the richly bedecked noblemen the millions of the poor. And I feel like saying to these noblemen, 'There is no salvation for India unless you strip yourselves of this jewellery and hold it in trust for your countrymen in India.' I am sure, it is not the desire of the King-Emperor or Lord Harding that in order to show the truest loyalty to our King-Emperor, it is necessary for us to ransack our jewellery boxes and to appear bedecked from top to toe. I would undertake, at the peril of my life, to bring to you a message from King George himself that he expects nothing of this kind.

"Sir, whenever I hear of a great palace rising in any great city of India, ... I become jealous and say, 'Oh, it is the money that has come from the agriculturist.' Over seventy-five per cent of the population are agriculturists. As Mr. Higginbotham told us last night in his own felicitous language, that they are the men who grow two blades of grass in the place of one. But there cannot be much spirit of self-government about us if we take away or allow others to take away from them almost the whole of the results of their labour. Our salvation can only come through the farmer. Neither the lawyers, nor the doctors, nor the rich landlords are going to secure it."

Gandhi then refers to the extraordinary security in the city apparently to ward of any attack by freedom fighters opting violent means. Gandhi decried violence irrespective of the purpose for which it was resorted to and asserted that such acts were not sanctioned by Indian civilisation. "I honour the anarchist for the love of his country, I honour him for his bravery in being willing to die for his country; but I ask him: Is killing honourable? Is the dagger of an assassin a fit precursor of an honourable death? I deny it. There is no warrant for such methods in any scripture.... the bomb thrower creates secret plots, is afraid to come out into the open, and when caught pays the penalty of misdirected zeal."

Soon after, Gandhi was interrupted but he continued. Ultimately even the president left and meeting ended. Mrs. Besant strongly condemned Gandhi's speech, but he felt no remorse, for what he said was truth, even if a bitter truth.

Conflict Resolution Through Soul Force

One of the major contributions of modern civilisation is the escalation in violence. Violence has always been there ever since man emerged as Homo sapiens. Prior to that he has passed through various stages of animal existence, which ran for several millennia. Animals prey on other life forms both vegetation (*Jad*) and other animals (*Chetan*). Homo sapiens too were guided by those instincts for a along time. Man was however "a special creation of God precisely to the extent that he is distinct from the rest of His creation. (*Young India*, 13-2-30) As cultural heritage grew, man produced his own food and tended to be less violent. All cultures in the world developed philosophies that promoted love, compassion, human brotherhood and simple living and high thinking.

"In eating, sleeping and in the performance of other physical functions, man is not different from the brute. What distinguishes him from the brute is his ceaseless striving to rise above the brute on the moral plane." (*Harijan*, 7-4-46) If we turn our eyes to the time of which history has any record down to our own time we shall find that man has been steadily progressing towards *Ahimsa*. Our remote ancestors were cannibals. Then came a time when they were fed up with cannibalism and they began to live on chase. Next came the stage when man was ashamed of leading the life of a wandering hunter. He therefore took to agriculture and depended principally on Mother Earth for his food. Thus, from being a nomad, he settled down to civilized stable life, founded villages and towns, and from member of a family he became member of a community and a nation. All these are signs of progressive *Ahimsa* and diminishing *Himsa*. Had it been otherwise, the human species should have been extinct by now, even as many of the lower species have disappeared. (*Harijan*, 11-8-40)

"Man is not brute. He has risen to a higher state after countless births in the brute creation. He is born to stand, not to walk on all fours or crawl. Bestiality is as far removed from manhood, as matter from spirit." (*Young India*, 29-4-26). "Man is higher than the brute in his moral instincts and institutions. The law of nature as applied to the one is different from the law of nature as applied to the other. Man has reason, discrimination, and free will such as it is. The brute has no such thing. It is not a fee agent, and knows no distinction between virtue and vice, good and evil. Man being a free agent knows these distinctions, and when he follows his higher nature shows himself far superior to the brute, but when he follows his baser nature can show himself lower than the brute. Even the races regarded as the most uncivilized on earth accept some restrictions on sexual relations. If it be said that restrictions itself is barbarous, then freedom from all restrictions should be the law of man. If all men were to act according to this lawless law, there would be utter chaos within twenty four hours. Man by nature being more passionate than the brute, the moment all restraint is withdrawn, the lava of the unbridled passion would overspread the whole earth and destroy mankind. Man is superior to the brute in as much as he is capable of self-restraint and sacrifice, of which the brute is capable." (*Young India,* 3-6-26). And this superiority lies in his inclination towards nonviolence, *Ahimsa*, love, compassion, which together constitute the Soul Force.

"The world is full of *Himsa* and Nature does appear to be 'red in tooth and claw.' But if we bear in mind that man is higher than brute, then is man superior to that of Nature. If man has a divine mission to fulfil, a mission that becomes him, it is that *Ahimsa*. Standing as he does in the midst of *Himsa*, he can retire into the innermost depths of his heart and declare to the world around him that his mission in the world of *Himsa* is *Ahimsa*... Man's nature is then not *Himsa*, but *Ahimsa*, for he can speak from experience his innermost conviction that he is not the body but *Atman* and that he may use the body only with a view to self-realization. And from that experience, he evolves the ethics of subduing desire, anger, ignorance, malice and other passions, puts forth his best effort to achieve the end and finally, attains complete success. Only when his efforts reach that consummation can he be said to have fulfilled himself, to have acted according to his nature. Conquest of one's passions therefore is not superhuman, but human, and observance of *Ahimsa* is heroism of the highest type, with no room therein or cowardice for weakness. (*Young India,* 24-6-1926).

A civilized society is at peace with nature; it is free from exploitation of man by man. Human dignity and welfare are the prime concerns of such a society. The common people live under the shadow of three freedoms:

Freedom from fear;
Freedom from want;
Freedom from ego.

Civilized people are courageous and morally strong. They are prepared to die for the right cause than to yield to threats and temptations.

"Non-violence is not only a cloistered virtue confined only to the *Rishis* and the cave dwellers. It is capable of being practiced by the millions, not with full knowledge of its implications, but because it is the Law of our Species. It distinguishes man from the brute, but man has not shed the brute in him. He has to strive to do so. This striving applies to the practice on nonviolence, not to the belief in it. I cannot strive to believe in a principle: I either believe in it or I do not. And if I believe in it, I must bravely strive to practice it. *Ahimsa* is an attribute of the brave. Cowardice and *Ahimsa* do not go together any more than water and fire." (*Harijan*, 4-11-39).

"(1) Non-violence is the law of the human race and is infinitely greater than and superior to brute force.

(2) In the last resort, it does not avail to those who do not possess a living faith in the God of Love.

(3) Non-violence affords the fullest protection of one's self-respect and sense of honour but not always to the possession of land or movable property, though its habitual practice does prove a better bulwark than the possession of armed men to defend them. Non-violence in the very nature of things is of no assistance in the defence of ill-gotten gains and immoral acts.

(4) Individuals or nations, who would practice nonviolence, must be prepared to sacrifice (nations to the last man) their all except honour. It is therefore inconsistent with the possession of other people's countries, *i.e.* modern Imperialism, which is frankly based on force for its defence.

(5) Non-violence is a power which can be wielded equally by all – children, young, men and women or grown up people,— provided they have a living faith in the God of Love and have, therefore, equal love for all mankind. When nonviolence is accepted as a Law of Life, its must pervade the whole being and not applied to isolated acts." (*Harijan*, 5-9-36).

"Scientist tell us that without the presence of the cohesive force amongst the atoms that comprise this globe of ours, it would crumble to pieces and we would cease to exist. And even as there is a cohesive force in blind matter so must there be in all things animate; and the name for that cohesive force among animate beings is Love. We notice it between father and son, between brother and sister; friend and friend. But we have to learn to use that force among all that lives, and in the use of it consists our knowledge of God. Where there is Love, there is Life; hatred leads to destruction. (*Young India*, 5-5-20)

"Passive resistance is a method of securing rights by personal suffering, … reverse of resistance by arms When I refuse to do a thing that is repugnant to my conscience, I use soul force. For instance, the government of the day has passed a law which is applicable to me. I do not like it. If by using violence I force the government to repeal the law, I am employing what may be termed body force. If I do not obey the law and accept the penalty for its breach, I use soul force. It involves sacrifice of self." (*Hind Swaraj* p. 71).

"Everybody admits that sacrifice of self is infinitely superior to sacrifice of others. Moreover, if this kind of force is used in a case that is unjust, only the person using it suffers. He does not make others suffer for his mistakes. Men have before now done many things which subsequently were found to have been wrong. No man can claim that he is absolutely in the right or that a particular thing is wrong because he thinks so, but it is wrong for him so long as that is his deliberate judgment. It therefore means that he should not do that which he knows to be wrong, and suffer the consequence whatever it may be. This is the key to the use of soul force. (*Hind Swaraj* p. 71)

"To use brute force, to use gun powder, is contrary to passive resistance, for it means that we want our opponent to do by force which we desire, but he does not. And if such a use of force is justifiable, surely he is entitled to do likewise by us. And so we should never come to an agreement. We may simply fancy, like the blind horse moving in a circle round a mill that we are making progress. Those who believe that they are not bound to obey laws, which are repugnant to their consciences have only the remedy of passive resistance open to them. Any other must lead to disorder." (*Hind Swaraj* 72)

"Passive resistance is an all-sided sword; it can be used anywhere; it blesses him who uses it and him whom it is used. Without drawing a drop of blood, it produces far reaching results. It never rusts and cannot be stolen. Competition between passive resistance does not exhaust. The sword of passive resistance does not require a scabbard. It is strange indeed that you should consider such a weapon to be a weapon merely of the weak." (*Hind Swaraj* 73).

"Truly, men were less unmanly when they settled their disputes either by fighting or by asking their relatives to decide for them. They became more unmanly and cowardly when they resorted to the courts of law. It was certainly a savagery when they settled their disputes by fighting. Is it any the less so, if I ask a third party to decide between you and me?" (*Hind Swaraj* 51)

Our ancestors "saw that kings and their swords were inferior to the sword of ethics, and they therefore, held the sovereigns of the earth inferior to the *Rishis* and *Fakirs*. A nation with a constitution like this is fitter to teach others than to learn from others.... The ordinary rule was to avoid courts....the common people lived independently and followed their agricultural occupation. They enjoyed real Home Rule." (*Hind Swaraj* p. 56)

DUTIES PRECEDE RIGHTS

Gandhi did not give as much emphasis to Rights as to Duties. If all followed their duties, the rights of all will remain secure and protected. Further, securing rights through duties generates brotherhood; it does not generate conflicts. Yet at the same time he put certain standards before humanity to hollow. He considered life in general and human life in particular very sacred. It has a dignity that must be respected. And it was the duty of everyone to safeguard this dignity, particularly of women, children and weaker sections of the society.

Each man is born free and he should remain free all through his life. He should have freedom from all basic needs: food, clothing, shelter, knowledge, health, security and self-respect. And these needs should be met at a level, which economy and ecology could, permit. Gandhi was not against comforts provided that the needs of all were met adequately. He wanted to help create a civilisation, which ensured human dignity and freedom.

In a truly modern civilisation, people would not hanker after rights; they would honestly follow their duties. In fact, they would consider protection of other's rights as their duty. Gandhi considered rights and duties as complementary to each other. But there is some difference. If all performed their duties honestly, the rights of everyone else would be automatically protected. There would be love and affection among the people because performance of duty means sacrifice for others. Its *vice versa* is, however, not true. If all got their due rights, it need not be because everyone performed his duties well;

it might be because a government by law has forced people to concede the rights of others. Other people have been forced to concede something that someone considers to be his right.

Let us examine it in some more details. Duties are voluntary; they are not demanded; they are willingly given. Performance of duties is possible only if there is willingness to sacrifice, to give. It requires a feeling of love for others. It also calls for the recognition of the dignity of others and their rights. Duties are never complete if we do not have a desire to care for others and share their sorrows and pains. Duty is equivalent to *Ahimsa*, Love, Compassion, and Sacrifice.

Rights on the other hand are obligatory and demanded. They are conceded only on demand often backed by force of one kind or the other. Anything taken by force creates resentment and ill-will. When rights are secured through soul force, the difference between rights and duties is narrowed, if not totally removed. Gandhi launched *satyagraha* movement to convince the British to perform their duties of not taking away the rights of Indians to be free. Instead of forcing the British to concede the rights of Indians, Gandhi tried to remind the British of their duties to concede freedom to India.

Duties are neither extracted nor forced upon a people. A slave or a bonded labour is not duty bound to serve his master. Indians were not duty bound to serve the British. Oppressed are not duty bound to serve the oppressed. Services of the above categories are not duties; they are slaveries of the mind. To recognize the rights of others is also the duty of each and every individual. But which rights? In a society where there is glaring display of wealth and brute force, we cannot expect the poor, dispossessed and weak to recognize the rights of a few powerful persons to keep the poor under their heels. It is, therefore, the duty of oppressed to fight for their rights by peaceful means; by changing the hearts of the oppressors. Nonviolent way of securing rights amounts to asking the oppressor to recognise and perform his duties. It is in this context that rights and duties become two sides of the same coin.

Swaraj is the Ruling Creed

In a civilized society the spirit of *Swaraj* reigns supreme. It is not that there are no self-seekers, bad characters and wayward lunatics; it does however mean that they do not rule the society; they remain on the margin creating problems here and there, but unable to disturb the dynamic stability of the social system.

Self-esteem is the hallmark of *Swaraj*. Those who respect themselves, they respect others too. Those who perform their duties are also to secure and enjoy their rights. Unfortunately, the word *Swaraj* was and still is equated with political independence. Gandhi used this term in a very comprehensive sense to mean self control by the individual over his senses, by the community over its local jurisdiction, by the nation over its sovereignty and by the humanity over human destiny.

Nothing should be done that would adversely affect *Swaraj*; and since colonialism was a direct and very crude affront to *Swaraj*, Gandhi fought against it using the means which enriched *Swaraj*. In a society of *Swaraj*ists all will perform their duties well and the rights of all will, therefore, be fully protected.

COOPERATION PERVADES ALL WALKS OF LIFE

Modern civilisation is based on competition. In fact competition is a way of life and everyone is engaged in competing against others for limited resources. No matter what field of activity we look at, competition is the prime mover. Modern economics would become irrelevant if we take competition out of it. The same is the case with political science. Darwin's theory of evolution would lose its base without competition for resources among and within the species.

Gandhi theorized that competition is based on animal instincts. As man progresses in his evolutionary journey, he forsakes competition and adopts cooperation as a mode of social behaviour. In a cooperative living, everyone has a place for each contributes according to his abilities and get according to his needs. Mental or physical prowess becomes a joint 'property' not owned by individuals for their self-aggrandizement. It is a social property kept by individuals as trustees. Cooperation also ensures participation by each and every member of the society.

Gandhi developed the theory of oceanic circle to explain his concept of cooperation. It involved maximum autonomy with maximum interdependence. When we throw a stone in water, a series of circular ripples are formed. The inner ripples are more prominent while the outer ones less. Ultimately the outer most ripple is almost invisible. The tank in which the stone is thrown is the human society formed of innumerable drops of water. The drops do not have their identity. The ripples have. The innermost ripple may be likened to the individual; the next one to the village or community and so on until we get to the outermost, which is global society. Inner ripples are more prominent than the successive outer ripples. The links between these ripples weaken in terms of intensity as distance increases.

Gandhi's opposition to cut-throat competition was total. He did not subscribe to the view that evolution of species resulted from competition among them for survival or resources. He was well conversant with Darwin's theory of evolution of species and Adam Smith's economic theories based on competition. He considered both theories of the same genre emanating from the mindset of industrial civilisation. Darwin theorized that it was the survival of the fittest, which ultimately produced Homo sapiens. Gandhi turned the table and said it was cooperation, not competition.

The goal of evolution was already fixed. All species worked for the achievement of the goal even if unknowingly, *i.e.* instinctively. Many of them advanced on the road and then disappeared; many others left behind, advanced ahead. Millions and millions of the species appeared and disappeared before an animal with large enough brain emerged to take control of the future evolution from nature. Darwin saw all this guided by competition; Gandhi saw it otherwise and felt it was cooperation among the species that brought man into being.

It is cooperation that brought family into being; the community too is the product of desire to cooperate and so is the society. The United Nations in recent years is some total of the present stage of cooperative spirit among the nation states of the world. Cooperation is what keeps this universe functioning forever. Cooperation is, however, not always good. Cooperation in immoral things is highly destructive; it is highly constructive when it pervades in good deeds. Similarly, competition in what is moral produces good results; but the one in immoral things is highly destructive of both the individual and the society.

In modern industrial society, there is cooperation in what can broadly be called immorality; it is lacking in moral activities. Similarly, there is lack of competition in good things (truth, nonviolence, love, compassion, sacrifice etc.) but it is present in all other spheres. Without competition, there can be no modern economics and politics. No one can prosper economically unless he can out compete others.

Competition divides people; cooperation unites. No wonder then that there is so much disunity in the society today. There is disunity at the global as well as individual level. All this is reflected boldly in the violence that prevails in the world.

ALL HAVE EQUAL ACCESS TO BASIC NEEDS

In a civilized society, no one should be deprived of his basic needs. And since there is so much poverty and deprivation in the world, modern civilisation could not be counted as modern, was Gandhi's contention. "America is the most industrialized country in the world, and yet it has not banished poverty and degradation. That is because it neglects the universal manpower and concentrates power in the hands of the few who amass fortunes at the expense of the many." (*Harijan*, 23-3-47)

He was critical of socialism too. "Socialism was not born with the discovery of the misuse of capital by capitalists. As I have contended, socialism, even communism is explicit in the first verse of *Ishopnishad.* What is true is that when some reformers lost faith in the method of conversion, the technique of what is known as scientific socialism was born.... I accepted the theory of socialism even while I was in South Africa. My opposition to socialists and others consists in attaching violence as a means of effecting any lasting reform." (*Harijan*, 1-6-47) Further, socialism has only one aim that is material progress. "I want freedom for full expression of my personality.... Under the other socialism, there is no individual freedom. You own nothing, not even your body." (*Harijan*, 4-8-46) "As I look at Russia where the apotheosis of industrialisation has been reached, the life there does not appeal to me. To use the language of the Bible, 'What shall it avail a man if he gain the whole world and lose his soul? In modern terms, it is beneath human dignity to lose one's individuality and become a mere *cog* in the machine. I want every individual to become a full blooded, fully developed member of the society." (*Harijan*, 28-1-39)

Gandhi advanced the concept of Sarvodaya, which was based on three basic principles:

(1) that the good of the individual is contained in the good of all;
(2) that the lawyer's work has the same value as the barber's, inasmuch as all have the same right of earning their livelihood from their work;

(3) that a life of labour, *i.e.*, the life of the tiller of the soil and the handicraftsman is the life worth living.

In order that the tendency in the people to accumulate wealth is kept under control, Gandhi advanced the theory of *Trusteeship*. Gandhi wanted complete equality in so far as the basic needs of the people were concerned. In fact he wanted the basic needs of all including animals to be met satisfactorily. But at the same time, he wanted people to have incentive to remain economically active and produce more. This naturally would lead to some people having more than what they need. They would be rich but there would be no poor because the basic needs of all would be satisfactorily met.

To ensure that those who were rich did not use their property for ulterior purposes or to control others, he advanced the theory of *Trusteeship*. Explaining the theory he said, 'Everything belonged to God and was from God. Therefore, it was His people as a whole, not for particular individual. When an individual had more than his proportionate portion he became trustee of that portion for God's people.

"God who was all-powerful had no need to store. He created from day to day, hence men also should in theory live from day to day and not stock things. If this truth was imbibed by the people generally it would become legalized and trusteeship would become a legalized institution. He wished it became a gift from India to the world. Then there would be no exploitation and no reserve as in Australia and other countries for Whitemen and their posterity. In these distinctions lay the seeds of a war more virulent than the last two. As to the successor, the trustee in office would have the right to nominate his successor subject to the legal sanction." (*Harijan*, 23-2-'47, p. 39)

The idea underlying the concept of trusteeship is two-fold:

(1) All humans are born equal and hence they have the right to equal opportunity. This means that all must have their basic needs fully satisfied.

(2) All humans, however, are not endowed with equal intellectual and physical capacity. Some would have greater capacity to produce than others. Such persons must treat themselves as trustees of the produce beyond their basic needs.

There are lot of misgivings about Gandhi's insistence on equity. Let us see what he says on this issue. "I cannot picture to myself a time when no man shall be richer than another. But I do picture to myself a time when the rich will spurn to enrich themselves at the expense of the poor and the poor will cease to envy the rich. Even in a most prefect world, we shall fail to avoid inequalities, but we can and must avoid strife and bitterness. There are numerous examples extant of the rich and the poor living in perfect friendliness. We have but to multiply such instances." (*Young India*, 7-10-1926)

The above quotation admirably sums up the Gandhian concept of economic equality. Gandhi further elaborated his ideas in the *Harijan* of 18-8-40 and said: 'Economic equality of my conception does not mean that every one would literally have the same amount. It simply means that everybody should have enough for his or her needs....The elephant needs a thousand times more food than the ant but that is not an indication of inequality. So the real meaning of economic equality is: *from each according to his ability to each according to his need.* If a single man demanded as much as a man with wife and four children, that would be a violation of economic equality.

'Let no one try to justify the glaring difference between the classes and masses, the prince and the pauper, by saying that the former need more. That will be an idle sophistry and a travesty of my argument...The contrast between the rich and the poor is a painful sight. The poor villagers are exploited by the foreign Government and also by their own countrymen—the city dwellers. They produce the food and go hungry. They produce milk and their children have to go without it. It is disgraceful....I do not want to taboo everything beyond and above the bare necessities, but they must come after the essential needs of the poor are satisfied. First thing must come first.' (*Harijan*, 31-3-46)

MICROPOLIS IS THE BASIC UNIT OF HUMAN SETTLEMENTS

Considerable literature exists on Gandhi's concept of village. We would take up this issue in succeeding chapters. Here suffice it say that the concept of Gandhi's village was not akin to the village as it existed in his time or exists in our times in India. There are certain characteristics of village, which Gandhi considered to be ideal for human survival and development. Village has a human size; it is not so big like a metropolitan city in which man as an individual and as member of a community is lost. Second, village is typified by face-to-face communication. Each one knows the rest of the people living in it. Third, it is known for cooperative spirit. Fourth, it is most suited for *Swaraj* at the grassroots level. And fifth, it has perfect synergy with nature.

It is true that none of above qualities exist in our villages today. But they do point to a better future. Why else we call our earth as global village. Gandhi wanted these qualities to be strengthened and new ones to be added. So far as the basic infrastructure was concerned. He wanted our villages to have their own architects, water supply and so on. In addition to all these facilities Gandhi village was humane, it was not a small city of filth and squalor; it was a micropolis in the real sense.

"Society based on nonviolence can only consist of groups settled in villages in which voluntary cooperation is the condition of dignified and peaceful existence. A society, which anticipates and provides for meeting violence with violence will either lead a precarious life or create big cities and magazines for defense purposes" (*Harijan*, 13.1.40. "I am convinced that if India is to attain true freedom and through India the world also, then sooner than later the fact must be recognized that people will have to live in villages, not in towns, in huts, not in palaces." (*A Bunch of Old Letters*, 1958)

"I hold that without truth and nonviolence there can be nothing but destruction for humanity. We can realize truth and nonviolence only in the simplicity of village life and this simplicity can best be found in the *Charkha* and all that *Charkha* connotes. I must not fear if the world today is going the wrong way. It may be that India too will go that way and like the proverbial moth burn itself eventually in the flame round which it dances more and more fiercely. But it is my bounden duty up to my last breath to try to protect India and through India the entire world from such a doom. (*A Bunch of Old Letters*, 1958)

"My idea of village *Swaraj* is that it is a complete republic, independent of its neighbours for its own vital wants, and yet interdependent for many others in which dependence is necessary. Thus every village's first concern will be to grow its own food crops and cotton for its cloth. It should have a reserve for its cattle, recreation and play ground for adults and children. Then if there is more land available, it will grow useful money crops, thus excluding Ganja, tobacco, opium and the like. The village will maintain a village theatre, school, and public hall. It will have its own waterworks ensuring clean water supply. This can be done through controlled wells or tanks.

"Education will be compulsory up to the final basic course. As far as possible every activity will be conducted on a cooperative basis. There will be no castes such as we have today with their graded untouchability. Nonviolence with the technique of *Satyagraha* and non-cooperation will be the sanction of the village community." (*Harijan,* 26-7-42)

"My ideal village will contain intelligent human beings. They will not live in dirt and darkness as animals. Men and women will be free and able to hold their own against anyone in the world. There will be neither plague, nor cholera, nor smallpox; no one will be idle, no one will wallow in luxury. Everyone will have to contribute his quota of manual labour.... It is possible to envisage railways, post and telegraph.... and the like." (*A Bunch of Old Letters*, 1958)

"There is nothing inherently impossible in the picture drawn here. To model such a village may be work of a life-time. Any lover of true democracy and village life can take up a village, treat it as his world and sole work, and he will find good results." (*Harijan*, 26-7-42)

Not many people have read about the model of a village Gandhi had in his mind. It we call this model as Gandhigram Model, then as stated earlier Gandhi had in mind a spatial community of about 5000 people having adequate economic base to afford all those facilities the model envisages. Such a community will be a micropolis, a small town, which will have the good things that a city has (modern public utilities) and a village has (openness, natural, simple, and environmentally clean). It will not have what is not good in villages and cities of India.

One of the prerequisites of the micropolises will be household manufacturing. Questions are raised regarding the competitiveness of village industries. Yes, there would be problems but if we take into account the fact that in future it is the self employment that is going to sustain people, not the government and industrial jobs as is the case even today, then information technology and processing of agricultural products at the place where they are produced is the only answer. One fails to understand as to why even the grains, the vegetables and fruits produced in villages should be exported to cities for processing? Moreover, integration of head, heart and hand is essential for the fullest development of human personality and this is possible only if our education is geared to it and we make a mission to keep this integration intact all though our life.

So with a slight modification in the concept of village and gram *Swaraj* enunciated by Gandhi, we can make it viable even in the twenty first century. In such a rural society, there would be space for cities too. But the cities would be clearing houses for their own and village products. I doubt that we can have autarchic villages, nor did Gandhi envisage such villages. Micropolises would generate lot of surplus for the cities and outside world and the cities too would generate surplus for the villages and outside world. Further both will exchange goods among themselves. Cities would have the necessary infrastructure to organize exchange services. But the exchange between the micropolises and metropolises will be on terms of equality: Both will be producers as well consumers of different products and both would be generative rather than exploitative.

Gandhi developed the concept of human size in all spheres of life. He wanted human size technology, human settlements, political system, production system and even human size thinking. I was told that once a western educated person approached Gandhi and told him that he waned to serve India and would like to have Gandhiji's blessings and of course guidance. Gandhi paused for a moment and then enquired of him the place of his origin and how he wanted to serve the country. After hearing him patiently, he told him to go to the village he hailed from and serve the people there. As to the things he could do, he suggested him to read his book on constructive programme and see how fast and well he could implement them in the fashion described in the book.

Gandhi was a true believer in Global Thinking and Local Action. In his opinion, world could be changed only by changing communities, and communities could be changed only by changing the individuals which joined hands to make it a corporate body. Changes have to begin from the bottom, not from the top. Anything that emerged from the top had an in-built system of control and direction leading to dependence instead of interdependence, competition instead of cooperation, suffocation instead of freedom. As such Gandhi was against large, big and huge things as a matter of principle. He was a votary of small size machines, small size production and small size houses, small size human settlements, etc.

BIOLOGICAL PRINCIPLES GOVERN LIFE

Universe is Not a Machine

Gandhi was a scientist *par excellence*. He called his autobiography 'My Experiments with Truth'. He never recommended anything to any one without first experimenting and testing it himself. His theories emerged from his experiments on the one hand and his worldview on the other.

Questions are often raised on Gandhi's views on progress or development. In his scheme of things economic progress cannot be separated from social, political, ethical and spiritual progress; human life is not compartmentalized; it is unified and synergic in the same way as nature is. To understand what progress is one has to understand the working of the nature of which human life is a part. There is nothing wrong is seeing it in compartments provided it is within the framework of a holistic vision.

Gandhi did not agree with the view that the universe could be compared to a machine, which could be assembled, manipulated, repaired and reconstructed if we know the physical laws that govern it. He distinguished the biological world from the physical world in terms of functioning. While the physical phenomena could be separated from each other without causing any damage to their functioning, the biological phenomena exist not because they are an assemblage of discrete parts but because there is interdependency among the parts and no part can exist outside the whole. There is something what we call life, which separates the biological phenomena from the physical ones.

The difference lies mainly in their functioning: one is an assemblage of non-living parts; separated from the whole it does not die. It may be destroyed though and in process of destruction it does not feel any pain. The other, *i.e.* biological is also an assemblage of parts of various sizes and levels but it form a united whole and cannot be separated from each other or from the whole. There is another difference. The physical phenomena do not reproduce while the biological ones do and, therefore, are marked with continuity. Death does not end the existence for they reproduce their likes before they die. The physical phenomena, however do not reproduce their likes, once destroyed, they are distroyed forever.

Modern science has the expertise to examine and understand the physical phenomena. The problem is that it treats even the biological phenomena as physical *i.e.* an assemblage of so many parts like a machine. An engine works because it forms a system of parts which work in unison once the energy it supplied from outside. Human body is also an assemblage of parts but the parts have grown out of the whole. The organs, the tissues and cells of human body have no existence outside the body; the body supports and nurtures them and they support and nurture the body. Human body functions like a machine but it is not a machine. All biological phenomena form an integral and living whole. Their parts, which we call organs, do not exist outside the living machine.

The mechanical approach to biological phenomena gives rise to a series of problems: human, ecological and others. It is this approach, which produced Darwin's theory of evolution and Freud's theory of Libido controlled human nature. It is also responsible for increasing violence against nature and fellow human beings. If humans are just like machines, then there is no 'sin' involved in killing or destroying them.

VOLUNTARY POVERTY ENSURES EQUITY

Earth has enough to meet everyone's need but not everyone's greed, said Gandhi. Unless people lived simply, there was no prospect of equality. Inequality results from accumulation of resources and wealth. This leads to two major consequences. Earth's resources are over used leading to pollution, exhaustion and shortages; and the economic gains are mal-distributed; some people living in luxury while many others living in poverty and pestilence.

For equitable distribution of earth's resources and economic benefits derived there from, our mindset has to change. We must move away from accumulation and grabbing what belongs to others on one pretext or the other; and create a culture of care and share. Simple living and high thinking emanates from this new mindset. What is important in life is not more goods but more and higher human values. This is one of the central themes of *Hind Swaraj*.

For the hungry, bread is, God, said Gandhi. Thus, unless the basic needs are satisfactorily met, it is difficult for man to remember God or to see God in all that exists on the earth. This means that body welfare in Gandhian praxis is not irrelevant. It is very relevant because it is through the body that man can perform his duties. But once the basic needs are met, body welfare should become secondary or even tertiary. The primary goal of life should hereafter be consistent movement towards super-conscious state of human evolution.

Gandhi gave a new concept of alternative development, *i.e. sarvodaya*. According to this model, none is evolved enough to be called developed. Everyone, rich or poor, needs development. The materially poor need more material development so that they can meet their basic needs; the materially rich need more spiritual development so that they can shed their material load painlessly.

This is, the model of a civilized society Gandhi envisaged. Individual is the most important. His freedom and autonomy and dignity should never be compromised. Yet, he is part of the global society to which he depends for certain purposes. Thus he came to the concept of village as the basic spatial unit of the society.

SELF-REALIZATION IS THE GOAL OF LIFE

In Gandhian paradigm, the aim of life is self-realization, which in turn means understanding the Maker of all that exists. Self-realization does not result from economic progress and body welfare; it results from moral progress and ethical behaviour and hence real progress means moral progress, not material progress. Economic progress, the chief pursuit of modern man, is accompanied by exploitation of both nature and man and both these acts are immoral for they violate the dignity of both. "True economics never militates against the highest ethical standards, just as all true ethics to be worth its name must at the same time be also good economics. An economics that inculcates Mammon worship, and enables the strong to amass wealth at the expense of the week, is a false and dismal science. True economics, on the other hand, stands for social justice; it promotes the good of all equally including the weakest, and is indispensable for decent life. (*Harijan*, 9-10-37)

The primacy accorded to morality and ethics by Gandhi did not preclude material progress. Man has to eat, clad himself, live in houses, and use various tools to get his work done. He needs schools, health clinics, security, agriculture, industry and a variety of other things. In fact, the more civilized he is, the more health and peace promoting basic goods and services he needs and creates. Gandhi lived a very austere life; he had practically no possessions. But he did not insist on his followers to live like him. All he wanted was to lead a simple life so that there were no poor and no rich.

A thorough study of Gandhian thought reveals that while laying emphasis on morality (right thought, right speech and right action), Gandhi was not totally against acquisition of wealth, so long as it was not used for dispossessing others or for wasteful luxuries. The wealth so created must first be used to meet the basic needs of all the people irrespective of the work they did. In other words, he considered basic needs to be part of the Human Rights. These needs were: Food, Clothing, Shelter, Education, Health, Security and Human Dignity (self-esteem). Further, the wealth created at the cost of ecology and environment was also undesirable. Thus he set five conditions for the acquisition of wealth:

(1) It should be produced without violating the moral and ethical standards,
(2) It should not pollute the environment,
(3) It should not be used for luxurious life style of a few,
(4) It should not be used to acquire power to oppress others, and
(5) It should be used for the welfare of all specially the poor;

It is apparent that the accumulation of wealth while meeting the above conditions would be a great boon for humanity. Gandhi emphasised the moral and ethical standards because these were the real directions in which human evolution has to proceed. Anything that comes in the way must be avoided and shunned. By de-emphasising luxuries, he gave primacy to the basic needs of the people. The use of wealth for the welfare of the poor would ensure equity in those needs whose satisfaction is the human rights of all. And much before people started talking of ecology and environment, he called for ecological limits to economic progress.

'Man is the measure of everything.' It is true. The welfare and progress of man must be the goal of all civilisations. But there is a catch in this saying: it lies in the definition of man and his progress. Modern civilisation treats man as a thinking life form superior to all life forms. He is the master of all he surveys and has the right to use all that exists in nature to his advantage; to satisfy his physical needs and sensual urges. More wealth he accumulates, more successful and progressed he is. The more sensual needs he satisfies, happier he becomes.

Gandhi looked at man differently. For him, man is the most evolved life form destined to evolve further. He evolved from animals. He became Homo sapiens when he got a brain size computer large enough to store information and convert it into knowledge. Having become human, he started behaving differently. And thus he moved from what we may call sub-conscious stage to conscious stage. He created grand narratives; he was able to perceive his Creator in his own image, give shape to Him and communicate with Him. He is still in the conscious stage trying to detach him self-from animal urges to become super-conscious human being. Real civilisation would help man use his energies to attain super-consciousness and not to satisfy animal urges.

INDIAN CAN SHOW THE WAY

Gandhi has repeatedly mentioned in *Hind Swaraj* that Indian civilisation in its original form offers a model of a truly modern civilisation. It does not however mean that other civilisations – Chinese, Greek, Roman and others – in their original forms were not equally great. They were. But Indian civilisation did not suffer from any major break and hence it has been less disturbed than other civilisations with the exception of the Chinese. All those civilisations, which gave primacy to morality were, in Gandhi's view, civilisations, which tried to take man towards his ultimate destiny, that is morally advanced man. Further progress of Greek, Roman and Latin civilisations was interrupted, and hence their moral growth was stunted.

Modern industrial civilisation is just three hundred years old but it has totally changed the base of European civilisation. And not only the European civilisation, but all civilisations, including Indian and Chinese have been affected adversely. In Gandhi's own words, Indian "civilisation is unquestionably the best, but it is to be observed that all civilisations have been on their trial. That civilisation which is permanent outlives it. Because the sons of India were found wanting, its civilisation has been placed in jeopardy. But its strength has to be seen in its ability to survive the shock. Moreover, the whole of India is not touched. Those alone who have been affected by Western civilisation have become enslaved. We measure the universe by our own miserable foot rule. When we are slaves, we think that the whole universe is enslaved." (*Hind Swaraj,* 56)

Responding to the statement of the revolutionaries that they would resort to guerilla warfare to defeat the British, Gandhi said "That is to say that you want to make the holy land of India unholy. Do you not tremble to free India by assassination? The millions of Indians do not desire it. Those who are intoxicated by the wretched modern civilisation think these things. Those who rise to power by murder will certainly not make the nation happy." (*Hind Swaraj* 60)

4

Development Means Spiritual Progress

ASCENT OF MAN HAS JUST BEGUN

Gandhi made a distinction between humans and animals in several ways but the most fundamental difference he discovered was related to the purpose of life and living. He considered man to possess three levels of consciousness:

(1) Sub-conscious,
(2) Conscious; and
(3) Super-conscious.

The three stages of evolution of man as perceived by Gandhi need to be understood better and hence a conceptualization thereof is given below.

Animal to Homo Sapiens

At this stage, man is guided by his instincts like animals although he does better than animals for he has a large enough brain to have a mind to appreciate the world around him and accumulate experience. The instincts are inherited from millions of years of animal existence. As time passes he accumulates experience and knowledge to create the rudiments of culture starting with stone tools and fire. His mind is still guided by instincts with occasional deviations resulting from accumulating experiences and power to think. His soul or conscience is almost dormant during this stage.

Man's strength lies in physical prowess for his artefacts and tools are primitive and his understanding of the nature is that of a subaltern. He uses the brute force to achieve his objectives. Love and compassion are limited to his siblings but unlike animals they are not always confined to their childhood. Violence is part of the dominant behaviour but his capacity to inflict damage to nature or his fellow humans is limited and localized.

The general tendencies among these early Homo sapiens is to move away from the animal in them but the inherited traits of several millennia overpower these tendencies. As such man is separated physiologically from the animal but not psychologically and behaviourally.

Homo Sapiens to Conscious Beings

During this stage, it is not only the body and mind of man that control his behaviour but also the soul or conscience. This leads to emergence of what we now call morality or the law that links the individual with the whole cosmos. Consciousness is the extraordinary power of the *Atma* (soul), which is infinite. It bestowed on the humans the capacity of conscious reflection, ideation and intelligence.

Consciousness is like a screen on which the human nervous system throws its invisible images. A well-integrated nervous system reflects a very well defined and clear picture. A nervous system distorted by the contradictions that plague modern man, gives a blurred and distorted image of the reality. Unless we take a conscious responsibility to channel our potentialities for the betterment of the world and to acquire divine like virtues, the images we receive would remain distorted.

Our capacity to accumulate knowledge and experience and thus build up a civilisation has both positive and negative implications. There is a struggle between the animal and divine in man. Animal, because of its long evolutionary history predominates. Unless an effort is made to cultivate the divine, the animal, being the innate wins. At times, the divine too sprouts, grows and opens up new vistas that lead humanity from happiness to bliss and that opens the door for the next evolutionary stage. Examples of these great souls are Buddha, Confucius, Christ, Zoroaster, Mohammad, Shankara and in our own times Mahatma Gandhi. In fact, each civilisation, big or small, has given rise to such great men and women, who treaded a futuristic path and showed to the world that humans are more that body and mind.

The mental consciousness geared to limited rationality and physical realities enhances man's physical strength manifolds. Better understanding of the laws of nature arms him with enormous capacity to inflict harm to both inanimate and animate world. Violence predominates, for man is superior to animal only in one respect, *i.e.* larger size brain. But the emergence of men and women, even if infrequently, who overcome the sensual urges and innate instincts, does change the course of human civilisation from violence to nonviolence, from self-centeredness to other-centredness. The duel between sensual and spiritual forces is the hallmark of this stage.

Humanity accepts the spiritual in principle and adopts the sensual in practice. There are, therefore, oscillations in cultural development. While the spiritual inspires man towards super-consciousness, towards divine virtues and self-realization, the sensual pulls him towards animal urges, towards violence and self-indulgence. Mental pollution produces a sort of disequilibria in the mind and propels the nervous system to ignore the inner call for sanity.

The growing disequilibria produce occasional burst of violence in the form of murders and wars taking away thousands or even millions of lives. In fact, it may at times take humanity to the brink of animal existence. Man builds weapons of mass destruction and destroys and burns cities and villages bubbling with life. He does not have the values and virtues to control these weapons and to use them wisely. The world becomes a global village more in what is animal in man than in what is human in him.

All is, however, not lost; the divine or super-human spirit keeps the candle lighted. People who sacrifice their lives for others are not scarce. Super-humans with conscience are also born in this very world. They are in a position to subdue their animal in them and demonstrate to the world that there was another and better way to happiness, not ephemeral but eternal. They won the hearts of the people and diverted them from material progress to spiritual progress making the former a means rather than an end of life. They have set the moral standards for behaviour, it is quite another thing that we fail to follow them for our animal background of several millennia still dominates our lives and living.

Ours is the conscious existence with good and evil in delicate balance. If the animal in us wins, we destroy ourselves; if the human prevails we move towards the bliss that the super-conscious stage promises. Choice is ours. Our present predicament lies in the fact that we have advanced too far mechanically without simultaneous spiritual advance. And hence our power to destroy has increased. But we have not regressed spiritually. Spirituality has seeped down to the people but the external world forces them to transgress the moral limits and opt for short-term benefits. Here lies the hope and urge to move towards the super-conscious stage.

From 'Civilized' Beings to Moral Beings

The super-human stage, also called super-conscious stage, is marked with complete departure of man from animal in him to become an enlightened human being. This is the stage when the common man is able to achieve what Gandhi called *Swaraj* and brute force is subordinated to soul force. This is not to suggest that evils will disappear from the world. It only means that they would not be the dominant forces in shaping human behaviour.

Let me hasten to say that what has been sketched above is not a utopia; it is possible, feasible, practicable and inevitable. Unless the evolution of Homo sapiens stops, which I see no reason to happen, man must move towards divinity. Conscience must prevail over the body and mind. In fact, even today we have people among us who are close to that stage of life and living. We need more of them. Today increasing number of people realise that happiness is not dependent on material prosperity; it depends on how much love and compassion we bestow on others and get from others; on how far we have gone from the animal in us.

Gandhi was indeed a super-conscious human being; although he never said it so. He considered himself a traveller on the way to self-realization: an experimenter with Truth. It may take centuries or even millennia before human society reaches the level Gandhi wished and worked for. We are still in the conscious stage marked with violence with intermittent non-violence. We honour those who show courage and win wars by destroying life and property, cultures and civilisations of the aliens, who are none others than our own brethren. We also honour those who work for peace and who sacrifice themselves for others. It is a strange world indeed but at the same time a very challenging one. It is struggling hard to come out of its animal past.

Gandhi aimed at self-realization or super-consciousness. According to his own confessions, he had not reached that stage but he was on the way. For Gandhi travelling on the road to super-humanhood is the privilege of each human being and he must try to make the best use of this opportunity. Self-realization was the goal of Gandhi's life. To reach that goal, he chose several objectives of living. But they all converged on one point: moral progress.

As such anything that did not raise human stature morally was retrogressive. He was critical of modern industrial civilisation because it did not give primacy to moral progress.

The true test of civilisation lies not in the bodily welfare but in the spiritual enrichment. Civilized people are morally strong; they are courageous in the real sense. They would be prepared to die for a right cause than to yield to threats and temptations, says Gandhi. Socrates was a civilized man; so was Christ felt Gandhi.

It would be pertinent to quote a few passages from *Hind Swaraj* to bring home the characteristics of modern civilisation as seen by Gandhi. "Its true test lies in the fact that people living in it make bodily welfare the object of life...Formerly, people in Europe ploughed their lands mainly by manual labour. Now one man can plough a vast tract by means of steam engine and can thus amass a great wealth. This is called sign of civilisation. ... Formerly, only a few men wrote valuable books. Now anybody writes and prints anything he likes and poisons people's mind. Formerly, men travelled in wagons. Now they fly through the air. ... This is considered the height of civilisation. ... Formerly, when people wanted to fight with one another, they measured between them their bodily strength; now it is possible to take away thousands of lives by one man working behind a gun from a hill. This is civilisation. Formerly men worked in the open as much as they liked. Now thousands of workmen meet together ...in factories or mines. Their condition is worse than that of a beast. Formerly, men were made slaves by physical compulsion. Now they are enslaved by temptation of money. ...There are now diseases of which people never dreamt before and an army of doctors is engaged in finding out their cures, and so hospitals have increased. ... These are all true tests of civilisation. And if anyone speaks to the contrary, know that he is ignorant".

"This civilisation takes note neither of morality nor of religion. Its votaries calmly state that their business is not to teach religion. Some even consider it to be a superstitious growth. Other put on the cloak of religion and prate about morality. But after twenty years experience, I have come to the conclusion that immorality is often taught in the name of morality. Civilisation seeks to induce bodily comfort and it fails miserably even to do so."

We cannot deny that modern industrial civilisation is by and large unconcerned with morality. It treats the society as a big machine, which has been tuned to produce goods and services for those who can afford to pay for them. For this civilisation, the evolution of man has stopped. All that man has to do to live happily is to fully participate in the work opportunities the civilisation creates. There are no higher goals to be reached except material. At time, there are outcries about the ill effect of what this civilisation produces. But soon, a remedy is suggested which does not cure the ill but postpones it and directs it in some other direction. As time passes, the ill effects accumulate and a major catastrophe sets in. Gandhi warned that modern civilisation had the seeds of its own destruction.

A related characteristic of modern civilisation is preference for bodily welfare. The British could succeed in colonizing India because Indians were allured by money, which trade with Europeans gave them and fell into their trap. They aided and abetted them to colonize India. But no matter who makes money his God, he falls from grace. "It would be folly to assume that an Indian Rockefeller would be better than the American Rockefeller. Impoverished India can become free, but it will be very hard for any Indian made rich through immorality to regain its freedom. I fear we shall have to admit that moneyed men support British rule, their interest is bound up with its stability. Money renders a man helpless."

Civilisation "is not an incurable diseases but it should never be forgotten that the English people are at present afflicted by it." Unless this affliction is removed, the disease would persist. The affliction would however go only if the civilisation returns to the path of sanity, *i.e.* it starts measuring all its achievements by moral standards. Only those things should be promoted that raise the moral standards of the people. Thus Gandhi's critique of modern civilisation was total. It is not one aspect of it, which has gone astray and hence can be corrected without a wholesale change in its very fundamentals.

'WAR IS TOO PRIMITIVE A TOOL TO CHISEL PEACE'

The greatest message of *Hind Swaraj* is message of Truth and Nonviolence. Soul force is more powerful than the brute force. Man has learnt through experience that war never ends in peace. How many wars humanity has fought; how many millions of people have died; and how many more are being prepared to die fighting wars so that wars do not come again. But each war leads to more and bigger wars. We are now waiting for an atomic war; for chemical and biological wars; and for laser wars. All these wars are being planned to bring peace. War appears to be too primitive a tool to chisel peace.

Gandhi found a new weapon to fight the conventional wars: *satyagraha* which could be used by individuals, groups and societies. To use this weapon, one has to be fully trained in non-violence in the same way as a soldier is trained in violence before he is sent to the battlefield. The non-violent fighter is called satyagrahi while the violent fighter is called a soldier. A *satyagrahi* is one who has full control over his senses. He would not indulge in violence (in thought, words, or deeds). He will face death valiantly in the hope that the killer would be reformed. Without proper training no soldier can survive, he would either surrender or face death within no time. In the case of the poorly trained non-violent *satyagrahi*, he would either become violent or run away.

One should not expect the masses to become so perfect *satyagrahis*. Even a few selected leaders would not reach that level of perfection. Gandhi considered himself to be an imperfect *satyagrahi* still learning through trial and error. The question then arises: how and who can train true *satyagrahis*? Gandhi's answer was favourable environment and regular practice. The first step in the training of a *satyagrahi* is the change in the prevailing worldview that only those who are physically strong and armed to defend themselves can survive. Unless the mind set of the trainee changes in favour of Truth, non-violence, love, compassion, duty, etc. even practical training would not do. This is borne out by the fact that Gandhi had to suspend his non-cooperation movement several times because the *satyagrahis* indulged in violence, his inspiration and leadership notwithstanding. They did not have the courage to face violence non-violently.

Worldviews do not change easily; very often people do not even know that they have a worldview, which determines their judgments. They tend to justify their indulgence in violence, anger, untruthfulness and other weaknesses. From the day we are born, we hear, see, feel and receive certain waves from the environment around. As we grow, the bits of information that come from various sources are internalized and synthesized to form what we call the worldview. All of us have our own worldviews but we are rarely conscious of it.

The worldviews that we inherit and nurture from early childhood form the building blocks of our attitude towards ourselves and others. Often they do not disappear with death for they are passed on to many others in the lifetime of an individual. That is the reason why bad characters tend to have sons and daughters with bad character. It would therefore be a very time consuming and difficult task to train people in *satyagraha*.

In a society of thieves, we cannot produce an honest man. And if per chance a 'Prahalad' is born, he would have to undergo torture, mental and physical, to remain honest. Most probably he would succumb to the temptations of thieving. But the process of change has to begin somewhere; and this somewhere is family and primary school. The parents and teachers therefore have a very critical role to play in the training of the children and youth who constitute the future generation.

KEY TO FURTHER LIES IN INDIAN CIVILISATION

Gandhi was the product of Indian civilisation in distress. He wrote *Hind Swaraj* when the country was in chains and its cultural foundations shaky. It was the time when industrial civilisation reached its peak; it swept Europe, then North America and then the Old World. Where ever it went it devastated the native culture and super-imposed the industrial culture it acquired not too long ago. One of the most spectacularly tragic outcomes of the Industrial Revolution was the annihilation of millions of people in South America, Australia, Africa and even in Asia – the people who were still a part of the pre-agricultural or agricultural civilisation, which lasted until the mid-nineteenth century in Europe and twentieth century in Asia.

Gandhi felt that India was eminently suited for a struggle based on inalienable and universally accepted, even if scarcely practiced, moral principles to change this satanic civilisation. Indian civilisation consistently laid emphasis on morality and spiritual advancement, and on using the material and physical achievements as means to promote unity, equity, and human dignity. Other cultural traditions (Greek, Persian, Chinese and many others) too treasured morality but Indian civilisation alone has survived without any major break to retain the original fervour. As time passed, other cultures, voluntarily or otherwise, cut themselves off from their roots and got more deeply involved in mundane affairs of material life, at times totally deviating from the path they started with. Indian culture in its essences has stood its ground and maintained unmatched continuity, consistency and persistency, the multi-directional pressures and onslaughts it faced notwithstanding.

The industrial civilisation, which has now engulfed the world, marks perhaps the most significant cultural deviation the world ever witnessed. India too was sucked in its whirlpool. Gandhi calls it interruption in the main current of cultural evolution. Yet, it was during the soaring heights of the industrial civilisation, that India produced a number of spiritual leaders who forced her to reconsider the path it was treading. Gandhi was the foremost among them. While others reminded India of its spiritual heritage, Gandhi went beyond and not only rediscovered Indian civilisation in its original form but also put it at the service of the humanity as a whole.

Gandhi hypothesized that only that civilisation could survive, which did not deviate from the Cosmic Law of morality otherwise known as the Law of Truth, Law of Life and Law of Love. He considered Indian civilisation unique in this respect. It is the only civilisation that accepts all life forms as parts of a single family (*Vasudhaiva Kutumbakam*). It is a civilisation, which measures its progress in terms of moral unfolding of human personality and upholds the supremacy of truth and non-violence. It is broad minded, accommodative, assimilative and dynamic. New comers were accorded an honourable place and were allowed to live as they pleased. True, these eternal tendencies of Indian civilisation were not infrequently disturbed by unwholesome external and internal pressures, but such disturbances were rarely allowed to cross the threshold limits of self-corrective negative feed backs. Further, such disturbances were often counterbalanced by the arrival of great spiritual leaders on the scene to put people back on the path of duty. If mythology is the dramatized folk expression of the main currents of a civilisation, then we stand assured that such disturbances were never allowed to put Indian culture upside down. Indians learnt through time to resolve conflicts peacefully and assimilate within their social fabric even such threads, which did not fit the texture of the fabric. Gandhi was greatly impressed by these tendencies.

Gandhi cautioned the revolutionaries against copying England. He told them that India's civilisation was older and more durable and Indians were superior to the British in many ways. The political institutions of Britain were not very effective and the elections did not bring to the parliament the most honest people. "If the money and the time wasted by parliament were entrusted to a few good men, the English nation would be occupying to day a much higher platform." Does it not apply to present day India?

Criticizing the parliamentary democracy in England, Gandhi wanted India to evolve a new democratic system based on equality, morality and self-reliance. "I pray to God that India may never be in that plight. ... It is generally acknowledged that the members are hypocritical and selfish. It is fear that is the guiding motive. What is done today may be undone tomorrow. ... When the greatest questions are debated, its members have been seen to stretch themselves and doze. Sometimes the members talk away unless the listeners are disgusted. Carlyle has called it the 'talking shop of the world.' Members vote for their party without a thought. Their so-called discipline binds them to it. If any member by way of exception gives an independent vote, he is considered a renegade."

Gandhi specifically mentions about prime minister acting for party, instead of for the welfare of the people. And people vote according to what newspapers say. He does recognize a great quality of Englishmen. "They will never allow their country to be lost. If any person were to cast an evil eye on it, they would pluck out his eyes. ... If India copies England, it is my firm conviction that it will be ruined." Alas, India copied England, and it is being ruined.

It is a superstition and ungodly thing to believe that an act of a majority binds a minority. Many examples can be given in which acts of the majority will be found to have been wrong and those of the minority will have been right. All reforms owe their origin to the initiation of minorities in opposition to majorities. If among a band of robbers a knowledge of robbing is obligatory, is a pious man to accept that obligation? So long as the superstition that men should obey unjust laws exists, so long will their slavery exist. And a passive resistance alone can remove such a superstition."

INDIA WILL RISE AGAIN

While thinking about India's future and its role in ushering a new world order, Gandhi faced a serious enigma. Why did India succumb to a satanic civilisation? How could a people 300 million strong and having a background of a magnificent past, be subjugated by a tiny European island nation? Gandhi was dismayed by the poverty, ignorance and inequality that prevailed in the country in his times. And he asked to himself: were the British stronger than Indians? Or, India had become weak and hence could not face even small bands of invaders? India's greatness was known from times immemorial. Who did not want to go to India: the Greeks, the Romans, the Central

Asian nomadic tribes (Aryans, Huns, Kushans, Moghals, to name a few) the Persians, the Arabs, the Portuguese, the Spaniards, the French, the Dutch, the English? Columbus wanted to circumnavigate the earth to reach India, it is quite another thing that he landed in an island of Central America, which he thought was India and named it so. Until the seventh century, all incoming tribes were totally absorbed in India's polity.

A new situation emerged when Moslems did not assimilate themselves fully in Indian culture. India devised a new approach to them: selective absorption. A great majority of Indian Moslems did not come from outside. They were Indians – Hindus, Buddhists, Jains and Animists who changed their religion willingly or otherwise. And those who came from outside, they settled down in India and became Indians. They adopted Indian music, Indian dance, Indian painting, and even Indian literary traditions. Some of them inflicted deep wounds on Inidan psyche but there were rulers like Akbar who tried to evolve a composite religion called Deen-e-Ilahi. By the end of the sixteenth century, a new synthesis was emerging in the cultural firmament of India.

India was invaded not once but very many times. The British were the last to come. The earlier invaders came and went back with the loot they could lay their hands on. Some of them stayed back and became Indians. India assimilated them. Even the Moghals and before them the Lodis and the Khiljis, just to mention a few, became Indians and had practically no links with the place of their origin, even if retaining their identity. The English were, however, a different stuff; they came to India to subjugate and rule it from England. They were interested in India as a perennial source of resources for industrialization. Fortunately, India was culturally advanced and population-wise well settled, so they could not treat it the same way as they treated Australia and North America. But they did bleed it for over two centuries without any respite.

Gandhi, after a thorough analysis of Indian history came to the conclusion that India lost not because it did not have the weapons to match the weapons of the foreigners but because it had deviated from its time honoured path of morality and thus lost the cultural superiority it commanded. How can a people be subjugated if they refuse to submit? A slave is a slave only so long as he cooperates with the master. On deeper analysis he came to the conclusion that fault lay not in the British but in Indians themselves. Indians became money minded and greedy;

they wanted to benefit from the British Raj even at the cost of their freedom and country's honour. British ruled India through Indians. And so long as the people of India wanted the British to rule over them, India would remain a British colony, concluded Gandhi.

The British rule had to end sooner than later, but how? It was possible to throw it out by using the same means the British used to capture India. They used physical force; Indians could use the same physical force to oust them from the country. The young revolutionaries were following that means. This is what the Americans did in 1776. The first war of independence in 1857 was a quacy organized physical onslaught on the British. Before that and even afterwards, many small scale rebellions took place in different parts of the country and many lives were lost. These were all acts of bravery and patriotism misplaced. Gandhi came to the conclusion that such a course of action suffered from two main infirmities. First, it involved violence, which was against the basic tenets of Indian culture, and second by acceptance of the means the British used, it accepted the superiority of the western civilisation. If violence breeds violence, then violence against the British would not breed love. And if Indian civilisation were superior to the western civilisation, India would degrade itself by adopting the methods of the western civilisation to solve its problems.

The British rule in India was unjustified; it had no moral basis. It was based on brute force. It had to go but not by brute force. British could be ousted from India without the use of violence and without the use of modern weapons of destruction. Indians must gird up their loins; they should come together on a common platform and refuse to cooperate with the British Raj. If the British use the brute force to subdue them, they should neither retaliate violently, nor give in. They should not budge even an inch and be ready to sacrifice themselves. They should fight the British Raj using their time-honoured weapon of non-violence, said Gandhi. And he added that India's fight should be against the British Rule, not against the British people for the British people were common sufferers with us; they were also the victims of industrialism. The real fight was therefore against the so-called modern civilisation, which has afflicted the people world over whether rulers or ruled. The British administration represented the political and economic power of modern civilisation.

Gandhi did not write so but I suspect he had a vision of a new world order, which must emerge as a logical corollary to what had been happening in the world. The first wave (agricultural) civilisation ended around 1700 AD; the second wave (industrial) civilisation, Gandhi perceived, must end by the end of the twentieth century; the third wave (information) civilisation would not last for more than a century. It would have to be followed by fourth wave (spiritual) civilisation, which must take roots before the twenty first century ended. Gandhi was thus not very much ahead of his time.

The edifice of *Hind Swaraj* that Gandhi built was founded on these convictions and considerations. If the law that governs the atom is the same as the one that governs the cosmos, then it must be the same for all life forms on planet earth. This law is expansive, inclusive, and centrifugal. The *Rig Veda* called it R'ta some five millenniums ago. The opposite of love is hate. Hate is contractive, exclusive and centripetal. It contracts and contracts until it finishes the one who is gripped by it. Hate produces material growth. The road to moral progress is strewn with Love. Moral progress means spiritual progress. Material progress is not the goal of man; the goal is spiritual progress. Material progress can at best be a means to accelerate spiritual progress.

TOWARDS A NEW FUTURE

Gandhi died but his message is alive. He has now risen from the Raj Ghat, not in flesh and blood, but in spirit, visions and missions to take humanity to its destiny. But the path is treacherous as it is evident from the violence that pervades the world to day. But there is silver lining too. Millions of people the world over have opposed the terrorist attack on America and American attack on Iraq. Gandhi's message is becoming the guide post for peace initiatives all over the world. The world forums quote him to prove their points. As the venom of terrorism spreads and conflict between man and man, between man and nature, and among the nations heats up, his relevance increases. 'Abjure violence and win your opponent with love' is the call of Gandhi. He bequeathed *Hind Swaraj* to us so that the generations to come are inspired to follow Truth and Nonviolence, become morally strong and move forward on the road to spiritually super human race.

As mentioned above, even in the lifetime of Gandhi, *Hind Swaraj* and all that it stands for, was not accepted by the English educated Indian intellectuals whether in the Congress Party, which he nurtured or outside it. His speeches at Muir College, Allahabad and Banaras Hindu University on economic and social matters in 1916 were treated with derision. It was only the common man of India, the real Indian who was illiterate and who could not read *Hind Swaraj* even though written so simply, who accepted Gandhi and whatever he had to say verbally or in writing. For them real *Hind Swaraj* was Gandhi himself. The following that Gandhi could command was so phenomenal that even those who had doubts about his theory and practice of truth and nonviolence bowed to his moral superiority and the logic underlying the theses he propounded and queued after him.

Hind Swaraj has become an oft-quoted book. Many great thinkers and futurologists have picked up the threads from Gandhi and offered models of what is in store for us in years to come and what should we do to usher in a new and peaceful world order. As one reads Capra, Rifkin, Mishan, Ellich, Naisbitt and several others both in the West and the East, one is wonderstruck by the versatility of Gandhi's thoughts.

The Gaia theory of the evolution of life on planet earth enunciated clear 50 years after *Hind Swaraj* was one of the building blocks of Gandhi's Whole Theory of Life. The moral crisis, violence, and environmental problems we face today, were foreseen by Gandhi even in 1908. He predicted the collapse of the Soviet Union as it was founded on violence as early as 1920s. He also saw the imminent downfall of capitalism as it was based on greed, which he considered immoral. The signs of fatigue are already there; globalization may be the last ditch effort to keep it afloat. The Third Wave by Mishan, the Turning Point by Capra, and the Mega Trends by Naisbitt published in 1970s and 1980s point to the same conclusions, which Gandhi arrived in 1908.

Independent India under the pressure of the prevailing circumstances rejected *Hind Swaraj* as the framework for national reconstruction. The real meaning of *Hind Swaraj* was lost. It was brought down to its literal meaning – political freedom of India. And to protect and strengthen the hard won freedom, the meaning of *Swadeshi* was also changed. Gandhi was declared as the Father of the Nation but the foundation on which Gandhi wanted the new nation to be built was postponed if not rejected. India tried to take lessons from both Marx and Adam Smith; little if at all from Gandhi.

Some recent political scientists have come to the conclusion that Gandhi has been rejected by India and Subhas Bose who was a votary of violent means has been accepted. Such conclusions are erroneous. Gandhi wanted to win *Swaraj* for humanity; Subhas Bose was interested in political freedom for India. Gandhi's goals were long term while that of Subhas, immediate run. Subhas called Gandhi 'the father of the nation'. India did adopt the Subhas model for it was easy to adopt but it did not reject Gandhi's perspectives. Gandhi had set the standards for future; Subhas had set the immediate political goals.

If we analyze the social, political and economic scene in India today, we realize that we did try to meet the immediate challenges in 1947 by adopting what Gandhi asked us to reject. After over 50 years, we realise that we committed a blunder. With the collapse of the Soviet Union, Adam Smith appears to have won the battle, but who will win the war, Gandhi or Adam Smith, only the future can tell. The signs and signals, even if feeble, appear to favour Gandhi. Gandhi's design of the future of India is now lodged in the museums named after him. When would they be taken out and put into use to build the India of the future, we do not know. It depends on us, our children and grand-children.

Some people are prone to ask: Is Gandhian model practicable; would it be even accepted by the world? I-Ching, a Chinese philosopher answered such questions long ago:

> After a time of decay comes the turning point. The powerful light that was banished returns. There is movement, but it is not brought about by fate. The movement is natural arising spontaneously. For this reason the transformation of the old becomes easy. The old is discarded and the new is introduced to measure accord with time; therefore no harm results.

PART II

BUILDING BLOCKS OF HIND SWARAJ

5

Gandhi's Own Experiences and Experiments

Cultural background of a person is clearly reflected in what he says, writes and does. Culture includes familial, societal, educational and spiritual mix that constitutes the outer and inner environment in which man lives. A person reacts to a particular situation in the light of his cultural background. Since this background differs from person to person, different people react to a particular challenge differently. Let us take the example of Gandhi's reaction to the challenge he faced when he was thrown out the train in South Africa. Many others before and after Gandhi passed through far greater challenges than him but how is it that Gandhi alone became a man of destiny for India and standard for measuring human progress for the world. Perhaps it was the providence; no two individuals are same, even the twin. There are as many religions as the people, said Gandhi. This being so, there was no possibility of replicating Gandhi biologically, psychologically and spiritually. Gandhi reacted to the situation he faced uniquely. There lies his greatness. And here lies the hope for humanity for each individual has a unique way of self-realization..

This chapter centres on the first 40 years of Gandhi's life (1869 to 1909); a period from birth to the writing of *Hind Swaraj*. Gandhi's receptivity and preparedness to react to challenges he faced depended on many factors. An attempt has been made here to capture the essence of some of them. They together constitute the inputs to culture that Gandhi acquired through time.

EARLY LIFE

Childhood

Let us begin with a short biography of Mohandas Karamchand Gandhi, the full name of Mahatma Gandhi. He was born in 1869 at

Porbandar, a small township on the northwestern coast of Kathiawar peninsula in Gujarat. His father Karamchand Gandhi was just a literate man but apparently highly educated otherwise. His mother, Putlibai was a pious lady of great moral standing even if traditional. His grandfather was the Diwan (prime minister) of Porbandar princely state; his father followed the family tradition and rose to the position of Diwan of Rajkot and later of Vankaner state. He belonged to a Bania sub-caste, which was well known for traditionalism and community solidarity.

Gandhi thus belonged to a middle class family of some status but as we will see later, not very strong financially. On the completion of high school education at Alfred High School, Rajkot in 1887, he proceeded to England for bar-at-law in the hope of following the family tradition of becoming the Diwan of Rajkot state.

Gandhi was not good at studies, nor was he an outgoing young man. He was an introvert and rarely participated in sports and other extracurricular activities. The only exercise he consistently did from his student days to the end of his life was brisk walking for long distances. He was married at the age of 12 to Kasturbai who was illiterate. Child marriages were common in those days; and girl's education was uncommon.

Influenced by the high moral, and religious standards of his parents particularly his mother, Gandhi maintained a strong moral code of conduct from early childhood. Two dramatic plays he had the chance to see: *Shravana Pitrabhakti* and *Harishchandra* left a very deep impression on him. After seeing these plays, he asked to himself: Why should not all serve their parents like Shravana and be truthful like Harishchandra? *Ramayana* by Tulsidas also left indelible mark on his life. A family priest recited it daily loudly enough to be audible to all. The character of Ram was so indelibly imprinted on him that even at the time of his death '*Hey Ram*' was the last word he uttered. He was always truthful to his parents, teachers and elders in general; never resorted to unfair means in school or outside and took special care to guard the purity of his character.

Despite strong moral footings, Gandhi did go astray in his school days. He was inspired by some of his friends to break the old traditions and become 'modern' by eating meat, smoking bidi (local cigarette), and visiting brothels. He did eat meat once but could not digest it; and he did not relish the bidi. He went to a prostitute too but could not gather the courage to indulge in sex. He escaped it just by the grace of God, so says he in his autobiography (*My Experiments with Truth*).

English Education

After passing the matriculation examination, the senior Gandhis decided to send him to England to study law. But they did not have enough money for the purpose. Further, his mother was totally against his education in a country where people were possessed by 'vices' like meat eating, drinking alcohol, etc. With great difficulty, the money was arranged and he got permission from his mother too on condition that he would avoid all evils while in England. His community leaders too were against his trip; they threatened to excommunicate him but he defied them in the hope of winning over them on return.

Gandhi set sail for England on September 4, 1888 from Bombay. His shyness came in the way of his mixing with co-passengers on board. While in England, he at first tried to look and behave like perfect English gentleman. This fad, however, did not last long. Being a vegetarian, he came in touch with the London Vegetarian Society. Meeting two prominent theosophists, Madame Blavatskey and Mrs. Annie Besant in 1889 brought him still closer to the richness of Indian culture. They introduced him to Arnold's *Song Celestial* (*Geeta*) and *Light of Asia* (Asoka) and the people who admired Indian culture and civilisation.

Gandhi entered the Inner Temple (Law School) on November 6, 1888. His three-year stay in England was eventful in many ways. England was passing through a period of great debate on freedom of thought. The Independent Labour Party was formed in 1887. The English edition of *Das Kapital* by Marx (1887) and *Fabian Essays* by Bernard Shaw (1889) stirred the minds of conservative England. Arnold's *Song Celestial* and *Light of Asia* earned many friends for India. At least in the intellectual circles, the assertion that India was not ready for representative government was being questioned. Lectures on Indian philosophy by Max Muller became highly popular. Gandhi could not remain untouched by the emerging scenario in favour of India.

Gandhi sailed back for India on June 12, 1891. On his return to India he tried for two years to establish himself as a lawyer at Rajkot and Bombay. In his first appearance in Bombay court, he became so nervous that he could not utter a word and slumped in the chair.

Failing to establish himself at Bombay, he returned to Rajkot after six months. At Rajkot too he could not make any headway, but being a good draftsman, he could earn enough to meet his expenses.

As the luck or destiny would have it, he got an offer from Dada Abdulla, a South African businessman of Gujarati origin and who knew the Gandhi family to help him fight his court cases in South Africa. He accepted the offer and in April 1893 he left for Durban.

SOUTH AFRICAN TRIALS AND TRIBULATIONS

On landing in South Africa he realized that Indians were looked down upon as uncivilized coolies. Gandhi by this time had developed a sense of pride in Indian culture and his education in England had given him some self-confidence to assert his rights. He could not be pushed around without protest. Within days of arrival, a Durban court asked Gandhi to take off his turban because it was not a prescribed dress for lawyers. Gandhi refused to do so. And this act of defiance got good publicity for him. His client was also happy with what Gandhi did.

Maritsburg Incidence

After a week, Gandhi was asked to go to Pretoria to handle a case there. He was booked in first class railway compartment. At Maritzburg, the capital of Natal, and in the middle of night, he was asked to change the compartment because a white passenger booked in the same compartment refused to travel with a coolie. On his refusal to vacate the berth, he was forcibly ejected and his baggage was thrown out on the platform. This bitter experience changed not only the life of Gandhi but also the colonial history of the three southern continents of the world: Africa, Asia and Latin America. The second half of the twentieth century was marked by the emergence of new nations and the man who triggered off the change was Gandhi and the event, which stirred the mind and soul of Gandhi was Maritzburg incident.

The train in which Gandhi was travelling steamed away. He was forced to shiver all night in the dark waiting room of Maritzburg. "There was a white man in the room. I was afraid of him. What was my duty, I asked myself. Should I go back to India, or should I go forward, with God as my helper, and face whatever was in store for me? I decided to stay and suffer. My active nonviolence began from that date."

Adding Salt to Injury

Many insults were in store for Gandhi. He left Maritzburg by evening train in a reserved berth for Charlestown from where he had to go by stagecoach to Sanderson in the evening. The stagecoach too was prearranged for him. A white passenger was also booked in the same coach. Only two persons could sit inside the coach. The white man and the leader of the coach sat inside. Gandhi was asked to sit besides the coachman. Apparently he was unhappy with this affront and deliberate injustice, but did not want to pick up another quarrel. His tolerance, however, produced an opposite reaction. After some time, the leader of the coach wanted to smoke. He came out and asked Gandhi to sit on the footboard so that he could sit besides the coachman and smoke. It was too much for Gandhi; he refused to budge. The leader started beating him and pulling him down. The co-passengers intervened in favour of Gandhi and he remained where he was. Next day, he took another coach for Johannesburg.

On reaching Johannesburg, he went straight to Grand Hotel, but there was no vacancy apparently because he was a coolie. He was lodged in some other smaller hotel. The following day, he went to Pretoria by train. Gandhi's mind was fully charged with agony of insults heaped on him by the ruling classes of South Africa. What disturbed him most was that despite their rich cultural heritage, Indians were ill treated and derided but no one protested. The same was the situation with regard to other coloured people: the Chinese, the Turks, the Arabs, etc. The situation with regard to the native Africans was much worse. They all had accepted their inferior position as given.

Gandhi Brings People Together

Gandhi was unhappy with the condition in which Indians and other Asians lived and made up his mind to do something concrete to change the situation. He requested an influential businessman Tyeb Haji Khan Muhammad to call a meeting of local Indians to discuss the problems they faced. It was the year 1994. Gandhi spoke to the audience and suggested a two-pronged strategy: self-improvement and protest through representation to the authorities. Under the first strategy, he advised people to be honest, to develop the habit of cleanliness and to maintain unity among themselves irrespective of the religion, caste and language. He also advised them to learn a bit of English to understand what was going around in the country they were living. And under the second strategy, he suggested the formation of a committee to represent to the authorities concerned for redressing their grievances. He offered to teach English to all those who so wanted and to devote time for the association.

Both the suggestions were accepted. A committee was constituted which held monthly meetings. Gandhi attended these meetings and became more closely associated with Indians and their problems. He found to his dismay that Indians were deprived of all their rights to pursue their vocation by a Transvaal Government notification in 1888. Indians were not allowed to open shops in white residential areas and those who were already there were packed off with small compensation. The only occupations open to them were those of waiters and coolies. Prior to that in 1885, a law was enacted to levy a poll tax of three pounds per head on all those Asiatics who entered the colony.

To develop a new culture of self-reliance and unity, Gandhi convinced Dada Abdulla (Gandhi's client who brought him to South Africa) and his adversary Tyeb Seth to settle their dispute outside the court through arbitration. Gandhi achieved this feat by sacrificing his own pecuniary interests. This single act of Gandhi boosted his image as a leader of Indian community and his stock as a lawyer.

By the end of 1893, Gandhi decided to go back to India. At Durban he was informed that a law was being drafted to de-franchise Indians. Gandhi advised his people to send representations to appropriate authorities and protest against the proposed law. People forced Gandhi to cancel his trip to India and help them secure justice. He had no choice but to agree. He offered to fight on behalf of the people without any professional fee. He drafted a petition and sent it to the South African legislature on June 28, 1894. A large number of copies of the petition were sent out to all those who mattered in this respect. Newspapers gave wide publicity to the document. The Bill was, however, passed. Gandhi did not relent; he sent a monster petition signed by 10,000 Indians to Lord Ripon, Secretary of Colonies in London requesting him to deny the royal assent to the Bill.

Realizing that his work as a lawyer was increasing and he had to appear in courts of different places, he applied for registration as an advocate in Natal Supreme Court through the white dominated Natal Law Society. The Society rejected his application obviously because he was an Indian. By this time Gandhi was so much used to fighting against injustice that he appealed against the decision of the Society in the Supreme Court and succeeded in getting himself registered.

The petition Gandhi sent to Lord Ripon had its salutary effect. Ripon did not give assent to the Bill. Thus, the petitioner Gandhi succeeded in achieving something without resorting to any violence. Having achieved some success, Gandhi tried to create public opinion against the injustice being perpetrated against the coloured people in general and Indians in particular. He approached the people of both British and Indian origins to pressurise the colonial administration to treat all British subjects as equal irrespective of the colour or origin.

While Gandhi was fighting on the South African front, it would be instructive to know the situation back home in India. Indian National Congress was formed in 1885 to function as a bridge between the British Government and the people of India and help redress the grievances of the people. The Congress started pressing the colonial administration to concede some participation of Indians in running the affairs of the country. Gandhi kept in touch with what was going on in India through Dada Bhai Naoroji who presided over the Lahore session of INC in 1893. He in turn kept Dadabhai informed of the situation in South Africa and the work he was doing there. Gandhi liked the idea of Indian National Congress. He decided to have a similar Organisation in South Africa. On August 22, 1894, the Natal Indian Congress was formed. It met every month.

Once the NIC was formed, he started acting on its behalf as its representative. Among the new activities he started were: adult education classes to teach English to Indians so that they understood what was going on in the world and also to articulate their own opinions. He arranged lectures on health and hygiene and their rights as British subjects. He drafted and published pamphlets to acquaint people with the pitiable conditions in which the Indians lived and worked in South Africa.

Search for Unity in Diversity

While the above public activities kept Gandhi busy, his spiritual journey took a new turn. He became a true believer in unity of human kind. Among his closest friends and supporters were Moslems and Christians. He maintained close contact with them, and had frequent discussions and dialogues. Gandhi was convinced that all religions were united on certain fundamentals like Truth, Non-violence, human brotherhood, love, compassion and dignity of individuals and hence they all should join hands on issues that go against these basic principles. May be some of them went astray more often than others, but they could not deny their basic tenets and they must join hands to create a world in which violence, inequality, hate and prejudices were very much lessened, if not eliminated. In this regard Indian civilisation had some lessons for the world. It had always been inclusive, nonviolent, and truthful. Whenever major deviations occurred, great men like Buddha came on the scene and put the society back on the right course.

By the turn of the nineteenth century, Gandhi had emerged as a leader of some political and cultural standing and his opinions could not be summarily ignored. His work got wide publicity in India too. In the Madras session of Indian National Congress (in 1894) which was presided over by Alfred Webb, the following resolution was unanimously adopted: *This Congress earnestly entreats Her Majesty's Government to grant the prayer of Her Majesty's Indian subjects, resident in South African Colonies, by vetoing the bill of the colonial government to de-franchise them.*

A Short Visit to India

Gandhi had been in South Africa for three years. He had already become a leading figure at least in the Asiatic circles. Because of abjured violence, he earned some sympathy among Europeans too. Even those who differed had a word of appreciation for him. His mind was set on his wife and child whom he had left behind in India. He, therefore, decided to return to India and bring his wife and child too.

On the eve of his departure, he was given a very touching farewell with a number of costly presents for himself, Kasturbai and his son. He thanked the people for the gesture. He felt honoured by the appreciation of the people for his services. But in line with his thinking about selfless service he returned the presents given to him pleading that whatever he had done, was his duty. All the gifts were presented to Natal Indian Congress and other public organisations. Gandhi returned with lots of goodwill from all sections of Indians: Hindus, Muslims, Parsis and Christians. He was 'bathed with the nectar of love.'

He landed at Calcutta. From there he proceeded for Rajkot by train. The train stopped at Allahabad for a few hours; Gandhi met the editor of Pioneer and apprised him of the work he was doing in South

Africa and the progress he had made. The Pioneer building where Gandhi met the editor is still there. It is now known as Food Corporation of India (FCI) building and is just in from of the Senate Hall of the University. By the time this book comes out, it may be demolished and replaced by a new building. In front of the building is a well. When Gandhi sent his name to the editor, the latter was busy wring something. Gandhi had to wait for about 90 minutes. He sat down on the platform of the well. When the editor saw the chit with M.K. Gandhi's name, he rushed out to receive him and profusely apologized for what had happened.

Gandhi reached Rajkot in 1896 and stayed there for some time. He published a Green Pamphlet giving details of the plights of Indians in South Africa. The pamphlet received good publicity in India. England and South Africa. Soon he met Ranade, Badrudin Tyabji, and Ferozshah Mehta at Bombay and Tilak, Gokhale and Bhandarkar at Poona. He acquainted them with the conditions in South Africa. From Poona he went to Madras and met the editors of Hindu and Madras Standard. He returned to Bombay via Calcutta where he met Surendranath Banerjee. Gandhi wanted to address a public meeting in Calcutta but could not do so because he received an urgent telegram from Natal (on November 12): "Parliament opens January return soon." He returned to Bombay and left for South Africa on November 30, 1896, this time with his wife and child.

Whites Attack Gandhi on Return

The steamer reached Durban on·December 18, 1896. A rumour was set around that Gandhi had brought two steamers full of Indians to settle down in South Africa. While the Asiatics were jubilant, the Europeans were unhappy and did not want him to return to South Africa. When they came to know that Gandhi was returning, some 2000 of them assembled to stop him and fellow Indian passengers from disembarking from the steamer. The police persuaded them to disperse but no sooner the passengers disembarked, the European crowd returned and attacked them. For safety reasons, Kasturbai and her son were taken out separately. Gandhi opted to face the crowd. Gandhi was given all the protection he needed. He had to go through a terrible ordeal, but he was not physically hurt.

Chamberlain, the Secretary of State for the Colonies asked the Natal Government to prosecute Gandhi's assailants. But Gandhi said:

"I do not want to prosecute anyone. I do not hold the assailants to blame. They were given to understand that I had made exaggerated statements in India about the whites in Natal and calumniated them.... I am sure that when the truth becomes known they will be sorry for their conduct." Soon, the press brought the truth out. Gandhi was declared innocent and whites were condemned.

During this visit, Gandhi stayed in South Africa for about six years (1896-1901). He got more deeply involved with the problems of Indians and his professional work also grew rather fast. As Gandhi's public activities multiplied, he realized that he must be fearless if he wanted to fight nonviolently. He, therefore, decided to become self-reliant and to lead a simple lifestyle. He started cutting down his personal expenses by washing his own clothes and trimming his own hairs. He also engaged himself in social service such as treating lepers and helping patients in hospitals.

Gandhi's inclination towards service of the sick and needy became more visible during the Boer War in 1899. Since he was asking for equal treatment as a citizen of the British Empire, he considered it his duty to help the empire fight the war successfully. He offered to organize an Indian Ambulance Corps. The work of the corps was highly appreciated. This experience gave a lot of confidence to Indians and taught them a great lesson in organizing the people for joint action.

Another Visit to India

Gandhi was keen on settling down in India and, therefore, he decided to return home for good and visit South Africa only when situation there so demanded. The local leadership in South Africa, he thought, was capable of handling the problems. He reached Bombay on December 19, 1901 and immediately left for Calcutta to attend the seventeenth session of the Indian National Congress. The Congress began with a tribute to Ranade who had just passed away. Gandhi moved a resolution in the subject committee of the Congress *on behalf of the hundred thousand British Indians in South Africa.* He was however disappointed when his resolution did not get the attention it deserved. The meeting however gave Gandhi an opportunity to get closer to Gokhale, Tilak, Surendranath Banerjee and other leaders and feel their pulse.

Gandhi stayed in Calcutta for a month and interacted with Gokhale and a number of Bengalee intellectuals. He paid a quick visit to Burma too (Burma at that time was part of India). On his way to Rajkot, he visited Allahabad, Benares and several other places in India in third class railway compartment. After a halt at Rajkot for a few months, he shifted to Bombay where he established a good legal practice. He interacted with Gokhale very frequently and learned about the problems of India and the trials and tribulations through which India was passing.

Gandhi could not stay in India for too long. On receiving a telegram from South Africa that Chamberlain was expected there, he decided to go back for a year leaving his family at Bombay. He left for Natal in December 1902. On reaching South Africa, he represented the case of Indians who, after the Boer War, were once again barred from entering Transvaal without permit. He was told bluntly 'you know the Imperial Government have little control over self-governing colonies.' Gandhi decided to stay put and fight this unjust law tooth and nail.

The Phoenix Settlement

As Gandhi's name spread in Asiatic as well European circles, his law practice and related activities grew fast. He could not handle them single-handed and therefore, decided to take the help of some theosophists. In 1904 he launched two major projects of great significance: *Indian Opinion,* a weekly magazine, and Phoenix Settlement of 100 acres near Durban. The latter became the hub of all activities of Gandhi and his colleagues who moved to the new settlement. *Indian Opinion* also was shifted there. The Phoenix Settlement consisted of two types of people: schemers and workers. The schemers were the producers: each schemer had 3 acres of land to work on. The workers were paid wages. Gandhi commuted between Phoenix Settlement and Johannesburg. He called his family back to Johannesburg in 1905 and settled down there for the law practice.

It was just a coincident that Gokhale in India started the Servants of Indian society the same year (1905) to 'train men prepared to devote their lives to the cause of the country in a religious spirit and seek to promote by all constitutional means, the national interests of the Indian people.' It had five main objectives:

(1) to create among the people by example and by precept a deep and passionate love of the motherland, seeking its highest fulfilment in service and sacrifice;
(2) to organize the work of political education and agitation, basing it on a careful study of public questions and strengthening generally the public life of the country;
(3) to promote relations of cordial goodwill and the cooperation among different communities;
(4) to assist educational movements, especially those for the education of women, the education of backward classes and industrial and scientific education; and
(5) to help forward the industrial development of the country; and the elevation of the status of depressed classes.

By this time, the revival of India as a united self-governing dominion commensurate with its great past, even if within the British Empire, had already gripped the minds of educated sections of Indian society. It was clearly reflected in the deliberations of Indian National Congress at its Benares session in 1905. Gopal Krishna Gokhale, the President of the Congress denounced the partition of Bengal and urged Lord Curzon to annul it. He declared "the devotion to the motherland, which is enshrined in the highest Swadeshi, is an influence so profound and so passionate that its very thought thrills and its actual touch lifts out of oneself India needs today above everything else that the gospel of this devotion should be preached to high and low, to the prince and the peasant, in town and in hamlet, till the service of the motherland becomes with us as overwhelming a passion as it is in Japan."

Gandhi was highly moved by these developments and tried to emulate them in his Phoenix Settlement. Along with his other activities he took keen interest in vegetarianism and religious unity. He had already won the confidence of the Muslims. In fact among the most influential followers of Gandhi were Muslims. Most of the major meetings were held in the quadrangles of the mosques. He focused his attention to various sects of Christianity. And he did prove successful in his endeavours. The theosophists gave him great support particularly at the time of crises and functioned as a bridge between Europeans and Gandhi.

The leading figures of resurgent India were aging fast. Apparently, India was waiting for a younger person like Gandhi who was thoroughly exposed to the outside world and deeply entrenched in India mentally and spiritually; who had some experience of fighting a colonial power; who was proud of his Indian history and culture; and who could follow a middle path to bring various sections of the Indian society: extremists, liberals and conservatives; Hindus, Muslims, Christians and others; rich, middle class and the poor together on a common platform.

The Zulu Rebellion

When did Gandhi become a full-fledged Satyagrahi? Not after his final return to India in 1914. The *Satyagraha* experiment began in 1906 in South Africa. The Zulu rebellion of 1906 gave him yet another opportunity to prove his loyalty to the Empire as also to render service to the Zulus. During the Zulu rebellion (1906), Gandhi saw the atrocities of the Whites on the sons of the soil. The Whites flogged the Zulus, but they refused to treat the wounded. Gandhi organized a very successful Ambulance Corps as he had done during the Boer War (1899) but the Whites did not like the corps to attend to them. The Zulus were grateful for the service rendered to them. The corps treated the White soldiers too.

As a volunteer of the corps, he realized that selfless service was not possible without voluntary poverty and *brahmacharya* (celibacy). Gandhi on return to Phoenix convinced Kasturbai on both the ideas. Apparently, he succeeded in his efforts. He started transforming his own life in consonance with the task he had undertaken. M.K. Gandhi, Attorney, Barrister-at-Law who was trained to fight the opposite side legally was on his way to becoming a hardcore Satyagrahi to fight the opponents with the weapon of love and non-violence.

BIRTH OF A SATYAGRAHI

Fight Against Registration Act

After the Zulu war Indians and other Asiatics staying in South Africa for eight years or more were asked to get themselves registered and carry the certificate of registration with finger prints wherever they go. Any Indian failing to comply with the regulations would forfeit his right to live in Transvaal; and would be liable to a fine of 100 pounds and deportation. The ordinance was published in the gazette extraordinary of the Transvaal Government.

Gandhi was convinced that the ordinance, if it became a law, would spell total doom for Indians. He called a mass meeting of Indians at Johannesburg to protest against the proposed Bill and declared "I have studied the whole of anti-Asiatic legislative acts throughout South Africa but have never come across anything like this present ordinance.... I know my countrymen. I know I can trust them and I know also that when occasion requires a heroic step to be taken, everyman amongst us would take it. There is only one course open to me, namely, to die, but not to submit to the law, even if everyone else were to hold back, leaving me alone. I am confident that I should never violate my pledge." At the conclusion of the speeches, all present, standing with upraised hands, took a solemn oath with God as witness not to submit to the ordinance if it became a law. Workers followed up the resolutions and continued to deliberate on the implications of the ordinance. *Indian Opinion* declared it to be a Black Ordinance.

Gandhi first sent memorials to the government requesting for reconsideration of the proposed law. As a result the clause relating to women was defeated in the assembly but the rest of the provisions of the ordinance was passed in the form in which it was drafted. Since Transvaal was still a crown colony (not self-governing colony) the ordinance had to be approved by the Secretary of the Colonies at London. On the suggestions of Gandhi, the Indian community decided to send a deputation to England to persuade the Imperial Government to deny imperial assent to the Act.

Lobbying Mission to England

H.O. Ali and Gandhi were the two members of the deputation. They left for England on October 3 and reached there on October 20, 1906. After meeting Dadabhai Naoroji, and through him the British Committee of the Indian National Congress, the deputation headed by Sir Lepel and consisting of Gandhi, Ali, Lord Stanley, Sir George Birdwood, J.D.Rees, Sir Henry Cotton, Mr. Harold Cox, Dadabhai Naoroji and Sir M. Bhawnaggaree, waited upon Lord Elgin, the Secretary of State for Colonies and presented a memorandum both in writing and verbally. The deputation also met Mr. Morley, the Secretary of State for India, the then British Prime Minister and about 100 members of the House of Commons committee for Indian Affairs.

Gandhi stayed in England for about six weeks and used this opportunity to meet Indian students who helped him in preparing document and mailing letters. He also contacted all those Englishmen who had sympathetic attitude towards India. Some English newspapers published leading articles and letters in favour of Indian cause and the methods they were using to get relief. Gandhi was not successful in his mission. While on the way back, he got the news that Lord Elgin had decided not to approve the ordinance. But it was a trick played by the authorities. Transvaal was to become a self-governing territory shortly with full powers to implement the ordinance without getting clearance of the Imperial Government. British government, therefore, decided to let the ordinance be implemented by the colonial government without imperial assent.

1906 was a momentous year for India too. Dadabhai Naoroji, the then president of the Indian National Congress, angry as he was at the partition of Bengal by Lord Curzon, declared at Calcutta that Indians should claim *Swaraj* as their political goal. Besides *Swaraj* the Calcutta Congress popularized *Bande Matram* as the national anthem. It also passed a strong resolution condemning oppression of Indians in South Africa.

On January 1, 1907 the Transvaal and Orange Colonies were granted self-government; they decided to implement the provision of the Registration Ordinance with effect from July 1. Indians were required to get themselves registered by July 31. Gandhi welcomed the challenge thrown by the Transvaal government and said "if we are conscious of the mark of slavery the act will put on us, we will meet it and refuse to submit to it. The brave rulers who know the value of action rather than any speech can only respond to bravery and practical action."

Satyagraha in Practice

Registration Boycott

As soon as the Transvaal and Orange River Colonies were granted self-government in 1907, the Transvaal legislature passed a law requiring Indians to register. The Transvaal Indian Association got into action. Pickets went from house to house to dissuade Indians from registering. The boycott was complete. Only 100 out of 1500 persons registered in July. The last date was extended several times but with no effect. The leading figures of the movement were arrested but new leaders emerged. Everyone followed Gandhi in pleading guilty and went to jail instead of paying the fine imposed on them. Gandhi requested the magistrate trying the cases of satyagrahis not to be lenient; let the guilty be deported within forty-eight hours as demanded by the prosecutor. After the court proceedings were over, Gandhi addressed a large gathering of Indians, Chinese, other Asiatics and Europeans and declared:

"We are going on with the struggle, no matter what happens to me or anyone else. If God's message came to me that I had erred, I would be first to acknowledge my fault and beg your forgiveness. But I do not think that I would ever receive that message. It is better to leave the colony than to lose our self-respect and honour. This is a religious struggle and we shall fight it to the end." It was during this period that the term *Satyagraha* was used for passive resistance. At Gandhi's initiative, Manilal Gandhi coined the term *sadagraha* (firmness in a good cause); Gandhi modified it and called *satyagraha* (the force which is born of truth and love or non-violence).

Gandhi was jailed on January 10, 1908 although he was arrested in the last week of December 1907 along with twenty-four others including Mr. Quinn, the leader of the Chinese community. It was Gandhi's first jail term. Each satyagrahi pleaded guilty and refused to furnish surety for bail. South African jails were full of *satyagrahis*.

Pressure was building up in England and India as in South Africa against the arrests of satyagrahis particularly Gandhi. General Smuts invited Gandhi to meet him on January 30 and agreed on a formula suggested by the latter according to which the Asiatics would voluntarily register provided that the Registration Act was repealed soon after. When Gandhi explained the contents of the agreement to a gathering of Indians, Chinese and friendly Europeans, a misled Pathan felt let down; he assaulted Gandhi when he went for voluntary registration the following day.

Gandhi was badly bruised. From the sick bed he telegraphed the Attorney General that the Pathan whose name was Mir Alam should not be prosecuted because he was not at fault. Gandhi stayed with Rev. Doke whose family attended on him. After ten days stay with Dokes, he moved to Polak's house in the suburbs of Johannesburg. By April, Gandhi was back on the job. Most Indians had by that time voluntarily registered.

Burning of Registration Certificates

General Smuts, however, went back on his words and did not repeal the law. The *satyagraha* or passive resistance as it was commonly known then, was restarted. Gandhi informed the Transvaal Government "if the Asiatic Act is not repealed in terms of the settlement, and if the government's decision is not communicated before a specific date, the certificates collected by the Indians will be burnt, and we shall humbly take the consequences." He appealed to Indians to burn their registration papers and defy the ban on entry on a mass scale without indulging in any kind of violence. A Holi (burning of bad things) of the certificates was organized. Hundreds of people were arrested but Gandhi was spared. Gandhi wrote to General Smuts to arrest him also. Being out of jail, he kept the *Indian Opinion* busy giving the latest information about the movement to the people. 'The news was read to the assembled Indians who greeted it with continuous loud cheers.'

When the certificates were being burnt Mir Alam who was imprisoned for having assaulted Gandhi, also came. By that time Alam was released from jail. He apologized for what he did and joined Gandhi in *Satyagraha*. Gandhi was arrested on September 29, 1908 and sentenced to pay a fine of 25 pounds or two months imprisonment with hard labour on October 15. Gandhi chose the latter. It was Gandhi's second jail term. He was jailed because he could not produce his certificate while returning from Natal. After 12 days he was transferred from Volksrust to Johannesburg jail. From the railway station he was marched under guard and before sunset in convict's dress and with a bundle on his shoulders.

While in jail he was invited to meet with General Smuts. In the mean time he got disturbing news about Kasturba poor health. He wrote a letter to her on November 1908, which is quoted below to enable the reader to understand the spiritual journey Gandhi had already travelled.

"I have received West's telegram about your illness. I feel heart-broken, but I cannot come to look after you. I have sacrificed all in the *satyagraha* struggle. I can come out only if I pay a fine and that is not to be done. You must not lose heart. If you regulate your diet, you will certainly get well. But even if it is my fate to lose you, then all that I can say is that it will not be something bad for you to die in separation while I am alive. I love you so much that even if you are dead you will always be alive to me. I repeat, what I have told you that I shall never marry again. You should depart with faith in God. Such death will also be in accordance with *satyagraha*. My struggle is not only political; it is also righteous struggle, and is therefore entirely pure. In it life or death do not make any difference. I have the hope that you will go through everything with the same view in mind. That is what I ask of you."

On his release from Pretoria jail on May 24, he exclaimed "whether our number be large or small, I earnestly pray God to give us strength to carry the burden until we have reached the goal." He started attending to his legal work; and soon left for Durban to meet Kasturbai. He took her to Phoenix Settlement and gave her naturopathy treatment. She recovered from anaemia she was suffering from in about a year.

Gandhi took up fight against injustice with greater vigour. In an interview to *Natal Mercury* he said "the Indians have gone through the struggle for the last two years and over 2000 have gone through the prisons of the Transvaal. The government consider that it would be possible to starve us into submission. But I believe that we have amongst ourselves a very large and sufficient number of people to carry on the struggle, in the face of all odds."

On January 15, 1909 Gandhi returned to Transvaal. He had no certificate to enter the colony. He was ordered out. But came back soon after. He was rearrested but not charged. On February 25, he along with seven others was fined 50 pound or three months imprisonment for refusing to produce certificates of entry. He preferred jail. The movement continued with greater vigour. Gandhi also got the opportunity to read books and meditate. Among the books he studied were those by Ruskin, Mazzini, Tolstoy, Emerson, Thoreau, Carlyle, and others. He also studied *Patanjali Yog Darshan, Manusmriti,* and *Upanishads*. Gandhi was a voracious reader and he was quite conversant with the literature of relevance to him.

YET ANOTHER MISSION TO ENGLAND

Gandhi decided to go to England again to convince the Imperial Government about the injustice being perpetrated on Asiatics and to pressurize the government of Transvaal to concede their just demands. It was the time when General Smuts and General Botha too happened to be in England to discuss the future set up of South African colonies. He stayed in London for about four months.

Just before he reached London, Shaheed Madanlal Dhingra had killed Curzon Wyllie on July 1. Gandhi did not succeed in his mission but used the opportunity to warn the Englishmen that such acts would multiply if the imperial policy towards the colonies in general and India in particular did not change.

The visit, however, gave an opportunity to Gandhi to meet the leaders of the suffragette movement. He learnt from them how the British women were using passive resistance. A section of them was using violence to which Gandhi observed: 'They have their own weapon. Why should they copy the evil ways of men.' He also came in contact with well-known terrorists in London. They tried to dissuade him from nonviolence. He instead tried to bring them to the path of truth and nonviolence. Gandhi was impressed by their bravery and patriotism but felt that their zeal was misguided and misplaced. "Those who believe that India has gained by Dhingra's act and other similar acts in India, make a serious mistake. Dhingra was a patriot, but his love was blind. He gave his body in a wrong way, its result can only be mischievous", said Gandhi.

Gandhi felt quite frustrated with the Generals Smuts and Botha. "The more I see them, the more am I tired of calling on persons considered to be great.... Everyone seems to be wrapt in his own thoughts. Those in power have scarcely any sense of justice for its own sake. They care for maintaining and magnifying their own position. Had it been a question of justice, pure and simple, it would have been decided long ago. To drudge in this way, to waste one whole precious day in trying to see at the most one or two persons goes against the grain of a satyagrahi. Far better to go to jail and suffer. If our demand is granted, it would be more on account of the harships endured by those who have gone to jail than as a result of the labours of the deputation; and if we fail, the reason would clearly be that we have not suffered enough." Even Sheth Habib was so frustrated that he did not want his community which controlled the Asiatic business to suffer any longer. Gandhi's constituency was, however, different. It were the poor people, the indentured labourers.

Gandhi wrote to Tolstoy telling all that he was doing and the sufferings that Indians were going through in South Africa and India. Tolstoy complimented him and wished him success. Gandhi left

London disappointed on November 13, 1908. On the ship deck he penned several articles for *Indian Opinion* on the ship stationery, which later were put together to form *Hind Swaraj*, his most seminal book and the subject matter of this volume.

During his stay in England, Gandhi was thinking not only of South Africa but also of India. He talked to people of different shades of opinion to concretize his own thoughts. On October 9, 1909, he wrote to Lord Ampthill a letter, which contains ideas, which formed the basis of *Hind Swaraj*. Among the major points he raised were:

(1) Impatience with the British rule was widespread in India and so was the hatred of the British;
(2) The above being the case, repression would be counter productive;
(3) British people were obsessed with commercial selfishness and hence the British Government would not concede the civil rights of Indians;
(4) The fault lies not with the British people but with modern civilisation which is a negation of the spirit of Christianity;
(5) All that shines as modern—the railways, machines, the style of life etc. are a true badge of slavery of the people both Indians and Europeans;
(6) Rise of large cities like Calcutta and Bombay was a matter of sorrow, not of congratulation;
(7) India has lost because her villages are destroyed;
(8) Violent methods are built in the modern civilisation and so is immorality;
(9) I share the national spirit but I do not agree with those who want to use violence directly or indirectly to win freedom for the country because it is immoral and against the spirit of Indian civilisation;
(10) Rulers must rule according to the wishes of the people; the moment they fail in their primary duty, people must refuse to recognize them and cooperate with them.

The above ideas were enveloped in a book, which Gandhi wrote on board S.S. Kildonan Castle while returning from England to South Africa between November 13 and 22, 1909. About 50 pages he wrote with left hand because his right hand could not write any further.

The book was written in Gujarati under the title *Hind Swaraj*, which in English means Indian Home Rule.

Hind Swaraj was written when Gandhi was forty years old. He sent a copy of the book to Tolstoy. Tolstoy commented: "I have read your book with great interest, for I consider the question there dealt with – passive resistance – to be of very great importance, not only for India, but for the whole humanity."

On return from England Gandhi stayed in South Africa until 1914 end. He left South Africa only after the struggle he launched was crowned with success. The Asiatics got their basic human rights. But of greater significance was the perfection of the method of nonviolence, satyagrah, which was later used in India, the USA and many other countries of the world and which appears to be the only way to solve problems the industrial civilisation has forced on humanity. This is the only way for peace and harmony; for culturally and morally rich life; and of course for human survival and development.

6

Gandhi's Interpretation of Indian History

History of the world as documented by Europeans especially the British suffered from two great deficiencies: it was not the history of the people as such; it was only the history of kings and the wars they fought. If there was some reference to the history of the common people, their lifecycle and trials and tribulations, it was incidental. In fact history books tended to ignore and down play the role common people played in setting the society right and in disciplining the rulers. Secondly, the history as presented by a overwhelming section of historians was not scientific as claimed by them. It was highly biased in favour of western imperialism and the alleged role it played in controlling, restructuring and civilizing Asia, Africa and Latin America. The only good thing that came out of it was the fact that war had never brought peace. Each war was fought to bring peace but it always proved to be a precursor of another and often a bigger war.

Violence breeds violence, said Gandhi. It has never solved the problem of discord—local or global, nor would it solve such problem in future either. Violence, according to Gandhi, was against the Cosmic Law, the Super Law that has kept the universe in harmonious motion for billions of years. Had violence been a dominating force in the universe, no life would have been left on this earth. Indian sages experimented this Law and brought it down to their own life and environment. If one has to look for a civilisation, which pined for peace and harmony, love and compassion, sacrifice and nonviolence, one has per-force to look to India. And hence the people of India must relearn from their own civilisation and reject untruth and violence as the means to solve their problems.

It was from this understanding of Indian culture and its potentials that he labelled the industrial civilisation of the West as a disease. 'Its deadly effect is that people come under its scorching flames believing it be all good.' He advocated an alternative civilisation free from the evils of modern civilisation. According to him, India possessed the basic ingredients of the real 'modern civilisation'. It must go back to its eternal values of *Vasudhaiva Kutumbakam*, truth and non-violence.

WHAT IS TRUE HISTORY?

Gandhi noted another major weakness in the history as presented by Europeans. History records only the political events and wars. It is divided into periods based on the reign of kings and emperors. Only when information about the rulers is absent or scant, it tells about people, cultures and civilisations. Gandhi believed that man was moving towards perfection – from animal to super-conscious human; towards *devatwa*. The evolutionary process one observes in nature is part of a grand design to unravel the hidden potentials of life ordained in man. Historian he felt had not tried to record the flow of events that made man what he is at a given point of time and the lessons he must learn to ensure his ascent to realize the inherent potentials. Instead, history captures and records interruption in the flow.

Gandhi was not against the study of interruptions as such. What he objected to was the neglect of the main currents in order to record the details of the interruptions therein. What is being interrupted was considered insignificant and the interruptions became the central issues. Gandhi hinted at a new approach to historical studies, and approach which Toynbee, perhaps the greatest historian of the twentieth century, suggested a quarter century later. According to him societies and civilisations, not nations, kings, and periods of time, should be the significant units of historical studies. Toynbee identified twenty-six civilisations, including the arrested ones; and after careful study of each of them concluded that civilisations grew by responding successfully to challenges under the leadership of creative minorities; they decline when the leaders fail to respond creatively. (Toynbee, *A Study of History*, 1934-54, Vol 10.

Julius Huxley calls man a part of "the stream of life. He is part animal and part human." What distinguishes him from animal is civilisation or culture. While modern anthropologists in general consider those traits of civilisation, which are extensions of man's animal origin, as part of progress he has made, Gandhi considered it as regression for they keep man animal. In Gandhian praxis, only that part of progress, which takes man away from the animal, towards humanity, is real progress. Gandhi's complaint is that historians highlight only the regressive aspects of civilisation.

Real progress, according to Gandhi, lies in the transformation of animal in man into human in him. Material progress must enhance the real progress. Material progress is not to be shunned; it must continue for human survival and development but its must remain within the perimeter of spiritual progress. History should give primacy to how man has struggled to achieve spiritual progress and how this journey has been interrupted from time to time by men, machines and institutions created by man.

The tendencies that make humans super humans in consciousness are slow; they are not clearly visible to those who do not see and think in long terms; but the wars and conflicts come suddenly and make stunning impacts. Look at the sacrifices all life forms make to keep the earth alive. If the parents do not sacrifice their own needs and comforts, no life can survive on the earth. In the later part of life too people save more people than they kill. All this forms part of human progress. But why is it that that these things do not find a place in the history books. We read only the wars and killings which are nothing but temporary interruptions in human progress. History we read is the story of these interruptions presented in a biased manner. A murderer becomes a hero because he committed the crime for a 'just cause'. War waged by the government of a country to which one belongs is a 'just war'; and the one waged by the other side is always 'unjust'. When our soldiers die on the war front, we honour them as 'martyrs' but when soldiers of the opposite side die we disgrace them as 'enemies'. The opposite side is always portrayed as treacherous, immoral and even savage. One rarely gets real history of man and his civilisation)

Life is not a random assemblage of discrete events; it is a constant flow of energy. A true history would lay greater stress on this behind the scene flow of life. "History as we know it, is a record of wars of the world, and so there is a proverb among Englishmen that a nation, which has no history, that is no wars, is a happy nation. How kings played, how they became enemies of one another, how they murdered one another, is found accurately recorded in history and if this were all that had happened in the world, it would have ended long ago. If the story of the universe would have commenced with wars, no a man would have been found alive today" *(Hind Swaraj*, p.67).

The moral thread that binds all life together has been described differently by different cultures. Gandhi called it Soul Force. "Thousands, indeed tens of thousands, depend for their existence on a very active working of soul force. Little quarrels of millions of families in their daily lives disappear before the exercise of this soul force. Hundreds of nations live in peace. History does not and cannot take note of this fact. History is really a record of every interruption of the even working of the soul force." Elaborating this point further, Gandhi says, "Two brothers quarrel; one of them repents and reawakens the love that was lying dormant in him; the two again begin to live in peace; no body takes note of this. But if the two brothers take up arms or go to law ... their doings would be immediately noticed and would probably go down to history. And what is true of families is also true of nations. ... History then is a record of the interruption of the course of nature; Soul Force being natural is not noticed in history" (*Hind Swaraj* p. 70)

That is why, "the kings and statesmen are termed the makers of history and sometimes it is said that the historian only records the history which they make. History in this connection is obviously not the record, but the thing to be recorded" (Enc. Britain. Vol II, p. 594) and human beings as they are cannot be unbiased even if they want to be so. Everyone has his own mindset, which filters the things that enter his head. He sees things in the form and complexion his mindset permits.

Gandhi concluded that the history of India is not just the history of kings and wars; it is not the history of cowardice, chaos, and dishonesty as depicted by English historians. "Macaulay betrayed gross ignorance when he libeled Indians as being practically cowards. They never merited the charge. Cowards living in a country inhabited by hardy mountaineers, and infested with wolves and tigers must find an early grave." Apparently Gandhi was paying Macaulay in the same coins. The message is clear. There were some cowards but they were among many more braves. To the charge that before the British took over the administration of India, there was chaos; there were *Thugs* and Pindaries who robbed and killed people, Gandhi in his characteristic way says: "If you give the matter some thought, you will see that the terror was by no means such a mighty thing. If it had been very substantial thing, the other people would have died before the advent of English." (*Hind Swaraj* p. 38)

Real history, yet to be written, would not be the account of kings and wars. It would be the account of how man struggled for several millenniums to rise above the animal urges and moved towards the human state. Only that civilisation which was marked by continuity in spiritual attainment and auto-change could truly reflect that history. A study of ancient civilisations prove that peace rather than war, harmony rather than conflict, compassion rather than hate, duties rather than rights, and sacrifice rather than greed were the main tendencies of all civilisations. In case of India, these tendencies have remained unbroken. In India, progress was always seen in moral and ethical terms. All other departments of life: economic, intellectual, technological, social etc., were designed to support these tendencies. India should revive its cultural heritage and find its own way of fighting the British Raj

Gandhi felt that true history of India was yet to be written. Indian historians of the time generally followed the British line; they repeated what the British said about India. But there were exceptions. Gandhi was very appreciative of *Economic History of India* written by R.C. Dutt. "When I read it, I wept; and as I think of it again my heart sickens."

FOREIGNERS CANNOT WRITE TRUE HISTORY OF INDIA

The worldviews of different cultures and communities differs widely. The British worldview cannot be the same as the Indian worldview. There are very few writers who transcend the dominant political and cultural assumptions of their own time and place. What we get as history is Euro-centric. The early European historians especially those of British origin wrote as missionaries engaged in civilizing the world. Even today we live in the world created by a handful of provincial British experts of the nineteenth century.

James Mill in his History of India, wrote of Indian history as nothing but record of the perennial battle between two religious communities: Hindu and Muslims. He considered the East India Company as the harbinger of peace and civilisation. Incidentally, he never visited India. There were no Indians of comparable competence to tell Mill that he was an ignorant man as far as India was concerned. No wonder then, the British used the divide and rule policy to pitch Hindus against Muslims to prolong their rule. History books written by Marxists in the twentieth century went to the other extreme. They openly extolled violence and dictatorship of the proletariat. The colonial era is gone and so is the soviet era but the traces of both are present in different garbs even today. Even today the exploitation of the weaker nations and peoples by the richer nations continues in the name of globalization, liberalization and privatization. The world continues to be divided into rich and poor, super powerful, powerful and week. America can justify its attack on Iraq to find WMD's which Iraq never had anyway. And the whole world including the United Nation's, the conscience of humanity, has succumbed and accepted it as given.

"They (English) have habit of writing history; they pretend to study the manners and customs of all peoples. God has given us a limited mental capacity; but they usurp the function of the godhead and indulge in novel experiments. They write about their own researches in most laudatory terms and hypnotize us into believing them. We in our ignorance then fall at their feet." (*Hind Swaraj* p. 46). Hence anything written by the British about India and Indian civilisation must necessarily be taken with caution. History taught in schools and colleges of India was based on the writings of nineteenth and twentieth centuries British historians. It was highly distorted. It highlighted the British achievements and depreciated whatever was Indian. True there were some Europeans who did excavate the vast Indian literature to bring to attention of Europe what it was missing, but such cases were few and their voices treated as deviant. Indian historians, barring a few very honourable exceptions, followed the British line. They too debunked Indian contribution to philosophy, science and humanities as unhistorical and speculative. Even the war of independence India fought against the British in 1857 was termed as Sepoy Mutiny. It was partly designed to rule over India and partly natural because they saw everything Indian through colonial glasses. They could not understand Indian culture and people; they could only interpret them in the light of their own cultural standards. They thus failed to present a real history of India. And the Indians educated as they were in English tradition followed suit.

Every attempt was made to belittle India and Indians. Even the school textbooks presented Indians as backward and traditional and unfit to hold responsible positions. There was a deliberate use of Mercator projection in school atlases so as to show the British Islands three or four times larger than their real size. Gandhi was critical of history as such for, according to him, it never recorded the progress humanity made in its journey towards its destiny—to turn out, better human beings, different from animals not in look because that had been done by nature itself but in nature and culture. According to him there was a secular and persistent tendency to move in that direction but each progressive step was interrupted by the animal in man: wars, conflicts, killings; annexation of land and property; destruction of cultural monuments, religious places, forcing people to change their style of life and belief system; deceits and immoral doings by a powerful minority.

Gandhi's comments on history and historians apparently emanated from the fact that Europeans in general and British in particular, notwithstanding some noteworthy exceptions, have looked down upon other peoples and cultures; and even in the face of evidences to the contrary, have tried to portray the superiority of the west. Gandhi saw a design in history to spread British language, religion and power. The destruction of the village industries and institutions was portrayed as the triumph of modernity. In South Africa, he could see this tendency in the most oblique form. He was horror stricken to see that worst injustices were done in the name of justice and fair play. The blacks were the white man's burden and the white man had put this burden on him without the black man ever asking for it. It is these very white men who were writing the history of those who were being tormented.

Gandhi postulated that India from times immemorial had given overriding importance to morality and ethics. Material development was always subordinated to the requirements of moral development. The country fell when it deviated from this mode of progress and opted for material development minus moral development. One of the mechanisms for ensuring this was the *varnashrama dharma*, of course in its original form wherein all were born *sudras*, they had to be reborn through appropriate *karma* to become *dwijas*. The *Brahmin* had no power or possession – material or political; his power lay in morality. His job was to keep the flag of morality flying higher and higher. And he was to sacrifice himself, if need be, to maintain moral standards of his own self and the society at large. When even the *Brahmin* fell from the moral pedestal, the social fabric was torn to pieces, and India became a colony. It was the allurement of the British trade and commerce, which kept India in bondage, Gandhi postulated. It were not the British who subjugated India; it were the decadent Indians who invited the British to rule over them. No one can enslave an unwilling non-cooperating slave – individual or nation, said he. Maybe, the non-cooperating slave will be killed, but if the other potential slaves too refuse to cooperate, the slave driver will have no way of perpetuating the system of slavery. He postulated that India would be free the moment Indians return to their cultural roots and follow their *Dharma, i.e.* duty as prescribed by their cultural traditions. That did not mean return to the past; it meant recapturing the past to create a new future.

Gandhi also asserted that India became a nation much earlier than the concept of modern nation was born. It is not the British who unified India: it was unified before the British came, and no matter who ruled the country, he always dreamt to rule over the whole of geographical-cum-cultural India, not just a part of it. India's geography gave a unique opportunity for the people of the subcontinent to merge individual and regional interests into a larger whole without losing their specific identities, *i.e.* to see unity in diversity and to evolve a culture of synthesis and accommodation. Another recurring and persistent feature of Indian civilisation has been spiritual development focusing on nonviolence, peace and harmony. It produced great souls like Buddha, Mahavira, Shankara, and Guru Nanak who brought people back to the spiritual path. And the number of saints and philosophers is a legend. No other culture produced an emperor like Asoka who renouned war after winning a war.

Gandhi was of the view that these tendencies of Indian civilisation were weakened because of foreign invasions and colonial rule and that the time had come to give them new impetus and perfect them not only to bring India back to its moorings but more importantly to bring peace and harmony in the world marked by hatred, conflicts and wars.

HISTORY OF INDIA AS GANDHI KNEW

Some 5000 years ago, a civilisation akin to that of Sumerian civilisation in the valleys of Euphrates and Tigris in present day Iraq emerged in the Indus and Saraswati valleys covering the eastern flanks of the present day Pakistan and western states of India. Traces of the still older New Stone Age civilisations, if one may so call them, have been found practically all over the Indian subcontinent. Who these earliest settlers were is not yet clear. If linguistic archaeology is any guide, some of them probably came from the Southeast Asia, while others from West Asia once the Homo sapiens became humans. They remained in India for a long time and developed an advanced civilisation comparable to Mesopotamian and Egyptian civilisations. The boundaries of this civilisation are still changing as new archeological evidences come to light. It is however clear that its epicenter or to be more precise, its nuclear zone was in the region bounded by river Yamuna in the east, Sind in the west, Himalayas in the north and southern Gujarat in the south.

Archaeological findings reveal that the Harappans were quite mobile people; had trade with contemporary Mesopotamian and Egyptian civilisations around 2750 BC. The sea route followed the Indus and the Arabian Sea coast, while the land route passed through the present-day Afghanistan, Iran, Iraq and then on to Egypt and Black and Caspian Sea regions. One should not rule out some sort of link with other parts of the Indian subcontinent. Most probably, the itinerant Harappan traders had spread out further east of their cultural perimeter to Ganga valley, Malwa and south Gujarat which were inhabited by people of Neolithic culture or post-Neolithic culture.

The villagisation of the Indus-Saraswati civilisation appears to have been complete by 2750 BC. And then started the urbanization process based on trade and commerce on the one hand, and agricultural and household industrial development on the other. This civilisation appears to have developed a unique blend of rural and urban traits in both material and spiritual aspects of life. The towns functioned as generative centres. Beyond their perimeter were less advanced agricultural and paleolithic communities.

For reasons still unknown, this civilisation died by 1500 BC although its remnants lasted up to 1300 BC. Historians attribute several reasons for its decline: ranging from Aryan invasion to tectonic uplifting of the lower reaches of Indus valley and the resulting floods and river capture by a tributary of Jamuna. We should not forget the fact that other contemporary or preceding civilisations also met the same fate, may be for similar reasons. What appears to be a common factor is the over use and misuse of natural resources in building cities and pyramids and resulting ecological imbalances.

While writing *Hind Swaraj*, Gandhi did not have the idea of this civilisation because the excavations at Harappa, Mohenjodaro and sites in the Saraswati basin started only in 1922. The Indus script is yet to be deciphered; we do not know enough about this civilisation to pass any final judgment on its spiritual foundations. All that we know about it is its material richness. The artefacts found in excavations do however show a link between this and the Vedic civilisation that followed it. It would be better to say that the Sindh-Saraswati civilisation in its declining phase merged into the Vedic civilisation. So even if Gandhi had known about it, his conclusions about Indian history and civilisation as given in *Hind Swaraj* would not have been materially different.

Vedic Civilisation

What Gandhi considered to be the earliest record of Indian civilisation was the Vedic literature and the oral traditions that remained ingrained in the minds and hearts of the people of India. Vedas compiled during 2500-1500 BC were not the records of events; they recorded the human interaction with nature and fellow human beings and grand synthesis they evolved to withstand any upheavals. It is perhaps the largest and spiritually and philosophically the richest literature any civilisation ever produced. Apparently, it resulted from the fusion of three streams of people: the *Aryans* (at least a part of them being new comers), the Harappans (on the move from Indus valley to the east and south) and late Paleolithic, Mesolithic, and Neolithic peoples (who were almost ubiquitously distributed in the rest of the country. Who the Aryans were, is still an unsettled issue. According to one theory, they came from Central Asia and belonged to a group of pastoral people, who branched off in different directions in search of new and vacant lands in Persia, southern Europe, and India. Another theory suggests that they formed part of an ethnic group that occupied a large landmass extending from Northwest India to Persia and central Asia. According to this theory, the Harappans were also a sub-group of this larger group with the same language but different dialect and script. And according to the third theory, Aryans were Indians but they had frequent interaction with Central Asian pastoral peoples.

Irrespective of the origin of the Aryans, the linguistic archaeology points to a close link between them and Central Asian peoples. But the fact that the literature produced by them did not refer to geography and history of the place of their origin, points to their Indian base, if not Indian origin. Aryans were not a homogenous people; they had linguistic and cultural differences emanating perhaps from the areas they occupied. They were perhaps present in the Indus-Saraswati valleys when the Harappan civilisation declined (1500-1300 BC). They must have tried to extend their area of influence to fill the gap left by weakened Harappans and thus were partly responsible for the decline of Indus-Saraswati civilisation. They fought amongst themselves for supremacy; and assimilated the weakened and out-migrating Harappans as well as the other indigenous people through bonds of marriage and community living. Sanskrit with Devnagari script was the language of the Aryans. It has close links with Persian, Latin, Greek, Pushtu, and the languages of Central Asian republics, indicating that they were closely related to each other either through common origin or frequent interaction.

The Vedic civilisation borrowed heavily from the Harappans in matters religion, family structure, social organisation and governance. Many of their gods and goddesses – the *Shakti*, the Shivalinga, the Bull, the Peepal tree, and swastika sign were Harappan; they were adapted by the Vedic peoples. The Aryans however did not adopt the decadent urban culture of Harappans; instead they remained agricultural and explored the open fertile lands in the Ganga valley and later, in the Indian Peninsula. With the ascendancy of the Vedic civilisation, people were no longer set against nature. They pronounced loudly: *Mata Bhoomih putroaham prithivyah* (earth is the mother; we are its children). Unlike the Harappans who specialized in the use of bronze, Aryans were well versed in the use of iron. Iron was probably known to Harappans too, but they did not possess the skill of iron forging. It helped Aryans break new and hard soils and clear forests.

Indus valley and the adjoining fertile regions constituted the most immediate and rich homeland of the Vedic peoples. It is here that the *Rig Veda*, the ancient most written book, was composed. The Purush Sukta of this Veda had detailed the division of society into four *varnas*, occupational classes. During the later Vedic period (1000 to 600 BC) other three *Vedas, Brahmanas, Aranyakas* and *Upanishads* were composed. As population grew, they moved east and southward and intermingled with other tribes to evolve a unique culture and social organisation, which is typically Indian, not found anywhere else in the world. The centre of power shifted to Indraprastha, the land of Kurus (close to Delhi).

Vedas particularly the *Rig Veda* is the depository of all the knowledge people in India had from times immemorial. Vedas tell not only about the world at the time they were composed, but also the knowledge passed on through generations of sages and scholars through word of mouth (*shrutis and smritis*). Vedas tell how humans cooperated with nature to carve out a niche for them selves to produce one of the oldest, richest and most humane civilisations of the world. *Rig Veda* was composed during 2000-1500 years before Christ. Other three Vedas were composed later between 1500-900 BC.

The people who composed Veda were not yet spread over the whole of geographical India. They were comfortably placed in the rich river valleys of what now constitutes Punjab (both India Pakistan),

Northern Rajasthan, Haryana and west U.P., *i.e.* between Sindh and Jamuna rivers. Rest of the Indian subcontinent was inhabited by microlithic, mesolithic and neolithic tribes. Since the Vedic people alone have left the written records of what they were, we know more about them. Further, they have left to posterity something that is unmatched and highly revealing. It does not however mean that other peoples had nothing to contribute in the making of the Indian civilisation.

Vedic civilisation lasted for about 1000 years. Early Vedic society was marked with simplicity. The Aryans had seen the failure of the Harappan civilisation and perhaps knew the causes thereof. They did not try to revive the Harappan ways because the very bases of the Harappan civilisation, *i.e.* trade with the outside world, was no longer possible. Further, the Aryans were pastoral with some training in agriculture. They, therefore, adopted the agricultural techniques of Harappans and moved further east to settle down in the virgin lands of the Ganga valley.

During this period population was limited and practically the whole of the land was covered with dense and often impenetrable forests. Advance parties set up villages and collectively cleared the forests for agriculture. Emphasis was laid on cooperation, skills and collective work. The land and water resources were in plenty; all that was needed was hard work and protection from wild animals and other groups of people already there trying to establish their own settlements.

The early Aryans, to be successful in their new ventures, laid special emphasis on community life and their moral code therefore was more communal than individual. "We find a systematic attempt to build up *sam hridays* (for *sahridays*), literally, concord, *i.e.* the unity of hears, *sam jyanam,* unity through common understanding, at all social levels." Individual wrongs were not ignored but there was greater stress on collective morality. The *Rig Veda,* therefore, asks people to follow the Cosmic Law or Natural Law, which for them was the moral law (R'ta) so that the welfare of all was assured. The Vedic hymns praise moral values and uphold the glory of the moral law. Individualism had not yet taken roots and hence one finds only a few references to individuals with great moral standing in the society.

The highest and the largest unit of social organisation was the *jana, i.e.* group of kinsmen. Among the *janas* were Bharats, Kurus, Purus, etc. Head of the *jana* was the king assisted by a wiseman, may be a priest. King was charged with the responsibility of defending the *jana* against the neighbouring *janas* and other tribesmen.

It is interesting to know that the concept of Law of Nature or Cosmic Law discovered by the early Aryans has continued as a guiding principle to this day in India and despite increased emphasis on individual morality in later years, its relevance has not diminished. Its violation is still frowned upon by Indians in general. Gandhi was sold to this concept; he exhorted the people to sacrifice their individual interests so that the others both individually and collectively live in peace.

During the later Vedic period (1000 BC – 600 BC) the Aryan society became more complex. Population increased and the small towns on the crossroads and sacred places started emerging to handle the surplus agricultural produce and emerging handicrafts. One hears of towns like Kaushambi, Asandivat, Kampilya, and Kashi. And the country saw the emergence of several *janapadas* some of them with democratic governments on the pattern of Greek city states. It heralded the second urban revolution in ancient India, this time based on internal rather than external trade. The institution of hereditary kingship took its roots and the tribal states based on extended kingship were replaced by territorial states having several tribes or *janas* during this period. Apart from farmers a new class of people who engaged themselves in trade and commerce emerged. There is frequent mention of rich merchants called *Shresthin.* According to some historians, the development of trade guilds began during this period.

As individuals acquired more political and economic power, curbs on the misuse of power were brought about by codification of individual morality. This period is, therefore, known for the codification of moral principles for individuals. We see the emergence of sages with great moral standing; we also observe great changes in the social organisation. Through intermarriage and contacts, many of the tribes were assimilated in the Aryan society. The Harappans too appear to have become part of it. This apparently resulted in hierarchic ordering of individuals and groups, which ultimately produced what is known as *varnashrama* system. It was a system, which engendered interdependence yet at the same freedom for each group to progress at its own pace and in its own style. The ordering was hierarchic but social interaction was marked with liberality and recognition of rights of individuals and ethnic groups.

The unity of all life remained the main pillar of Vedic religion; ashramic divisions were never accepted as a hindrance in ascendance of humans to divine life where morality reigned supreme. Every living being existed by virtue of the manifestation in him of a universal and all pervading force called God or Brahman. All were therefore equal; they had equal rights and no individual had the privilege to curb the rights of others. Even animals and birds were given an honourable status; they were allowed to share the gifts of nature.

Ramayana and Mahabharata Culture

Ramayana was written sometimes between 1500 and 1000 BC. Let it be clear that this is not the period when Ram or Krishna lived and when *Mahabharat* took place. It is period of composition of the *Ramayana* and *Mahabharat* treatises. *Ramayana* tells how one should live to strengthen social solidarity and moral principles. What was presented philosophically in *Vedas* and *Upanishads* was put into practice by Ram and his whole family in real life situation. Ramayana still constitutes the standard to evaluate man and his activities.

Mahabharat constitutes the penultimate demonstration of the power of love and observance of once duty. *Gita*, a portion of Mahabharat is one of the most popular and widely read spiritual treàtises. It tells how man is nothing but a perpetually fight between the forces of good and evil both within and outside and how one should fight the evil without sacrificing the moral principles.

The beauty of these two books lies in the fact that the ideals they propound have percolated down to the commonest man in India. The philosophy underlying them is known and understood by the leaders and laity alike. And despite tremendous pressures exerted by modern civilisation, the common people of India still have faith in it and try to follow to the extent they can. Gandhi was encouraged by this ground reality and felt that the situation was not so hopeless and India could still show the way to the world.

The Culture of Ahimsa Parmodharmah

By the end of sixth century BC, the Vedic culture went through a process of transformation. It revolted against violence in popular culture and the desire of the people to return to the culture of nonviolence and peace increased. This gave rise to two great men, Buddha and Mahavira, who taught *Ahimsa* as the basic religion of humanity. Buddha declared *Ahimsa Parmodharmah* (non-violence the greatest religion)). Mahavira too said the same thing in a different mode.

There are no records of the two great contemporaries whose teachings became world's two great religions, meeting together, but their message did meet and reverberated through out the length and breadth of India, all the way from Gandhara in the northwest to Assam in the East and Kashmir in the north to Kanyakumari in the south. The whole of geographical India was united by an umbrella culture of peace and harmony.

The concept of *Vasudhaiva Kutumbakam* and the ideas of the dignity of the individual were further broadened to recognize the right of each individual to shape his destiny according to his own perception of reality. But the political unification of India still had to wait for few more centuries. India was divided into several *Janapadas*: both kingdoms and republics covering the whole of north, east and central India. Of them, Koshala and Magadha emerged as most powerful. And thus centre of power shifted from Indraprastha near Delhi to Pataliputra in the East.

Buddha (563-485 BC) and Mahavira (540-468 BC) rekindled the spirit of love, nonviolence, compassion, and tolerance to the conflict prone society of the time. Bindusara (550-490 BC) tried to expand and unite the land from west to east; he could achieve only a limited success. Alexander invaded India during 327-325 BC but his expedition did not prove a success. He returned to Greece leaving his commander behind to rule the remnants of the area he won. He too appears to have been so deeply impressed by Indian culture that on return to his homeland and in the year of his death he proclaimed an edict, which resembles that of Asoka the Great.

The impact of Buddhism and Jainism continued but the Vedic religion too remained vibrant. There was no conflict among them in so far as the essence was concerned.

By the time the teachings of Buddha, Mahavira and other teachers took the form of religions by their names, the Vedic phase of Indian civilisation had reached its full circle. Shramic ideology, which was in some ways distinct from the Vedic ideology about God, Cosmos and Atma (soul), was present during Vedic era too. Some people were probably inclined towards it because the prevailing ideology did not satisfy their quest for self-realisation. Buddha and Mahavira did not start on a clean slate. The tendencies to do away with rituals were already there; they gave new meaning, rationale and structure to it.

Buddha declared that all life existed by virtue of individual force, not cosmic force, called *karma.* Thus in Buddhism, individual morality alone could make man really human. Every individual was required to improve himself by a patient training of the will and the purification of thoughts and feelings. But the social restructuring that began in the later Vedic period continued during the Buddhist period. Buddhist and Jain sources are replete with references to servants, slaves, debtors, and poor. Asoka edicts ask people to treat their servants kindly.

It was an age of large kingdoms, armies and fierce wars. People were tired of conflicts. They wanted to settle down and lead a peaceful life. When Buddha and Mahavira taught an alternative philosophy of life based on truth and nonviolence, people were highly attracted to it. The Shramanic philosophy taught the impermanence of material gains; their transcendence was the only means of liberation from worldly miseries. This was unlike the Vedic philosophy, which preached group action and firm faith in a God that pervaded all that existed.

One of the great moral advancement of this period was the extension of the notion of morality to all life forms. During the Vedic period, God existed in all lives but animal sacrifice reflecting the older tribal ritual persisted. During this period that chapter was closed. Philanthropic disposition was another important feature of this period. *Karuna* (compassion), nonviolence, and love towards one and all were to be the means to achieve salvation. Charity *(dana)* in Vedic period was more related to service rendered; during the Buddhist period it was related to compassion; a desire to help others in need.

Chandragupta Maurya (320-297 BC) assisted by his teacher Vishnugupta (Chanakya), consolidated his rule over northern India with Pataliputra as its capital. His grandson Ashoka (274-232 BC) unified practically the whole of India into one empire and thus engraved once again in the minds of the people the geographical-cultural-political unity of the subcontinent. To protect the empire from external dangers, he extended his empire to the former Greek territories of Aria, Archosia and Paropamisadae in northwest India, and thus laid down a defence policy, which was followed even by the British in nineteenth century. His empire did not extend up to Kanya Kumari but he maintained good relations with the southern most kingdoms.

ALEXANDER'S OATH IN MESOPOTAMIA

Here is what Alexander the Great, the greatest military and cultural leader of his time said at the city of Opis in Mesopotamia in 324 B.C., the year of his death.

His vision for the New World Order in East and West still remains a noble but unfulfilled vision.

Alexander mentions the name of his own god, Zeus, but he swears with the others to 'the god father of all humanity.' He says he had a vision that behind the local gods there was a great omnipotent god who moves the universe.

OATH BY ALEXANDER THE GREAT

'NOW THAT THE WARS ARE COMING TO AN END, I WISH YOU PROSPER IN PEACE. MAY ALL MORTALS FROM NOW ON LIVE LIKE ONE PEOPLE, IN CONCORD AND FOR MUTUTAL ADVANCEMENT. CONSIDER THE WORLD AS YOUR COUNTRY WITH LAWS COMMON TO ALL AND WHERE THE BEST WILL GOVERN, IRRESPECTIVE OF TRIBE. I DO NOT DISTINGUISH AMONG MEN, AS THE NARROW MINDED DO BOTH AMONG GREEKS AND BARBARIANS. I AM NOT INTERESTED IN THE DESCENT OF THE CITIZEN, OR THEIR RACIAL ORIGINS. I CLASSIFY THEM USING ONLY ONE CRITERION: VIRTUE. FOR ME EVERY VIRTUOUS FOREIGNER IS A GREEK, AND EVERY EVIL GREEK WORSE THAN A BARBARIAN. IF DIFFERENCES EVER DEVELOP BETWEEN YOU, NEVER RECOURSE TO ARMS, BUT SOLVE THEM PEACEFULLY, IF NECESSARY I SHALL BE YOUR ARBITRATOR. YOU MUST NOT CONSIDER GOD LIKE AN AUTOCRATIC DESPOT, BUT AS A COMMON FATHER OF ALL, SO THAT YOUR BEHAVIOUR MAY RESEMBLE THE LIFE SIBLINGS HAVE IN A FAMILY. ON MY PART, I SHALL CONSIDER YOU ALL EQUAL, WHITES OR BLACKS, AND I WISH YOU WOULD BE NOT ONLY SUBJECTS OF THE COMMONWALTH, BUT PARTICIPANTS AND PARTNERS. AS MUCH AS THIS DEPENDS ON ME, I SHALL TRY TO BRING ABOUT WHAT I PROMISED. THE OATH WE MADE OVER TONIGHT'S LIBATIONS, HOLD UNTO AS CONTRACT OF LOVE.'

Source:

1. The philosopher Eratosthenis (375-294) from Alexandria, who was director of the famous library of Alexandria. He heard it from Alexander's Comrades that were ear witness.
2. Pseudokallisthenis, Vol. C
3. Major General Kostas Konstantinidis (Ret), a member of ex-NATO Generals for Peace and Disarmament.

Consolidation of the Indian nationhood was accomplished by war and bloodshed. Ashoka defeated the Kalingas of present day Orissa; the war claimed lives of thousands of soldiers and common people. Ashoka felt very much grieved and concluded that war that unleashed so much violence and suffering on the people was unethical. He decided never to fight another war. He saw a new role for India, a role that was clearly defined by Buddha. It was a spiritual role. India must teach the world, the folly of violence, hatred, and greed And he set upon to spread the message of Buddhism in India and its neighbouring countries. And thus he not only consolidated forever the idea of one political India but also the idea of a cultural India with a message: future of humanity lay in truth and nonviolence; in compassion and human brotherhood; in a non-killing society. Ashoka sent ambassadors to spread Buddha's teachings to such far off lands as China, Central Asia, Southeast Asia, etc. the imprints of which we see even today on the hearts and minds of the people of these regions.

The decline of the Moryan Empire during the second century AD was accompanied by invasions from the West (180 BC – 200 AD) and division of India into several small principalities. The Andhras under Satvahanas declared their independence. Greeks who were thrown out by Chandragupta Maurya regrouped in Bacteria and occupied Punjab and Sind. In 183 BC Demetrius (Greek King) occupied Pataliputra. Fortunately he had to go back to Greece. Greeks were followed by Sakas, Parthians, Kushanas. In the mean time the Satavahanas in the third century AD were weakened and broke into several principalities. Meander the last Greek king died in 145 BC. Gandhara school of Art was the gift of the Greeks. The Sakas occupied Ujjaini and Mathura. Saka era is their gift. Among the Kushan, the most famous king was Kanishka who became Buddhist and tried to spread the religion in his empire. Kanishka's empire brought India closer to West Asia specially Iran and Greece and Rome and gave stimulus to trade as well human relations with the outside world. Once inside India, the foreigners found Indian soil hospitable and elevating; they stayed back and became sons of the soil. So great was the attraction of Buddha, Ashoka and of course of the Indian soil and society that they had no incentive to go back home.

Classical Age

The classical age of India began by third century BC. It was the period when new Vedic literature was created and *Puranas* started taking the shape. It was also a very creative period in Indian history. Agriculture progressed to cover new areas and urbanization process restarted all over the country. With the arrival of the Guptas on the political scene of India, the political map of India and the style of governance changed phenomenally. Chandragupta I ascended the throne of Pataliputra in 320 AD. Samudragupta (340-380 AD) extended his empire to Nepal in the North, Kanchi in the South, Punjab in the West and Assam in the East. The records of his victory stand engraved on the Ashokan pillar at Allahabad.

It was an era of religious synthesis and consolidation and flowering of literary and Puranic writings. Chadragupta II (Vikramaditya 380-414 AD) was the most enlightened of the Gupta Kings. He ushered in a golden age of Sanskrit literature. Kalidasa and eight other literary figures adorned his royal court. He had matrimonial relations with Vatakas, the chief power in the Deccan peninsula. Villagization of India was almost complete and several great cities emerged all over the country. Practically the whole of geographical India was united by a common culture and expanding trade and commerce. Agriculture made new strides.

The imperial power of Guptas ended in 470 AD. Two kingdoms of some consequence centered at Ujjaini in the West and Pataliputra in East took control of Northen India. With the weakening of the central authority and emergence of many mini-kingdoms, the Indian political scene changed once again to attract foreigners from the West. Ephithalits invaded the country in 510 AD and overthrew Mihirgula (512-28 AD). Harshvardhana (606-647 AD) made another attempt to unite the geographical and cultural India into a single political entity. He was a devout Buddhist and a great patron of letters. He extended his empire to practically the whole of Northern India but could not move much beyond the Vindhyas to the south because of the resistance of Chalukyas of Vatapi (Badami).

Medieval India

Period extending from 650 to 1200 AD was a period of dynastic rivalry and Moslem penetration in India. The Moslems occupied Sind in 712. The Gurjara-Pratihara Rajputs who ruled over Rajasthan could have stopped them from further advances but they had to fight on two other fronts: in the east was the Pal dynasty of Bengal, and in south were the Rastrakutas. With the defeat of Prithviraj Chauhan in 1192, India had to face the Moslem onslaught.

In the south, there were two centres of power: Maratha and Tamil. Deccan was under Chalukyas (550-757 AD). Rastrakutas came back with some force once again in 973-1190 AD but remained a middle level power. The Yadavas of Deogir (1187-1312 AD) acquired some power to be reckoned with. Further south in the Tamil land, the Pallavas of north Indian origin overran Chola, Pandya, and Chera kingdoms in 7th century. They remained there until the end of 9th century. They were replaced by Cholas who reached great heights in all walks of life under the reign of Rajaraja (985-1014 AD) and Rajendra (1014-1044 AD). The Cholas became a great Naval power. They controlled the south, defeated the Pals of Bengal and sent expeditions to Ganges, Malaya and Indonesia. They were succeeded by the Pandya dynasties in 12th century but their triumph was short-lived. By 1310, the Moslem onslaught destroyed them as a power to reckon with.

The early medieval period of Indian history is generally known as the feudal period. During this period, the central authority of the country was weakened and so many small principalities declared their independence. There was a political turmoil due to frequent feudal wars and the emergence of landed aristocracy, which was known for luxurious life and ostentatious living. The ruling chiefs and rapacious officials resorted to arbitrary and excessive taxation. Even village heads became agents of the feudal lords.

Most of the *Puranas* composed during this period give vivid details of the characteristics of the Kali age. They did not criticize the prevailing situation but they predicted what would happen when the Kali age came. It was left to the people to infer and compare the prevailing situation with the one ascribed to *Kali Yuga*. One finds that even the village life was highly disturbed. Villages were essentially self-governing. Village or gram was so much a part of the culture of the time that its organisation was considered ideal for the organisation of individual life. In *Agni Purana* an individual is conceived as a village pradhan and the five external sense organs as five families inhabiting the village. Sankaracharya in his commentary on Brahmasutra has given a similar simile. But some of the village headmen (gramakutas) were so unpopular that Brahmins were prohibited from partaking food given by them.

During this period, the institution of village headmen appears to have been corrupted. It happened because the institution of headman gradually became hereditary. Headmen turned into small feudal chiefs paying tributes to bigger feudal chiefs. There were village assemblies but they probably lost their decision-making power. Even the allocation of the agricultural land, which was traditionally done by the Gram Sabha (village assembly) fell under the jurisdiction of the *gramapati* (headman) sidelining village assemblies.

Despite these deteriorations, villages were self-sufficient in most of their basic needs. There was no difference between the producer and the consumer and almost everyone was a prosumer to use Toffler's term. And there was a code of conduct – *gramdharam* or *gramachar*, which was to be followed by the *gramapati* as well as the inhabitants of the village. Cases of some *gramapatis* breaking these rules were probably more frequent during this period.

Buddhism, which was the main religion of India until 700 AD was marked with increasing unpopularity partly because of its inability to check the growing menace of militant Islam, and partly because of loosening of Buddhist ethics in Sanghas and outside. Proliferation of different sects within Buddhism each claiming to be original and superior to the rest also created confusion in the minds of the people. Jainism too had important areas of concentration. Most religious leaders (monks) became too ritualistic and the essentials of Buddhism were sidetracked in so far as its practice was concerned. We need not go further into the causes of decline of these two great religions in India, but if one has to identify a single most important factor it was the loosening of both individual and corporate morality.

The Vedic religion had not disappeared during the ascendancy of Buddhism; it became ritualistic often referred to as Brahmanism. Buddha and Mahavira did not denounce Brahmanism; they only propounded a new philosophy and the approach to put it into practice. Their approach was positive and additive rather than negative and destructive. The two philosophies were, however, not foreign to the Vedic religion. As time passed the distinction between ritualistic Buddhism and Brahmanism narrowed down. Further with increasing pressure of Islam on Indian polity and society, all Indian religions had to come together to protect themselves.

Arrival of Shankaracharya as the new and very powerful exponent of Vedic religion in eighth century AD paved the way for the emergence of Brahmanism otherwise known as Hinduism as the chief religion of India. Many of the Buddhist monks became Hindus monks. And thus Buddhism, which spread even to far off lands like Central Asia, East

Asia and Southeast Asia shrank in terms of adherence in its homeland. In this regard it should, however, be noted that the basic tenets of both Buddhism and Jainism were incorporated in Hinduism and hence the differences among Hinduism, Buddhism and Jainism at the popular level were so few that there was no major problem in changing over from one to the other or being follower of all three simultaneously. Even today, Hindus in India have the same devotion and respect for Lord Buddha and Lord Mahavira as they have for Hindu *Avatars*. In fact Lord Buddha is accepted as the ninth Avatar of Lord Vishnu.

Hinduism had developed a rich philosophical tradition, which ranged from monism, *vishisht*-dualism to dualism and then on to atheism. It had something for everyone for God appears in the form in which a person seeks Him. So long as its basic tenets of acceptance of Vedas as God given and the adherence to Truth and Non-violence were ensured, it mattered little in what form one worshiped the God. It was so liberal that it accepted different religions and sects as different paths to reach the same God. And hence there was no need to quarrel about the methods of worship. It accepted Buddha as an avatar of Vishnu and Buddhist values like non-violence as integral parts of Hinduism. The agility of Hinduism became perhaps one of the reasons for the decline as well continuance of Buddhism and Jainism in the country. Together, the Indian religions (Sikhism added later) had their indomitable impact on even those religions which came from outside such as Christianity and Islam.

The conquest of India by West and Central Asian Moslems preceded Arab consolidation in Sind since 710 AD. With the decline of Abbasi Caliphate, new power centers emerged in Persia, Turkestan and Afghanistan. A Turkish slave named Mohammad of Ghazni raided India over a dozen times. He reached up to the Ganges and was responsible for destroying the Somnath temple in Gujarat. But his rule did not extend beyond Punjab. The Ghaznis were driven out from Punjab by a rival Moslem invader from Ghur called Mohammad Ghori in 1186. He defeated Prithviraj Chauhan in 1192. He was, however, assassinated in 1202 and a new slave dynasty under Kutbuddeen Aibak laid the foundation of Delhi Sultanate, which ruled over Delhi until Babur arrived on the scene in 1526.

It must have been a traumatic period for people of India. Most of the Indians lived in villages and the villages were so self-reliant that it did not matter much who ruled at Delhi. So long as there was no interference with their religion, traditions, social system and agricultural base, they did not mind who the ruler was and what his religion was. A new situation arose in which uncivilized foreigners descended on the country for mindless destruction.

Plundering and destruction of temples and looting of villages by the marching armies must have aroused very hateful feelings against the invaders but there was no coordinating force to bring the people together against their common enemy. India was divided into too many principalities each fighting the other. Some sided with the invaders in the hope of getting help to defeat their own neighbours. Unlike Japan where the shoguns joined hands to wage a war against a common enemy entering the country from outside, Indian rulers had lost touch with the concept of Indian nationhood, which developed as early as Vedic times. They were more interested in fighting their own brethren than to join hands to face the marauders and invaders. This applied to both Muslim and Hindu rulers.

It was the period of great confusion in India. People especially the farming community went through very difficult times. The rulers tried to extract as much from the people as physically possible. From the people's side, there was a sort of non-cooperation, which often took the form of wholesale desertion of villages. This situation weakened the hold of the Sultanate too. It shrank in authority as well as territory and remained confined to only those areas where army was posted. It was particularly the case in thirteenth century. In fourteenth century, the situation improved and the sway of the Sultanate extended from Kashmir in the north to Madurai in the south, even if loosely. But this did not last long and the political confusion engendered by people's antagonism continued to grow.

Of the 33 Sultans who ruled over Delhi, none is known for anything great. Balban (1296-1316) was perhaps the most powerful among them. They were ruthless and very oppressive of Hindu peasantry. Allauddin Khilji imposed land tax equivalent to half the produce. The Sultanate could not stabilize itself for it could not control the Hindu chieftains nor could it leave the peasantry alone. In the Peninsula, the situation was equally confused. The Yadvas were there but they were not in a position to work with the neighbouring kingdoms to jointly face the common enemy.

Mohammad-bin-Tughlaq (1325-51) shifted his capital from Delhi to Deogir, which according to him was the geographical center of India. He was one of the cruelest rulers India ever had. After his death, his successor Feroz Shah (1351-88) could not hold on. The

Sultanate disintegrated and anarchy prevailed. Taimur Lane attacked Sind and indulged in unprecedented massacre of the people. The Lodi dynasty took control of the Sultanate in 1451 AD. Lodies were Pathans from Afghanistan. They could not control the powerful Rajput and Moslem principalities. In the peninsula, the Bahmani kingdom was divided into five principalities. South of river Krishna and Tungabhadra was the mighty empire of Vijaynagar (1509-95). It was founded on the ruins of Chola power. It reached its greatest extent and height under Krishna Deva Raya. The rulers of this dynasty were highly accomplished but remained confined to their origin. A combined onslaught by Moslem kings of the Deccan wiped this empire out in 1595.

A descendant of Taimur Lane and Jenghij Khan, Babur was forced out of his homeland and took shelter in the mountains of Afghanistan. He defeated Ibrahim Lodi at Panipat in 1526. He is considered to be the founder of Moghul empire in India. But in reality it is not so. He captured Delhi but after his death his son Humayun who was an incompetent ruler, lost the throne to Shershah Suri, a rebel Afghan soldier, in 1544. He is credited with the construction of Grand Trunk Road linking Peshawar with Patna via Delhi. Shershah's successors, however, could not hold on. There was anarchy in the country. Humayun regained power in 1555 but he died a year later.

Real Moghul impire began with Akbar the Great (1556-1605). He ruled from Kabul in the west to Ahmednagar in the Deccan. Akbar's rule is considered to be a watershed in Moslem rule in India. He was liberal; understood the culture of India, and tried to unify the people cutting across religious divides. Further, Akbar was a true Indian; he was born here and had no emotional links with outside.

With the arrival of Akbar on the scene, the situation changed drastically. He abolished all discriminatory laws and rules against the Hindu population and declared a policy of equality before law. While it is true that the roots of the anti-Hindu policies of the Sultanate era did not cease altogether, it was during this period that the people of India felt somewhat relieved and started cooperating with the government on their own.

He launched a number of programmes including land surveys, famine relief, encouragement to scholarly activities, and dialogue among various sections of the society. He even launched a new religion called Deen-e-Ilahi, which took good things from various religions. It was a synthesis of all religions. He was a naive in this sense for religions are not created like this. But he deserves commendation because his intentions were good and pious.

Tulsidas who wrote *Ramacharit Manas* lived during Akbar's time. Many Moslems wrote great books taking Hindu philosophy and gods and goddesses as their favourite subjects. A sort of synthesis of ideas and ideals started in this period and if this tradition were continued India would have become something like Indonesia with a Hindu culture but several religions. Unfortunately it was not to be so.

Akbar's son Jehangir proved to be an incompetent ruler; he was a drunken despot. His wife, Nur Jehan, was controlled by a junta, which ruled the country. His son Shah Jehan (1627-58) ruled the country not very competently. He had a passion for buildings and monuments, the most famous of which is Taj Mahal. Shah Jahan was dethroned by his son Aurangzeb in 1657 and imprisoned in Agra fort. Had his elder son Dara Shikoh succeeded him, the history of India would have been different. He was not only a competent and scholarly person but also liberal like his great grandfather Akbar. Aurangzeb ruled India for about 50 years (1658-1707); expanded his empire to areas where even Akbar did not reach, but also set in motion the disintegration of the Moghul empire. He was a bigot Muslim; he alienated Hindus almost completely and impoverished the peasantry. By the time he died, the empire was in distress. His successors proved incompetent, even if less exacting. Marathas defeated the imperial army in 1737 near Delhi. And to make the confusion more confounded, Nadir Shah invaded northern India in 1739, and defeated the imperial army at Karnal. He unleashed his furry on the people of Delhi and massacred thousands of them. He returned with the Peacock throne, the only symbol of the Moghul empire still with the emperor.

Marathas controlled the remnants of the Moghul impire but were defeated by Ahmedshah Durrani (in 1761) who invaded India ten times between 1747 and 1769. Durrani got support from all Moslem principalities but the Marathas failed to get the support of other Hindu Rajahs. Whatever the case, there is no doubt that India in the middle of the eighteenth century was in turmoil; it offered fertile ground for Europeans to overpower the petty kings and rule the country.

From Company Raj to British Raj

On December 31, 1600 just five years prior to Akbar's death in 1605, Queen Elizabeth granted charter to the Company of Merchants of

London to trade with East Indies where the Dutch were already there. In 1613 they received imperial firman to establish a permanent factory at Surat. In 1614 Sir Thomas Roe arrived as the first English ambassador to the imperial court at Agra. By 1619 trading posts were established at Agra, Ahmedabad and Broach. In 1661 the island of Bombay came in the hands of the British as dowry from Portugal and in 1687 it replaced Surat as the company's head quarters on the west coast.

On the eastern coast, the first English settlement was erected at Masulipatnam in 1611. Local Hindu ruler permitted them to build a fortified factory at Madraspatnam in 1639. Fort St. Johns was built the following year. Moghuls, when they overran the area, did not disturb the British. A factory was built in Hooghly in Bengal in 1651. Calcutta was founded during the second half of the seventeenth century.

In 1717 the then Moghul emperor issued a firman giving the English East India Company exclusive privileges for trade. By that time the imperial power had become so week that the provincial governors ignored the firman and charged the company necessary dues. When the company tried to cheat the government the Nawab Siraj-ud-Daula captured the British settlement in Calcutta in 1776 and allegedly incarcerated 146 English prisoners in a small room called Black Hole. To avenge this outrage, Robert Clive sailed from Madras with a force and recaptured Calcutta. A treaty was signed but with help of Mir Jafar, the British defeated the Nawab at Plassey in 1757. Mir Jafar was appointed the new Nawab; British became the de facto rulers of Bengal.

The Moghuls appointed Mir Kasim as the new Nawab. He asserted his authority and came in conflict with the company officials. He could not stay for too long and Mir Jafar became the Nawab once again. Shah Alam, the titular Moghul emperor tried to recapture Bengal. His forces were defeated at Buxar in 1764. The emperor was forced to grant Diwani, the right to collect the revenue in Bengal, Bihar and Orissa, to the East India Company.

The British Raj begins with the battle of Plassey in 1757 when the East India Company became the *de facto* ruler of Bengal. Thereafter it was only a matter of time before the British suzerainty extended to the whole of India. Warren Hastings became the governor of Bengal in 1772. Tipu Sultan in Mysore was defeated in 1799. The so-called Sepoy Mutiny, in effect the first countrywide war of independence in 1857 forced the British government to take over the reigns of the Indian subcontinent from East India Company.

The British brought many social and economic changes. They refrained from interfering with the religion of any community in India. This was in contrast to the Moslem rulers with a few honourable exceptions. Most of the invaders who came to India and settled down permanently and became Indians. As such the resources of India remained in India. The problem if any lay in mal-distribution, not in siphoning off. In case of the British it was just the other way round. The British remained foreigners and their rule remained foreign. They were here not to serve India and its people, but serve Britain and its people by taking away whatever they could from India directly or indirectly. One of the consequences of the British rule in India was thus the draining off of its resources.

The second major consequence was the weakening the country economically by destroying its cottage industries, which were a major source of employment both in villages and towns. Destruction of cottage industries enabled British industry to get raw materials from India and sell the finished products at the price determined by them. Thus the self-sufficiency and self-reliance that marked the rural economy of India until then was lost. It has not been able to recover the ground since then.

The third and very subtle consequence of British Raj was the undermining of Indian culture by introducing English education that alienated the people from whatever was Indian. People came to believe that Britain was the model of a progressive and modern country and whatever was practiced there must be progressive and modern and hence worth emulation. European civilisation was admired and Indian civilisation was looked down upon by many of the English educated Indians. This problem continues to haunt India even today.

India, Renaissance

A Hindu religious reform focusing on India's great cultural heritage began in the second half of the nineteenth century. Prominent among the reformers were Raja Ram Mohun Roy (Brahmo Samaj), Dayanand Saraswati (Arya Samaj), Ramkrishna Paramhansa and his disciple Swami Vivekananda (Ramakrishna Mission) and several others. English education was introduced with a view to make Indians lackeys of the British but it had opposite impact too. Indians came to know what was happening in the world and how India with its great past deserved a far better position in the world. Educated Indians demanded reforms in various fields and formed societies to deliberate on political and social affairs.

Indian National Congress, the first political organisation was formed in 1885 and its first annual session was held at Bombay the same year. Seventy-two delegates from different parts of the country attended the session. The use of the term 'National' was a clear enough indication that nationalistic feelings were surging through the country and geographical-cum-cultural India, which asserted itself rather persistently even if not with the same vigour to politically unify the Indian subcontinent gathered new strength. India was united several times even in times when it was so difficult to politically control such a large land mass. Thanks to the improvements in transport and communication and anti-Indian policies followed by the British, unity of India and a firm faith in its destiny as a great nation took deep roots. In was on the move again.

The second session of the Indian National Congress was held in 1986; the number of delegates attending rose to 440, 33 of them being Moslems. 1248 delegates attended the 1888 session of INC. By the end of the century, the character of the Indian National Congress changed from being moderate to anti-British. It called for the boycott of British goods on the lines of Chinese boycott of the American goods.

By 1907, the leadership of the Congress party shifted from Gokhale, a moderate professor, to Bal Gangadhar Tilak and Arobindo Ghosh, both of them nationalists with anarchist leanings. Congress was converted into an anti-British party. The anarchist movement was first started in Poona; its mouthpiece was *Kesari*, a journal published by Tilak. The movement spread to Bengal where secondary schools became the recruiting centers for volunteers to carry out attacks against the British institutions and officials. In 1908, the hideouts of the conspirators were raided and 35 of them were arrested; 15 of them were found guilty. They were so well organized that an approver was shot dead in jail; the public prosecutor was assassinated in Calcutta; and deputy superintendent was killed while leaving the court. Between 1909 and 1914, the anarchist movement spread to the whole of the country. In 1909 Curzon Wyllie, a functionary of India Office was assassinated at the Imperial Institute in London. The same year, Arther Jackson, district magistrate of Nasik was done to death. In 1911, Robert

Ashe, the district magistrate of Tinnevelly in Madras was killed and the famous Delhi Bomb attack seriously injured Lord Hardinge.

The British were frightened and tried to introduce some changes known as Minto-Morley Reforms (1907) to mollify Indian urge for greater participation in administration of the empire. Two Indians got place in the Secretary State's Council at London; and soon in the Governor Generals Council at Delhi. The Councils in provincial capitals were enlarged and their powers enhanced. Since the election to the Councils was indirect, most of the members were lawyers. Since the ex-officio members predominated, the people's voice was never heard in these Councils.

Indian Moslem League was formed in 1906 to safeguard Moslem interests *vis-à-vis* the Indian National Congress.

It is here at this stage that M.K. Gandhi entered the scene. He met the revolutionaries in London and tried to convince them of the futility of violent change they were committed to. Gandhi felt that what the British were doing in India was unethical and unjustified. India must get rid of them sooner than later. But how? If India uses the same means, which the British used and are using, there is no difference between the oppressors and the oppressed. Gandhi read through Indian history, which has been narrated above in nut shell and came to the conclusion that India had always upheld morality and ethics and her pre-eminence in ancient times lay not in power to destroy but in power to create. He argued with the revolutionaries to abjure violence and come to the path of non-violence.

CONCLUDING REMARKS

Beginning of the nineteenth century marks a watershed in British Raj in India as also in recent Indian ethos. It was a century, which produced a great number of Indian poets, writers, scientists, political thinkers, historians and nationalists. Further, the very forces, particularly the English education, which tended to alienate people from their culture and traditions, generated a new wave of rethinking on the so-called modern civilisation and a revaluation and reassertion of Indian cultural traditions. The *Vedas*, *Upanishads*, *Ramayana*, *Mahabharata*, *Geeta*, *Puranas* etc. were read by some Europeans and highly lauded as the books of great philosophical and cultural significance. The positive attitude of Europeans about Indian civilisation rather forced the English educated Indians to feel proud of India's past and potential future and to discard their appreciative attitude towards whatever was European. They felt ashamed that a small island country of Europe was ruling over India. A feeling that Indians alone had the right to rule over India spread like a wild fire.

It was at this crucial juncture that Gandhi arrived on the scene. To a great extent Gandhi was part of the rethinking that was going on in the country ever since the last quarter of nineteenth century. People were highly moved and agitated: some took to the violent path and decided to kill or get killed. Some wanted to fight the battle constitutionally to get self-government. Gandhi took the spirit underlying all these ideologies and chiseled a new and typically Indian tools to fight the British. The people of India liked it; they called Gandhi a Mahatma and followed him to the end. When his last journey crawled through the streets of Delhi on January 31, 1948, there were ten million mourners, perhaps the largest funeral procession ever witnessed in the world.

We discussed this issue to some extent in the preceding section. Let us look at it in greater details. Gandhi was critical of history as written in his time on several counts. First, he objected to the very approach to history. History is not the record or analysis of the doings of the rulers and the wars they fought. It must be the record of what people did in order to make this world a better place to live. To him history was not neutral to human destiny. Unless a historian has a point of view on human destiny, he cannot assess the events that take place in terms of desirable and undesirable. To say that history is neutral to ethics, is to condemn it as baseless. If human destiny lies in peace and harmony, then anything that disturbs peace must be wrong. If any country forcibly occupies other countries, the action must be treated as unethical and wrong. Secondly, Gandhi was opposed to the very idea of writing of the history of people and cultures about which the writer has no knowledge and unbiased attitude. The fact that winners in wars are always considered to be brave and right, is indicative of this drawback. The British historians always justified British occupation of India because Indians were White Man's burden; they had to be civilised by the British.

7

Contemporary Political Thinkers and Activists

Indian renaissance produced a number of luminaries who were exposed to western thought and ongoing industrial revolution but were thoroughly soaked in Indian thought and culture. These people were exposed to what was going on the world over especially in Europe and America and wondered why India with such a great past became a colony of Britain. They wanted to take up arms against the British as Americans did in 1776 to free themselves. They studied the history and geography of India and came to the conclusion that Indian civilisation in its essence was the best and the oldest living civilisation of the world. It fell into evil days partly because it was covered by a dead weight of unhealthy traditions, which might have come in response to the challenges it faced in the past. It also might have degenerated for it remained demoralized to such an extent for the last few centuries that Indians themselves lost faith in it and tried to discard it in favour of the western civilisation.

The Indian renaissance took five main routes:

(1) political reforms through constitutional means;
(2) revolutionary changes through violent means;
(3) social change through legal means;
(4) modernization through scientific and liberal education;
(5) cultural revival through historical studies and literary and religious activities.

Among the great men and women who can be placed in the first group and who tried to secure rights of the people of India through political participation and constitutional advancement were Dadabhai Naoroji, Justice Govind Ranade, Ferozshah Mehta, Gopal Krishna

Gokhale, Mohammad Ali Jinnah, Motilal Nehru, etc. The second group consisted of persons like Shyamji Krishnavarma, Sri Aurobindo Ghosh, Bal Gangadhar Tilak, Bipin Chandra Pal, Lala Lajpat Rai, (Bal, Pal, Lal) and a host of other well known revolutionaries who laid down their lives for the motherland. Raja Ram Mohun Roy (1772-1833), Mahatma Phule, Ramswamy Naiker, etc. belong to the third group. The fourth group had Madan Mohan Malaviya, Sir Syed Ahmed Khan, Jagdish Chunder Bose, C.V. Raman, Meghnath Saha, etc. who convinced Indians that they were no inferior to Europeans even in educational and scientific fields. And the fifth group consisted of Bankim Chandra Chatterjee, Dr. Anand K. Coomaraswami, R.C. Dutt, Rabindranath Tagore and Mohammad Allamah Iqbal, Swami Vivekananda, Raman Maharshi; and Swami Dayanand Saraswati who reminded the people of their great past and equally great future. Interestingly many of these leaders were born within a span of 20 years from 1860 to 1880: Swami Vivekananda was born in 1863; Mahatma Gandhi in 1869; Shri Aurobindo in 1872; and Raman Maharshi in 1879.

Gandhi did not belong to any of these groups; he was a bridge that transcended them all. He was sympathetic to them all for they all wanted India to rise again and spread its cultural fragrance all over the world. He thus formed a sixth group, which took whatever was good and in conformity with Indian civilisation from other groups and prepared a path of salvation that was typically Indian yet global in relevance.

Since they were contemporaries or near contemporaries they were aware of each other's thoughts and activities. Mahatma Gandhi had interacted personally with Shyamji Krishnavarma, Swami Dayanand Saraswati; poet Rabindranath Tagore, Madan Mohan Malaviya, Annie Besant, Motilal Nehru and many others on several occasions. Gandhi has referred to the history of India by R.C. Dutt in *Hind Swaraj*. Apparently he had read the book. If there was no mention of some of the important personalities like Aurobindo Ghosh, Veer Savarkar and Swami Vivekanand in *Hind Swaraj*, it was not because he was not was not in full agreement with them.

The young revolutionaries and their leaders like Tilak and Veer Savarkar were very much in the mind when Gandhi wrote *Hind Swaraj*. He appreciated their courage and devotion to the motherland, but did not consider their methods right. It was Tilak who proclaimed complete independence as the birth right of Indians. Gandhi had great regard and respect for him. But he was not in agreement with him in so far as the method of achieving *Swaraj* was concerned. *Hind Swaraj* was written in response to the activities of these revolutionaries. Only a few days before Gandhi reached London (on July 1, 1909) in his second lobbying mission, Madan Lal Dhingra, an engineering student at the Imperial College, had killed Sir William Curzon Willie, an ADC to the Secretary of State. That had very much embarrassed Gandhi. He resolved to talk to them and to bring them on the path of truth and non-violence.

The groups mentioned above had considerable impact on the evolution of Gandhi as a Mahatma and liberator of India by a means no one else had tried in the past. Their goals were common; they wanted India to play its assigned role in the world, as a great civilisation. For some the greatness lay in its religion, culture and mind, for others in its potentials as a mighty nation, and for still others in its civilisation. The means they adopted were different but the objectives were common. Gandhi accepted their goal, but not the means. He devised his own means, which was as pious as the goal. For him means and ends were interchangeable. The goal of freedom of India, the land of one of the oldest civilisations of the world, the land of Ram, Krishna, Buddha, Mahavira and Shankaracharya; the land of Ashoka, Harsha and Akbar, could not be soaked in blood. India must win its freedom using methods and approaches, which were unique and novel, and which were typically Indian. It must be in tune with its civilisation.

India, according to Gandhi was not enslaved by the British people but by the British government. British government was the product of the industrial civilisation paraded as modern civilisation. It could not be expected to liberate people. Modern civilisation in reality was yet to be borne. The British people too were the slaves of this civilisation, which Gandhi termed Satanic. India's fight must be against the root cause, *i.e.* modern civilisation first, not against the British people who must be treated as common sufferers. And the weapon to be used must be the one that did not exist in the toolbox of modern civilisation. India had to reopen the toolbox of its own civilisation and select the chisel, which would carve out peace not war. Non-violence was Gandhi's chisel to give shape to new India, an India of peace and harmony, of selfless service and self sacrifice and of love and compassion; and *satyagraha* was the hammer that made the chisel produce miracles.

Gandhi, success lay partly in the circumstances in which he was placed; in the ideas and works of the people who were his contemporaries or near contemporaries and above all the Indian heritage of several millennia. We propose to discuss a few of those who influenced Gandhi before he wrote *Hind Swaraj*. Names of several important leaders like Dr. Bhimrao Ambedkar, Jawaharlal Nehru, Subhas Chandra Bose and several others do not figure here because they arrived on the scene after 1909.

This chapter gives a short biography and work of persons falling under the first two groups: liberal constitutionalists and the great revolutionaries. For others, the reader is referred to the next chapter.

THE LIBERAL CONSTITUTIONALISTS

Dadabhai Naoroji

Dadabhai Naoroji was born in Bombay on September 4, 1825, almost 45 years before Gandhi. His father, Maneckbhai Panlanji Dordi was a Zorostrian priest with a poor economic base. He lost his father when he was four; his mother Maneckbai brought him up and arranged for his education at the Native Education Society, Bombay. Dadabhai was rated very high as a student. At the age of 15, he was awarded Clare's scholarship. Professor Oriebar called him 'Promise of India'. He was appointed professor of mathematics and philosophy at Elphinstone Institute, Bombay at the age of 20. Dadabhai had deep love for India and he had a firm faith in its great future. He was a champion of girls' education and volunteered to teach free at the first girls school opened in Bombay.

He went to England with K.R. Cama and M.H. Cama to join their business in London. Soon he left the Camas and became professor at the University College, London where he worked for ten years. Dadabhai never lost the opportunity to ventilate the grievances of Indians in appropriate forums. He was a very active member of the East India Association. He was honoured with a purse of Rs. 25,000 in Bombay for the services he rendered for the country and its people in England. He became the Diwan of the state of Baroda in 1875; was twice elected to Bombay Municipal Corporation. He was the moving spirit behind the Indian National Congress, which had its first meeting in 1885 in the Gokuldas Tejpal Hall near Gowalia Tank, Bombay.

Naoroji went back to England in 1886. He was elected the president of INC at Calcutta in 1886 and had the distinction of being the first

Asian to be elected to the House of Commons. His speeches in the parliament were read with great interest. He wrote 'Poverty and Un-British Rule in India', which gave the vivid details of how British rule ruined Indian economy and polity. It aroused considerable nationalistic feelings among the educated sections of the Indian society.

On his return to India, he received a welcome greater than the British Viceroy of India (*Times*, London). Wherever he went, he was received with great spontaneity all over the country. People lovingly called him Dadabhai but he felt embarrassed by the title. The Shah of Iran wanted to decorate him but he declined to accept the offer. When his term as member of the House of Commons ended he served as a member of the Royal Commission. He got Din Shaw Wachha, Gopal Krishna Gokhale, Surendanath Banerjee, and Subramanian Iyer in the Commission and organized a campaign to educate the British about the conditions in India and the demands of the Indians. M.K. Gandhi, across the Arabian Sea in South Africa, was so much enamoured of Dadabhai Naoroji that he regularly consulted him on all important issues through letters and telegrams.

In 1906 Dadabhai was re-elected as president of the Indian National Congress. He was 80 years old then. He succeeded in patching up the conflict between the extremists and the moderates at the Calcutta Congress and declared *Swaraj* or Self-Rule as the goal of the Congress. Dadabhai Naoroji passed away in 1911. Sir Narayan Chandravarkar paid tributes to the Grand Old Man of India in following words:

"If we take stock of his life and his example, may we say with perfect justice and trust that in his career in all he did, in all he suffered, and in all he taught, he was the Prophet Zoroaster's religion personified, because he was the man more than anybody else of pure thought, of pure speech, and of pure deeds. ... The sun that rose ninety-three years ago, over India, is set, say, it is set to rise again in the form of regenerated India, for Dadabhai lived and worked for us with the devotion which must remain for all of us an inspiring example."

When the revolutionaries branded Naoroji as a collaborator with the British, Gandhi had this to say in *Hind Swaraj*:

"That opinion is not justified. Had not Grand Old Man of India prepared the soil, our young men could not have even spoken about Home Rule.... I must tell you, with all gentleness, that it must be a matter of shame for us that you should speak about that great man in terms of disrespect. Just look at his work. He has dedicated his life to the service of India. We have learnt what we know from him. It was the respected Dadabhai who taught us that English had sucked our life-blood. What does it matter today that his trust is still in the English nation? Is Dadabhai less to be honoured because in the exuberance of youth, we are prepared to go a step further? Are we, on that account, wiser than he? It is a mark of wisdom not to kick away the very step from which we have risen higher....He will always command my respect.... We must admit that he is author of nationalism."

Gopal Krishna Gokhale

If Tilak was the leader of the extreme wing of the Congress, Gopal Krishna Gokhale was the leader of the moderate wing. He was born on May 9, 1866 in Ratnagiri, the place where Tilak was born. Gokhale was greatly influenced by Ranade whom he regarded his guru in public life. Dadabhai Naoroji and Ferozshah Mehta were the other figures in public life who influenced Gokhale.

When Ferguson College was opened in 1885, Gokhale became a lecturer there. He left the service in 1902 to devote his time to public life. In 1889, he joined the Indian National Congress and became its joint secretary in 1895 and president in 1905. He founded the Servants of India Society and Ranade Institute of Economics in 1905.

Gokhale was a frontrunner social reformer. He deprecated caste system, and untouchability and championed the cause of women's emancipation. He called for primary education for all. Gokhale was appreciative of English education for it helped enlightened sections of the people what was going on in the world but considered British rule absolutely disastrous for the country. He sought home rule for India within the British Commonwealth. He advocated constitutional means to secure home rule. While appreciating the benefits of the British rule, he never failed to criticize the unjust policies of the government.

Gokhale advocated rapid modernization of agriculture and pleaded for industrial and commercial education for Indians so that they could secure opportunities for livelihood in non-agricultural sectors. He was in favour of mechanization and mass production. He was a great orator and the Government listened to what he said. He was highly respected by the people of India for he was honest, sincere and totally devoted to national development. His approach to India's future was dual: social reform and political advancement. Gandhi treated him as his political *guru*.

On the criticism levelled against Gokhale by the revolutionaries, Gandhi had this to say in *Hind Swaraj*. "Professor Gokhale occupies the place of a parent. What does it matter if he cannot run with us? A nation that is desirous of securing Home Rule cannot afford to despise its ancestors.... how many Indians were there like Professor Gokhale, when he gave himself to Indian education? I verily believe that whatever Professor Gokhale does, he does with pure motives and with a view to serving India. His devotion to the Motherland is so great that he would give his life for it, if necessary. Whatever he says is said not to flatter anyone but because he believes it to be true. We are bound, therefore, to entertain highest regard for him."

Surendranath Banerjee

Born in 1848, he was one of the great liberals of Indian politics who steered the Indian National Congress until his death in 1925. He graduated from Calcutta University in 1868 and proceeded to England for higher studies. Passed the Indian Civil Service Examination in 1869 and returned to India to join as assistant magistrate at Sylhet. He was dismissed from service for reasons other than political and was not even allowed to enroll as a barrister. He was the founder of Ripon College now known as Surendranath College.

He was an eloquent speaker. He was able to influence many a young men who were interested in social change under the banner of Brahmo Samaj to join the nationalist movement. In 1876 he founded the Indian Association and toured the whole country ostensibly to protest against the reduction of age for civil service examination from 21 to 19 years but the real intention was to enroll the youth for the service of the country. His tour more than anything demonstrated that India was geographically and culturally one and it was possible to organize a pan-Indian movement against the British.

He was imprisoned for contempt of court (because he made an adverse remark against the Chief Justice of Calcutta in his newspaper *Bengalee*). People protested and observed hartal all over Bengal and protest meeting were held all over the country. This was followed by an All-India Political Conference under the aegis of the Indian Association. The first session of the conference was held in 1883 and the second in 1885. These conferences had delegates from every part of the country.

Immediately after the conclusion of the second session of the Conference, the first session of the Indian National Congress was held in Bombay in 1885 wherein the National Conference was merged with the INC because the goals and objectives of the two were the same. The second session of the Congress was held at Calcutta and Surendrababu played a leading role since then. He became its president twice (1895 and 1902). He was a leading figure of agitation against the partition of Bengal in 1905. Banerjee ruled the minds and emotions of the people of Bengal; he was the uncrowned king of Bengal and a respected leader of the whole country.

Surendranath Banerjee was a leading moderate in Congress. After 1906 the extremist wing got hold of the party and his influence started declining. In the meantime the Home Rule League got underway and Mahatma Gandhi emerged on the scene after his return from South Africa. On the issue of Montagu-Chelmsford Report, the moderates walked out of the Congress in 1918.

Surendranath accepted the Ministry and Knighthood. He became so unpopular tnat he lost the election for Bengal Legislative Assembly in 1923. Thereafter he retired from active politics. He was a member of the Indian Legislative Council for many years. Even though Surendrababu died unwept, his contribution to national regeneration was in the last decade of the nineteenth century and first decade of the twentieth century was unmatched. Gandhiji met Surendranath Banerjee several times and whenever he visited Calcutta he made it a point to meet him and learn about the conditions prevailing in the country.

THE GREAT REVOLUTIONARIES

Balgangadhar Tilak

Born in 1856, Tilak was a journalist and the leader of the extreme wing of the Indian National Congress and the foremost nationalist before Mohandas Karamchand Gandhi. Before becoming a full time journalist in 1890, he studied law at the famous Deccan College and taught at the Pune English School (1880-85) and Furgusson College (1885-90). He revived the Ganapati festival in 1893 to arouse patriotic ferver; later it became the rallying point for the nationalist movement in western India. Two years later, he initiated the Shiva Ji festival for the same purpose.

He was highly critical of the British Raj. He was charged for sedition and imprisoned in 1897. The same year Tilak organized the extreme wing of the Congress Party. In 1907 it demanded complete independence for India from the British. He was once again imprisoned 1908 and this time for six years. In 1916, he founded the Home Rule League to fight for India's cause. The Congress adopted his advocacy of complete independence for India only after his death in 1920.

Bipin Chandra Pal

Described as one of the mightiest prophets of nationalism, Bipin Chandra Pal, along with Bal Gangadhar Tilak and Lala Lajpat Rai formed a trinity, that stood for achieving complete independence from British rule through courage, self-help and self-sacrifice. He was a teacher, journalist, writer and librarian; he started his public life as a supporter of Brahmo Samaj started by Ram Mohun Roy. Then he turned to Vedanta and ended up as the follower of Vaishnava philosophy of Sri Chaitanya. He married a widow of a higher caste twice to break the social taboos of the time and supported the Age of Consent Bill, 1891. He wrote a series of articles on the makers of modern India such as Ram Mohun Roy. He started a number of journals such as *Paridarshak*, 1896, *New India*, 1902, and *Bande Matram*, 1906.

Pal was born in 1858 in a village in Sylhet (now in Bangladesh) in a well to do family; he cut short his education at the intermediate stage when he came under the influence of the then Bengali leaders like Keshab Chandra ,Sen and Pandit Shivnath Shastri. He was imprisoned for six months on the ground of his refusal to tender evidence against Sri Aurobindo in the Bande Matram sedition case.

He attended the first Indian National Congress in 1885 as delegate from Sylhet. Later in 1920, he opposed Gandhi's Non-cooperation Movement. Soon he retired from politics but continued to express his views on national issues. He died in 1932.

Lala Lajpat Rai

Lala Lajpat Rai was born in an Agrawal (trader) family in Punjab in 1885. His father was a teacher. Young Lajpat received his education at several places depending on where his father, Munshi Radha Krisna Azad, was posted. His mother Gulab Devi inculcated strong moral values in all children.

Lajpat joined the Government College at Lahore in 1880 to study Law. While in the College, he came in touch with the future freedom fighters like Lala Hans Raj and Pandit Guru Dutt. They became fast friends and joined the Arya Samaj movement. He passed his Vakilship examination in 1885 and started practicing Law at Hissar where some of his friends were also practicing.

While practicing law at Hissar, he participated in Arya Samaj activities and engaged himself in collecting fund for the Dayanand College. He was also an active member of the Indian National Congress. He shifted to Lahore in 1892.

Arya Samaj broke into two factions: the College faction wanted both English and Sanskrit to be taught in schools while the Gurukul faction wanted only Sanskrit, to the exclusion of English. Lala was with the College faction and ultimately succeeded in bringing the two factions together. Thus began the DAV college movement. He worked for the orphans and his services during the famine earned great respect and adoration for him. Famine stricken people fled to cities like Lahore. Lala gave them shelter in his own house. 1905 earthquake in Kangra district gave yet another opportunity to the Lala to serve the people.

He worked relentlessly against the partition of Bengal. Lala was arrested for creating turmoil in Rawalpindi in 1907 when he went there to protest against the arrest of five fellow lawyers. He was deported to Burma and lodged in Mandalay jail for six months.

He left for Britain in 1914 to campaign against the British Raj in India. When the World War I broke out in 1919, Lala ji was not allowed to return to India. He decided to go to the USA on the same mission. He founded the Indian Home League Society of America and wrote a book called 'Yong India' with a preface by Colonel Wedgewood, a member of British Parliament. It constituted the most damaging indictment of British Raj in India. He could return to India only after the War was over. He presided over the special session of Congress held at Calcutta in 1920.

Lalaji supported the Non-cooperation movement launched by Gandhi in 1921 against the Rowlatt Act. He was arrested in December 1921 and was imprisoned for a year and half. When the movement was withdrawn by Gandhiji, Lala again diverted his attention to social and educational activities. He moved a resolution in the Central Legislative Assembly in 1927 refusing cooperation to the Simon Commission. The resolution was passed. Lala joined the protest again the Commission. Police resorted to lathi charge to disperse the peaceful crowd. Lala was injured. He almost recovered from injuries but was so tormented by the cruelty of the British Raj that he passed away on November 17, 1928 of heart failure.

Shyamji Krishnavarma

Krishnavarma (1857-1930) was born in Gujarat and was a gifted linguist. He was brought to Oxford by Sir Monier Monier-Williams, a Sanskritist to assist him in translating Indian classics. He graduated in 1882 from Balliol College. A great admirer of Herbert Spencer, he was influenced by Russian Revolution and wanted India to be liberated like Russia. He instituted several scholarships to bring young Indians to England and train them in revolutionary activities. He was the founder of India House (1905) in which Gandhiji also stayed for some time in 1906. He published Indian Sociologist, which was dedicated to Herbert Spencer. Gandhi was in constant interaction with Krishnavarma until 1906. Thereafter it appears the relations cooled down and finally, ended, may be, on a sore note.

Krishanvarma was a genius. He was instrumental in promoting violent struggle against the British; he brought many a youth from India to England and Germany. Gandhiji was conversant with what Varma was doing. He tried to dissuade him from the path of violence but apparently without any success. But Gandhiji did appreciate the devotion and sacrifice of the revolutionaries. He considered such sacrifices wasteful. It were not the British who were responsible for India's subjugation; it was the western civilisation, which had mesmerized both the British and the Indians. The enemy was the British Raj, not the British people; then why violence against latter? Argued Gandhi.

Sri Aurobindo Ghosh

The fourth son of Kishnadham Ghosh and Swarnalata Ghosh, Aurobindo was born on August 15, 1872. His primary level education was completed at Loretto Convent School, Darjeeling and St. Pauls' in London. He passed the ICS examination but did not attend the interview. During his stay at Cambridge for bachelor's degree, he joined the India Majlis, a newly launched Organisation of Indian students. Among Aurobindo's contemporaries at Cambridge were Ferrers, Robert Pentland Mohaffy, Felix Zavier De Souza, K.G.

Deshpande and Sir Harisingh Gaur. He left Cambridge in 1893 and returned to India.

Aurobindo joined the state service of Baroda state. He was lecturer in a college; when he left Baroda after 13 years, he was the principal of the College. From his younger days, he was not particularly interested in creature comforts, he lived like a *Brahmacharin* and never kept account of the salary he received from Baroda state. He was a prolific reader and writer, apart from being a very good orator. He was at his best when the subject matter pertained to religion and philosophy. He was married to Mrinalini Bose at the age of 21.

During 1890s secret societies were being formed in India to wage war against the British. There was one in Maharashtra presided over by Thakur Ramsingh. Efforts were made in Bengal too but without much success. Aurobindo, on leave from Baroda, started a society at Deoghar under Satyen Bose. While he continued to be active in the revolutionary movement, he developed spiritual inclinations and engaged himself in *Sadhana*. "My own experience is that the brain becomes *Prakashamaya* – full of light. When I was practicing *Pranayama* at Baroda, I used to do it for five to six hours in the day, three hours in the morning and two hours in the evening. The mind worked with great illumination and power.... along with this enhanced mental activity, I could see an electric energy all round the brain."

In 1905 he wrote his famous letter to his wife asking her to go along with him even though people think of him as mad. He considered himself an uncommon man destined to do something great for the motherland. He wished his wife worked with him or at least followed him. "I have three madnesses. I firmly believe that the accomplishments, genius, higher education and learning and wealth that God has given me are His. I have a right to spend for my own purposes only what is needed for the maintenance of the family and is otherwise absolutely essential. The rest must be returned to God.... Hindu scriptures say that one who receives wealth from God and does not give it back to Him is a thief."

"My second madness is this. If God exists, there must be some way to experience His existence and to meet Him face to face. However arduous this path is, I have made up my mind to follow it.... Within a month (of practice) I have realized that what the Hindu religion says is not false. I am experiencing in myself the signs of which it speaks."

"My third madness is that while others look upon their country as an inert piece of matter – a few meadows and fields, forests and hills and rivers – I look upon my country as the Mother. I adore her, I worship her as the Mother. What a son would do if a demon sat on his mother's breast and started sucking her blood? Would he quietly sit down to his dinner, amuse himself with his wife and children, or would he rush out to deliver this fallen race. It is not physical strength – I am not going to fight with sword and gun but the strength of knowledge... God sent me to earth to accomplish this great mission."

Aurobindo became the first principal of National College, Calcutta in 1906. Same year he started *Bande Matram*, a newspaper. It called upon the youth to die for the motherland, oppose injustice, awaken manhood in the nation, punish treachery and perfidy against India. He attended the Calcutta session of the Indian National Congress in 1906 wherein a resolution laying down independence as the goal was passed. It was presided by Dadabhai Naoroji. The moderates – Sir Ferozshah Mehta, Surendranath Banerjee, and Gopal Krishna Gokhale – were opposed to the resolution. Dadabhai Naoroji even though a moderate went with the majority.

In 1906 Aurobindo went to Surat to attend the Congress session. There he met Sakhare Baba, a Maharashtrian Yogi who was intensely interested in the question of Indian independence. From Surat he went to Baroda to meet Yogi Vishnu Bhaskar Lele who promised to help him in his *sadhana*. *Bande Matram* office was searched in 1907. Aurobindo was one of the accused but was set free because of the paucity of evidence against him. His inclination towards Yoga and meditation grew and, as he says, an inner voice guided him in his *sadhana*. He did not need any guru or guide any longer.

In 1908 Khudiram Bose tried to kill Kingsford, the magistrate of Muzaffarpur. He was hanged. Aurobindo was not aware of this but he too was arrested and put in Alipur jail. He was finally acquitted and released in 1908. "My idea was an armed revolution in the whole of India. What they did at that time was very childish, killing a magistrate and so on. Later it turned into terrorism and dacoities which were not all my idea or intention, Bengal is too emotional, wants quick results and can't prepare through a long course of years. We wanted to give battle by creating a spirit in the race through guerilla warfare..." (Purani Evening Talks, III series, Sri Aurobindo Ashram).

Sri Aurobindo was by this time known as a revolutionary and his name was always linked to freedom struggle in the eastern part of India. In the mean time his interest in *yoga sadhana* grew and he decided to move down to Chandernagor, a French enclave near

Calcutta and from there he moved to Pondicherry near Madras. He reached Pondicherry in 1910. Mrinalini Devi, his wife died in 1918. In 1914, Mother from Paris met Sri Aurobindo and joined him in his search for divinity in 1920.

Sri Aurobindo left the revolutionary struggle (desire less work) for freedom of India and returned to his reliance on the use of spiritual force against the aggressor and had the satisfaction of seeing the tide of the Axis powers in the Second World War change into a tide of rapid crushing and finally overwhelming defeat. He also saw India becoming free on his 75th birthday on August 15, 1947. On that occasion he issued a statement:

"August 15, 1947 is the birthday of free India. It marks her the end of an old era, the beginning of a new age. But we can also make it by our life and acts as a free nation an important date in a new age opening for the whole world, for the political, social, cultural and spiritual future of humanity.

"August 15 is my own birthday and it is naturally gratifying to me that it should have assumed that vast significance. I take this coincidence, not as fortuitous accident, but as a sanction and seal of the Divine Force that guides my steps on the work with which I began life, the beginning of its full fruition. Indeed on this day, I can watch almost all the world movements, which I hope to see fulfilled in my life time, though then they looked like un-practicable dreams, arrival at fruition or on their way to achievement. In all these movements free India may well play a large part and take a leading position.

"The first of these dreams was a revolutionary movement, which would create a free and united India. India today is free but she has not achieved unity.... But by whatever means, in whatever way, the division must go; unity must and will be achieved, for it is necessary for the greatness of India's future.

"Another dream was for the resurgence and liberation of the people of Asia and her return to her great role in the process of human civilisation. Asia has arisen; large parts are now quite free or are at this moment being liberated; ...There India has her part to play and has begun to play it with an energy and ability, which already indicate the measure of her possibilities and the place she can take in the council of the nations.

"The third dream was a world union forming the outer basis of a fairer, brighter and nobler life for all mankind.... For unification is necessity of Nature, an inevitable movement. Its necessity for the nations is also clear, for without it the freedom of the small nations may be at any moment in peril and the life even of the large and powerful nations insecure.

"Another dream, the spiritual gift of India to the world has already begun. India's spirituality is entering Europe and America in an ever-increasing measure. That movement will grow; amid the disasters of the time more and more of eyes are turning towards her with hope and there is an even increasing resort not only to her teachings but to her psychic and spiritual practice.

"The final dream was a step in evolution which would raise man to a higher and larger consciousness and begin the solution of the problems, which have perplexed and vexed him since he first began to think and to dream of individual perfection and a perfect society. This is still a personal hope and an idea, an ideal, which has begun to take hold both in India and in the West on forward-looking minds. The difficulties in the way are more formidable than in any other field of endeavour, but the difficulties were made to overcome and if the Supreme will is there, they will be overcome. Here too, if this evolution is to take place, since it must proceed through a growth of the spirit and the inner consciousness, the initiative can come from India, although the scope must be universal, the central movement may be hers.

"Such is the content which I put into this date of India's liberation; whether or how far this hope will be justified depends upon the new and free India."

Veer Savarkar

Among the many follower of Krishnavarma was Savarkar (1883-1960) who was sent to London by Tilak. Savarkar was deported to Andaman's in 1910 in connection with Willie's assassination by Madan Lal Dhingra. While in London he translated Mazzini's Life (from English to Marathi) and wrote Indian War of Independence in Marathi. Gandhiji did interact with Savarkar but they did not share each other's views and ultimately agreed to disagree and parted company)

Savarkar was the first Indian leader to call for Swadeshi and the first one to perform a bone fire of foreign clothes in 1906. Even before Tilak proclaimed *Swaraj* as 'our birth right', Savarkar demanded absolute political independence for India. Bombay University took away his bachelor degree in 1911 for his political views (it was restored in 1966). He also lost his law degree for the same reason. He was the first to declare the so-called Sepoy Mutiny of 1857 as the first war of Independence in his book 'War of

Independence of 1857 which was proscribed both by the Governments of India and Britain. He refused to recognize the authority of the British law. His arrest and deportation was contested in the International Court of Justice, at the Hague. He was the first political prisoner who was deported for 50 years.

Savarkar composed poems on prison walls with pebbles and thorns and remembered over 10,000 lines of his poems until they reached India through the words of mouth. He designed the first Indian flag, which was unfurled in Stuttgart International Socialist Congress in 1857 by Madam Cama. He built a temple where the priest was an untouchable. He was the president of Marathi Sahitya Parishad and was honoured by Sikh Gurdwara Pabandhak Committee (SGPC).

Savarkar was a rebel and revolutionary; he was not a Hindu fanatic, nor did he believe in fads associated with Hinduism. He fought Hindu Orthodoxy because it came in the way India's regeneration as a great modern nation. He never subscribed to the idea of cow being sacred; he called it a useful animal. He advocated one man one vote and opposed any political weightage for the Muslims. He was also totally opposed to religious conversion. But he was all for making India militarily strong so as to successfully face aggressors from abroad.

Unlike Gandhi, Savarkar welcomed mechanization and wanted India to develop and possess superior weapons of war to defend itself. On violent revolution, he said in 1909: 'whenever the natural process of national and political evolution is violently suppressed by the forces of wrong, then revolution must step in as a natural reaction and therefore, ought to be welcomed as the only effective instrument to re-enthrone Truth and Right. You (British) rule by bayonets and under these circumstances it is a mockery to talk of constitutional agitation when no constitution exists at all. But it would be worse than a mockery, even a crime, when there is a constitution that allows fullest and freest development of a nation. Only because you (British) deny us a gun, we pick up a pistol. Only because you deny us light, we gather in darkness to compass means to knock out the fetters that hold our Mother down.'

Savarkar breathed his last on February 26, 1966. For about 22 days before his death he stopped eating anything and lived on just a few spoonfuls of water daily. Among the many tributes paid on his death, four of them deserve to be reproduced here.

Savarkar was a national hero, a symbol of courage, bravery and patriotism, an 'abhitirth' in the long battle for freedom.

— Rajagopalachari

Savarkar was a great figure of Contemporary India and his name is byword for daring and patriotism. He was cast in a mould of a classic revolutionary and countless people drew inspiration from him.

—Indira Gandhi

'Savarkar was a great patriot and an illustrious son of India; anyone living in this country who loved and drew inspiration from the great heritage of India and was loyal to India was a Hindu. Revolutionaries like Savarkar created an atmosphere, which made it possible for Mahatma Gandhi to succeed. It would be unpatriotic if the people of India failed to give Savarkar a prominent place in the history of India.'

—M.C. Chagla

Gandhi did not approve of Savarkar's approach to ousting the British from India but he had a great influence on his thoughts.

—Madam Bhikhaji Cama

Others

Among the other persons subscribing to revolutionary approaches to Indian Independence were V. Chattopadhyay (1880-1930) and Taraknath Das (1884-1958). The former was the brother of Sarojini Naidu. He edited *Talwar*, a monthly journal and lived in Germany and USSR. He was an active member of the communist party but was killed apparently for anti-party activities by Soviet Union's firing squad sometimes in 1937-40.

Taraknath Das (1884-1958) was a member of Bengal Secret Society (Anushilan Samiti). He was based on the west coast of the USA (usually San Fransisco). He published a magazine called *Free Hindustan*. He was also Spencer's follower. The famous letter of Tolstoy to a Hindu was addressed to him.

Madam Bhikaji Rustom Cama was born in 1861 and died in 1936. She was based in Paris. Cama was a pioneer in Indian women in politics. Along with Hardayal, she revived Bande Matram, earlier edited by Sri Aurobindo and banned by the Government of India. In 1907 she moved a resolution in the Stuttgard Congress of the Socialists demanding *Swaraj* for India. The resolution was seconded by Comrade HM Hyndman, a British Marxist.

8

Contemporary Social Reforms and Intellectuals

Gandhi was influenced by the Indians who excelled in different walks of life, other than politics. Even though he lived in South Africa and was deeply involved in securing the rights of Indians there, he appears to have considered his South African sojourn and his rebirth as a Satyagrahi only as a prelude to and preparation for his entry into public life in India. He kept in touch with what was going in India. To be relevant to India of early twentieth century, he picked up threads from the leading figures of the time working in field like social change, art, science and literature and weaved a socio-political fabric, which was traditional yet modern, religious yet secular, nonviolent yet militant and local yet global.

This chapter gives some biographical details of some of the social reformers, educationists, scientists, poets, writers and artist whose works influenced Gandhi. It is hoped that the chapter would benefit those who are not conversant with the life and work of these contemporaries of Gandhi. Let it be clear to the reader that only a select few who influenced Gandhi in shaping his vision of India on his return from South Africa in 1914 have been discussed.

SOCIAL REFORMERS

Mahadev Govind Ranade

Born in 1841, Justice Ranade studied at Elphinstone College in Bombay and became a teacher and journalist. He questioned the beliefs and customs of the then Hindu society and became an active reformer. In 1869 he joined the Widow Remarriage Association and in 1870 the Prarthana Samaj. To begin with, he launched an intellectual tirade against superficial dogma unsuited to a great civilisation like that of India. Later he became a social activist.

He was appointed a judge in Poona where he joined a group of very committed social reformers. Soon after becoming a judge, he lost his wife. He was keen to marry a widow but his father, knowing the mind of his young son, selected a suitable girl in great hurry and despite his protests he was married to Ramabai Ranade who later became one of the great social reformers of India.

In the later part of his life he tried to bring a compromise between the radical reformers and traditionalists and focused on widow remarriage, female education and child marriage. His greatest contribution is the building up of National Social Conference (1887) to spearhead the social change movement in the country. He believed that in ancient India women enjoyed a very important position and that they must regain that position once again. He also argued that revolutionary change was inherently Indian and no outside force can change the situation.

He hoped to see Indian society moving from constraints to freedom and credibility to faith; from unorganized to organized life and from bigotry to tolerance and from blind faith and fatalism to a sense of human destiny. He warned his critics that not to change would be suicidal for Indian society.

Ranade recommended four methods to accomplish social change:

(1) using arguments with examples from *shashtras* and oral traditions,
(2) using morality as the standard measure for all actions,
(3) using legal means, and
(4) if nothing works, inciting social rebellion.

At the second annual meet of the National Social Conference (1889) over 500 persons pledged to support widow marriage and female education

Ranade played an important role in building up of the Indian National Congress. He died in 1901. Gandhiji used to get all the information about Ranade's activities in South Africa.

Mahatma Jyotiba Phule

Jyotiba Govind Phule (1827-1890) was born in Poona in a family of gardeners, which supplied flowers to the Peshwas. His early life was not a smooth one but taking inspiration from both Indian and American leaders, he became a prolific writer and one of greatest social reformers of the nineteenth century in India. He wrote both in Marathi and English. His well-known book *Gulamgiri* (slavery) was published in 1872.

Phule's was concerned with the fate of the lower middle and lower castes and the women in India and incessantly fought for their emancipation. He believed that Brahmins domination of the Hindu society was the major cause of the social ills in India. He opened a school for non-Brahmin girls in 1848 where his wife became a teacher. Later he opened more schools and libraries for the non-Brahmins. He also opened orphanage for the children of Brahmin widows who were not allowed to remarry.

Phule worked as part-time teacher in a Scottish Mission School and raised funds from Christians and was very favourably disposed to the British rule in India because it helped low caste people to get out of the shackles of the Hindu caste system. He wanted free education for all up to the age of 12, advocated vocational and technical education, and demanded change in the Hindu marriage rules to dispense with Brahmin priests.

In 1873, he formed an association for human rights and social justice. Phule received recognition for the social work he was engaged in and became an inspiration for many a leader like Dr. Bhimrao Ambedkar to carry forward the movement he had launched.

Periyar E.V. Ramaswamy

Periyar E.V. affectionately called Thanthai Periyar played a major role in changing the social structure of the southern states in general and Tamil Nadu in particular. To begin with, he was an ardent follower of Mahatma Gandhi and a member of the Congress party. He was even the president of the Madras Presidency branch of the Indian National Congress. Later Periyar parted company with Congress. He felt that the party was dominated by the Brahmins who in his opinion always worked against the interests of the non-Brahmins. Periyar discarded Khadi and adopted black dress. Even after leaving Congress, he continued to be a very good friend of Rajaji, a staunch Congressman at that time.

Periyar sided with the Justice party and worked against the Congress party, Gandhi and Rajaji. Later the justice party was reorganized as DK (Dravida Karzhagam) party, the parent body of many Dravidian parties in Tamil Nadu.

According to Periyar:

(1) there was no God and those who believed in God were barbarians;
(2) people were swindled by the Brahmins in the name of God; and
(3) DK party alone could bring social change and create a casteless society.

Till his death he worked hard to protect the interests of the depressed classes and for the welfare of the non-Brahmins. He died at the ripe age of 94. Like Gandhi, he published articles in his party organ *Kudiyarasu*. Karunanidhi the president of the DMK was the editor of the journal.

Periyar never compromised his ideology for the sake of power. He called DK a social reforms party and did not participate in electoral politics. He did, however, supported one party or the other during elections.

He donated his property to a Trust to carry forward his mission through DK. After his death his wife headed the trust and the party. The party gradually disintegrated but his mission is still alive even if in a weakened form.

EDUCATIONISTS

Madan Mohan Malaviya

Born at Allahabad in 1861, Madan Mohan Malviya was a contemporary of Gandhi. He was educated in Muir Central College (now part of Allahabad University) graduating in 1884. He became a teacher and editor of Hindi weekly *Hindustan* at Allahabad. He did his graduation in law 1891 but he did not opt for the legal profession.

Malviya ji was closely associated with the Indian National Congress; he attended most of the annual meetings of the party. He invited the Congress to hold its sessions in Allahabad in 1887 and 1892. He was elected president of the party four times (1909, 1918, 1932 and 1933). Despite being a strong supporter of the Congress, he founded Hindu Mahasabha in 1906 to oppose the 'divide and rule' policy of the British government. We all know his role as an educationist: he founded the Banaras Hindu University. He was thus a multi-faceted personality and therefore, to put him in any specific group or category is difficult.

Realizing the role of print media in arousing nationalistic feelings and in ventilating people's grievances, he started a Hindi weekly called *Abhydaya* in 1907, which became a daily in 1915. He also started Leader, an English daily from Allahabad and quite a few monthly journals and magazines. He was the chairman of the board of directors of the *Hindustan Times*. He was elected member of the UP Legislative Council in 1902 and of the Imperial Legislative Council in 1909. He vehemently supported compulsory primary education, stopping of export of indentured labour to South Africa and elsewhere, nationalization of railways, industrialization of the country, etc. He joined the non-cooperation movement started by Gandhiji and refused to seek the election to the Imperial Legislative Assembly in 1921.

Banaras Hindu University is the greatest contribution of Malviyaji. Here he combined the teaching of Arts and Sciences and brought together all the disciplines in a sprawling campus along the Ganga. Malaviya was a great reformer; he wanted to take all sections of the society including the Pandits of Benaras who had a firm faith in Varnashrama dharma with him. He was totally against untouchability and injustice done to women.

Mahamana Malviya as he was reverentially called in the later part of his life occupied a very high position in Indian public life and was a great support to Gandhiji in his movements against social evils and British Raj. His public activities were numerous. Apart from freedom struggle, he advocated rapid economic development of the country through agricultural improvements and industrialization, improvement in the position of Hindi language, women, and Harijans, *i.e.* the untouchables. On some issues he, however, differed with Gandhi. He did not like the boycott of schools and colleges, nor did he like the burning of foreign clothes. He was also opposed to the boycott of the visit of Prince of Wales in 1921. He considered responsive cooperation better than civil disobedience. Yet the relations between the Mahatma and the Mahamana remained cordial and understanding.

Sir Syed Ahmed Khan

Sir Syed Ahmed Khan was born at Delhi on October 17, 1817; he died on March 27, 1898 at Aligarh. An author, jurist and educator, he founded the Mohammedan Anglo Oriental College at Aligarh which later became Aligarh Muslim University. He came from a family, which had been close to the then British administration. His father received an allowance from the Moghul administration. His maternal grand-father had twice served as Prime Minister of the Moghul emperor of the time and had also occupied position of trust in the East India Company. His brother has started a printing press in Delhi and one of the earliest Urdu newspapers.

After his father's death, the family found itself in financial crisis. Young Syed joined the East India Company as a clerk in 1838 and three years later qualified to become a sub-judge. His first major book, *Ahar Assanadid* (Monuments of the Great) giving the antiquities of Delhi was published in 1847. His pamphlet, *The Causes of the Indian Revolt,* was widely read by both Indians and the British. It pointed out the shortcomings of the British administration, which led to the revolt.

Realizing that education alone could help the Muslims of India get out of the ghetto mentality, he started schools in Moradabad (1858) and Ghazipur (1863). He set up a Scientific Society, which published translations of many educational texts and issued bilingual journals in Urdu and English. During a visit to England in 1869-70, he prepared plans of 'a Muslim Cambridge'. A Muslim School was established at Aligarh in 1875 and it was upgraded as Mohammedan Anglo-Oriental College in 1877.

Sir Syed wanted Hindus and Muslims to have parity in jobs. So he planned to develop the college into a university. He was the founding father of the Two Nation Theory. He was a staunch patriot and generous person and if one studies him carefully, his idea in the early stages of his life was not to partition India into two different countries.

'I look to both Hindus and Muslims with the same eyes and consider them as my own eyes. We Hindus and Muslims live together under the same soil and under the same government. Our interests and problems are common, and therefore I consider the two factions as one nation.' The membership of British Indian Association he formed in 1886 was open to both Hindus and Muslims. But he later felt that the Congress party was working against the interests of the

Muslims. Congress he felt was so functioning that under their rule Muslims would be eliminated as a nation.

He felt hurt when in 1876 Hindus launched a movement to replace Urdu with Hindi as the official language. Speaking at Benaras, he said, 'I am now convinced that the Hindus and the Muslims, as their religion and way of life was quite distinct from one another, could never become one nation'. And added 'now I am convinced that these communities (Hindus and Muslims) will not join wholeheartedly in anything. At present there is no open hostility between the two communities but it will increase immensely in the future. And thus he became the prophet of the well-known Two-Nation Theory, which led to the division of India in 1947 into Secular India and Islamic Pakistan. The partition lead to communal riots which took lives of over a million Hindus and Muslims; it left behind more Muslims in India than in Pakistan and thus nullifying the apprehensions of Sir Syed that Hindus would wipe out the Muslims if they lived in united India. Yet another crushing blow to the Two-Nation Theory occurred in 1971 when East Pakistan separated from West Pakistan not because of two different religions but because of two different cultures)

LITTERATEURS

Bankim Chandra Chatterjee

Bankim Chandra Chattopadhyay (1838-1894) was among the first graduates of Calcutta University. He served as an official of Indian Civil Service from 1858 to 1891. He was a great literary figure of his time. He wrote the first novel in Bengali language. Initially he wrote novels in English. His first fiction to be published was *Rajmohan's Wife*. *Durgeshnandini*, a historical romance published in 1865 made him famous. Important among his novels were: *Rajani* (1877), *Krishnakanter Uil* (1878), *Rajsimha* (1881), *Kapalkundala* (1886), *Anandmath* (1882), and *Sitaram* (1886). Despite their shortcomings, they were highly popular and had a considerable influence on Bengali and later other Indian language literature.

He founded *Bangadarshan,* a Bengali monthly in 1872 in which some of his later novels were serialized. Bankims novels weaved stories around romances with common household themes laying emphasis on traditional morality.

Anandmath is not so much famous as a novel as an harbinger of patriotism. It gave to India its national song: *Bande Matram* (I worship Mother India). It became a rallying point for many a young man who sacrificed himself so that India became free from the British rule, in the first decade of the twentieth century. Many of the young men whom Gandhi met in London before he wrote *Hind Swaraj* were highly surcharged by patriotism and were ready to teach the British a bitter lesson.

Rabindranath Tagore

Born on May 6, 1861 at Kolkata, Rabindranath Tagore was a towering and epochal figure in India whose influence extended beyond the country of his birth. He was a multifaceted genius whose impact on Indian renaissance was indeed great. He synthesized several great movements of the nineteenth and early twentieth century that triggered what we may call Indian renaissance: Brahmo Samaj, started by Raja Ram Mohun Roy, Arya Samaj launched by Swami Dayanand Saraswati; cultural revival set in motion by Swami Vivekanand; educational reform started by Pandit Ishwar Chandra Vidyasagar, intellectual resurgence created by Madhusudan Dutt and Bankim Chandra Chatterjee. He was the first Asian to receive Nobel Prize for Literature. A poet, author, composer of songs, artist, educator and ardent advocate of human brotherhood, Tagore was a true representative of what Indian culture and civilisation stand for.

He was the youngest of the fourteen brothers and sisters. His father, Debendranath Tagore was a Sanskrit scholar and a leading member of the Brahmo Samaj established by the great social reformer of the eighteenth century, Raja Ram Mohun Roy. His early education was completed at home. In school his interest in lessons was minimal. Often he used to get absorbed in the dreams of his own creation. He was born poet. His first poem appeared when he was just seven years old. His first book of poems was published when he was seventeen.

In 1878 he went to England for further studies but returned empty handed as he did not find the studies interesting. Rest of his life was engaged in writing poems, melodious songs, novels, short stories, plays and essays on topics ranging from literary to social issues. He also wrote travelogues and books for children. The bulk of his work was in Bengali. *Geetanjali*, which fetched Nobel Prize for literature in 1913 was translated in English by Tagore himself. He passed away on August 7, 1941.

Tagore was a contemporary of Gandhi; they admired each other but at times differed too. They never were misunderstood by each other though. The prefix 'Mahatma' was the gift of Tagore as the suffix 'Father of the Nation' was that of Subhas Chandra Bose. Tagore called Gandhi 'a Mahatma in Peasant's garb'. Tagore was a great support for Gandhi. His personality comes out clearly from the quotation from Leonard Gordon's book *Brothers Against the Raj: Biography of Subhas* and *Subhas Chandra Bose.*

"Tagore was never in full agreement with any of the political leaders, though in the last decade of his life, he was sympathetic to the approach of Jawaharlal Nehru. Tagore never entered politics quite so directly after his disillusionment with *Swadeshi*. He remained, however, a frequent and penetrating commentator on the development of the movement and his relinquishment of his knighthood after the Jalianwalla Bagh incident in 1919 was widely applauded in India. Certainly from the year of his Nobel Prize, 1913, Tagore stressed his international concerns and shrewdly denounced the excesses of nationalism not only in India, but also in Japan, China and the West.

In October 1921, Tagore published his first major essay on Gandhi and Non-coopration, *The Call of Truth*, which argued that truth was of both the head and the heart; while Gandhi stressed inner truth and love, he was fostering blind, unquestioning obedience to his message of *Charkha* by one and all. Tagore wanted Indian economists and leaders to fully investigate whether this made any economic sense. Tagore had his doubts and he resented that all were told to simply 'spin and weave'.

Tagore also objected to the burning of foreign cloth because it was foreign.... Like Gandhi Tagore believed that inner *Swaraj* and cultivation of the Self were vital and some aspects of Gandhi's constructive programme were not foreign to the oft repeated teachings of village reconstruction and paths to Indian revitalizaion, which Tagore had put forward."

Gandhi and Tagore differed on Subhas Chandra Bose's election as president of the Indian National Congress. But one thing on which they both agreed wholeheartedly was nonviolence. Tagore was totally against the use of force against individuals, groups, races, and countries. They had tremendous respect and affection for each other.

Mohammad Allamah Iqbal

Sir Mohammad Allamah Iqbal (1873-1938), was erudite scholar, poet and philosopher. He is regarded as the spiritual founder of Pakistan even though his poem *Sare jahan se achha Hindostan hamara, ham bulbele hain iski ye gulistan hamara* (Our India is the best land in the world; we are its bulbuls and it is our garden) is still considered in India as one of the best patriotic songs. He was born in Sialkot now in Pakistan and was a scholar of Arabic, Persian and Urdu.

He taught English and philosophy in Islamia College and Government College at Lahore from 1901-1905. From 1905 to 1908 he was in Europe at the universities of London, Cambridge and Munich. He qualified as a barrister and earned Ph.D. degree.

On his return, he taught at the Government College Lahore, practiced law and wrote poetry. He became famous after the publication of his Persian poem called Secrets of the Self in 1915. A follow up volume Mysteries of Selflessness was published, only after his death, in 1953. These poems called on Muslims to practice self-sacrifice in the interest of botherhood and justice for the greater good of others. His masterpiece *Baan-e-Darra* (Song of Eternity) was published in 1932.

His political thoughts underwent change after his return from Europe. Earlier he was an ardent nationalist and believed that all those who lived in geographical India formed one nation. His poem *Sare Jahan Se Achchha Hindostan Hamara* (No land is better than India in the world) is still sung in India. But his views changed and he started propagating nationalism based on race, religion and culture. And thus emerged the two-nation theory, which culminated in the partition of India in 1947. In fact Iqbal went a step further and advocated Muslim Brotherhood extending beyond national boundaries.

In 1930, he addressed the Allahabad session of the Muslim League as its president and the urged the Muslims of the north and western provinces to demand independence from both Britain and India and work for the creation of Pakistan (Nation of the Pure). Two years after he died in 1938, Muslim League voted in favour of Pakistan. Iqbal the universalist who sang the song of one God and one humanity, died as a representative of Muslims and Muslim God.

The fate did not favour the grand design of Iqbal; the Nation of the Pure has not yet seen a government that truly represents those who created it. Gandhi stood for Hindu-Muslim unity; he worked for a nation, which was united by geography, race and culture. Iqbal worked for a nation, which was united by Islam. Gandhi proved right when Pakistan was divided in 1971 to form a new nation called Bangladesh based on culture and geography, not religion.

SCIENTISTS

Sir Jagadish Chandra Bose

Born on November 30, 1858 in Bikrampur village near Dhaka, Jagdish Chandra Bose's father Babu Bhagawan Chandra Bose was Deputy Magistrate of Faridpur district in Bengal. He was a very popular person always helping the poor and needy. He tried to spread education both among the poor and women. The family being religious in temperament, Jagdish became well versed in stories of *Ramayana* and *Mahabharata*.

Jagdish was very fond of nature; he loved plants and animals. He used to go to the bank of the river and see the fishermen catching fish and telling all shorts of stories about the depth of the river and monsters living therein. At the age of nine he had to leave his home to join St. Xavier School at Calcutta. While in the boarding house, his interest in nature did not wane; he grew some flower bearing plants to study their root system and kept some frogs and fishes to study their behaviour. His main subject was physics but he was more interested in botany. He received his BA honors degree in 1877.

He went to England for higher studies in 1880. On return from England with B.Sc. Honors in Physics from London University and BA in Natural Sciences from Cambridge University, he was appointed professor of physical sciences at the Presidency College, Calcutta. London University honourned him with Doctorate and Cambridge with MA degrees.

Sages in India from times immemorial believed that plants had life but it was for Jagdish Chandra Bose an imminent scientist to prove that they had life and feelings as other life forms had. His other contributions were in the field of radio physics and optics. He also established the first indigenous research institute in India: Bose Vigyan Mandir (Bose Research Institute) in Calcutta.

Bose worked under very adverse co0nditions and proved that Indians could advance the frontiers of knowledge as well or even better than others. Even though Nobel prize for the invention of telegraphy went to Marconi, Bose is credited to have been the first inventor. He died in 1937 at Giridih, then in Bihar.

Sir C.V. Raman

Chandrasekhar Venkata Raman or CVR as he was popularly known was born in 1888 in Tamil Nadu. He was a brilliant student. After acquiring his bachelor degree from Madras Presidency College, he did his MSc. in 1907. Due health reasons he could not go to England for further studies, nor could he appear in Indian Civil Service Examination as at that time the examination was held in England.

He accepted the Palit chair in Physics at the University of Calcutta in 1917. Raman had a special interest in optics of colloids and the physiology of the human vision. He studied the structure and properties of diamonds and the structure and optical behaviour iridescent substances such as agate and pearls. He was honoured with Nobel Prize in Physics in 1930 for the discovery of Raman Effect. Raman too proved that Indians were second to none in inventing and discovering new theories, principles, tools and techniques even in adverse educational and research conditions.

SPIRITUAL LEADERS

Swami Vivekananda

No single Indian has done more to acquaint the West with Indian philosophy and religion than Swami Vivekananda. His life was totally dedicated to unraveling the hidden secrets of Indian culture and propagating the same in the western world, which was so ignorant about it. It was said that he was the reincarnation of German scholar Max Muller.

Vivekananda was born in Calcutta in 1863. His father's name was Vishwanath Dutta. His name was Bireshwar but his parents lovingly called him Biley. He was like any active and alert child. When Biley grew up he was given the name of Narendra Nath. From his early age he had great faith in God. Narendra had the opportunity of singing before Sri Ramakrshna Paramhansa at one his friend's house. Ramakrshna appreciated his song. Then onwards he got attracted to him and used to meet him from time to time at Dakshineswar.

Soon he became his disciple. Sri Ramakrishna passed away in 1899. Narendra Nath took *Sanyas* soon after.

Swami Vivekananda went on a tour of India to acquaint himself with the real condition of the country. He was pained to see the poverty of the masses. He was distressed to see children not getting the opportunity to go to school and sick people having no access to hospitals, doctors and medicines. At Kanyakumari he meditated and told his disciples at Madras that 'India was like a person who had been asleep for hundreds of years. Our people have lost faith in them selves. He would go away to far off lands and bring that faith in them again. Now I go but when I return I shall awaken the sleeping millions of my people.'

A Parliament of Religions was going to be held at Chicago in the USA in 1893. Swami ji decided to go there. 'I will go there. I will tell them about the ancient religion of India. I will tell them what I know, and I will learn from them the things they know'. He sailed for the USA on May 31, 1893. While addressing the delegates of the conference he said:

"I am proud to belong to a religion which has taught the world both tolerance and universal acceptance. We believe not only in universal toleration, but we accept all religions as true. I am proud to belong to a nation, which has sheltered the prosecuted and the refugees of all religions and all nations of the earth. I am proud to tell you that we have gathered in our bosom the purest remnants of Israelites, who came to Southern India and took refuge with us in the very year in which their holy temple was shattered to pieces by the Roman tyranny. I am proud to belong to a religion, which has sheltered and is still fostering the remnants of the grand Zoroastrian nation. I will quote to you, brethren, a few lines from a hymn, which is everyday repeated by millions of human beings. 'As the different streams having their sources in different places all mingle their water in the sea, so, O Lord, the different paths which men take through different tendencies, various though they appear, crooked or straight, all lead to thee.' "

"If the Parliament of Religions has shown anything to the world it is this: it has proved to the world that holiness, purity and charity are not the exclusive possessions of any church in the world, and that every system has produced men and women of the most exalted character. In the face of this evidence, if any body dreams of the exclusive survival of his own religion and the destruction of others, I pity him from the bottom of my heart, and point out to him that upon the banner of every religion will soon be written, in spite of resistance: 'Help and not Fight.', 'Assimilation and not Destruction', 'Harmony and Peace and not Dissension'.

Elsewhere in the USA he said, "That is a glorious thing that there should be so many paths, because if there were only one path, perhaps it would suit only an individual man. The more the number of paths the more the chances for everyone of us to know the truth. If I cannot be taught in one language, I will try another." Thus his benediction was for every religion.

Swami Vivekananda told his disciples to go beyond the self and work for others. 'What is the good of that spiritual practice or realisation which does not benefit others, does not conduce to the wellbeing of the people sunk in ignorance and delusion, does not help securing them from the clutches of lust and wealth? Do you think, so long as one *Jiva* endures in bondage, you will have any liberation? ...Every *Jiva* is part of yourself—which is the rationale of all works for others. As you desire the wholehearted good of your wife and children, knowing them to be your own, so when a like amount of love and attraction for every Jiva will awaken in you, then I shall know that Brahman is awakening in you. Not a moment before. When this feeling of all round good of all without respect to caste or colour will awaken in your heart, then I shall know you are advancing towards the ideal. Elsewhere he tells his *Sanyasins*: 'See how simple they (the poor people who came to Belur Matha) were. Can you mitigate their misery a little? Otherwise, of what good the wearing of the *Gerua* robe? Sacrifice of everything for the good of others is the real *Sanyas*. Sometimes I feel a desire to sell the Math and everything, and distribute the money to the poor and destitute.... Seeing the poor people of our country starving for food, a desire comes to me to overthrow all ceremonial worship and learning, and go round the village to village collecting money from the rich by convincing them through force of character and *Sadhana*, and to spend the whole life in serving the poor.'

Swami ji passed away on July 4, 1902. He was then only 40 years old. If we have to sum up his teachings in a few words, 'God is present in every *Jiva*. There is no other God besides that. Who serves *Jiva* serves God indeed.' The whole world is one family. And the future of this family lies in a new civilisation rooted in the principles of Vedanta.

To this end he gave a clarion call to the people of the world:

Uttishthat jagrat prapyavarannnibodhat
Arise! Awake! And Stop Not Till The Goal Is Reached.

— Kathopanishad

To manifest the divinity, which is in man, is the ultimate goal of human life. Says Vivekananda.

The concept of God that Gandhji's arrived at (Truth is God) is so close to Swami's thinking. Gandhiji's and Swamiji's views on western civilisation are similar and so are those on the potentials of Indian civilisation to usher in peace and harmony. Gandhiji must have heard about Swami ji's activities both in India and abroad.

Annie Besant

Annie Besant was a British by origin but she was more Indian than many Indians. She gave her entire life to the service and propagation of Indian culture. Born in 1847 in a middle class family of very modest means in England, her father died when she was barely five. Her mother could not meet the expenses of even her early education. At 19, she married young Rev. Frank Besant. They had a daughter and son within four years of marriage.

Realizing that religious service alone was not enough to alleviate poverty and suffering, she stopped attending the communion. This made her husband force her out of the home. She started living with her daughter in London and soon broke away from Christianity. She became a freethinker and atheist and in 1874 joined the Secular Society. She also worked for the radical paper *National Reformer* with its editor Charles Bradlaugh. They jointly wrote a book advocating birth control. They were imprisoned for 6 months for 'obscene libel'. She wrote another book entitled *The Laws of Population*. This time her husband claimed her daughter on the ground that it was not ethically safe for her to live with Annie.

Her life began in hardship and she lived much of her early life in hardship. Left alone to shape her future, Besant's journey was incredibly eventful. She took up the job of a governess. This enabled her to support her children and ailing mother. It was during this period that she was influenced by proactive atheist Charles Bradlaugh.

During 1880s Annie continued to write against Christianity and the unhealthy conditions in which the poor mill workers particularly the women workers had to live. She earned a science degree from London University. In 1887, she met Madame Blavatsky who in 1875 had founded the Theosophical Society and became a theosophist. After Madame Blavotsky's death in 1891, she took charge of the main faction of the Society.

Annie Besant moved to India to study Hindu religion in general and Vedanta in particular. She developed keen interest in the theory of Karma, reincarnation and nirvana. She also came closer to the vegetarian movement. She often returned to England to speak on women's suffrage. Her daughter lived with her in India. She died in 1933 in India which she considered to be her real home.

In India Annie lived like Indians. She wore saries, abandoned almost all furniture and ate vegetarian meals on leaves (instead of plates). She was so much in love with India and its civilisation and she spoke so movingly on the future of India that the huge audience that gathered to listen her was moved to tears. She spoke of compassion to all living things and considered European worldview and mindset as the greatest enemy of the world.

Annie was popularly known as Dr. Besant even though she never practiced medicine. She did not have Ph.D. degree either. She was also called Annie Militant even though she advocated passive resistance. She was also called 'mother' because her love and compassion was all embracing. She was a ferocious mind, championing the movements for India's self-government, Women's suffrage. George Bernard Shaw once said 'she is the greatest orator in England, and possibly in Europe'.

She struggled all through her life for Truth. "That one loyalty to Truth I must keep stainless, whatever friendships fail me or human ties be broken. She may lead me into the wilderness, yet I must follow her." And she did succeed in her mission, admirably. When she lost her control over the Theosophical Society, Mahatma Gandhi wrote "I wish to express my admiration for this long record of service, and the amazing energy and courage that lay behind it. I cannot forget, though it is many years ago, the inspiration I drew from her in my boyhood and then again in my experiences of political activity."

"Never forget that life can only be nobly inspired and rightly lived if you take it bravely and gallantly, as a splendid adventure in which you are setting out into an unknown country, to meet many a joy, to find many a comrade, to win and lose many a battle."

She passed away in 1933.

Raman Maharshi

Raman Maharshi was born in 1879 as Venkataraman Iyer in the village of *Tiruchili* in Tamilnadu. He lived with his uncle in Madurai after his father's death in 1991. He was religious minded person from his younger days. His life took a drastic turn when he was about sixteen years old. A powerful fear of dying suddenly attacked Raman, but instead of trying an escape from it, he faced it boldly and tried to investigate it. He laid still as a corpse and distanced himself from the body and mind pretending to be as dead as possible. He entered the condition of silent Beingness and from thereon knew himself as pure Awareness. All fear of death vanished from him.

After this event Raman Maharshi lost all interest in household life and ascended the Arunachalamalai (Arunachala Holy Hill) about 187 kilometres from Chennai. He advised the people to know themselves by meditating on Who Am I? Countless people who went to the Hill during the life-time of the Maharshi had the feeling of being uplifted to a world which gave Ananda – supreme spiritual bliss. They saw in him a sage who was totally removed from worldly things and feelings. He was a saint of matchless purity and a true witness to the eternal Vedanta. The Maharshi recommended concentration on 'I' or the meditation on 'who am I?' as the short-cut to the realization of the Self.

His life revolved round the message of compassion. He talked to the people at their own level; he would patiently talk to the children and painstakingly bind their torn books. He loved animals. It is said that leopards, dogs, cows, monkeys, snakes, squirrels. peacocks, and other birds used to gravitate towards him. Gently he would ask the leopard to sort out the problems between two quarrelling monkeys and remain unperturbed while a snake slithered over his legs.

He believed that Consciousness or Soul existed in all life forms, he respected even plants; he called trees 'standing men' and human beings as 'walking men'. He admonished a woman devotee for plucking *tulsi* (basil) leaves. "If you cannot get the leaves why not pinch yourself and do the *puja*? If it pains you to pinch your own body, is it not painful for the tree when you pluck the leaves."

Thousands of people from all over the world visited him and received his blessings but he never recognized any one as his disciple. He insisted that Consciousness alone is the teacher and *guru*. Seated in silence, he would suddenly fix his eyes on some one and that one would become directly aware of his own nature.

Paul Brunton describes his experience with Maharshi thus: "Maharshi turned and looked into my face, I, in turn gazed expectantly at him. I became aware of a mysterious change taking place with great rapidity in my heart and mind. Old motives which have lured me on, begin to desert me. The urgent desires, which have sent my feet hither and thither, vanish with incredible swiftness. The dislike, misunderstandings, coldness and selfishness, which have marked my dealings with many of my fellows, collapse into the abyss of nothingness. An untellable peace falls upon me and I know now there is nothing further that I shall ask from life."

"When the mind unceasingly investigates its own nature, it transpires that there is no such thing as a mind. Get rid of the 'I' thought. When I cease to exist, there is no grief and there is peace." His teaching is best exemplified not just in the way he lived, but especially in his death. In 1949 at the age of 70, a tumor was discovered below his left elbow. This was operated several times without anesthesia. Being malignant, the tumor grew at an amazing pace. When devotees begged him to cure it with his yogic powers, the Maharshi replied: 'Who is there to have such a thought? Who is there to will this?" Through suffering great pain, he sought to alleviate the grief of the devotees – not the easy way by removing suffering and postponing death, but fundamentally by making them realize that the body was not Maharshi. "They take the body for Bhagavan and attribute suffering to him. What a pity! They are despondent that Bhagavan is going to leave them and go away, but where would I go? I am here."

After his death, the body was interred in the north wall of the temple at the ashram. A hall of silence has been built over the Samadhi where devotees sit in meditation as they did before the living Ramana. As the late Arther Osbourne, a close devotee of Maharshi said: "Even now, those who sit before the Samadhi find the grace of Bhagavan as powerful and as sweet and subtle as during his body's life time. Some who lived there have remained. Some who went away have returned. Many more will come. For according to his promise, he has not left us. He is here in our hearts. He is here at Arunachala."

There is no reference of Mahatma ever meeting the Maharshi but at the spiritual level they inspired each other. Maharshi tried to achieve *Moksha* through *Gyan Yoga*; and the Mahatma through *Karma Yoga*.

Maharshi Dayanand Saraswati

Before being called Maharshi Dayanand, his name was Mool Shankar. He hailed from Gujarat. He was the son of Tax Collector, Karsanji

Tiwari. He left home in search of God and travelled all over India right from the caves of Vindhyachal to Himalayan peaks. On his way, he met several yogis and highly enlightened people. Finally, he met an old monk Swami Virjanand at Mathura who satisfied his desire and quenched his thirst.

Swami Virjanand was blind. He guided Mool Shankar for two and half years and taught him Vedic traditions, particularly the deeper meaning of Vedas and real meaning of truth of life. Now Mool Shankar was enlightened and was given the name of Rishi Dayanand by his guru.

Rish Dayanand travelled throughout India to spread the teachings of Vedas and real meaning of truth of life. He started reforming the society and preached the people through Speeches, Discourses and Writings. He debated with learned pundits and in the presence of thousands of people made them speechless. He wrote many books, important among them are *Satyarth Prakash, Rigvedadi Bhashya Bhumika, Rig Veda* and *Yajurveda Bhashya*, and *Shankar Vidhi*. The last book explains the sixteen different rituals and means of worship according to Vedic tradition.

Rishi founded Arya Samaj in 1875 in Mumbai to organise the followers of Vedic religion. He was thereafter called Maharshi Dayanand. He got lot of support and following from Gujarat. A large number of sethias became his disciples and followers. He died of a deadly poison administered in food on Diwali day, on 30th October, 1883. Among his great followers were Swami Shraddhananda and Mahatma Jyotiba Phule who kept the torch of reform in Hindu religion lighted.

Gandhiji was not a religious leader as such; he was a spiritual activist trying to learn from each religion the insights they provided on God in His most abstract form and the human destiny. Being born in a Hindu family, he was proud to be a Hindu and tried to reform it wherever and whenever he encountered something that was irreligious in it. Swami Dayanand Saraswati's crusade against obscurantism and dead load of the traditions that obscured the real image of Hinduism finds a place in Gandhiji's life.

CONCLUDING REMARKS

The contemporaneous spiritual leaders intellectuals and reformers discussed above must have made impression on Gandhi in his formative years. When we compare the lives, philosophies and writings of these great men in totality with the life, philosophy and writings of Gandhiji, we find that Gandhiji absorbed them all and weaved them to conceive a philosophy of his own. Gandhi was a great synthesizer, a man of synergy. He could take whatever he found good anywhere and used it to the best advantage of Indian people and Indian culture. Gandhiji was very much a product of the his time.

Hind Swaraj has the imprints of the ideas of these and many other Indian leaders as well as those of foreign origin like Tolstoy. In fact he combined in him Swami Vivekananda, Sri Aurobindo, Ramana Maharshi, Swami Dayanand Saraswati, Mahatma Phule, Bal Gangadhar Tilak, Gopal Krisna Gokhale, Madan Mohan Malviya, Dadabhai Naoroji, Annie Besant, Savarkar and many others. But he was none of them individually. He brought religion down to earth yet at the same time took spirituality to a high water mark. He saw in the poor the face of the God and Truth and Non-violence as the foundation of all religions. And service of the poor he considered to be the means to achieve *Moksha*. And since man did not live by bread alone, he gave a totally different meaning to development, progress and civilisation.

Progress means spiritual, moral and ethical progress, but it could not be achieved so long as the basic needs of man remain unfulfilled, and human dignity is not only respected but also given a practical shape. A society riddled with inequity and exploitative social and economic structure, a mind tormented by fear and anger, and a limitless material development un-circumscribed by ethical norms and standards must land humanity in great distress sooner than later.

Gandhi was a thinker, a social reformer, a spiritual leader, a liberal politician and a revolutionary at the same time. He was a Mahatma who combined in him whatever is potentially good and abiding in human personality. Gandhi was convinced of the continuity of the basic tenets of Indian civilisation; it was not just a Hindu civilisation. It was synergic Indian civilisation incorporating whatever was *satyam, shivam* and *sundaram* in all religions and peoples who made India of his time.

9

Gandhi's Exposure to Western Thought

It is generally believed that Gandhi was not a well-read person and that he was more of a saintly statesman who tried to win India's freedom through non-violent means. While the second part of the conjecture is correct to a great extent, the first part is not correct. True, he was not a scholarly person in the mould of modern pedagogy; he was, however fully acquainted with the latest thinking on the subjects of his interest. He did not read much about what was bad in western civilisation, but he read a lot about the alternatives suggested by various thinkers. When he wrote *Hind Swaraj* he was fully convinced through learning, experiences and analysis that modern civilisation was a disease, which needed treatment. Many others had felt the same way earlier but they did not go beyond suggesting remedies. Gandhi wanted to go a step further. He took all that he found efficacious in all the medicines suggested earlier and tried to experiment them in India.

There were two main reasons why he selected India for the inauguration of a beginning of a new civilisation. He had already worked with Indians in South Africa where he found the medicine *i.e. Satyagraha* quite efficacious. Secondly, no other people would have so willingly accepted his approach. Indians by nature were quite receptive to it. It is quite another matter that they did not practice it for the last several decades. In a war torn world of colonial exploitation, who would have accepted non-violence as a means of winning freedom and ushering in a new civilisation except Indians?

Gandhi was well acquainted with Indian culture from early childhood. By studying the alternatives suggested by western thinkers, Gandhi's convictions about global urge for morality and ethics and the role of Indian civilisation in playing a catalytic role in ushering in a new civilisation of peace and harmony was further strengthened and sharpened. In this chapter we propose to review some of the influences of western thought, literature and art on Gandhi in his formative years, *i.e.* before he wrote *Hind Swaraj* in 1909.

GREEK AND ROMAN THINKERS

Gandhi was exposed to western thought in jurisprudence, politics, history, theosophy, vegetarianism, Christian theology, industrial revolution, condition of labour in industrial cities, morality, nonviolence and civil disobedience when he was in England for his higher studies and while in South Africa fighting for the rights of the indentured Indian and other Asiatic immigrants. As a student of Law he was introduced to Greek and Roman thought, He had learnt some Latin to study Latin classics in law and society. Apparently he had studied Plato's Apology and may be even Republic. He was well acquainted with Socrates and Aristotle.

These exposures brought to his mind certain general tendencies both in western and eastern thinking which he considered to be universal tendencies uniting the humanity as a whole. Desire for peace, respect for life, dignity of the individual, love of nature, living in conformity with the laws of biology, self-government, democracy and freedom were general human cravings. But there have been frequent deviations from these general tendencies, which have become the subject matters of historians.

Gandhi also came to the conclusion that there was a law, which was higher than the common law and it was the moral law, which governed the nature as well as man. The moral law being superior must get priority over any man made law. He was quite aware of Darwin's theory of evolution; he did not however agree with him in its entirety. He believed that the evolution of man was built in the very origin of the universe and it occurred not so much because of competition among the species but because of the cooperation among them and between them and the environment.

The three Greek philosophers who appear to have had great influence on him are Socrates, Plato and Aristotle.

Socrates

Socrates lived in Athens, Greece in the fourth century BC. He altered the western though profoundly by exemplifying life of a saintly person in search of Truth and preparing Plato, his pupil, to write in great detail through a dialogue between the two about his philosophy.

Socrates taught that every person had full knowledge of ultimate Truth contained within his soul. This potential knowledge can be spurred to conscious reflection to make the person aware of it. He was highly critical of injustice prevailing in the then Athenian society. He was asked to stop his teaching, which allegedly corrupted the youth. He refused to relent and was persecuted and finally sentenced to death. Socrates welcomed death instead of choosing to live a life of untruth.

Mahatma Gandhi called him a great Satyagrahi. He appears to have tried to emulate Socrates in his own life. He advised his people to be introspective and devote less time in finding fault with others. Only a clean person can fight the evils with courage and conviction. He truly believed that India would gain independence the day Indians clean themselves both internally and externally and demonstrate their moral superiority over the British.

Plato

As stated above, Plato was the pupil of Socrates. He was one of the most creative and original thinkers in the West. He was born in 428 BC; he died in 347 BC. Plato in his early youth tried to involve himself in Athenian politics but he felt disillusioned with the leadership of the time and decided to become a disciple of Socrates. Plato witnessed the death of Socrates at the hands of the Athenian democracy in 399 BC.

In 387 Plato founded the Academy in Athens (often called the first university in Europe) where teaching of various disciplines from Astronomy to Ethics was arranged. Aristotle was one of the students of the academy.

Plato's wrings were in dialogue form. Some philosophical ideas were advanced and discussed by two or more persons. The earliest collection of Plato's work includes 35 dialogues and 13 letters. They represent Plato's attempt to communicate the philosophy of Socrates. Usually the dialogue begins with a question by some one. Socrates pretends to be ignorant and calls some one who claims to be knowledgeable to answer. Then he starts asking searching questions to prove that the knowledgeable person was really ignorant. Socrates emerges as the wiser one because he at least knew that he did not know. Such knowledge is the beginning of wisdom.

Plato's theory of knowledge goes deep into the nature of knowledge itself. True knowledge is not changeable; it is permanent. Gandhi called it Truth. The knowledge, which is based on appearance or responses of the senses to the physical environment is not permanent, nor is it true either.

Gandhi appears to have liked the approach of imparting knowledge through dialogue and separating truth from untruth. *Hind Swaraj* is also in dialogue form and it is a treatise that tries to separate truth from falsehood.

Aristotle

Aristotle was born in Macedonia. He was with the Plato's Academy in Athens for twenty years first as a student and then as a teacher. On Plato's death in 347 BC, Aristotle left for Assos in Asia Minor whose ruler was his friend. As the ill-luck would have it, the Persians captured Assos and executed his friend. He then moved back to Macedonia and became a tutor of Alexander, later known as Alexander the Great.

On Alexander becoming the King in 335 BC, Aristotle returned to Athens and established his own school, the Lyceum. On Alexander's death, he retired to a family estate and died in 322 BC.

Like his teacher Plato, Aristotle too tried to write his ideas in dialogue form but did not succeed. His lecture notes on almost every subject of relevance are excellent documents that portray the Greek thought of the time. He considered the universe to be spherical and finite with earth as its centre. In biology he thought that the species were fixed and they reproduced like ones. He considered psychology to be a study of the soul. According to him each thing is the product of a multitude of causes, not just one cause. Likewise, he had his doctrines on politics and other aspects of life.

NINETEENTH CENTURY THINKERS

Gandhi was influenced by the philosophies and thoughts of European and American intellectuals of eighteenth and nineteenth centuries. This was a period of great change in the West. Industrial Revolution was proceeding at a great pace and the value system of the society was undergoing change. Many great thinkers of the time revolted against such changes and tried to bring the society back to what they thought was the path of sanity. Some of those whose impact on Gandhi was considerable and who made Gandhi go beyond the border of South Africa and India and to work for the emancipation of the humanity as a whole, are discussed below even if only cursorily.

Count Tolstoy

Among the several Europeans and Americans who inspired and influenced Gandhi, Count Leo Nikolaevich Tolstoy (1828-1910) was the foremost. He has listed six books of Tolstoy in the appendix of *Hind Swaraj* to be read by those who wanted to understand his book better. These books deal with the colonial question of India, Christianity, in its original form, as an ethical religion, a critique of modern civilisation and other socio-political issues. Gandhi sent a copy of *Hind Swaraj* for Tolstoy's perusal soon after its English translation. Tolstoy replied: "I have read your book with great interest, for I consider the question there dealt with – passive resistance—to be of very great importance, not only for India, but for the whole of humanity."

On his young days, Tolstoy wrote his first book *Confessions* (1884): "I cannot recall those years with horror, loathing and heart-rending pain. I killed people in war, challenged men to duels with the purpose of killing them, and lost at cards; I squandered the fruits of peasants' toil and then had them executed; I was a fornicator and cheat. Lying, stealing and promiscuity of every kind, drunkenness, violence murder – there was not a crime I did not commit.... Thus I lived for ten years."

Sick of the society which gave him a character of the type mentioned above, Tolstoy developed a unique Christian philosophy which espoused non-resistance to evil as the proper response to aggression, and which put great emphasis on fair treatment of the poor and working class. He also rejected the state while seeking answers to the questions of morality and look within and God for the answers. His other notable books were *What Then Must We Do*? (1886), and *The Kingdom of God Is Within You* (1894).

Gandhi was so moved by his '*The Kingdom of God Is Within You*' that he serialized it in *Indian Opinion*. Practically all religions of Indian origin especially Jainism and Buddhism proclaimed nonviolence as the weapon of civilized human beings. In Hinduism too Gandhi found nonviolence as the guiding principle. Tolstoy showed to Gandhi that Christianity as revealed by the New Testament taught nonviolence and morality. Of course there were other aspects, which would have not fitted in the basic framework of nonviolence and morality, but Gandhi, as Tolstoy, considered them peripheral.

The problem according to Tolstoy was not Christianity but the institutionalization of Christianity, which justified the state and physical force (war) to punish those who did not adhere to the Christian morality and rejection of conscience, inner upwelling of feelings and ideals in response to some hidden power which may be called God or anything else by the so-called scientific disciplines. Religion is the means to understand the true meaning of life: whence it came, what was its purpose and whither would it go after its physical tenure on the earth was over. It was, therefore, the real source of wisdom. The very denial of it, according to Tolstoy, had denied humanity of its eternal source of strength.

Tolstoy was convinced that morality was the bedrock of human development. It alone could measure progress. Improvement in the external conditions of living could be useful only so long as it helped moral progress. Even if all external conditions were realized and man had material goods he desired, he would still not be at peace. Morality alone could bring him to peace.

Gandhi was so much sold to Tolstoyan ideas and ideals that he started a settlement, an ashram, in South Africa called 'Phoenix Settlement' to practice the principles he had laid down and made the reading of '*The Kingdom of God Is Within Us*' a compulsory reading for every inmate of the settlement. Later, Gandhi developed similar types of settlements called Ashrams in India first at Ahmedabad (Sabarmati Ashram) and the second at Wardha called Sevagram Ashram.

Another idea of Tolstoy that impressed Gandhi was the meaning he gave to Art. He did not subscribe to the theory of art for art's sake; if beauty and aesthetics lie in the harmony in nature and in the inner happiness of man, art that separates itself from both cannot be called art. Gandhi arranged the translation of Tolstoy's *What is Art*? in Gujarati.

Scholars in India have a rather superficial and at times erroneous understanding of Gandhi's interest in art, aesthetics, beauty etc. He was a very keen observer, loved everything that was artistic. But his meaning of art was different. A pure soul was beautiful, nature was beautiful, any sacrifice that removed the misery of man and enlightened his soul was beautiful. He saw a close link between aesthetics and other departments of life including political action that aimed at liberating man from external and internal bondages. For example, the inventions of spinning wheel or Singer sewing machine were acts of art.

Tolstoy wrote extensively on the pitfall of industrial civilisation. Three books listed in the appendix of *Hind Swaraj* deal with this subject. These are: *How Shall We Escape*?, *The Slavery of Our Times*, and *The First Step*. A review of all these books would take lot of space. They contain sharp criticism against various aspects of modern civilisation particularly the exploitation of workers, peasants, consumerism and lack of moderation. Gandhi's thinking was similar but he derived it from Indian cultural traditions and thoughts. After reading Tolstoy he felt emboldened to assert with confidence and also realized that the Christian civilisation as such was not the same as modern industrial civilisation.

Tolstoy's famous *Letter to a Hindoo* gave Gandhi a practical avenue to kill two birds with one stone: to liberate India peacefully and to take humanity back from violence to non-violence.

John Ruskin

Born in London in 1819, Ruskin was the son of a rich wine merchant. He graduated from Oxford. He was one of the most influential art critics of all time. He published '*Modern Painters*' (1834) and then a series of books of the same title (*Modern Painters II to V*) between 1846 and 1860 wherein he defended J.M.W. Turner and the pre-Raphaelites. His other books on Art included *The Seven Lamps of Architecture* (1849), and *The Stones of Venice* (1851-53). It is said that he wrote a popular story *The King of the Golden River* (1851) for his youthful wife, who afterwards chose to divorce him for his alleged impotence.

Ruskin was associated with Arundel Society and taught at the Working Men's College. He delivered a series of addresses in 1850s, which showed his growing interest in politics and economics. The addresses were published in *The Lectures on Architecture and Painting* (1854), *The Political Economy of Art* (1857), *The Two Paths* (1859), *Unto This Last* (1860), *Essays of Political Economy* (1862-63), *Time and Tide* (1867) and *Munera Pulveris* (1872). In these lectures Ruskin denounced greed as the guiding principle of English life and argued against competition as the way to progress and in favour of a sort of Christian socialism. He translated his convictions into reality by donating much of the sumptuous property he inherited from his father after latter's death to institutions engaged in educating the poor.

Gandhi owed much to Ruskin in so far as his economic thinking was concerned. Two books by Ruskin influenced him immensely: *The Political Economy of Art* which consisted of two lectures entitled *A Joy for Ever and Its Price in the Market* delivered in 1857 at the Art Treasure Exhibition in Manchester and *Unto This Last* (1860). Both the books contain a scathing attack on modern civilisation in general and the 'pseudo-science' of Ricardo and Mill, the two celebrated economists of the time, in particular. The new political economy according to him aimed at meeting the luxuries of a few, not the basic needs of the many. In his view blankets must get priority over 'silk laces'. 'As long as there are cold and nakedness in the land around you, so long there can be no question at all that splendor in dress is a crime.... As long as there are any who have no blankets for their beds, and no rags for their bodies, so long it is blanket making and tailoring we must set people to work at.' It is apparent that Gandhi adapted much of what Ruskin said to the situation prevailing in India including the idea of appropriate technology.

The second book had still greater impact on Gandhi's thinking. He read this book in 1904 while travelling by train from Johannesburg to Durban. Gandhi was so overwhelmed by it that 'I could not get any sleep in the night. I determined to change my life in accordance with the ideal of the book... I translated it later into Gujarati, entitling it Sarvodaya.' He learnt three things from this book:

(1) good of the individual lies in the good of all;
(2) wages should not differ according to the nature of work. The lawyer's work is as important as that of a barber or peasant; and
(3) life of a peasant or artisan is worth living.

The book has four chapters: Introduction, I – The Roots of Truth; II – The Veins of Wealth; III – Even-handed Justice; and IV – Ad Valorem, Conclusion. 'Unto This Last' was first serialized in Indian Opinion and later paraphrased into *Sarvodaya,* a term he used for his economic philosophy now known all over the world as an alternative development philosophy. Ruskin's idea of social affection (as opposed to self-interest) was transformed into compassion by Gandhi. Gandhi took from Ruskin the value of manual work and handicrafts as something necessary for self-esteem and self-realisation. It involved creativity apart from a source of livelihood. A teacher may be less paid but less wages could be amply compensated by respect he commanded in society. It could be so for all other activities including scavenging. A person who cleans must be treated superior to one who makes thing dirty.

Gandhi was so much sold to Ruskin's views that he immediately set upon the establishment of Phoenix Settlement where members joining the community lived a life according to the dictates of the above three convictions. Later he started the Tolstoy Farm near Johannesburg and two Ashrams in India (Sabarmati near Ahmedabad and Sevagram in Wardha near Nagpur), on the same pattern.

Gandhi felt convinced that *Swaraj* without Sarvodaya would be meaningless. Sarvodaya was not possible unless the middle classes in India opted for restraint on consumption of goods and accumulatiorr of wealth. And neither of the two conditions would be met unless people reached a threshold of moral development. Gandhi, therefore, thought of a different pattern of economic, social and political development within the framework of the cultural traditions of India. It so happened that Ruskin, Tolstoy and many others advocated a similar line. 'We must transmute ourselves into gold by leading a life of virtue'. Ruskin died in 1900.

Ralph Waldo Emerson

Emerson (1803-82) was a leading philosopher, poet and essayist in America. He set the tone of American literature of his time. He represents the American pragmatism and his influence still persists in American thinkers like John Dewey, William James and Friedrich Nietssche. Among his great friends were Henry David Thoreau, Margaret Fuller, and Thomas Carlyle.

He was a transcendentalist and his first book *Nature* (1841) gave ample evidence of this. His address '*The American Scholar*' (1837) made him highly popular among the youth, which started believing in the maxim 'one thing in the world of value is active soul'. He said from the public platform that 'historical Christianity has fallen into error' and it 'destroys the power of preaching. Emerson represents American soul and America that gave Emerson is not the one represented by the present political thoughts and institutions. It is the

American ideal of democracy and the experience of freedom that gave to him the moral and political vision reflected in his lectures and poems. It is the American sense of equality that made him the 'the philosopher of democracy'. According the John J. Chapman 'if a soul be taken and crushed by democracy till it utter a cry, that cry will be Emerson.'

Among his series of celebrated essays written between 1841 and 1860 are: Self Reliance, Circles, Experiences, Representative Men, English Traits, Conduct of Life, and Fate. He also wrote poems.

Gandhi was greatly inspired by Emerson. He considered his essays 'teaching of Indian wisdom in western garb.' He read Emerson's some of the essays in 1909 in Pretoria jail.

Henry James Sumner Maine

Maine was born at Leighton England on August 15, 1822. He was a very studious student partly because his health during his student days was not good. He graduated from Cambridge in 1844 and became a Tutor in Trinity Hall. Later he became a student of Roman Law and Jurisprudence in the Inns of Court but his practices of law never reached a respectable level. He married his cousin in 1847 and had two sons.

He was offered a job in India and remained Vice-Chancellor of Calcutta University for seven years. His deteriorating health forced him to return to England in 1869. He joined the Oxford University as Corpus Professor of Jurisprudence. On the basis of his experience of village life in India and reading of German literature on the subject he published his first book entitled *Village Communities in the East and West* in 1871. His last lectures were published in Dissertations on Early Law and Custom in 1878. Maine was a skilful synthesizer of discrete ideas and information. It was well reflected in the book.

Maine was given a place in the Council of the Secretary of State for India. In 1878 he quit his job at the Oxford and became a professor in Cambridge University. His health however never improved and he passed away in 1888.

Maine was a kind gentleman. Because of his poor health, he did not have access to relevant literature and hence many of his ideas were half-baked. His study of India villages is however still a classic and Gandhiji was highly impressed by his essays on the subject.

Henry David Thoreau

Thoreau (1817-1862) is a well-known American naturalist, philosopher and writer of eighteenth century. He believed in the dignity of the individual. His personality, thinking and philosophy is well reflected in *Walden*; or Life in the Woods published in 1854. The book is a record of his experiences in self-built cabin at Walden Pond near Concord, Massachusetts where he spent two years in near seclusion.

He was born at Concord and educated at Harvard University. During 1830s and 1840s he taught at schools in Concord and New York. He lived with Emerson for two years (1841-43) because he like Emerson was transcendentalist, *i.e.* philosophers who believed that God lived in nature and human beings and each person has to realize his potentials himself and seek the truth in his own ways.

The transcendentalists tried to free America from European conventions and thoughts. Both Emerson and Thoreau were the chief protagonists of this line of thinking. Among the other transcendentalists were philosopher Bronson Alcott, social reformer Margaret Fuller and literary critic George Ripley.

During 1845-47 he lived in a hut on the shores of Walden. He kept detailed records of everything he did in these natural lives and produced his most famous book Walden. He wrote in the book about the pleasures one could get from withdrawing from the hum-drum of the busy life for a while and about the opportunity one got to understand himself better through meditation, self-reliance and self-sufficiency. While in the woods he grew his own food. Apart from Walden the only other book he published during his life time was *A Week on the Concord and Merrimack Rivers* (1848).

He stayed with Emerson again during 1847-48 and then with his parents and sister. But he always supported himself by doing gardening, carpentry, land surveying etc. He spent lot of time on reading Latin, Greek, French and English literature and interaction with his neighbours and acquaintances.

Thoreau opposed the Mexican War (1846-48) and refused to pay poll tax imposed by the American government. He preferred to go to jail. He clarified his stand in his famous essay 'Civil Disobedience' (1849). In this essay Thoreau has discussed the philosophy behind civil disobedience as a method of protest, which Gandhi converted into *Satyagraha* to oust the British colonialism from India.

During his life, Thoreau was not known beyond his close circle. As the ecological crises deepened, the value of what he wrote and lived became known widely. He articulated the view that humans are not outside nature and they can function best if they are conscious of this fact.

Edward Carpenter

Born in 1844 at Brighton in England, Edward Carpenter was ordained by Trinity Hall Cambridge University in 1870. After serving as curate in a neighbouring church for about four years, he became a lecturer in astronomy, science and music in Brighton University. His father's death left him quite rich financially.

Carpenter was highly influenced by the work of John Ruskin and William Morris. He started developing the idea of a utopian future with primitive communism as the basic philosophy. He soon joined the Socialist League and came to be known as poet of democracy. Towards Democracy (1883), and England's Ideal (1887) and a series of songs like England Arise were highly popular in 1890s. In 1893, he with several other like-minded persons like George Bernard Shaw and Ramsay Macdonald formed the Independent Labour Party 'to secure the collective ownership of the means of production, distribution and exchange'.

Carpenter was a pacifist and opposed Boer War. He played a very active role in 'No Conscription Fellowship' and wrote several antiwar pamphlets such as Healing of Nations (1915) and Never Again (1916). Gandhi was highly impressed by his books 'England's Ideals' and 'Civilisation, Its causes and Cure'. Some of his ideas perhaps had their roots in Carpenter. His views on modern civilisation are quite similar to those of Carpenter. England's Ideals taught him to treat Englishmen as friends and oppose English rule as a negation of the very principles of justice, democracy, and fair play that England professed and hence an enemy to fight against. He died in 1929.

Being a homosexual he wrote several pamphlets defending homosexuality. But he stopped further publications on the subject after the House of Commons banned homosexuality.

John Stuart Mill

Mill was born in 1806 when the reformist trend in England had just started. As a student he was a brilliant boy. By the time he was 12 years old he had already learnt Aristotle in original and the works of Scottish economist Adam Smith and English economist David Ricardo.

Mill's father was a strict disciplinarian and he imbed some of his sterling qualities. He was studious, punctual and highly intelligent. He concerned himself with the struggle between liberty and authority for its history went back to ancient times of Greeks and Romans. In olden days the struggle was between people and rulers who were considered to be antagonistic to the people they ruled. Liberty was the state where people were free from the tyranny of rulers.

In his essay 'On Liberty' he elaborated his political thesis, which Gandhi found very useful in formulating his ideas about a truly modern civilisation. According to him, democracy was introduced to set limits on the powers of the rulers who were to be elected for a short period so that they did not develop vested interests. In due course of time, the majority rule became an accepted principle of governance only to be realized later that majority need not always be right.

There was no recognized principle by which the propriety or otherwise of activities of the rulers could be tested. He, therefore, set a principle: 'that the sole end for which mankind is warranted individually or collectively in interfering with liberty of action of any of their number is self-protection. That the only purpose for which power can be rightfully exercised over any member of the civilized community, against his will, is to prevent harm to others. His own good either physical or moral, is not a sufficient warrant. He cannot be rightfully compelled to do or forbear because it will be better for him, or entreating him, but not for compelling him, or persuading him, or visiting him with any evil, in case he does otherwise. To justify that, that the conduct from which it is desired to deter him must be calculated to produce evil to some one else. The only part of the conduct of any one, for which he is amenable to society, is that which concerns others. In the part, which merely concerns himself or his independence is, of right, absolute. Over himself, over his own body and mind, the individual is sovereign.'

Lord Ampthill

Ampthill as a member of the House of Lords vigorously supported and fought for the just cause of Indians in South Africa. His speech during the debate on Asiatic Registration Act was one the factors responsible for Gandhi's very favourable attitude towards the British people. He called for complete equality before the law for all the British subjects and any discrimination against any section of them was against the constitution of the British Empire. Further, "the Registration Act, without solving the immigration question in any shape or form, degrades British Indians residents of Transvaal and its incidence changes the cherished maxim of the British Constitution, namely, that every man has to be presumed to be innocent until he is proved to be guilty, and that, rather than an innocent man should suffer, guilty ones should go unpunished. This act presumes every Indian to be guilty and throws on him the onus of proving that he is not so, that to say that he has not entered Transvaal in a *bona fide* manner. ... The Act is like locking up the honourable men in cells, so that that thieves may not steal." (*Indian Opinion*, 29.6.1907)

Sir William Wedderburn

Wedderburn was a member of the Indian Civil Service (1860-87). He was born in 1838 at Edinburgh, Scotland. His first assignment was at Dharwad now in Karnataka state as assistant commissioner. He became a district and session judge in Poona in 1872. At the time of his retirement in 1887, he was the Chief Secretary of Bombay Presidency.

Weddenburn was deeply interested in the problems of Indian peasantry. Poverty, famines and indebtedness made him think of the ways and means of improving the situation. His readings about Indian villages brought him to the realization that Indian villages were very prosperous in ancient and medieval times and that they functioned so autonomously that changes in the government at Delhi did not make much of difference to them. This brought him close to the Indian National Congress and its leaders. After retirement from service he decided to stay put in India and did not go back to England. He presided over the fourth annual session of the Indian National Congress held at Bombay in1889.

On his brother's death, he became a baron in 1879 and entered the Parliament in 1893 as Liberal member and intervened several times on behalf of India. He was the chairman of Indian Parliamentary Committee (1893-1900). He represented India on the Royal Commission on Indian Expenditure. He also participated in the Indian Famine Union established in 1901 to find the causes, consequences and remedies for recurring famines in India. Weddenburn came to

India in 1904 to attend the Bombay session of the Indian National Congress; he presided over its Allahabad session too in 1910.

Weddenburn believed in the principle of self-government. He envisaged a continuing good relations between free India and the British Commonwealth and was happy that the British Government in 1917 put the progressive establishment of self-government in India as its policy goal. He was accused of being disloyal officer because he incessantly pleaded for Constitutional Reforms in India. He considered the Montegu-Chemsford reform granting local self-government as the crowning glory of his life's work.

In his presidential address at the Bombay session of the Congress, he said: "What are the practical objects of the Congress movement? They are, to revive the national life, and to increase the material prosperity of country, and what better objects could we have before us? Lastly, as regards our methods, they are open and constitutional, and based solely on India's reliance upon British justice and love of fair play."

The efforts of persons like Weddenburn later brought fruits and India fought its battle against British Raj constitutionally under the inspiring leadership of Mahatma Gandhi and decided to remain a member of the Commonwealth of Nations.

Robert Harborough Sherard

Robert Sherard is better known as a friend of Oscar Wilde. Born in London in 1861, he was educated at different places in Europe and finally settled down in Paris to pursue his writing career. It is in Paris that he met Wilde in 1883. The friendship however did not last, as Wilde was interested in homosexual relations, which Sherard was not. Sherard supported himself mostly through journalism. He was a prolific writer of novels, biographies, reminiscences and social criticism. In all, he wrote 33 books.

Sherard continued to be a loyal friend of Wilde and tried his level best to save him from imprisonments. He visited Wilde in prison during his second two-year sentence. On Wilde's death in 1900, Sherard wrote his biography entitled 'Story of an Unhappy Friendship'. His second book was Twenty Years in Paris (1905).

Sherard was a difficult man to get along. He spoke French, German, Italian and, of course, English. He was a very intelligent and idealistic man always in love with nature. He married thrice and all the marriages ended in divorce. He was nevertheless highly respected in his life-time. He died in London in 1930.

Max Nordau

Born in Hungary in 1849 in a Jewish family, Nordau drifted away from Jewish community. He studied medicine in Pàris. He was a controversial writer always critical of contemporary European culture, behaviour and literature. He is best known for his book *Conventional Lies of the Society* (1883) wherein he attacked egotism, irrationality, and nihilism prevalent in the society.

Later he went back to Judaism and became its active member. He was the first speaker at the First Zionist Congress; he gave details of the pitiable condition of the jews in different parts of the world. In 1920 he gave the idea of shifting half a million Jews from Europe to Eretz-Israel but no one took it seriously. Soon after he died in Paris.

Giuseppe Mazzini

Born in 1805, Mazzini was an Italian patriot and revolutionist. His youth was spent in literary and philosophical studies. He was imprisoned briefly. This forced him to go out on exile in Marseilles where he set up a secret society called Giovine Italia (young Italy) which campaigned for Italian unity under a republican government.

Mazzini's influence extended all over Europe. The radicals and revolutionaries considered him their peer. During 1848, a rebellion broke out in Milan, the Papal States, and the two Sicilies. Mazzini became one of the leaders of the Roman Republic. The Republic however did not last and Mazzini had to go on exile once again to resume propaganda from outside Italy. He organized uprising in Milan in 1853 and a unsuccessful expedition to South Italy.

Mazzini was sentenced to death in absentia. But he continued to visit Italy secretly. He founded a newspaper in London called Pensiero ed azione (Thought and Action). He supported Garibaldì but unlike Garibaldi, he was a republican. He was also not in full agreement with Camillo Benso-di-Cavour, the then Sardinian premier. Although both wanted the unification of Italy, Cavour relied on French help while Mazzini on Italian people. and their moral strength.

Mazzini's work was inspired by his moral strength. His program was not only political but also deeply social aiming at human development on religious and moral basis. He wanted Italian people to unite and fight for justice and liberty themselves without relying on the help of other countries. For that he wanted the people to be morally strong.

Mazzini's literary style was remarkably sophisticated. He wrote on a large number of subjects covering the fields of philosophy, politics, and literature. Gandhi was highly appreciative of Mazzini's approach to self-reliance, moral strength and patriotism. He died in 1872.

Herbert Spencer

Known for synthetic philosophy, this English philosopher was born in 1820 and died in 1903. He interpreted all phenomena according to the principle of evolutionary progress. He was to the social sciences, what Darwin was for natural sciences and Freud was for psychology. He divided the phenomena into two segments: those, which were unknowable, and those, which were knowable. In the first category was the supreme power from which everything came and which could not be understood except intuitively. In the second category fell the phenomena, which were the manifestations of unknowable power. He further categorised these into biological, psychological, sociological and ethical spheres.

Romain Rolland

Romain Rolland was born in 1866 in Nievre district of France. He studied philosophy, literature and music. After working for quite some time as a school teacher he came to Sorbonne in 1903 where he gave a very unique course on the history of music.

His debut in literature began in 1897 with *Saint-Louis*, a five-act play. He wrote too many great books in the field of music and literature to list them here. He was awarded Nobel prize for his masterpiece in Literature in 1915 entitled *Jean-Christophe.* The book describes 'how a powerful nature which has the noblest and most urgent desire for truth, moral health and artistic purity, with an exuberant love of life is forced to overcome obstacles that rise up ceaselessly before it; how it attains victory and independence; and his character and his intelligence are significant enough to concentrate in themselves a complete image of the world.'

Romain Rolland's concerns were truth, altruism and art. His *Jean-Christophe* has taken its place in world literature among the most original, the boldest, and the healthiest works of the twentieth century. He persisted in the quest for peace and was attracted by the non-violent movement of Gandhi about whom he wrote a book in 1924. He was very much influenced by Buddhism and Indian mysticism. We are not sure whether he and Gandhi knew each other before he penned *Hind Swaraj*, but they must have communicated with each other telepathically for their routes were different but the goal was the same: to seek the truth and peace. Both Roman Rolland and Gandhi were so original that they could not be indifferent to each other.

EUROPEAN WOMEN WHO INFLUENCED GANDHI

Gandhi had a very special regard for women; he considered them stronger than men in many respects. In his program women were always in the forefront and he firmly believed that the women were the harbingers of peace. During his South African days he was greatly supported by several European women specially in securing settlement with General Smuts. A brief sketch of some of them is presented below.

Helena P. Blavatsky

Helena P. Blavatsky's contribution to the revival of Indian thought specially the Hindu and Buddhist in the nineteenth century through the medium of Theosophical Society is unmatched. She was not liked by the practiceners of Buddhism in the West nor was she so popular even in the East. Yet we cannot but agree with S. Radhakrishnan one of India's leading philosophers and political figures that: 'when, with all kinds of political failures and economic breakdowns we were suspecting the values and vitality of our culture, when everything round about us and secular education happened to discredit the value of Indian culture, the Theosophical Movement rendered great service by vindicating those values and ideas. The influence of Theosophical Movement on general India society is incalculable.' Blavatsky was the founder of the movement.

Gandhi was well acquainted with work being done by Madame Blavatsky. It was through the Theosophical Society that he came to know many of the British sympathetic to India, Indian Home Rule and Indian civilisation.

Emily Hobhouse

Emily Hobhouse was the daughter of a churchman in Britain. She dedicated herself to a movement against the Anglo-Boer War. She visited the camps of Boer refugees where children and women were kept and earned their affection and reverence. In that process she came close to Boers like General Jan Christian Smuts and General Louis Botha.

She had met a number of Indians at the house of her uncle Lord Hobhouse who was a member of Council of the India and later of Privy Council. She had great regard for India. She was pained to see that the Boers who fought the British joined hands with them to oppress the Indians in South Africa. She went to South Africa in 1913 to unveil a memorial to Boer women but had to stay put because of poor health. It was the time Gandhi needed support and she was only too ready to render it.

Olive Schneider

Olive Schneider was a prominent South African writer of the late nineteenth century. She vehemently opposed Boer War of 1899-1902 and was virtually interned by the British. Gandhi might have met Olive as early as 1907. Indian Opinion in its editorial in 1909 highly commended her for a letter she wrote on race relations.

When Gandhiji left for England as the head of a delegation to put the case of Indian before the British authorities in 1909, Olive to the dislike of the whites went with her sister to the ship at Cape Town to shake hands with Gandhi. Gandhiji later wrote, 'she performed this ceremony most heartily in the presence of a huge crowd and both the sisters were quite for a few minutes with us. Fancy the author of Dreams paying a tribute to passive resistance'.

Still later in 1925, Gandhiji in his speech on South Africa in the Kanpur session of the Congress said:

"I claim the privilege of having been a close friend of that great poetess and philanthropist and that most self-effacing woman – Olive Schneider. She was a friend of the Indians equally with natives of South Africa. She knew no distinction between white and black races. She loved the Indian, the Zulu, and the Bantu as her own children. Such precious men and women have also been born and bred in South Africa.

And Olive had equally great regard for Gandhi. She told Sarojini Naidu in 1914: "Tell your young Indians that Mr. Gandhi is the greatest spirit that as ever came to South Africa; he is the Mazzini of the Movement."

Elizabeth M. Molteno

Molteno came from a rich South African family. Her father was the first prime minister of the Cape Colony and her brother was the first speaker of the South African parliament. Tired of riches and luxuries, she took to teaching but lost the job because her opposition to Anglo-Boer war and her support to Emily Hobhouse. She went to England and met Gandhi there in 1909 and discussed his activities and emerging thoughts.

On return to South Africa in 1912, she visited Phoenix Settlement and wrote to Gandhi "Your Phoenix is a poem – a dream of loveliness." She bought a cottage just a couple of km from Phoenix and stayed there during the crucial phase of *Satyagraha* to lend a helping hand to Gandhiji. He stature did facilitate the movement and prepared Gandhi to return to India in 1914 to take a bigger challenge there.

She addressed an Indian meeting in 1914. According to the *Indian Opinion* of January 7, 1914, she said: ...After the Boer War I saw that Boer and Briton would have to unite, but would they try to do it at the cost of their dark brothers? Broken-hearted I went to England. For eight long years, I remained away from Africa – in body – never in soul and spirit. And England and Europe have sent me back with this message to white South Africa: 'Open your hearts – your souls – to your brethren of colour'. We are in the twentieth century. Rise to the heights of this glorious century. Try to comprehend the words of DuBois – that grand and sympathetic soul: 'The 20th century will be the century of colour." "And I say it is also a century of women. She too is divine and supreme. She too must play her God—appointed part – and in this 20th century her part will be a great one."

On January 12, 1914, she welcomed Mrs. Sheikh Mehtab and Hanifa Bibi, the two Moslem women passive resisters. And soon after she addressed another meeting to welcome a group of women passive resisters from Transvaal.

EUROPEANS WHO WORKED WITH GANDHI

Henry S.L. Polak
Hermann Kallenbach
Allan Octavian Hume
Reverend Joseph J. Doke
L.W. Ritch
William Hosken

THE BOOKS THAT GANDHI READ

A general feeling that Gandhi was not a well-read person particularly in modern scientific fields and that is why he talked of morality prevails among Indian intellectuals. The feeling is however erroneous. Gandhi was a very fast reader; he was able to separate the essentials from the non-essentials and absorb what was relevant. He used to look at some books, glanced through others and read those, which he thought had originality. Since he was jailed several times, he got ample opportunity to read and write there.

His source of knowledge was not books alone however. He used to meet a variety of people and discuss with them at length the contemporary issues ranging from birth control to religion and world peace.

Some of the books he appears to have read are listed at the end of *Hind Swaraj;* they are also discussed by Parel in his recent book *Gandhi: Hind Swaraj and Other Writings*. The list appended to *Hind Swaraj* is given below but it need not be a complete list of books Gandhi read and consulted. Gandhi perhaps mentioned only the books that he could recall and which impressed him most. In a few cases the titles were not complete.

The Kingdom of God is Within You	— Leo Tolstoy
The Slavery of Our Times	— Leo Tolstoy
What is Art?	— Leo Tolstoy
The First Step	— Leo Tolstoy
How shall We Escape?	— Leo Tolstoy
Letter to a Hindoo	— Leo Tolstoy
Civilisation, Its Cause and Cure	— Carpenter
The White Slaves of England	— Sherard
The Fallacy of Speed	— Taylor

A New Crusade	— Blount
On the Duty of Civil Disobedience	— Thoreau
Life Without Principle	— Thoreau
Unto This Last	— Ruskin
A Joy Forever	— Ruskin
Duties of Man	— Mazzini
Defense and Death of Socrates	— From Plato
Paradoxes of Civilisation	— Max Nordau
Poverty and Un-British Rule in India	— Naoroji
Economic History of India	— Dutt
Village Community in East and West	— Maine
Bhagvat Geeta	— Arnold
Ramayan	— Tulsidas

10

Gandhi's Valuation of Modern Science and Technology

GANDHI, THE SCIENTIST

I do not claim to have originated any new principle or doctrine, I have simply tried in my own way to apply the eternal truth to our daily life and problems.... Well, all my philosophy, if it may be called by that pretentious name, is contained in what I have said. You will not call it 'Gandhism'; there is no ism about it. And no elaborate literature or propaganda is needed about it.

Hind Swaraj has been lauded as seminal; it has also been criticized as a work of a crank. Some have even seen in it a big game to subvert India's independence movement and a sinister design to halt progress. The main import of the book has generally been lost because the critics looked at it only in bits and pieces. The book has presented an alternative worldview, a new paradigm for progress or development. Its title appears to focus on India, but the contents have global scope and relevance; it is for the humanity as a whole. What Gandhi has presented is a model, logical model, which should be pursued. It cannot be implemented as a short-term project. A model is a model; when put in practice it has to be modified in its details for the environment in which it has to be implemented changes through time.

The vocabulary used in *Hind Swaraj* is the one current in the first quarter of the twentieth century. Gandhi does not make a distinction between culture and civilisation; culture is subsumed in civilisation. At present civilisation is considered to be the physical manifestation of culture. Gandhi lifted the concept of civilisation from Gujarati and said it meant good conduct. Even today, a civilized person is supposed to be one who possesses good manners. Similarly, the term 'progress', in Gandhian praxis is the same as 'development'. In his time the term 'development' was not in currency. The term 'progress' thus subsumes development although development is more subtle and specific than progress.

Gandhi was a scientist *par excellence*. His life was nothing but his experiments with truth. He wanted scientific discoveries and inventions to be used for the welfare of humanity. He did not believe in miracles and even rejected the sacred books where they went counter to scientific laws and human dignity. Gandhi was a rationalist through and through but his rationalism was not blind and limited to physical and material sphere of the world. He found science in spirituality and spirituality in science. Transcending the distances between body, mind and soul, he put man far above the status of just another species. He gave a spiritual purpose to human life and the scientific laws that contradicted that purpose were rejected for they did not take man to his goal.

Gandhi was not mesmerized by scientific discoveries and inventions because he was aware of the limitations of science. But he was deeply concerned with and intested in application of science and technology for it affected both man and nature. This is not a place to elaborate this point further. Science deals with the external world; Gandhi was more deeply interested in the internal world of man. He was not interested in the brute force; he was interested in the soul force.

There is no aspect of Gandhi's life, which is not marked with rationality and logic. He never accepted anything given as many scientific theories do. He carried the logic to its final conclusions beyond a given stage. Gandhi's spiritualism was thus very close to that of Kabir who was rationalist yet a spiritualist.

Science tries to uncover the mysteries of nature; it cannot go beyond that to uncover the spiritual side of man. So Gandhi was interested in science to the extent that it enabled man to keep his body and mind in healthy state. But when it affected them adversely, he condemned it right away as he did with respect to machinery. Let me quote here what he had to say about technology as represented by machines. Recognizing that machine by itself is neither moral nor immoral, he was not against machines as such:

"How can I be when I know that even this body is a most delicate piece of machinery? The spinning wheel is a machine; a little toothpick is a machine. What I object to is the craze for machinery, not machinery as such. The craze is for what they call labour—saving machinery. Men go on 'saving labour' till thousands are without work and thrown on the open streets to die of starvation. I want to save time and labour not for fraction of mankind but for all. I want the concentration of wealth, not in the hands of a few, but in the hands of all. Today machinery helps merely a few to ride on the backs of millions. The impetus behind it all is not the philanthropy to save labour, but greed. It is against this constitution of things that I am fighting with all might."

Of the two methods of scientific analysis, *i.e.* deductive and inductive, Gandhi used both. He always experimented with things that he wanted people to follow. He never prescribed anything without experimentation. Thus he not only made his colleagues and associates science minded but also brought science outside the laboratory to the homes of the people. What to eat, when to eat, how much to eat, what to wear, what type of habitat one should reside in, what is the relationship between man and nature, how to handle diseases, and many other mundane issues he experimented with and found answers.

As regards method of analysis, let us be clear that he considered synthesis more important than analysis. Science, in his view, must involve itself with both. Without synthesis it is difficult to understand the ultimate truth. Analysis only dissects and divides; synthesis puts knowledge together. If knowledge is one and united, it can be understood only through synthesis. Yet, analysis is not unimportant for the day-to-day life of individuals has to be broken down in sectors and parts to deal with the problems they create.

Since Gandhi tried to bring science and religion together so that both were purified, let us note that science is analysis based while spirituality is synthesis based. There is a single Law of Truth, which hold the universe together. If religion is purged of its unscientific elements and science of it irreligious element, both could stand on a common platform. This is what Gandhi tried to do during his life time.

Let us discuss a few of the theories and laws, which Gandhi propounded or discovered, which are of catalytic importance for human progress.

THE LAWS MODERN SCIENCE FAILS TO DISCOVER

Cosmic Law

Gandhi has referred to the Cosmic Law that binds all that exist in the universe. It is all-pervasive, nothing stands apart from it. He is the Brahma of Hindus, the God of Christians, the Allah of Moslems. He defines God as Truth, so it is the Truth that is the Cosmic Law. "God is not a person.... The truth is that God is the force. He is the essence of life.... He is eternal. And yet strangely enough all are not able to derive either benefit from or shelter in the all-pervading living presence." (*Harijan*, 22-6-47)

The Cosmic Law that Gandhi has repeatedly mentioned in his writings has a scientific meaning. Perhaps he derived this meaning from contemplation over what the ancient books of India reveal. Recent cosmological researches point to similar, if not the same conclusions. How the universe came into being is still a mystery. Our universe appears to have been born some 20 billion years ago. It was born out of nothing or something that is neither matter nor anti-matter. The seers call it God; the scientist the anti-chance. No one knows what caused it to be born? What was the seed, and the seed of the seed? There are several hypotheses. According to one, which appears to be most plausible, there were several universes earlier. They were borne and then they died. Our present universe also was born and since anything that is born must die, it would also die to be born again. According to Charles Townes who discovered the Black Hole in the center of our Milky Way, immorality eludes all cosmic constituents; they are as much a part of the karmic birth and death cycle as we are. (see *Hindustan Times editorial*, Jan., 2003)

What applies to the Universe also applies to the galaxies, to all the stars, planets and their satellites. It applies to the earth, to the moon and all individual elements thereof. It applies to each of us, to our organs, tissues and each of the cells. Nothing is permanent. New Stars are born while many others are being swallowed by the Black Holes. Astronomers have been able to observe nebulae giving rise to stars and black holes sucking star systems. Yet the universe remains healthy; it is not chaotic, no single galaxy or solar system can deviate from the assigned role. Our earth functions as a part of the solar system, which in turns functions as a part of the Milky Way and the Milky Way functions as a part of the thousands of other galaxies which go to form the universe. Each has a role to play but has no freedom to violate the laws that govern the functioning of the universe as a whole. Of course there are disturbing forces. Something new comes up and some old structures die. Even our tiny earth has earthquakes, ice ages, etc. and in our own life times there are accidents, droughts, floods, diseases etc. but none of these can disturb the long term general functioning of the system as a whole. Universal forces work out an optimum birth and death ratio and optimum level of functioning of each element thereof so that the universe does not cease to exist before its pre-set time expires; nor does our solar system, our earth, our body and each cell of the body. The sages have said: *Yatha Pinde Tatha Brahmande* (as in the atom so in the universe).

The cosmic law applies to all equally. No one even a galaxy can violate the law. Had it done in the past, the cycle of universes would have been closed long back. Fortunately, no single entity of the universe has been endowed with power to interfere with the Cosmic Law except the man. He is endowed with a brain large enough to think and create images, to detach himself from the whole and commit even hara-kiri. Man is governed by the Law of Life, which is an integral part of the Cosmic Law. He cannot violate the Cosmic Law but has been enabled to violate the Law of Life to end his journey before time, if he so chooses knowingly or unknowingly.

Whole Theory of Life

Gandhi postulated that the economic, social and moral degradation of India had its roots in the deviation of the country from the fundamentals of natural principles as enshrined in Indian culture. It happened because of the foreign influence and oppressive pressure of those who commanded power during the last few centuries. Removal of the foreign rule, therefore, became his immediate target. His long term target was however, thorough change in the mindset of the people and a thorough cleansing and transformation of all departments of life—cultural, social, economic and political – contaminated as they were and still are by the so-called modern civilisation.

He was looking for a new meaning of progress and development to convince the people of the futility of the western model. He rightly ascribed all problems India faced in his time to the western model. India slid back instead of moving ahead during the 200 years of British

Raj. Interestingly, during the same period the condition of England at least in material terms improved a lot. He further said, that not only England and India, the whole world moved backwards morally during that period. He postulated the concept of Sarvodaya (universal arising) – development of all. According to him, the economically rich people needed 'moral development' so that they could share their wealth with others. Rich should become more human by getting rid of greed, tendency to accumulate, insensitivity towards other humans and life forms. The poor need economic development in order that they can secure their basic needs of food, clothing, shelter, education, health, security, and self-esteem. Unless the rich develop humanaly, the poor will remain poor; and unless the poor develop socio-economically, the rich will remain in fear of violence and guilt. The future of both is bound together; they have to work together, support each other to create a more livable society.

He further postulated that the separation of man from the beast over a million years ago set in motion a new trajectory of evolution – from physical evolution to spiritual evolution; and from nature's control to self-control which he called *Swaraj*. He concluded that the future of man depended less on nature and more on himself. With brain size bigger than any animal ever had or will ever have, man got the capacity to control nature; to see beyond the present; to link himself to the past; to actively participate in the creation of his own future.

He looked within and found the model he was looking for in India's own civilisation. There is some evidence to suggest that Gandhi studied the cultural history of major civilisations of the world before he came to the conclusion that many civilisations disappeared in the past because they could not maintain a balance between the moral and material dimensions of life. He mentions Egypt, Greece, Rome, etc. He did not mention the Indus valley civilisation probably because it was not known at that time. He concluded, and rightly so, that most ancient civilisations in their initial stages maintained balance between material needs and ecological imperatives. But once on a high pedestal, they lost the balance, and were gripped by cancerous growth. Only those civilisations survived, although they could not escape being bruised, which did not neglect the moral dimensions of life. He has singled out Indian civilisation as the one.

Gandhi analyzed the main tendencies of the Indian civilisation and stumbled on a General Theory of Human Progress, which he called the Whole Theory of Life. Future of humanity lay in moral advancement; material development was necessary but only as long as it helped in attaining a high standard of moral life. All must have adequate material means to maintain physical health because only a healthy body can produce a healthy mind and thought. All must have all other basic needs in adequate quantity and quality. But no one should have so much that he wields economic power over others. In order that greed does not prevail over need, moral strength must be the standard for measuring human progress.

The crises that modern industrial civilisation faces today are the consequences of the man's progressive control over nature and his fellow beings and the loss of control over his own mind. Gandhi contemplated and looked around and found that the civilisation, which has enslaved India, has also enslaved the whole humanity both physically and mentally. He foresaw more conflicts and wars in the future and more ecological disasters as the umbilical cord that linked man with nature got snapped. The so-called modern civilisation promoted primordial animal urges, and suppressed the urge to love and sacrifice for others. It was the root cause of the prevailing upsurge of violence in the world.

Gandhi also observed that the improvement in physical quality of life in the West was accompanied by the deterioration thereof in the rest of the world. He theorized that such anomalies would further increase so long as moral standard of life remains low. One cannot be materially rich without keeping others poor. And if all achieve the living standard of the West, this earth, given the limits of nature, would not remain worth living. He felt that humanity could not be at peace unless the material development of man was circumscribed by his moral development.

So the new paradigm of progress has to be based on following tenets:

(1) Earth is a live system; it follows certain bio-cybernetic laws to maintain itself in dynamic equilibrium. Man too must not violate these rules while developing its economy, polity and technology.

(2) Earth has enough to meet everyone's needs but not everyone's greed. As such man must live in harmony with nature and within the threshold limits of the biosphere.

(3) Stability of biosphere is essential for human survival and development and hence nothing should be done that disturbs it.

(4) Each activity performed at the individual, family, village, city, regional, national and global levels must conform to the bio-cybernetic laws.

(5) In order that man continues to move forward on his evolutionary path to become a better human being, moral development is a must. Ecological balance, equity, growth form three sides of the triangle of socio-economic development. And moral growth forms the circle, which circumscribes the triangle.

(6) Human Rights have now become one of the main concerns of the Civil Society. The Human Rights of individuals and whole nations have been so trampled by the so-called developed peoples that the issue had to be addressed in right earnest. But unless Rights and duties go together, not much can be achieved. The time has come when Commissions on Human Duties are also appointed along with those of Human rights at different levels – global to local.

(7) To achieve all the above, globalization of the society is a must for the whole world constitutes one single family. But it should not be confined to the economic field. The moral concerns should get equal priority, nor should it dilute the principles of self-reliance and development from below.

Law of the Species

Life occurs in a limited space on the earth and nowhere else that we know of. It, however, does not occur everywhere on the earth in same variety and luxuriance. A thin skin, just a few kilometers thick at the junction of earth's lithosphere and atmosphere known as biosphere forms the habitat for all life forms. The specific conditions that support life vary with the availability of temperature, oxygen, light, nutrients, water and other requirements. The living species, all the way from plants to human beings, are collectively part of the biosphere. There are several million species of organisms; over 30 million of them if all the microbes are included.

The lithosphere, the atmosphere and the biosphere cannot be separated from the earth. In the very process of evolution of earth from its origin some 14 billion years ago (from a gaseous ball going round the sun, to hot magma and then on to further cooling to form the crust, the atmosphere and the hydrosphere and then finally the biosphere) aimed at the evolution of Homo sapiens and finally super humans not in physical but moral terms. The living space formed by interaction among the lithosphere, the atmosphere and the biosphere is so thoroughly integrated with the interior of the earth that its true nature can be understood only by a synergic mind.

Within the biosphere, no life form or species is independent of others as free standing unit. Each one is the product of an evolving environment dependent on its own special circumstances of time and space on the one hand and physical, chemical and biotic conditions on the other. No species has come into being without these connections to the rest of the species and the environment around or by the selective pressure exerted by over thousands of generations of life forms and unimaginable stretches of time. The general functioning of nature is symbiotic: living together for mutual advantage and sacrificing for each other.

The development path of all biota is marked by greater specialization, progressive branching of the evolutionary tree, increasing dependence piled on dependence, and more species surviving and living in more diverse and complex environmental settings. The tropical forests and coral reefs are commonly thought to be ultimate in evolutionary expression. A hundred species of tress per hectare is a common occurrence in the Amazon basin forests, their importance to man depends not only on potential direct benefits but also on indirect benefits derived from their roles as environment sinks and in arousing our feeling of aesthetics, ethics and compassion.

The biosphere is the product of the evolution and continuing interaction among the species over time. While no single species may be essential to the normal functioning of the biosphere, all species together constitute the driving force that maintains it in balance. Asking as to which part of the biosphere is important is meaningless. Each part is important because it is linked to the other parts. Yet, if we have to single out the most important element of the environment from the point of view of biotic diversity, it is the forests that harbour the largest number of species and generate maximum amount of photosynthesis, respiration, annual flux of carbon, nitrogen and sulfur. They must be protected at all cost. Unfortunately, the forests are the major targets of human intrusion into nature.

The expansion of the human influence brings about change in the chemistry of environment. Acidification of rain, climatic change, destruction of soils, and the wholesale scrapping of the earth to put in roads, locate industries, extract minerals, and expand agriculture are some of the examples of human interference with the natural processes. As population increases, the demand for space also increases. Rarely do people realize that the space is not inert. Interference with it means interference with its self-regulative power, with its biodiversity and with its capacity to support life.

The preservation of inherent diversity and its self-regulatory and life-supporting capacities involves acceptance of the fact that we live in a matrix of natural system that dominates the biosphere and operates at little or no expense to society so long as the basic structure of the matrix is maintained intact. Once violated, the cost in the maintenance of the system accumulate slowly to begin with and then exponentially. Our interest in the earth is thus rooted not only in self-interest but also in the larger interest of all life forms.

The emergence of life and various forms thereof on planet earth was not just a matter of chance. If the physical environment created the necessary conditions for life to come into existence, life itself was no less instrumental in giving rise to several elements of the physical environment. Oxygen in the atmosphere, for example, was the product of living organisms. So much so that even some of the rocks like the limestone were created by these organisms. The interaction between the lithosphere and the biosphere was more sympathetic and cooperative than coercive and competitive. Darwin was thus only partially right when he postulated that the evolution of life resulted from natural selection and survival of the fittest.

The living species and the environment around them are tightly coupled and therefore have evolved as a single system in the same way as the mother and her baby in the womb. Our inability to see the earth in its totality is the root cause of the current ecological and environmental problems. It appears that Indians, Chinese and Greeks in 1001 BC were far more realistic and sensitive about it than we are in 2001 AD. Indians equated the earth with Mother and Greeks called it Gaia. In Europe the arrival of the pastoral Aryans reversed the trends; they transformed the living earth into a physical planet. But in India the Aryans behaved differently; they merged into the human ocean of India and looked at earth as source of sustenance and hence as Mother.

The *Atharva Veda* proclaimed: 'Earth is the mother, we are her children.' (*Mata bhoomih putroham prithivyah*). And our Upanishads asserted that 'the whole world constitutes one single family' (*Vasudhaiv Kutumbakam*). These were not words of the primitive minds fearful of the awesome and unpredictable nature. These were the words, which came from a systems view of the universe and from the realization of a built in unity between man and the rest of the biosphere. These words came out of deep contemplation, experimentation and learning. They did not see the earth in pieces, they saw it synergistically and concluded that the pulsating life on the earth was as much, if not more, a product of harmonious interaction between the physical and the biological earth and between humans and other species of life. They saw a thread of unity running through them all. Gandhi in the twentieth century captured this great primordial truth and capsuled it in his Whole Theory of Life.

Gandhi felt that the physical evolution of man ended the moment he was endowed with a thinking, imaging and recalling brain. But the evolutionary process did not stop; his mind continued to evolve, not so much physically as cognitively to take him to his ultimate destiny, which was none other than self-realisation (*Moksha*). Man evolved from animal and he set upon a different path. The self-realisation of animals lies in meeting the sensual urges; of man it lies in transcending the sensual urges. Human mind has the potentials to create monsters, which would destroy the earth, his home; it also has the potentials to transform the earth into a 'heavenly abode': a place that is marked with peace and harmony rather than violence and conflict; cooperation rather than competition; sacrifice rather than greed; and tolerance rather than hate. Man has to rise above his physical needs; he has to aspire the higher spiritual and moral needs. Here in lies his *Moksha*.

Humans ever since they left the body and mind of the chimpanzee have been oscillating between two extremes. Some reach the great intellectual heights to become scientists, technologists etc., while some others, even if less frequently, reach great spiritual heights of truth, ahimsa, love and compassion. The former excel in reasoning while the latter in spiritual awakening. A great majority of the people, however, lives an ordinary life triggered into action by their senses and trying to meet their day to day needs. From time immemorial, great teachers descended on earth to redirect man's energy towards super consciousness. Ram, Krishna, Buddha, Mahavira, Zoroaster, Christ, Mohammad, and Sankara are the historical figures of this rare category.

Many others like Tolstoy, Einstein, Emerson, Ramkrishna Paramhansa, Raman Maharshi, and Gandhi came in the recent past. They were the contemporaries of our parents and grand-parents. They all transcended their sensual urges, and intellectual reasoning to reach great spiritual heights and inspired man to become truly human.

The destiny of man lies in his intellectual-cum-spiritual evolution. Let spiritual not be confused with religious. Religion is only a by-product of the path shown by a great soul to achieve spirituality in a particular context of time and space. While the fundamentals of all religions are the same and eternal, the methods they prescribe to achieve spirituality differ and may not always stand the test of time. The methods, which often take the form of rituals, must therefore, be treated as secondary but the adherents of practically all religions refuse to do so. Religions tell how to become better human beings. But more people and animals have been slaughtered in the name of religion than even the greatest pandemics have done so far. Killing represents a precipitous fall of man from religion.

Earth is not an assemblage of inert rocks and waters; it is alive. The life that makes this earth unique among the planets is one universal whole manifesting in different forms ranging from plants to human beings. All religions ask its adherents to practice truth, nonviolence, peace, harmony; all religions teach love, compassion, and sacrifice. They also teach in a variety ways, how to maintain the natural balance, which enables the earth to keep itself alive.

HOW THE ORGANIC SYSTEMS FUNCTIONS

What is a natural balance and how does it get disturbed? To know this, one has to appreciate that the living organisms cannot be compared to machines. The machines are created; the live organisms evolve. A machine can thus be understood in terms of its parts but the organisms can be understood only in terms of the processes involved in their formation and subsequent development. As F. Capra says in his Turning Point "machines are constructed by assembling a well-defined number of parts in a precise and pre-established way. Organisms, on the other hand, show a high degree of internal flexibility and plasticity. The shape and form of their components vary within certain limits and no two organisms have identical parts. Although the organism as a whole exhibits well-defined regularities and behaviour patterns, the relationships between its parts are not rigidly determined.' Yet the organisms function smoothly, because the coordinating activities do not rigidly constrain the parts but leave room for variation and flexibility, which enables the organisms to adapt to new circumstances.

"Machine function according to linear chains of cause and effect, and when they break down, a single cause for the breakdown can usually be identified. In contrast the functioning of the organisms is guided by cyclical patterns of information flows known as feedback loop. For example, component *A* may affect component *B*; *B* may affect *C*; and *C* may feedback the influence to *A* and thus close the loop. When such a system breaks down, the breakdown is usually caused by multiple factors that may amplify each other through interdependent feedback loops. Which of these factors was the initial cause of the breakdown is often irrelevant."

This non-linear interconnectedness of living organisms indicates that the conventional attempts of biomedical and bioengineering sciences to associate diseases or environmental problems with a single cause is highly mistake. It also questions the apparent fallacy underlying genetic determinism. A living organism is a self-organising system, which exhibits a certain degree of autonomy, for example, in establishing its size according to internal principles of organisation, independent of environmental influences. This is not to say that living organisms have no relation with the environment. They interact with it continuously but the environment does not determine the internal organisation. It only influences their behaviour and functioning.

This relative autonomy of the self-organising systems sheds new light on the age-old philosophical question of free will. From the systems point of view, both determinism and freedom are relative concepts. To the extent that it depends on it through continuous interaction, its activity will be shaped by environmental influences. The relative autonomy of the organisms usually increases with their complexity, and it reaches its culmination in humans.

To maintain their self-organising capacity, the living organisms have to function as open systems having continuous interaction with the environment around them. They have to exchange energy and matter with their environment (metabolism) to stay alive, *i.e.* not to reach the stage of internal equilibrium. Equilibrium means death. Thus the living systems are marked with dynamic stability. "We replace our cells, except for those in the brain, within a few years, yet we have no trouble recognising our friends even after long periods of separation. Such is the dynamic stability of the self-organising systems." This happens because our cells retain their identities through time.

An essential characteristic of self-organising systems is self-renewal. A machine does the work for which it is made. Organisms keep themselves engaged in renewing themselves. Cells breakdown to build up structures, tissues and organs. Pancreas replace their cells every 24 hours, the stomach lining every 72 hours, white blood cells are renewed every 240 hours (ten days), and 98 per cent of the proteins in the brain is turned over in less than one month. This capacity to renew itself and maintain the system stable persists under a variety of environmental circumstances.

The power of the regenerating capacity of the organism decreases with its increasing complexity. Starfish can regenerate its entire body; lizards and crabs, their lost limbs; and higher animals and humans can renew their tissues to heal wounds. But there is limit to regeneration. With aging, this capacity weakens and death is the ultimate fate. To get over the death, the species have found a super repair capacity that is reproduction, a characteristic of all life forms.

In the process of their interaction with the environment for self-maintenance, all living systems oscillate within a limit without undergoing any structural change or major changes in internal functioning. Such a state is known as homeostasis. The organic systems adapt themselves to the environment within the limits set by the homeostasis. For example, if a person goes up to the mountains, he may start panting; his blood pressure may go up. When he comes down to the normal place of his residence, his panting stops and the blood pressure becomes normal again. If the person stays on the mountain for some days, he will go through a further process of adaptation, leading to complex physiological changes. This is called somatic changes. Acclimatization, habit forming and addiction are other cases of this process. But there is a limit. If he tries to climb further up, he would cross the threshold limits of homeostasis. His system would collapse.

Thus life on planet earth depends on the stability and smooth functioning of each element of the biosphere. It follows certain rules to remain in business. Let us look at these rules in some details:

(1) Negative feedback;
(2) Efficient Functioning;

(3) Energy Conservation;
(4) Symbiosis; and
(5) Biological conformity.

Negative Feedback

Like other dynamic systems, the biosphere too is self-regulating within the norms prescribes by the solar system and universe as a whole. Any disturbance in any part of the biosphere permeates the whole system and defense mechanism is triggered off instantaneously. The principle of interlocking self-regulation applies to the living systems and represents the greatest difference between bio-cybernetic and man-made control engineering. In the latter the guide values are given from outside while in the former they are built in the system itself. If we want the man made economic and social systems to be sustainable, we must learn from nature and make them conform to the laws that govern the natural systems to the extent humanly possible.

Over the last 10,000 years or so, man has projected the principles followed by the biological system into the mundane world in a very strange way. He has analyzed these principles to develop sciences and then converted the scientific knowledge into practical technologies. For example, the pumps, levers, filters, batteries, aerodynamics, and even writing and printing are direct imitations of nature. But what we have failed to learn from nature is its Organisation – biocybernetic principles mentioned above. We use a great variety of truncated knowledge without caring for 'before' and 'after' of the product. We get so much mesmerized by our own creativity in a limited sphere that we fail to see its consequences for our biosphere and civilisation. We hit at individual targets, instead of looking at the total system. To move forward we do need a causal-logical thinking, but unless it is linked to feedback control system learning, we will continue to suffer from uncontrolled growth. In other words, we have to create a symbiotic relationship between non-communicating straight line thinking of modern sciences, social sciences included, and circular thinking of the folk cultures to evolve an ever-communicating spiral model of development.

Technology imitates nature but only superficially. It learns from nature how an action produces proportionate reaction. For example, the burning of coal produces heat, which can be converted into energy to drive machines, So we produce coal, convert it into energy and then use the energy so generated to drive various kinds of machines to do the work which was once done by human or animal power. We thus have coal based energy system, which was integrated with a larger industrial system. The burning of the coal added to the carbon dioxide in the atmosphere, which modified the microclimates to begin with affecting adversely the health of the people. In due course, it became a major ecological hazard because it changed even the macroclimates.

Now in nature nothing like this can happen. Nature would not allow the carbon dioxide to increase to an extent that it adversely affected the health of the plants, animals and human beings. The self-control process (negative feedback) would be activated the moment the amount of carbon dioxide crossed the limits already imposed by the biosphere. Natural violations of the rule have occurred only at the time of major diastrophic movements such volcanic eruptions, climatic changes, etc. And each time it happened, it resulted in catastrophic changes in the evolutionary process of life. If human beings now create the same conditions, the impact on life on planet earth cannot be other than catastrophic.

Efficient Functioning Overrides Growth

In natural systems functioning gets priority over growth. Let us take our own body. Until death, it is totally geared to proper functioning. If we follow all the laws that govern the natural systems, diseases would become scarce. Each cell of our body is self-regulating, multi-functional, self-producing, and symbiotic with adjoining cells and with the higher-level systems like tissues and organs of the body. In order to function efficiently, it does not grow in size. It multiplies itself at a given speed -- never slower or faster. Whenever it multiplies faster than the naturally prescribed speed, it becomes cancerous. Whether it is malignant or nonmalignant depends on the speed of division. We thus learn that healthy cells do not grow in size; they only divide themselves at a given speed. Permanent functioning through sub-division at a given rate ensures the health of the cells. Erratic growth or multiplication leads to death.

There is a lesson for us. We suffer from growth mania. We want higher economic growth, technological growth, knowledge growth etc, but we have rarely given thought to the implications these growing artificial systems have on the ecology and environment; culture and society. Economic growth has so far been accompanied by environmental pollution, violence, poverty and social disintegration. We have already reached a stage where man is prepared to sacrifice himself in order that he can eliminate his presumed opponents whom he might have never seen, even at the cost of his own life. He loves killing and kissing death.

This is not to suggest that growth is anathema to natural systems. Does our body not grow? It does, but not at the cost of smooth functioning. Disproportionate, untimely, or abnormal growth signifies disease, not health. Same way growth that is not subordinated to smooth functioning should be treated as a disease. If our economic system just grows but does not function well enough to remain in health, it must lead to cancer and death. Similarly, our civilisation and each subsystem of it – big or small—all the way from individuals to families, communities, nations, occupational sub-systems like agriculture, industry, social services, and spatial systems like cities, towns and villages must remain at dynamic equilibrium, *i.e.* in a state of functioning and in harmony with each other, to remain healthy. Our civilisation is a subsystem of the larger system of biosphere, which is a sub-system of Mother Earth. It must follow the laws that govern the Mother Earth. Many ancient civilisations died because they failed to remain at equilibrium and at a high level of efficiency. Our civilisation too may go the same way if it does not develop self-regulatory mechanisms to control unhealthy growth.

As systems grow in size, their complexity increases. If the growth disturbs the functioning, the systems get derailed. If growth is accompanied by smooth functioning, then the system remains healthy. Unfortunately most of the man made systems just grow unmindful of functioning. It is easy to manage a small village but very difficult to manage a city which has grown to an enormous size. A simple life keeps the body system in order. When it is surrounded by an enormous array of goods, gadgets and fast moving machines, it gets complicated. Pressures are built from all directions; health is impaired. The large systems need different styles and structures of management. But we tend to manage them as if they are still small. We manage metropolises in the same way as we manage villages as if they are just enlarged villages. They are not. Unlike a village, which is marked by homogeneity in all spheres, large cities contain hundreds of neighbourhoods and a great variety of people. In a household industry everything is so simple to manage. The rules that apply in the management of a household manufacturing would be totally misfit in the management of a modern factory, a modern irrigation system, a modern waterworks, and a modern powerhouse.

Whether the system is small or big, it has to function well to keep itself alive. It should be self-regulated as are the natural systems. Further, it should not be seen as independent of the other systems of the same class or different classes together forming the bigger social or economic systems. Each system consists of a number of sub-systems; it is a part of a higher level system. For the proper functioning of a system, its subsystems must function efficiently. It should not grow or expand unmindful of its impact on its subsystems on the one hand and sister systems on the other. It should also adhere to the guide values of the larger system of which it is a part.

In a society marked by cutthroat competition who cares for the implications of what one does for other peoples and institutions? Who bothers about what happens to others so long as one's own interests are served? Gandhi was right when he laid emphasis on the Law of Love, on human brotherhood and on cooperation. He was opposed to greed based economic development; he wanted it to be need based. He was opposed to large scale operations; he wanted smaller units within the control of man. He wanted less of technology, because its misuse often derails the functioning of the natural systems.

Energy Conservation

The nature not only gives us the fundamentals for the organisational structures of the systems but also the most efficient methods of maintaining them. They utilize the already existent forces and energies by controlling and diverting them in desired directions. Tit for tat is not the principle followed by the natural systems. It follows the jiu-jitsu principle. The brute force applied from outside is not repulsed by brute force. By means of energy cascades, energy chains and energy coupling, nature achieves a very high degree of energy efficiency.

The waste of one element of a natural system becomes the feed of the other elements. Thus there is constant exchange of energy among the various elements. Even the minute natural systems, like our cells, generate their own energy; and if they take energy from outside, like the plants, the source is inexhaustible like the sun.

Multiple use is another method of saving energy. All viable systems prefer the products and processes with which they can kill many birds with one stone. As such a system to be stable must follow this principle. Everything we produce must be put to multiple uses. In fact this is how people in olden days used to live.

Recycling is another method of energy saving. A beneficial reintegration of the wastes into a living circulatory process of the participating systems is one of the fundamental rules the natural systems follow. In fact, there is no waste in nature. Our artificial systems are full of wastes, the waste, which are not reused and therefore pollute the environment. In our thinking, there is only cause and effect, and beginning and end. But in the circulatory systems of the nature there is no difference between cause and effect and between base materials and wastes.

When Gandhi said that ends and means are two sides of the same coin and they are inseparable, he was only interpreting the natural laws. When he said that each system from top to bottom must be self-supporting (*Swadeshi*), he was only echoing the call of nature. And when he said that each unit—individual, family, community, district, state, nation and the earth itself should be self-managing and dynamically stable (*Swaraj*), he was only trying to remind us the principles on which nature worked.

Symbiotic Relationship

Symbiosis means coexistence of different species of organisms and systems to their mutual advantage without a built-in process of exploitation. In the biological sphere, one finds widely varying forms of symbiosis – from intestinal bacteria, which live on man's food and give him vital vitamins in return to global open symbiosis between the animal and vegetable world via the circulatory system of photosynthesis and respiration. Symbiosis helps nature save lot of raw materials, energy and transportation costs. There are multiple and free benefits for the participating systems.

More the differences among the natural systems greater is the symbiosis. That is why nature does not believe in homogenization. Even in a small space, so many species of plants and animals exist. The lion preys on animals when it is hungry. Once the hunger is satiated, it settles down for rest and does not bother for tomorrow. It is not greedy; it does not accumulate and store; and it has no sense of enmity with the animals he preys on. So, the animal population remains stable as does the lion population. There is symbiosis among the two. But the example is too narrow in scope. In fact the whole forest habitat is bound in one symbiotic system.

Look at our own artificial systems. Large industrial systems, energy systems, towns and cities, monocultures in the agricultural, industrial and service fields stand separate from each other. There is no symbiosis among them. All of them produce huge amount of waste that cannot be recycled. Industries produce solid, liquid and gaseous wastes. So do the cities, powerhouses, atomic plants, and even little community stores and individual households. It is possible to create a sort of eco-system in industry: metal industry cooperating with paper industry, construction with coal industry, food with water purification industry, and so on. The development of symbiosis is, however, a communication task, more than the technological task.

This gives a clue to why Gandhi was so much against the industrial growth mentality. In fact *Hind Swaraj* is nothing but a direct condemnation of this mentality. He felt convinced that industrialism would ruin humanity. But he was not against industries as such. He was against the mentality underlying industrialism.

Compatibility with Nature

The health of Nature and Man is closely interrelated with ecology and economy. A deteriorating natural environment adversely impacts the health of man. To take care of the deteriorating health, man has to invest heavily in hospitals, doctors and medicines. This ultimately proves a costly proposition. When rivers lose their ability to purify themselves, when the air is unable to clean itself, when soil fails to re-fertilize itself, and when humans lose their natural immunity against diseases, the society has to bear a heavy social burden.

Think of the number of lives lost due to diseases, which are caused by environmental pollution and social stresses, the number of man days lost due to sickness and debilitation, and amount of resources invested in treatment of diseases. If we take care of the ecology, we would have less of diseases, will need less of doctors, medicines and hospitals, and will have a more active labour force.

Every product, every process, every function and every organisation has to be compatible with the biology of Man and Nature. The concrete jungles of our cities, the dung heaps of our villages, the smoke and solid and liquid wastes of our factories, and death traps of our roads have polluted human biology too, apart from the natural environment in which man lives. These concrete jungles are getting devoid of even dwarf plant life. Large scale clearing of forests has robbed the earth of is pollution sinks.

Gandhi was right indeed when he said that man would ultimately have to live in villages, not in cities and that he would have to adopt small scale activities instead of large scale projects like big factories and powerhouses. He was totally opposed to industrial mentality. He wanted man to be as self-reliant as possible and this he could do only by living with nature.

MAN-NATURE RELATIONSHIP

Man's Impact on Nature

Man has been a major agent of change particularly during the last few centuries. Ever since the emergence of the Homo sapiens, the earth has been subjected to continuous anthropogenic changes, slowly to begin with. The first wave of changes were brought about by the domestication of plants and animals and consequent agricultural revolution and permanent human settlements. After over two millenniums, came the era of modern science and technology and consequent change in the mode of production popularly known as Industrial Revolution which armed man with power to explore the interior of the earth, ocean deeps, and the outer space. The prospects of material prosperity were widened beyond expectations even if limited to Western Europe and Anglo-America to begin with. Among the late beneficiaries were only a few small countries. The negative implications of the Industrial Revolution were, however, far greater. The material prosperity of Europe and America was accompanied by acute poverty and deprivation in the rest of the world. In fact the prosperity of Europe and America and later of Japan was dependent on the poverty of the rest of the world.

Another implication of the Industrial Revolution was the ecological crisis that we face today. The air, water, land and plants, which support life on planet earth, have been polluted to an extent that no one is now safe – rich or poor. Climate change may shrink the land surface by millions of hectares chasing people from low-lying areas out. Ozone layer depletion may lead to skin cancer pandemic. Already millions of people have become victims of environmental pollution. More are likely to come in is grips. Man is on the verge of becoming an endangered species.

Ecological disturbances affect the biological systems. At first the complexities of the biotic systems are reduced: the forests become less diversified and many animal species are lost forever. And if the disturbances continue, all the tree species may be lost and replaced by equally diversified species of shrubs. A similar process can take place in the animal kingdom too. Unfortunately, the ecosystem once destroyed cannot be brought back to its original state. Such changes are irreversible, yet we continue to destroy our plant and animal life.

Gandhi in *Hind Swaraj* therefore insisted on living within the limits of nature. There are certain laws, which govern the functioning of nature. Any tempering with them can only invite disaster. He is being quoted by the United Nations to bring home the realisation that as long as man follows the present style of life and adheres to a world view, which violates the natural laws, the possibility of his continuing physical existence cannot be assured and hence the question of his advancing towards his moral destiny does not arise.

Man's Impact on Society

When Gandhi wrote *Hind Swaraj*, India was suffering from acute poverty. Gandhi contended that the Western civilisation by its very nature must keep some countries poor so that Europe and America can remain rich and richer. Gandhi was not off the mark. During the last 90 years, not much has changed in so far as disparities among the poor and the rich countries is concerned. India's GDP in 1980 was 172 billion dollars while that of the USA, 2008 billion dollars (12 times larger). Fifteen years later in 1995, India's GDP increased to $324 billion and that of the USA to $ 7000 billion (21 times larger). When converted into per capita income, the relative position of the two countries becomes more disgusting.

The disparities noted above are not limited to India and the USA: they run across all countries and peoples of the world. Many countries have lower per capita income than India; and a few have higher than that of the USA. The same situation prevails inside various countries. In India for example the per capita income of Punjab state in 1996-97 was Rs. 18,213; of Bihar it was only Rs. 3835. Similar glaring disparities exist between towns and villages; and groups of people.

The problems of inequity are not limited to economic sphere. Look at the 2001 census data of India: of the 1.02 billion people almost one third (36%) have never gone to school; they are illiterate, 25 per cent being males and 47 per cent females. In the state of Bihar, 52 per cent of the people are illiterate. As against this, in Kerala only 9 per cent of people are illiterate. The expectation of life at birth was 61 years in 1996. It stood at 67 years in Kerala. When we compare these figures with that of the developed parts of the world (77 years) we realize how man has treated his own fellowmen.

No matter which aspect of life we take into account, we find vast differences among nations, regions, localities and peoples. While one third of the population of the world lives in material comforts, an equal number leads a below human standard life. The tragedy is that both the poor and rich, contribute equally in making this earth unsuitable for any form of life to survive for too long.

It is said that as national income increases, disparities in distribution of income decrease. This is, however, not borne out by facts. Lowest 20 per cent of the people in the USA share 11 per cent of GDP; in India the lowest 20 per cent share 8.5 per cent of income. The upper most 20 per cent of the people share 42 per cent of the GDP in the USA; the India its counterparts share 42.50 per cent.

Today the world is divided into two groups of countries: North and South, developed and underdeveloped, industrialized and unindustrialized, rural and urban, and so on. These divisions are likely to persist unless there is some major shift in the social and economic management of the global economy. With the present (2001 AD) per capita income of $ 400 per annum, India would take so many decades to reach the income level of the USA ($27,000) even if the US economy stops growing and Indian economy grows at the rate of 10 per cent per annum.

What are the causes of these disparities? One may attribute part of the responsibility to the mal-distribution of natural resources, but major factor responsible for it is the mindset and the worldview that promotes accumulation and a tendency to have control over nature and fellow human beings. It is greed, not need that causes disparities. There is enough food in the world to feed every one well; there are enough resources in the world to wipe out poverty, to remove illiteracy; and to eradicate diseases. The money that people spend on tobacco will be sufficient to provide elementary education to children still out of school; and that they spent on liquor would be sufficient to give health facilities to all. If the greed for goods and services is brought down to need level, poverty will be eradicated and the ecological problems we face today will become part of history.

Man's Impact on Man

Man has inflicted lot of harm on himself – his physical health, his mental balance and his spiritual growth. The industrial civilisation is known for high speed. In fact, speed is one of its main characteristics. High speed results from desire to change fast, which in turn produces unprecedented changes in all aspects of life. When Gandhi said that trains spread plague, he was figuratively right. Recent studies on spatial diffusion of innovations, diseases and ideas prove his point. As pointed out in chapter 10, speed by itself is not to be condemned. Speed comes in the way of patience, cool thinking, contemplation, concentration, meditation, love and compassion. It generates confusion and cluttering of the mind. But there are several benefits of speed. High speed computers help us understand the environment around us especially if the causative factors are too many. Speed also helps man do many things he could have not done specially in the field of technology. The ill effects of speed can, however, be tempered and moderated. Speed need not bewilder people and make them lose control over their own creations.

There are two ways of handling speed: one, reduce it to the level of human comprehension; and two, create institutions and conditions, which can counter its ill effects. For example, speed decreases physical distance between man and man yet it does not bring people closer to each other. It tends to divides people more than to unite them. Meeting face to face and touching each other gives a feeling of togetherness, love and emotional attachment. What we need to do is to strengthen institutions, even create new ones, which bring people together; which promote human brotherhood; which give peace to the mind and body. In other words, the scientific and technological revolution must be accompanied by a spiritual revolution. The greatness of Gandhi lay in merging the two and thereby cleansing both of obscurantism.

Gandhi was against speed as a matter of principle, but it did not mean that he wanted to go back to wheelbarrow days. In a spiritually surcharged society, speed would not go uncontrolled; it would be used selectively to enrich human life not only by the ecstasy of the intellectual achievements but also by that of the spirit. The human touch that speed kills would then be restored.

PART III

RELEVANCE OF HIND SWARAJ

11

Pre-Independence Assessment

IMMEDIATE REACTION

Reaction of the Colonial Government

Hind Swaraj was proscribed by the then Government of Bombay Presidency soon after its publication because it had the potential of spreading disaffection among the people of India against the British government. The note written by the Gujarati interpreter to the British Government on March 15, 1915 on the issue of banning the book is reproduced below:

> "I have given sufficient matter to form an opinion whether the book is seditious or not.... Nowhere the author of the book advocates revolt or the use of force against the British government in India. But, he openly advocates passive resistance to subvert British supremacy, advises all people not to cooperate with government. If this idea takes hold of the mind of young inexperienced men, it might lead to systematic strikes among government servants of various classes as well as public works such as railways, posts, telegraphs, etc. Sure it is a very dangerous thought to the safety of the government. The sooner it is suppressed the better."

The official circles were not alone in criticizing the book even if for different or just the opposite reasons. It did not get a favourable response in India. The revolutionaries were of course critical of it for they found it diversionary. But there were critics even among the moderates.

Gokhale's Cryptic Remarks

When Gokhale saw the English translation of *Hind Swaraj* during his visit to South Africa in 1912, he considered it so crude and hastily conceived that he prophesied that Gandhi himself would destroy the book after spending a year in India. Nine years later in 1921, Gandhi said: "with deference to the memory of the great teacher, I may say that his prediction has failed to come true.

This, however, does not mean that Gandhi's respect for Gokhale diminished even the least. He considered him his political guru; and Gokhale did everything possible to give the leadership of the freedom movement in the hands of Gandhi. Speaking at the Lahore Congress in December 1909, Gokhale moved a resolution on South African situation and paid a glowing tribute to Gandhi:

> "After the immortal part which Mr. Gandhi has played in the South African affair, I must say it will not be possible for any Indian, at any time, here or in any other assembly of Indians, to mention his name without deep emotions and pride. Gentlemen, it is one of the privileges of my life that I know Mr. Gandhi intimately and I can tell you that a purer, a nobler, a braver and a more exalted spirit has never moved on this earth. Here the huge congress gathering rose to its fact and accorded three hearty cheers for Gandhi. "Mr. Gandhi is one of those men, who living an austerely simple themselves and devoted to all the highest principles of love to their fellow beings and to truth and justice, touch the eyes of their weaker brethren as with magic and give them a new vision. He is a man who may be well described as a man among men, a hero among heroes, a patriot among patriots, and we may well say that in him Indian humanity at present time has really reached its highest watermark." (Tendulkar, Vol. 1, p. 112)

And then let us see what Gokhale has to say about Gandhi after having seen *Hind Swaraj* during his South African visit in 1912:

> "Only those who have come in personal contact with Mr. Gandhi as he is now, can realize the wonderful personality of the man. He is without doubt made of the stuff of which heroes and martyrs are made. Nay, more, he has in him the marvellous spiritual power

> to turn ordinary men around him into heroes and martyrs.... In all my life I have known only two men who affected me spiritually in the manner that Mr. Gandhi does – our great patriarch, Mr. Dadabhai Naoroji, and my late master, Mr. Ranade – men before whom not only are we ashamed of doing anything unworthy, but in whose presence our very minds are afraid of thinking anything that is unworthy.... India owes an immense debt of gratitude to him.... At every gathering the leading Europeans, when they come to know that Mr. Gandhi was there, would immediately gather around him anxious to shake hands with him, making it quite clear that though they fought him hard and tried to crush him in the course of the struggle, they honoured him as a man." (Tendulkar, p. 131)

Not until 1919, did *Hind Swaraj* become widely known in intellectual circles in India. All of them, however, did not like it. S. Dange, a noted communist leader, in his book *Gandhi versus Lenin* (1921) and M. N. Roy in his book *India in Transition* (1922) dismissed it as mere humanitarianism based on ignorance of the laws of class struggle. It is quite another thing that at least Dange changed his views so enormously in the later stages of his life that he almost became a Gandhian. Sir Shankar Nair, a leading lawyer of India (he was also the president of Indian National Congress) in his book *Gandhi and Anarchy* (1922), castigated Gandhi for advocating anarchism through *Satyagraha*.

The reception of *Hind Swaraj* in the USA was warm. An American edition of the book entitled *Serman on the Sea*, edited by H.T. Mazumdar and introduced by John Haynes Holmes (1924), an American Christian liberal, was published in 1924. In India the book remained neglected by both liberal and revolutionary leaders. The British were, however, happy that it appeared to make no impact on the people of India!!

ARYAN PATH SYMPOSIUM—1938

The first evaluation of *Hind Swaraj* or Indian Home Rule by the British writers and intellectuals took place in 1938 via Volume IX (September 1938) issue of now defunct *Aryan Path.* A copy of the book was sent to a large number of people both Indians and Europeans for comments. The editorial note of the journal containing the comments is indicative of the high esteem Madam H.P. Blavatsky who started the journal accorded to the book.

"How many even among the thoughtful seriously took to heart the warning given in the last quarter of the last century, that modern civilisation was no civilisation and that it would soon die a violent death if it persists in its mode of life? The West was too intoxicated with its scientific inventions and the rest to think of 'those higher and nobler conceptions of public and private duties which lie at the root of all spiritual and material improvements'. More, the intoxicated West has reeled into the East, and many had taken his bravado and brawl to be words of knowledge and strength and infested by his company, had begun to follow his example. Japan was the first to succumb and she has already begun to reap the evil effects, as has the Continent of Europe.

Madame Blavatsky, looking on the plane of causes, which were leading modern civilisation from guilt to punishment, condemned it as degraded. India's living leader – the greatest man in the public world today – experiencing some of the effects of the drunken civilisation proclaimed it 'as civilisation only in name'; for it 'takes note neither of morality, nor of religion'. Speaking of India, Gandhiji made a distinction: "It is my deliberate opinion that India is being ground down not under the English heel but under that of modern civilisation". For this curse of civilisation, Madame Blavatsky gave – between 1871 and 1891 – a cure in her writings, which contain principles and applications, but these were not practiced on any large scale even among those who called themselves Theosophists. When Gandhiji wrote *Hind Swaraj* in 1909 and advocated in his own way and words almost the same cure, there were many and not only 'a dear friend' who called him – 'Thou fool !"

In 1909, the drunkard was drinking still; the East was still in the grip of glamour produced by Western civilisation. Then came the first world war, which demonstrated how true was the vision of Madame Blatvastky, how prophetic were the words of Gandhiji. That war was fought to stop further wars; but the leaders who produced the Treaty of Versailles were so full of the intoxication of their civilisation that they manufactured the germs of future wars fancying that they were sowing the seeds of future peace. Recent events clearly prove that even the Second World War has not proved to be the last war. As our civilisation advances, more weapons in number as well as ferocity are becoming available to man for newer wars.

The very bases of modern civilisation are competition, self-interest, preying on others, conflicts and wars. Our philosophy, economics, sociology, psychology, geography, history and sciences in general are designed to break the whole into parts and not to harmonize the parts to enable the whole to function better. If the current trends continue and the conflict between man and nature on the one hand and man and man on the other does not end, this civilisation must come to a crashing halt sooner than later. Those who feel that man has reached a level of mental development that a recovery is still possible suggest a variety of panacea, some utopian while others realistic but partial. "Civilisation is not an incurable disease", wrote Gandhi in 1909. He gave a detailed outline of the steps to be taken to save it from catastrophe. *Hind Swaraj* presents in nutshell the model of a new civilisation he had in his mind. It gives in some details and effectively what is wrong with modern civilisation and why it must be transformed into a truly modern civilisation.

By an irony of fate, a large number of Indians, especially among the youth, are still under the influence of Western socio-political doctrines. Even those doctrines, which the West itself has found wanting in many respects are still being pursued by educated men and women in India. India has a special claim on Gandhi. Gandhi wrote *Hind Swaraj* for Indians, more than for anyone else. In fact its first edition was in Gujarati. Not only India's future is bound up with her acceptance or rejection of Gandhiji's teachings in building her own civilisation founded upon moral principles, but that of the world also. An increasing number of thinkers in the West are beginning to appreciate the ideas contained in *Hind Swaraj*.

Then follow the comments by Europeans interested in India. Some of these comments are reproduced below for ready reference.

Frederick Soddy

Professor Frederick Soddy, a well known chemist and economist concluded his review by saying: "Having just returned from a visit of India, the reviewer can honestly say he saw little outwardly there to suggest it, except, perhaps a certain race consciousness. On the other hand, the internal combustion engine seems to have been at least as busy there as elsewhere in altering the mode of livelihood of peoples, not to attempt any more profound analysis of the situation."

Professor Soddy suggestsed that people should read *Hind Swaraj* and make their own opinion about it. "If you want to know anything about anyone outstanding, probably the worst thing to do is to read other peoples' impressions about him and his work." He was right. He examined the book only outwardly and missed its finer and seminal points to conclude that it was based on fancied assumptions.

Soddy's comments are subtle and penchant. He has reviewed the book chapter by chapter. On the preface he says that 'while admitting that the time was not ripe for it (discarding of modern civilisation)' it was less ripe after 30 years in 1938 and 'short of time going backward or a similar miracle, the likelihood of India ultimately doing so seems remote.' Certain features, even the whole of the philosophy may survive, as founded on one of the eternal verities, incorporated with the positive achievements of modern civilisation, which, just as much as they, are also founded on the eternal verities. The days when this self-satisfied assumption of the superiority of one sort of truth over another was considered the highest form of it seem to have passed away. But then in Gujarati, civilisation means good conduct, which rather begs the question!"

Soddy refers to Gandhi's criticism of modern civilisation as destructive, "the destructive criticism then takes in its sweep railways, lawyers and doctors, the very institutions we have hitherto considered to be good, the argument (the 'seminal' one) being that India is and always has been one nation in spite of the wide differences in religion. The lawyers forment religious and civil quarrels and if they abandon their professions, the English could not rule for a day. No lawyer, no Courts, no English."

D.G.H. Cole

"Thirty years ago when Gandhi wrote *Hind Swaraj* "the foundations of Western Civilisation looked stable – under Western eyes. England might 'lose' India – some of us hoped she would, in the sense of losing the power to rule over the Indians as subject peoples. But we were hardly thinking of the possibility that England itself—the England we knew changed out of all recognition by the events of less than two hundred years – might be swept away, and all the civilisation of Western Europe melt into a mangled mass of twisted metal work and torn flesh, the harvest of human inventiveness mishandled by human devilment and fear. But today who among us has confidence that this Western civilisation will survive at all? It is not 'doomed'; but it is threatened, and it grows plainer that it can be saved from destruction only if it can be quickly and radically transformed from within."

"*Gandhi's case against the West looks, then, infinitely stronger than it looked, to us Westerners, thirty years ago.* For it does seem as if all our material advances in machine mastery were unloosing upon us, not the plenty for which we had hoped, but an overmastering capacity for destruction. Nor is it merely that we have grown more efficient in dealing with death and mutilation. We have also grown more cruel – or some of us have; and those of us who are untouched by the recrudescence of cruelty know not how to prevent its spread without dire risk of falling ourselves under its spell. We are torn horribly between the will to resist evil and the sense that in resisting it we may become evil and fail to achieve anything except an universal desolation. Stalin is perhaps troubled by no such fears: I do not know. He at any rate is trying to save the machine-age from destruction by developing further, on a basis of mass ownership and unrestricted consumption, the power of the machine. But we, further West watch the great Russian venture with growing anxiety, for there too we find cruelty and mass persecution and intolerance. And in the Western democracies, we arm feverishly for defense, without even the sense of creation and what the Greeks called Athlos that, I am sure makes dictatorship an exciting experience to many in Nazi Germany as well as in the Soviet Union.

"And yet, I am not a Gandhist. I do not believe that Western civilisation is, of sharp necessity, at enmity with the human soul. I do not believe that science is man's curse, or that the world would be better without doctors or without machines. I do care about the body as well as the soul, and about the enjoyment of the body. I do not believe that the peasant life is the best, or that home spun is preferred to that of machine made, or that it would be better for men to sweep all their discoveries of the past two centuries aside, and go back to take up their lives again at a point, I know not where in history, before these things have become their masters. I make no judgment for Indians concerning the road they should travel; for I am not competent to make judgment. But for myself and men and the women I know, I am not prepared to say that Western civilisation is inherently false to the souls of men."

Western civilisation does have many weaknesses, which Gandhi very rightly points out in *Hind Swaraj*. But so has the Indian civilisation. These weaknesses crept into it in the course of history.

Gandhi advocates efforts to remove them. Such efforts should not be limited to Indian civilisation; they should be addressed to Western civilisation too. I believe that we can save and ennoble our western civilisation if we will: that we can make a better world without wholesale destruction of the very roots of our life.

"I do however agree that politics will not save us, and that something must happen simultaneously in the mind (or souls) of many of us, if our civilisation is to be saved at all. I agree that for us, as well as for Indians, Swaraj must be an individual as well as political experience, It must come to as something that fills us with a power to deny fear. To day our fears are hurling us towards destruction. Fear breeds counter fear; it causes us to huddle together under this or that dictator, to cry out for protection or for an aggression, which is the self-assertiveness of panic. If there were no fear, the might of the dictators would melt in an hour, and 'democracies' would turn democratic in the twinkling of an eye. There will be no rulers and no ruled; no bullies and no victims. We should be civilized people; masters of ourselves and strong enough to make ourselves without peril the masters of nature."

"If there were no fear! But Gandhi knows, much better than he knew thirty years ago, that fear cannot be driven out of men's minds by exhortation. A man here and there may conquer fear; but not even a saint can dispell it wholly from him. I think, Gandhi admits that because of the fearing men's minds, he must work in any movement that involves cooperation of many for a common end, for something that falls short of his ideal. Alone, he can aim directly at his ideal – for its realisation in himself. Corporately, ... he must work for parliamentary *Swaraj* in accordance with the wishes of the people of India."

We have all, individually, to face this problem of translating our ideals into political practices. Indeed, we have to face two problems. We have both to discover terms on which we work with others towards the realisation of our ideals, and, as individuals, to translate into action, personally as well as politically, our ideals of ourselves. Gandhi solved long ago, the second of these problems. That is his immense strength – that he is as near as man can be to *Swaraj* in a purely personal sense. But I think, he has never solved, to his own satisfaction, the other problem – that of finding terms of collaboration that could span the gulf between man and man and between acting alone and helping others to act in accordance with their lights, which involves acting with them and as one of them – being at one's self and someone else, someone's self can and must regard and criticize and attempt to value.

"Indeed, I think this problem is insoluble in any final sense. It requires constant adjustments and accommodations; and unless a man is very firmly seated in himself, his alter ego all too easily ceases to be objective to him, and usurps the place of his soul. Gandhiji's strength is to have made himself proof against that usurpation; and we in the West shall go down to defeat unless we can find guides and leaders who are also proof against it.

"But, to make ourselves proof, need we be ascetic as Gandhi is? And need we put our own civilisation behind us? If we must, then there is nothing before us but bloody destruction to clear the encumbered way; for it is impossible, in the West, to make a movement on these terms. If our civilisation is radically wrong, it will destroy itself; and in proportion as we are skilled in science the work of destruction will be horrible and the suffering intense. Men in mass cannot be led against all their ingrained habits and values. The Gandhi of this book could not be, in the West, a leader, but only a martyr at most."

"If the fault of our civilisation is but superficial, however pervasive and disastrous, if our men are men underneath the veneer, and our technicians and scientists ready enough to work for good human ends given but half a chance, then we need not despair. We shall need leaders who are masters of themselves as Gandhi is, but masters after our Western fashion, which is not his, or India's."

"*Swaraj*, for Gandhi, involves nonviolence, because no cooperation is the final effective weapon. So it is, I daresay, where a people of many millions is set against a handful of foreign rulers. But is it so when German or Italian airmen are massacring the Spanish people, when Japanese airmen are slaughtering thousands and thousands in Chinese cities, when German armies have marched into Austria and are threatening to march into Czechoslovakia, when Abyssinia has been bloodily bombed into defeat? Until two years or so ago, I believed myself opposed to war and death-dealing violence under all circumstances. But today, hating war, I would risk war to oppose these horrors. I would risk war; and yet, even now, the second self of mine shrinks back appalled at the thought of killing a man. Personally, I would much sooner die than kill. But may it not be my duty to try to kill rather than to die? Gandhi could answer that no such dilemma could confront a man who had achieved his personal *Swaraj*. I do not claim to have achieved mine; but I am unconvinced that the dilemma would confront me, here and now in Western Europe, less disturbingly if I had."

C. Delisle Burns

Burns was a University lecturer and editor of the International Journal of Ethics. He has stressed the point that Western Civilisation has far deeper roots than mechanical and hence there is possibility of its playing a far more constructive role in shaping the future of the world than what Gandhi perceived in *Hind Swaraj*.

Welcoming the book burn says: "A student of the history of civilisation will note, first, the governing principles of Gandhi's thought, which are in the main valid and would have been treated as undeniable, if we were not faced by the recrudescence of barbarism in Hitler's Germany. Gandhi's first principle is that moral distinction between good and bad, right and wrong. justice and injustice are of fundamental importance, as compared with more superficial distinctions between men in race, sex, religion or political opinion." Having said this, he finds some difficulties with the words Gandhi uses and the logic he presents to prove his points.

First of all the distinction between good conduct and right conduct is blurred. "The inquisitor who burnt heretics in the Middle Ages, no doubt had the best of intentions; but he could have learnt something from somebody else about right action." True Gandhi sets a standard for right action: force should not be used.... This means that their must be some practical means for the removal of oppression and redress of grievances other than the use of force." But what about the use of force for the maintenance of moral authority, say of a government. "Civilised life is the toleration of all opinions except one – that is the opinion of those who advocate and use intolerance against their opponents. But it is by no means certain that Gandhi distinguishes, at least in this little book, between force as an instrument of moral authority and the force used by any group of gangsters or political irreconcilables. He is right in saying that India" ought not copy the West and that "India has something of her own to contribute to the tradition of civilised life; and Indians ought to be able to ensure that no force is ever used except as the instrument of moral authority. But when moral authority becomes or is in dispute, there is always a danger that force may be used, not as an instrument of moral authority, but as a substitute for it." That is why Gandhi chooses Soul Force which in the Western parlance will be called truthfulness, "no one doubts in the West or the East that civilised life and a community worth living in, depend upon the reliability of its members and the tendency of most of them to treat the common good as superior to any private gain." This is a very definite improvement in what we in the West have learnt to believe about civilised life."

Burns however notes some serious problems with regard to Gandhi's choice of doctors, lawyers, machines etc, as the soul manifestations of Western civilisation. "We have in the West a great tradition of music and plastic arts, of drama and lyric poetry in many different languages, of selfless devotion to the pursuit of truth among scientist, and examples of religious and moral insight and enthusiasm which are not less great than those of any other civilisation. Unfortunately, the small groups of English men and women who control other countries and reside in them, are generally ignorant of the arts and the sciences of Western civilisation itself. Even missionaries, who go to alien races to spreads what they believe to be truth, are generally ignorant of the greatest achievements of Western civilisation in the arts and the sciences and the history of religion and morals. To condemn Western civilisation, therefore, because of the mechanisms, which are taken to be its characteristic expression, is to misunderstand what is being opposed."

"Another mistake in Gandhi's teaching is his condemnation of machinery as evil." Gandhi goes to the extent of saying that railways spread plague and evils of various kinds. "This is a fundamental philosophical error. It implies that we are as morally evil as any instrument which may be misused.... But it is ridiculous to treat as morally good or evil the mechanism which can be used equally by saints and villains....If Gandhi's teaching is to have its highest value in its emphasis upon moral issues and opposition to the pursuit of private wealth and power, it must be freed from the confusion which arises when mechanisms are given the moral qualities, which really belong to those who use or misuse them."

John Middleton Murry

John, a Christian socialist, called *Hind Swaraj* a great book: one of the spiritual classics of the world. Gandhi has reminded "us the way of nonviolence is a possible ...way out of the horrors into which the mass democracies of Europe are preparing to plunge. The greatest Christian teacher in the modern world is Gandhi; and *Hind Swaraj* (I believe) the greatest book that has been written in modern times." However, in spite of its clarity and beauty, it confronts us with awkward questions." First, his criticism of parliamentary democracy was scathing but his corporate life was devoted to the attainment of Parliamentary *Swaraj*. One finds it difficult to understand. Second, Gandhi's *satyagraha* in practice amounted to pressure tactics which can not go with his concept of non-violence and Love Force. Third, his condemnation of the technical civilisation of Europe as evil is not borne out of deeper understanding of Western civilisation. Machine is only a tool; it is not evil; much depends on who uses it and for what purpose. Is it not possible to control the machine with the power of Love? If it is, then why so much fuss about machines?

On the first question we need greater clarity on 'individual' and 'corporate' activity with respect to *satyagraha*, as it was used in Indian National Movement. "What is a non-violent means? Is non-violence, *faute de mieux*, really non-violence at all? Gandhi himself is acutely aware of the difficulty. His complaint the 'non-violence is not being carried out in the spirit of the book' is essentially a complaint that non-violence has become a mere technique of pressure."

The *Swaraj* that would emerge from the non-violent means would not be parliamentary democracy 'for the attainment of which his corporate activity is devoted.' "What Gandhi means by real *Swaraj* as distinct from and even diametrically opposed to Parliamentary *Swaraj*?" If by real *Swaraj*, he meant Kingdom of Heaven on Earth, then it must be an unattainable goal because the Kingdom of Heaven has its validity only in a supra-territorial condition. That must be the reason why Gandhi opted for small village communities as the building blocks of real *Swaraj*.

As regards the issue of machine, one may ask Gandhi if it would not be useful without doing any violence to the idea of real *Swaraj* to retain some of them. It would be impossible for the West to go back to the village community of medieval times. Further "...the same spiritual imagination which can conceive as a reality of society based on Love, can also conceive that such a society could just as well make true and humane use of the machine....Gandhi's apparent conception that any mechanical aid to the capacities of the unaided man is unnatural and evil is surely arbitrary" even if we give allowance to his acceptance of manually operated machines.

"The truth, the profound truth, of which Gandhi is one of the greatest prophets is that Nature – considered as the pattern of the harmonious life of man – is indeed our guide; but he forgets to emphasise that Nature grows and expands, and that the true guidance of Nature is discovered only in Man, and alas through human suffering. Thus and not otherwise, is the discovery made that Nature demands that Man should be guided by Love; and that if man does not submit his new powers and potencies to the rule of the Love, he must end by destroying himself. The guidance of Nature is not given as simple datum to Man; it is revealed to him by suffering. We cannot look back on any actual order of society – not even the village-community of India – and say 'There Nature reigned; there Love was supreme.' It was not. When man lacks the power to do evil, we must not speak of him as refraining from evil by the virtue of Love."

"To put the point otherwise, the asceticism of the spiritual leader is of different order from the simplicity of a poor peasant. Innocence is not the same as Imagination; any more than non-violence, *faute de mieux*, expresses the soul force of Love. So in the social history of mankind, the pre-machine community may be a far better, more human, and more spiritual society, than the mass society produced by the machine; but its weakness is that it has no power of resistance against the Machine. In so far as Gandhi believes that it has, he appears to me mistaken, though I profoundly agree with him that the only power which can resist the devastation of the Machine is the soul force of Love. But precisely that power is not in the pre-machine community; if it were, the machine would have done no harm. But it is not in any natural community, because it is developed only in the twice born soul.... Thus I am forced to the conclusion that ultimate social goal of the spiritual leader in the modern world should be not to withdraw backwards to the pre-machine community, but to advance forwards to the creation of a society capable of using the machine without incurring material and spiritual self-devastation."

J.D. Beresford

Mr. Beresford accepts the efficacy of the Law of Love in so far as the individuals are concerned but doubts its acceptance at the societal level particularly at the political state level. He felt that the non-violent struggle India has launched to gain freedom from the British may produce a state that might be ruled by the Law of Love. Her sons and daughters were then not free to shape her destiny. The problem is: Is there a sufficient number of Indians who recognise the great worth of the Law of Love, of *Ahimsa*, as a Way of Life on the earth.

"But as a matter of service to the present condition of India, Gandhiji's gospel will be of no more value than was the same gospel preached by Gautama to India twenty-four centuries ago. We praise and honour Gandhiji for his courage in bearing witness to the eternal truth. We know that if there were enough righteous men in India today, they might save the city. But the eternal purpose, so far as the mankind as a whole is concerned, cannot be served by any attempt to re-establish an earlier condition. The law of spiritual evolution demands change, no less than that of physical evolution. The appearance of this change that has come with such terrible increase of pace in the past half-century may be evil. It may bring suffering and death to uncountable millions throughout the world. But we have to accept it in the same spirit as that in which Gandhiji accepts British rule in India. In the midst of this wild, useless competition begotten by modern civilisation, we can still practice in our own lives, the law of love to mankind."

Hugh Fausset

He considers *Hind Swaraj* as a bold attempt to save India from 'modern civilisation which is eating into the vitals of the West' – in which, "we are now more ready to listen …for our self-complacence has received some rude shocks since then and we are being compelled by events to recognise the truth of Mr. Gandhi's claim that civilisation requires the use of a different and higher weapon for self-protection than that of brute force."

"While continuing to work individually for the ideal of self-rule …he admits that it requires a higher simplicity and renunciation than the people are today prepared for. And so he is ready to tolerate Parliamentary Home Rule, railways, hospitals, law courts, machinery and mills as at best necessary evils, which will die a natural death when enough people come into the possession of their true selves. It is likely, even in India, to be a long and painful process and for the Westerner in particular the problem though fundamentally a spiritual and moral one is perplexingly involved in the question whether we can use or must abandon the machine."

Agreeing in principle with what Gandhiji says about the evils of machinery, Fausset questioned his conclusion that industrial revolution was "no more than a terrible aberration from the rural economy of handicrafts to which man must ultimately return. Machinery, we may admit, represents a great sin, is in fact the outward embodiment of the split in man's being, which at present it deepens tending every where to deaden his creative spirit. Yet the machine, once it ceases to be an instrument of private power and greed, might, one imagines, be employed to liberate man in some ways from merely a creative servitude to matter for creative service and expression on a more spiritual plane. At any rate he will not be same when he has passed through the hell of the machine age as the countryman of the past. He will have either grown through the agony of self-consciousness into a fuller consciousness, or he will have been reduced to a mere automation. And I have enough trust in the indestructible vitality of the human spirit to be sure that it would not allow itself to be lastingly mechanised.

"The spiritually mature man, of course, cannot be in the servitude of machines, or to what they produce, because it is his very nature not to be attached by desire to things. And the spiritually mature society of the far future, if it is to exist, must be equally organic. But meanwhile the machine is doing certain services to us in the West by exposing with an inescapable ruthlessness the terrible consequences that must happen to men and nations who lose their integrity. Ultimately, I do not doubt it will compel us after much waste and suffering to reaffirm our humanity and the sovereignty of spirit. To speculate, therefore, on the future of the machine is waste of time. We should concentrate all our energy on the restoration of man to his true estate. And it is because Mr. Gandhi is devoted to this task with unflagging sincerity that *Hind Swaraj*, containing as it does the core of his teaching, is one of the best modern handbooks of that real revolution, which must happen in us all, if we are to fulfil the creative purpose of life.

"Since he wrote it (*Hind Swaraj*), the truth he enunciated that real home rule is self rule and that the way to it is passive resistance, that is soul force or love force, have been taken up and expounded by others, but by no one with a more lucid and persuasive simplicity than by him. For he not only preached passive resistance but practiced it in thought and act. The humility, the patience, the determined reasonableness of his approach to his fellowmen are nowhere more convincingly revealed than in his refusal to hate the English because they are the agents of a civilisation, which he deplores, in his desire to save them from it no less than his fellow countrymen and in his insistence that India has forged her own chains and can only be free when she has the strength to affirm through suffering and sacrifice her true spirit. To a world rapidly becoming quite irreligious he taught here the practice of religion which underlies all religions. It is still not too late for us to listen and learn."

Claude Houghton

After giving an appreciative note on the book, Claude picks up two points. "the first is that Western civilisation, with all its skyscraper glories, is a plague – and that, therefore, the greatest misfortune, which could overwhelm India would be for her to become wholly infected by it. The second, and the main, theme of the book is that love and love alone has power. It is madness, therefore, to fight evils with its own weapons. But this does not mean that one must serve it. One must resist it – passively. 'Passive resistance is a method of securing rights by personal suffering; it is the reverse of the resistance by arms. If I do not obey the law and accept the penalty for its breach, I use soul force. It involves sacrifice of self.'"

"To fight evil with its own weapons is to deny the righteousness of God. You do not believe in Him if you seek to avenge yourself. Who is the enemy? According to Karl Barth, it is he who incites you to render evil for evil. To strike a blow 'for the right' is to proclaim – God's impotence. It is precisely what your adversary has proclaimed. The fact that he has come in arms against you is proof conclusive. Meet him on his own level, with his own weapon, and you – become him! Hidden in your enemy is the image of God. It matters nothing that he has denied it. See only that image in him, serve only that image – serve it with love – and it will be made manifest. 'If thine enemy hunger, feed him, If he thirst, give him to drink,' Compel him by the power of love to reveal himself as he is in reality. Refuse to accept him at his own valuation. Judge not by the appearance, but judge righteous judgment. Affirm in him that which he is denying. To descend to his level, to fight him with his own weapons, is to collaborate with nightmare."

"Perhaps, in a last analysis, whatever is discussed in this book – be it Home Rule for India, or Civilisation – Gandhiji's main contention is that if, and only if, we have inner freedom, nothing and no one has power over us. If we are slaves to any one or anything, we have created this slavery.... We must take responsibility for ourselves. There are no short cuts – there are no scapegoats. If we find ourselves in chains, we have forged them link by link. And we must break them – link by link.

"In other words, Gandhiji asks us to do what is impossible for the 'natural' man who finds justice in the code: 'An eye for an eye, a tooth for a tooth.' It is possible only to the new, the risen man, who realises that we war not with flesh and blood but with principalities and powers; that our enemies are not outside the gates, but within them. Pride, envy, lust, sloth, inertia, greed – these are our enemies, because we have served them. They are the cause of the misery of man.

"And it may be that, with shadows lengthening and deepening across the world, more and more people will be impelled to attain in varying degrees this self-rule, which is the only freedom."

Gerald Heard

Comparing *Hind Swaraj* with Rousseau's Social Contract and Karl Marx's *Das Kapital*, Gerald considered it superior to both. The former two were crystallisation points, the catalytic agents around which precipitated the last two phases of Europe's Revolutionary Epoch – the political and the economic phases. *Hind Swaraj* is more significant because it does not mark, as did each of those, an end of an age but the beginning of a new order. They were symptomatic of western Man awakening to a new sense of self-consciousness – feeling himself to be 'born free but everywhere in chains'. Using the same technique, which had mastered him–violence–these newly aware individuals would break their chains and chain their masters. These Revolutions led, therefore, inevitably to reaction.

"The first psychological truth which every revolutionary must grasp, *Tat Twam Asi*—Thou art That – the occidental revolutionaries overlooked and all their work has only left new tyrants more firmly on the thrones. Mr. Gandhi, realising this fact, opened a New Path. He put into practice a new means, the right means which alone can lead to the right ends, for as Buddha taught, only correct means will lead to desired ends, wrong and evil methods can lead to only wrong and evil ends.

"The world-wide and age-long interest in Mr. Gandhi's experiment lies in the fact that he has attempted to make the method work in what may be called the wholesale or national scale. For millennia, saints and religious schools have shown that, on small, clear-cut issues, dynamic nonviolence, spiritual activism does work. Those who are the spiritual superiors of their physical assailants can conquer them by an attitude of spirit.

"What this generation needs to know is whether oppressed masses, meek (but many of them broken spirited), unarmed (but most of them debarred from the temptation, the test and the training which the offer of arms would give), whether such untrained numbers can win by nonviolence against an armed and resolute government. It seems unlikely. For what overcomes the user of violence when confronted with nonviolence is seldom the compassion, which is stirred by helpless misery and utter collapse. It is most commonly the realisation that the oppressed and the attacked could have used violence and did not, that though wronged they harbour no sense of wrong or injury, that they are fearless and friendly. When, to this, the oppressed can add something more and show, by their understanding action, that they have a true insight into their oppressor's needs that they understand his nature and action better than he does himself, and therefore, can show him how to satisfy his needs better than he can by his blind misguided self, then nonviolence becomes all powerful.

"Mr. Gandhi has attempted to solve the economic issue, at the same time as the political, by making every peasant his own manufacturer." But the third problem, *i.e.* psychological or mental stands unresolved. The moral height a commoner can scale is confined by the economic, political and physical conditions under which he lives. Any further spiritual advance, while still in the body, is possible only "if the pattern of the society, the way of creating material goods and the diet and routine, which each individual experiences is directed to one coordinating end, a higher consciousness, a continual unwavering awareness of a vaster reality than common sense discloses. This means a rational planned way of life for avowed intentional living – in short another Great Order, training its members so that in their noviciate they first master the psychiatry, ... in their mastership they become full members and work cooperatively a new psychologically based economy, ...; and finally. That means a new order of the society in their doctorate can pass back again into the world demonstrating the Path. Such an order may be the answer of the spirit to rising chaos. Should such an Order win the attention of mankind, it might recast human society. That, however, could only happen should mankind accept the authority of such an Order, when again we should have a dynamic caste pattern making of humanity a single organic whole.

The doctorate would be reborn Brahmin caste; the mastership, the director-administrative rank; the associate in training, the sub-administrative. Outside the order would be the technician, and craftsman rank, and finally, the simple routineer. There would be no tyranny in this. The Brahmin has no goods though directs power. Each individual in any rank may rise to another if he can stand the strain.

"Such seems the vision Nonviolence opens up. We may never attain that level in the world. Our ignorance and self-will may be too strong. But if we do, the world will always remember the name of Gandhi as one of its pioneers."

Irene Rathbone

"When we have a Hindu prophet – Gandhi – and the most cultivated women writer in England – Virginia Woolf—both saying the same thing, then East and West have indeed joined hands. 'Remain indifferent' they say, in effect, these two. 'Have nothing to do with violence. Ignore war preparations, ignore evil. Follow your conscience though it means derision, though it means death.'

"Passive resistance, Gandhi's doctrine is one of profound – irresistible – charm to certain minds. Which does not mean that its practice is easy. It requires a more stringent training, and greater fearlessness, than the warrior's. Nevertheless, its appeal is potent, and, as I say, to certain types, finally convincing, finally satisfactory." But to me it is not entirely convincing. It may be possible to follow Gandhi. I may embrace death rather than tread on a wrong path. But what about our children?

"The forms which evil is taking now in the world are so subtle and atrocious that it is no longer a matter of suffering one's own death, but the death of one's children. The modern tyrant says: 'You won't obey me? You refuse to accept my outlook and my rules? All right, your family shall pay the penalty.' Which human being would see his/her children being torn to pieces if by bowing to the tyrant (in this case the Nazis) and denying one's own conscience, the children could be saved. Gandhi does not even try to answer this question. Virginia Woolf too has remained silent and so has Aldus Huxley even; they were writing in the nineteen thirties, not in the first decade of the twentieth century.

She finds the economic system the main culprit. The marriage between Finance and Tyrants is the real problem, "but perhaps I could not have paid that book a greater compliment than to have found myself forced, by its tremendous honesty, to search my own honesty. I would implore people to read it. It is not dated – not in any essential way. It is suffused in light. It gleams with cogent passages; phrases at which the mind wistfully, assentingly smiles."

"There is no need whatsoever for the world to be either at peace under a shameful tyranny or at war under a righteous banner. No such choice confronts us – though it appears to. Then there are many other points on which the Western mind would move away. The question of machinery; of chastity; and of economics. Such views, however, need prove 'no deterrent to those wishing to drink at the deep well of Gandhi's wisdom. That well remains. It can never run dry. Easterners and Westerners will alike return from it refreshed: be enabled to pursue their varied, arduous journeys with quieter minds, firmer steps, and greater courage."

CONCLUDING REMARKS

It is clear that *Hind Swaraj* was not very favourably received in India partly because Indians were in search of a quick and sure way of getting self-government for the country. Gandhi's prescriptions as presented in *Hind Swaraj* were not political, they were spiritual. India wanted to take care of the spiritual after the political freedom was in hand. In a way, Gandhi reversed the order or at least mixed spiritual and secular to create a new approach to progress.

But it did not take much time before the Indians realised their follies and followed Gandhi, even without understanding or even caring for *Hind Swaraj*. They saw no difference between Gandhi the Mahatma and *Hind Swaraj*, the idea. It was easier to understand the man than the book, especially in a country where no more than 10 per cent of the people were literate. In fact, *Hind Swaraj* continued to influence and inspire the people of India, even if indirectly, until India got nearer to political freedom. It was specially after independence and the death of Gandhi who symbolised *Hind Swaraj*, that it became a library piece.

We are glad, thanks indeed to the crisis generated by modern civilisation, that *Hind Swaraj* is once again in currency after almost a century.

12

Post-Independence Assessment

GANDHI MARG: SPECIAL ISSUE

Gandhi Peace Foundation, New Delhi organised a symposium on *Hind Swaraj* in 1973. The purpose of the symposium was to assess its relevance to the then situation in India and to draw lessons from it for India's future development. The symposium was held at a time when the disenchantment with the process of development initiated in the country had risen high and there was a demand for change. The political structure led by the Indian National Congress was weakening fast and new political forces leading to J.P. Movement and the imposition of emergency in 1975 were emerging.

Among the participants were Sugata Sen Gupta, Badruddin Tyabji, R.R, Diwakar, R.C. Mazumdar, D.R. Mankekar, R.K. Patil, and Kodand Rao.

The discussion centred around the question of suitability or otherwise of Gandhian model of development. The participants expressed three different opinions but majority favoured the adoption of Gandhian model of development.

(1) *Western Model of Development is not suited to Indian genius:*

The Western model of development is not suited to newly developing countries like India for a variety of reasons. *Hind Swaraj* offered a better approach to handle the emergent problems of the country. It called upon the people of India to rediscover their own civilisational base. Over dependence on professionalism and machinery was injurious to the country because it tended to concentrate wealth in the hands of a few persons. "Gandhi realized that Indian masses could only secure a better life and find their true position in society if they were provided with the means to improve their own economic position.

(2) *Gandhian Model is not suited to modern India:*

Some participants considered Gandhi's prescriptions impracticable. Industrialization was necessary for the development of the country and society. The problems encountered were not unusual. Every country went through these pains. We should try to minimise those problems by appropriate policies and programmes.

(3) *It is possible to integrate the Western and Gandhian models.*

There were the integrationists too who wanted the modern industrial system and Gandhian economic system to be integrated to evolve a hybrid model. They wanted large scale industries to be backed by rural industries and handicrafts.

N. PRASAD'S 'HIND SWARAJ: A FRESH LOOK'

This book contains papers presented and discussions held in a seminar on *Hind Swaraj* at the Gandhian Institute of Studies, Varanasi in April, 1982. It was held at a time when India had just emerged from the trauma of Emergency; it was designed to offer guidelines for the new government at New Delhi to manage its business on Gandhian lines. The discussions hovered around *Hind Swaraj* but as it usually happens in intellectual meets, some of the papers presented were only indirectly related to the theme. As apparent from the conclusions and suggestion given in the last chapter of the book, the seminar was able to arrive at consensus on five main points. They are:

(1) Gandhi is being marginalised and the western thinking was overshadowing the Indian cultural heritage;
(2) Intellectuals should play a more active role in universalising Gandhi and his philosophy;
(3) Empirical studies on different aspects of *Hind Swaraj* be conducted to ascertain their applicability in current scenario;
(4) Efforts to bridge the communication gap between Gandhian academicians and activists should be intensified; and

(5) Gandhi should be brought closer to the common people through books and other means.

The book contains 17 papers contributed by eminent Gandhian scholars to the seminar. A summary of discussion following each paper has also been given. Introductory chapter by Nageswar Rao outlines the seminal character of *Hind Swaraj*. The book has reviewed the contributions of the symposia and discussions on *Hind Swaraj* held earlier, including the *Aryan Path* symposium of 1938 and *Gandhi Marg* symposium of 1973. *Hind Swaraj*, according to the seminar was not a final blue print of a nonviolent social order. Although Gandhi maintained all through his life that he had nothing to change in the text because what he had written had stood the test of time, he did make some changes from time to time. It did not thus present a final blue print even if the principles it enunciated were eternal. It presented the ideal conditions for an ideal state. Since Gandhi did not want to be consistent, what he wrote in *Hind Swaraj* could not be final. His was an evolving model.

Dev Dutt, in his paper '*Hind Swaraj*: Context and Text', points out that the book was almost ignored during Gandhi's active indulgence in Indian politics from 1915 to 1938. It was first taken note of by Annie Besant who organised a symposium on it in 1938 in Aryan Path, India's encounter with Britain was not political and economic; it was civilisational but Indians, in general, were more interested in Gandhi's leadership to win independence than in what India should look like after gaining freedom. *Hind Swaraj* did not tell much about how to win independence by defeating the British; it told about how to win *Swaraj* by sacrificing one self. It was not easily intelligible to the Indian elites.

In "Moral Foundations of *Hind Swaraj* and Nonviolence", Ramashray Roy asserts that *Hind Swaraj* minus morality is zero. "A fresh look at *Hind Swaraj* can, then, only frustrate an intellectual approach that seeks either to lay bare the structure of Gandhian thought as a means to reducing Gandhi to a formula or to sharpen one's understanding of the forces that have created or sustained modern civilisation in its present form." Gandhi's concern was man and his destiny. In his worldview, man's destiny lay in his moral evolution and hence, anything that comes in the way of this evolutionary process was condemned by Gandhi as satanic. This included modern civilisation, machinery, violence, and all that goes with them.

P.V. Pillai's paper "*Hind Swaraj* in the Light of Heidegger's Critique of Modernity' focuses on the nature of modern civilisation and suggests that the usual thinking that science is the mother of technology is not right. It is technology that is the mother of sciences. While Ramjee Singh's paper on 'Gandhi's Weltanschauung in *Hind Swaraj*' suggests that the history of mankind should not be seen in terms of economic and technological progress but in terms of "the progress of man along the steep and narrow spiritual path." Gandhi talks of God and truth but God nor Truth were able to deflect him from man who has a touch of God.

In his paper '*Hind Swaraj* and the Science Question' Sunil Sahastrabuddhey suggests that science need not be what it is if the middle level thesis about it is rejected. It is not just a means to understand nature; it can be liberating force too. And this is what Gandhi was hinting at when he criticizes modern science and technology in the book. 'Right, Left and Centre in the Science of Nature' is the title of the paper of J.P.S Oberoi. After examining the views of Hegel, Angels, Lenin, Marx, and Mao, he concludes that until the Renaissance and Reformation dualism was not the ruling paradigm in Europe, Goethe was not only a poet, he was a biologist too. China's Cultural Revolution was non-dualistic.

Modernity is impregnated with duality. Here the spiritual elites (scientists) and temporal elites (politicians) join hands to debar the common man from reaching anywhere near the goal of equality. But there has always been an undercurrent trying to assert that there must be truth in politics and nonviolence in science. It does not want arms created by scientist and environmental destruction created by industry to continue to kill people. Here lies the importance of Gandhi's *Hind Swaraj*.

Raghavendra Rao, in his paper entitled 'State and Society: A Swarajist Framework' has compared J.S. Mill's Essays on Liberty, Marx's economic and philosophical manuscripts and Gandhi's *Hind Swaraj* and raises a series of questions for further research. Continuing the dialogue further late Indira Rothermund, in her paper on *Hind Swaraj* and the Idea of Democracy, suggest some changes in the Gandhian framework for national development to make it possible for governments and people to pick up the threads from Gandhian philosophy.

'Gandhi and True Practice of Law' by Mira Sinha calls for decentralisation of the whole social and economic system as advocated in *Hind Swaraj*. Nageswar Prasad in his paper 'Technological and Institutional Basis of Gandhi's Theory of Decentralisation' points out that even during the days of freedom struggle there were two schools of thought on democracy. One advocated top down system with parliament at the top and local government at the village level, while the other wanted bottom up democracy. Gandhi went with the second view.

Hiteswar Sanyal's paper entitled Modern Development and the 'Gandhian Alternative' traces the beginning of the Swadeshi movement to 1905-08 struggle of peasants in Bengal within the framework of the British System. Gandhi's call to establish *Swaraj* from the bottom touched the vital cord of the Indian villages. Swadeshi was transformed into a movement to force the British out of India. In the same breath, T.K. Oommen, in his paper 'Gandhi's theory of Political Servitude and the Current Political Crisis in India', suggests that the crisis of Indian democracy could be overcome only through a militant counter-force. (Patabhiramayya, *History of Indian National Congress, 1885-1935,* Vol. I, Madras: 1935, p. 650.)

"I regard this rule as a curse. I am out to destroy this system of government.... I was believer in the politics of petitions, deputations and friendly negotiations. But all these have gone to dogs. I know that these are not the ways to bring the Government round. Sedition has become my religion." And this means non-cooperation with the 'unrighteous and unrepentant government', which in turn is possible only if we go through self-purification so that we are able to govern ourselves in all possible affairs and refrain from violence in any form. We must become true Satyagrhis. (see G.N. Dhawan, *The Political Philosophy of Mahatma Gandhi*, Ahmedabad: Navjivan, 1962, p. 228.)

'Gandhi's Critique of Education' by T.S. Anantu points out the importance of education as a means to convey the message of *Swaraj* to the people. *Swaraj* is not properly understood; people equate it with political independence. "I know India is not ripe for it" said Gandhi in *Hind Swaraj*. To straighten the record, the paper says that spiritual education did not exclude the analytical variety we are used to but "the cosmic religious experience is the strongest and noblest mainspring of the scientific research." Even modern science led to the *Advaita* philosophy. The author quotes what Albert Einstein said in Ideas and Opinions (1954) in this regard:

"The individual feels the futility of human desires and aims and the sublimity and marvellous order which reveal themselves both in nature and the world of thought. Individual existences impresses him as a sort of prison and he wants to experience the universe as a single significant whole."

Anantu, at the end of his paper, has summarized the difference between modern and Gandhian Education. It is reproduced below with minor changes for ready reference.

Modern Education	*Gandhian Education*
1. Aim: Acquisition of Knowledge	Aims: Human Transformation.
2. Method: gathering of information through sense perception and processing information though analysis	Transcending senses and control over thought. Sense perception and analysis also take place but are relegated to a secondary position.
3. Experiments take place in space outside the experimenter, with self (in the form of hidden paradigm or egocentric preoccupation) impairing the goal of perfect objectivity.	Experiments take place in inner space of experimenter as well, the aim being to gradually eliminate the self or ego and obtain perfect objectivity.
4. Brain development is confined to the left hemisphere.	Balanced development of both the brain hemispheres.
5. Analytical ability and memory are enhanced, Education is confined to intellect.	Primary stress on enhanced intuition, with better analytical abilities as by-products. Education goes beyond intellect.
6. Ethics, morality and other such values are accepted in theory, but are difficult to implement in practice.	Practice of ethics, morality, compassion and such values become the very basis of education.
7. Man is taught to become possessor and master of nature.	Man tries to become possessor and master of his own Nature.

(*Contd.*)

	Modern Education	Gandhian Education
8.	Relationship with others (nature including other creatures and human beings) becomes one of competition and constant struggle for survival and development.	Relationship with others is not of competition or struggle, but of cooperation and co-existence.
9.	Ecological balance is destroyed.	Ecological balance is preserved.
10.	There are rich people who live in luxury and poor people who cannot meet their basic needs.	There may be rich people but they do not live in luxury; and all can meet their basic needs.

Kishore Sant's paper on 'Gandhian Frame of Action' says 'Gandhi's life represents an ancient and ongoing pilgrimage of the human soul towards self-realisation and perfection.' And R.K. Patil in his paper on 'India's Development as Seen by Gandhi in *Hind Swaraj*' wonders how the character of modern civilisation as depicted by Gandhi could be changed given the present paradigm of development.

The last chapter of the book by Kishen Pattanayak focuses on 'Failure of Gandhi, Gandhians, and Gandhian Intellectuals' makes some remarks on Gandhi-Bose controversy and chides the Gandhians for not following the Mahatma in his true spirit. By 1937, says the author, Gandhi had lost the grip over congress. Nehru had become the real leader. Gandhi therefore resigned from the Congress. During the Second World War, Gandhi wanted to launch *Satyagraha*, but Nehru was against it. Gandhi's letter to Nehru in 1945 was meant to reassert himself and his model of future development. Gandhi referred to *Hind Swaraj* in this letter four times. He wanted a debate to settle the issue once for all. But Nehru spurned it by writing a very short and cryptic letter dismissing all that Gandhi wanted to discuss.

Nehru, according to the author, did not want to be clear for clarity was never his forte. His reply was full of ifs and buts. He blames Gandhi too for not being very specific in *Hind Swaraj*. In fact, he ought to have brought out another edition of the book to incorporate the new experiences he had gained and to accommodate, if necessary, the views of his critics as also of those who were sympathetic to his views but would have liked the book to be better worded and more specific to be intelligible to others.

Gandhi touched also everything in *Hind Swaraj* for he was the votary of a holistic approach to life. He was convinced that Indian civilisation would ultimately be the only Noa's Arc to take humanity beyond the mess it is in. Author agrees with both of these assertions but the way Gandhi presented his thesis was not intelligible to his successors. Gandhians failed to realise that Gandhian without militancy is no Gandhian. After all, the whole of *Hind Swaraj* is all war and no peace.

ANTHONY J. PAREL'S BOOK *HIND SWARAJ* AND OTHER WRITINGS

Anthony Parel's book is an excellent survey of Gandhian thought built around *Hind Swaraj*. The attempt is praiseworthy; there is nothing comparable to what Parel has produced. This book is important particularly because it has reached a much larger audience in the West than any other recently published book on Gandhi. Some of the documents the author has reproduced in the book were not easily accessible to those interested in the study of Gandhi and his philosophy.

What is original in this beautifully produced book is the 'Introduction' of 62 pages. Not that the other chapters do not constitute significant contributions; this chapter, however, portrays the editor's own perspectives on *Hind Swaraj*. A Note on the History of the Text (of *Hind Swaraj*) is also marked with originality. The letters exchanged between Gandhi and Tolstoy; Gandhi and Wybergh; and Gandhi and Nehru are reproduced and so are Gandhi's views on economic development and moral development (1916); machinery (1919-47); constructive programme (1941 and 1945); Gandhi's Quit India speech (1942); Gandhi's message to the nation issued before his arrest on August 9, 1942; Gandhi's political vision: the pyramid *vs.* the Oceanic Circle (1946), and Draft Constitution of Congress, 1948.

"*Hind Swaraj* is Gandhi's seminal work.... It is the seed from which the tree of Gandhian thought has grown to its full stature. For those interested in Gandhi's thought in a general way, it is the right place to start, for it is here that he presents his basic ideas in their proper relationship to one another. And for those who wish to study his thought more methodically, it remains the norm by which to assess the theoretical significance of his other writings including the *Autobiography*," says Parel.

Gandhi's intensions in writing *Hind Swaraj* have been grouped by Parel under six rubrics. These are:

(1) Gandhi harboured the ideas contained in *Hind Swaraj* for quite some time. He was inpatient to communicate them to people around him and world over specially the Indians who were his immediate concern;
(2) He wanted to clarify the meaning of *Swaraj*, which was far wider and deeper than political independence;
(3) Gandhi wanted to reopen a peaceful path of conflict resolution perfected by Indian civilisation and convince the people of India, especially the youth, to abjure terrorism and return to the Indian way;
(4) Gandhi wanted to tell his countrymen that it was not the British colonialism, which was their real enemy. The real enemy was Western Civilisation. So long as they remain mesmerized by it. They would remain slaves even if they get political independence;
(5) Gandhi was keen to see that Indians and British part political company as friends, not as enemies. He did not consider the British to be the enemies of Indians; the enemy was the modern (industrial) civilisation, which afflicted them both; and
(6) He wanted to use *Hind Swaraj* as a vehicle to give to India an updated version of dharma, which even a common man could understand and which would fit its people for life in the modern world. "I have used the language of politics, but I have really tried to offer a glimpse of dharma." Thus Gandhi wanted to make British occupation of India an opportunity to realise fully the potentials of Indian civilisation.

Parel then looks into the historical context in which Gandhi wrote *Hind Swaraj*. These include:

(1) The hold of modern industrial civilisation on the minds of the people all over the world, especially in the West. *Hind*

Swaraj challenged this civilisation and branded it as satanic. According to Parel, "Its critique of that civilisation is one of its main contributions to modern political thought."

While criticising modern civilisation, Gandhi was not negative and vindictive. He commended some of its contributions which Indian civilisation lacked or did not pay the attention they deserved – civil liberty, equality, human rights, prospects of improving the economic conditions of the poor, emancipation of women from tradition and religious toleration. He was critical of it because its tendencies were lopsides; because its concept and practice of freedom did not amount to *Swaraj*, in fact it negated it; it promoted rights at the cost of duties, economic progress at the cost of moral and spiritual progress, and it divided the world into We and They using religion, political dispensation, economic status, military might, education, etc. as dividers. It negated human brotherhood and the concept of *Vasudhaiv Kutumbakam*.

(2) The political situation in South Africa where he evolved as a Mahatma was another historical context in which *Hind Swaraj* was written. It was in South Africa that he first acquired the vision of Indian nationalism. In fact, South Africa was the foundation. Which he realised himself as a leader there. Parel rightly says that South Africa enabled him to transcend colonialism as the cause of the plight of Indians there. The culprit was the modern civilisation, which had caught the whole humanity by its neck.

South Africa freed Gandhi from many of the constraints he would have suffered, had he been in India. He could work without any social and religious pressures but also experiment his ideas in places like Phoenix settlement. But for his being in South Africa, he would not have got the opportunity to go to London on lobbying missions in 1906 and 1909 and thus acquire his diplomatic skills.

(3) The third historical context Parel identifies is the politics of expatriate Indians, specially of those based in London, which centred on preparation for violent struggle against the British. This brought Gandhi closer to many of the revolutionaries and prompted him to write *Hind Swaraj*.

(4) The Indian nationalist movement was yet another context in which the book was written by Gandhi.

(5) Gandhi's acquaintance with Western peoples, philosophers and thoughts was a major factor that shaped and sharpened his views as contained in *Hind Swaraj*.

Parel then discusses the intellectual sources of *Hind Swaraj*, both Indian and Western; the reception of *Hind Swaraj* in India and abroad; and Gandhi's contemporary influence.

ANTON PELINKA'S DEMOCRACY – INDIAN STYLE

Australian political scientist Anton Pelinka has produced a book, which concludes that present day India is not the India of Gandhi's dream. Pelinka is a professor at the University of Innsbruck and director of the Institute of Conflict Research in Vienna. According to him, India is closer to the dream of Subhas Chandra Bose. "It is industrial, it is modern, it is socialist, it is change driven and it walks the secular tightrope. It has put aside Mahatma Gandhi's tenets of non-violence and is a nuclear power. "Bose was not convinced that the best way to fight the British colonialism" was by nonviolence. He wanted to wrest freedom from the colonial masters by force of arms rather than the force of nonviolence.

Pelinka has explored Bose's impact on India before and after independence and how the controversial leader of the 1940s shaped India's political culture. "He was a secular nationalist and a socialist moderniser. He understood that Indian identity was above religion, caste and language." Bose led the Indian National Army (INA) wherein he maintained a certain balance of power by having one Sikh, one Hindu and one Muslim general. He had a woman too, at the top.

He has compared Nehru and Bose, Gandhi's two important protégés, and concluded that Nehru was Gandhi's good son while Bose was his prodigal son. The author further says that Indian democracy has been moulded not only by India's hoary past but also shaped by its encounter with the West.

As one goes through the history of freedom movement and entry of Gandhi into it in 1915, one would agree with Pelinka as far as the broad picture is concerned but once one goes into the details, one finds a number of pitfalls in the arguments he puts forward. Whether

Bose had a great impact on India, or he represented India's anti-British ethos and anger, engendered by Gandhi, is a matter of debate. Gandhi had created enough disaffection among the people of India before Bose or Nehru entered into the picture. In fact, the response of Indians to the British challenge was none different from that of Americans before 1776. The only difference one can notice is that Indians were more poverty stricken and resigned to their fate. They did not have guns the Americans had. Gandhi realised this drawback and tried to find a way out, which he got in Indian civilisation much before he came to India in 1915.

Bose represented angry India while Gandhi the wise India. Bose's goal was to liberate India and then run it on the pattern of the West. Gandhi wanted to liberate India but then run it on Indian line, the line, which could liberate the poor of India, nay the whole world. A deeper study of Gandhi puts the Gandhi-Bose controversy in a different mould. India may appear to veer round the Bose's image for it has adopted Western democracy, has nuclear bomb, and has retained the colonial institutions, but it has not run away from the Mahatma. The nature of the problems India is facing today was foreseen by Gandhi even in 1909 when he wrote his first book '*Hind Swaraj*'. Today, not only in India but the world over there is growing demand for what Gandhi had in view: direct democracy, decentralisation, nonviolence, respect for human dignity, spiritual development, etc. So even if Bose were alive and steered this country's political destiny, he would have not cast aside 'the father of the nation'. Maybe, he would have followed Gandhi more resolutely than Nehru did, for he was more deeply entrenched in Indian culture than Nehru was.

It is not correct to say that India has rejected Gandhi. If there is any leader in India who commands overwhelming respect and admiration among the people, it is Gandhi. He created a realistic dream for them and tried to realise it but failed. But the dream has not disappeared; it is still in the minds and hearts of the people of India. There is a general craving for it even if it is fuzzy and dim. Bose responded to the situation in real human way; Gandhi responded to the situation in a real superhuman way. Bose was concerned with the immediate future of India; Gandhi was concerned with the long term future of India and thereby of the world.

Today's India is neither Gandhi's India nor Bose's India; it is an India, which has been responding to the changing world scenario some times following Bose (nuclear denotation), at other times following Gandhi (India's recent peace initiatives *vis-a-vis* Pakistan and China). A stable pattern in accord with Indian civilisation and the memories of what Gandhi left behind as legacies will emerge not in the immediate future but in the distant one. And this future would be Gandhian for that alone can ensure a true democratic order, an order in which there is no poverty and humans are better humans.

CONCLUDING REMARKS

The four publications reviewed in this chapter point to the seminal character of *Hind Swaraj*. Its importance can be realised only if the reader considers this book as a Magna Carta of a new world order based on spirituality, fair play, justice, and inviolable human dignity. Gandhi, in this book, has given a direction in which humanity should move in order that it progresses towards it evolutionary goal. Those who still have a firm faith in Darwin's theory of evolution cannot derive much from it. For them, man's struggle against nature in general and his own fellow beings in particular is not over and it will not be over so long as he faces challenges from them. But those who believe, as even scientists now do, that man's evolutionary journey changed its direction when he acquired brain, they have much to gain from it.

Gandhi considers modern civilisation only as a phase in a long and continuing human history; such, if not similar, phases occurred in the past too. This phase is, however, overpowering because it is global in coverage and highly infectious. As such, it is the task of the whole humanity to overcome it and put the spiritual progress of man on the rails again.

Hind Swaraj offers the rationale and the means to reach the unreachable goal of self-realisation. It does not decry scientific progress, nor it denies the need to develop the economy. All that it says is that the means and the ends of modern civilisation are not the ultimate means and ends of humanity. And therefore man must move towards the ultimate means and ends and not get bogged down in the transitory aspirations that modern civilisation generates.

Gandhi commended Indian civilisation as superior to Western civilisation, not because of his ignorance of the latter or because he was being chauvinistic, but because the former still retained tendencies that lead man on the righteous path. Gandhi, therefore, wanted India to play a special role in this drama of human transformation and that it could do only if it were politically free and were imbued with the spirit of *Swaraj*.

REFERENCES

Anthony J. Parel (1997), *M.K. Gandhi: Hind Swaraj and Other Writings,* Cambridge: Cambridge University Press.

Anton Pelinka (2002), *Democracy: Indian Style.*

Gandhi Marg, Special Issue in on Hind Swaraj, 1973, published by Gandhi Peace Foundation, Deen Dayal Upadhyay Marg, New Delhi-110002.

Prasad Nageshwar, (1985), *Hind Swaraj: A Fresh Look,* New Delhi: Gandhi Peace Foundation, New Delhi.

13

Hind Swaraj in the Light of Recent Scientific Studies

A number of seminal and well-researched books emerged on the intellectual horizon during the last three decades uncovering the undercurrents of a new world order – an order, which, if not obstructed by any catastrophic event, will take humanity towards a spiritually rich, socially cohesive and materially contented life. That is to say that it will take man closer to his destiny and ensure his further evolution as a super-conscious entity. A sample of eight of these books has been selected for a comparative study with Gandhi's *Hind Swaraj*: four of them authored by scientists, while the other four by social scientists. The books by the scientists are reviewed in this chapter and by the social scientists in the next chapter.

These books offer some insight into Gandhi's oft-repeated references to Cosmic Law, Law of Love, Law of Species etc. in his writings and speeches. They would also help understand his theses on human destiny, purpose of life and theory of evolution. Gandhi was never precise on these issues for he considered them to be self-explanatory. But the new generation being less acquainted with the Vedantic literature and off beat scientific writings, finds difficulties in understanding the meaning of these 'Laws'. The books reviewed here throw some light on these concepts and point to the new direction in which further work needs to be done to understand Gandhi and *Hind Swaraj* better.

1. *The Ages of Gaia* by James Lovelock
2. *The Turning Point* by Fritjof Capra
3. *Entropy: A New World View* by Jeremy Rifkin
4. *Human Destiny* by Lecomte du Nouy

THE AGES OF GAIA: THE BIOGRAPHY OF OUR LIVING EARTH BY JAMES LOVELOCK

"Viewed from the distance of the moon, the astonishing thing about the earth, catching the breath, is that it is alive. The photographs show the dry pounded surface of the moon in the foreground, dead as an old bone. Aloft, floating free beneath the moist, gleaming membrane of bright blue sky is the rising earth, the only exuberant thing in this part of the cosmos. If you could look long enough, you would see the swirling of the great drift of white cloud, covering and uncovering the half-hidden masses of land. If you had been looking a very long geologic time, you could have seen the continents themselves in motion, drifting apart on the crystal plates, held aloft by the fire beneath. It has the organised, self-contained look of live creature, full of information, marvellously skilled in handling the sun."

Lewis Thomas, *The Lives of a Cell*

The Ages of Gaia is "about a new theory of evolution, one that does not deny Darwin's great vision but adds to it by observing that the evolution of the species of organism is not independent of the evolution of their material environment. Indeed the species and their environment are tightly coupled and evolve as a single system." The author has described in this book "the evolution of the largest living organism, Gaia" or in Indian terminology, Mother Earth.

James Lovelock considers earth to be a living organism. Its material and live elements have jointly worked to give the form in which we find it today. For the first 3.5 billion years, a billion years after its formation, it were the micro-organisms (meta-life), which worked with the physical environment to set in motion the process of transforming this planet into its own substance. They created the necessary infrastructure for the wild flowers, animals and human beings to emerge, survive, and prosper. All that exists on the earth today, the atmosphere, lithosphere, and biosphere has resulted from the radical intervention of the Gaia through the evolving diversity of various life forms.

But for the life forms, whose origin we have yet to know, and perhaps may never know, the earth would have been none better than the moon or mars. Its living organisms, working through and on the non-living inorganic materials, during the last several billion years, have 'converted the earth into a coherent system of life, self-regulating, self-changing, a sort of immense organism'. The concern of the ecologists and environmentalists is health of the human beings; the concern of Lovelock's book is the health of the earth.

All life forms today present on earth are part and parcel of the Gaia in the same way as different cells, which form the tissues and organs of our body. They co-evolve and contribute interactively to produce the optimal conditions for their own and Gaia's growth and prosperity. Gaia theory, therefore, calls for a planetary perspective, not just ecological and environmental perspective.

"The idea that the earth is alive is probably as old as human kind. But the first public expression of it as fact of science was by a Scottish scientist, James Hutton. In 1785, he said at a meeting of the Royal Society of Edinburgh, that the Earth was superorganism and that its proper study should be physiology. He went on to compare the cycling of the nutritious elements in the soil, and the movement of water from the oceans to the land, with the circulation of the blood. James Hutton is rightly remembered as the father of geology, but his idea of a living Earth was forgotten, or denied, in the intense reductionism of the nineteenth century– except in minds of isolated philosophers like Korolinko."

Lovelock suggests two new disciplines: geophysiology to study the processes involved in the efficient functioning of the earth as a live system and planetary medicine, to diagnose and cure the diseases inflicted on Gaia by human beings. I feel geography is the discipline, which is nearest to geophysiology but, somehow, it stayed away from this broad vision and narrowed its concern about the earth 'as the home of man'. In the geographic world, even plants, microorganisms and animals have become resources for development. Geography is man centred, not Gaia centred.

Lovelock says "I am happy with the thought that the Universe has the properties that make the emergence of life and Gaia inevitable. But I react to the assertion that it was created with this purpose. It might have been, but how the Universe and life began are ineffable questions." Lovelock, however, asserts, "unless life takes charge of its planet, and occupies it extensively, the conditions of its tenancy are not met. Planetary life must be able to regulate its climate and chemical state. Part-time or incomplete occupancy or mere occasional visits will not be enough to overcome the ineluctable forces that drive the chemical and physical evolution of a planet."

This book is reviewed here because Gandhi too believed in a live earth theory; he enveloped his idea in the law of the cosmos

(Cosmic Law). He also believed in the Lovelocks theory of evolution, which enveloped in the Law of Species. Gandhi's Cosmic Law bound the whole universe into a single entity so deeply and inextricately integrated that nothing could malfunction outside the threshold limits already inbuilt in the grand system, this included both living and non-living phenomena. As for the evolution of the species, Gandhi believed, like Lovelock, that various species of animals ultimately culminating in Homo sapiens would have not been possible without the joint effort of both organic and inorganic parts of the earth and cooperation and sacrifice by each of the species to ensure that the chain that must lead to the evolution of human species should not break. He believed that man should not violate the Cosmic Law, for it is the law that keeps the universe and the earth to perform their respective roles. Gandhi derived his concept of cosmic law from ancient Indian literatures and traditions. It is, however, discernible from the other religious traditions too.

Lovelock has tried to answer the question 'What is Life'. He asserts that no one has so far answered this question. Scientists have raised their hands up for they do not know it nor do they have the tools to know it. What is clear, however, is that life is not a social for everything is linked to everything else. To begin with, the cells had independent and separate existence; they now form communities to form living entities. It is also called homeostatis. Life has homeostatis properties. To know life, one has to study the whole. Even to understand the earth, one has to study it as a single entity linked to the universe as a whole. "Life and its environment are so closely coupled that evolution concerns Gaia, not the organisms or the environment taken separately."

There could be three approaches to the understanding of life: molecular biology, physiology and thermodynamics. Of these, the first two stand exhausted. The latter has two laws that concern us. The first law says that energy is always conserved and no matter how far it is dispersed the total always remains the same. It is never exhausted; it can only change its form. The second law says that when energy is put into action, part of it is wasted. And hence the total energy in the universe is always running down. Hot objects cool down but the cool objects do not heat up by themselves. All natural processes thus move towards disorder called entropy. Entropy is measured in calories per gram per degree (total quantity of heat added divided by the temperature). Greater the disorder, more the entropy.

Take the example of a lifeless snowflake. Quantity of heat needed to convert it into raindrop is 80 times larger than the quantity needed to warm the raindrop by a single degree of temperature. Thus the increase of entropy when snowflakes melt is 80 times larger than when they warm from – 1° C to the melting point. The environmental problems we face today are the results of the disorder generated by our consumption of fossil fuels. If there is something that does not come within the purview of entropy, it is life. Life has been evolving "to ever-greater complexity and is characterised by an omnipresence of improbability that would make winning a sweepstake everyday for a year, by comparison, seem trivial. Even more remarkable, this unstable, this apparently illegal, state of life has persisted on the Earth as a tightly coupled system so as to favour survival", says Schroidinger. According to Ludwig Boltsmann, more improbable a thing is, lesser the entropy it generates. Since life has no entropy, it is something that is improbably improbable. Schrodinger, in the absence of any better word, called it 'negentropy'. But according to Lovelock, even this term does not express the improbability of life on Earth. "...If some cosmic chef takes all the ingredients of the present Earth as atoms, mixes them and lets them stand, the probability that these atoms would combine into molecules that make up our living Earth is zero. The mixture would always react chemically to form a dead planet like Mars or Venus."

All living systems are open systems but they are enclosed systems too at the same time. The internal environment of animals and humans produces carbon dioxide as entropy; the plants produce oxygen as entropy. The two outputs are balanced because plants consume the carbon dioxide and animals and humans consume oxygen. Thus the living earth has no entropy. The environment in which life exists on earth was created by life itself in conjunction with the inanimate objects like rocks, air, water, etc. This is now well recognised by ecologists and some oceanographers, but the biologists and geologists and even physical geographers have yet to accept the truth that "Life has not adapted to an inert world determined by the dead hand of the chemistry and physics. We live in a world that has been built by our ancestors, ancient and modern, and which is continuously maintained by all things alive today. Organisms are adapting in a world whose material state is determined by the activities of their neighbours; this means that changing the environment is part of the game.

Lovelock gives the data pertaining to the Archeon before and after life emerged.

Gas	*Before life*	*After life*
Carbon dioxide	dominant	0.3 per cent
Nitrogen	unknown	99.00 per cent
Oxygen	0	1 ppm
Methane	0	100 ppm
Hydrogen	some	1 ppm

According to some scientists, the earth would have dried out in about 1.5 billion years, mid-way through the Archean. Even rainfall became possible because of evapotranspiration, "the pumping by tress and large plants of water from the soil to their leaves where it evaporates." Archean was the period when earth's operating system was populated wholly by the highly mobile and motile bacteria. Marshall McLuhan's global village with humans interconnected by telecommunication, is only a re-enactment of the Archean device.

Between the Archean and the Proterozoic, the appearance of oxygen as a major atmospheric gas was the primary event that marked a major change in earth's physiology. Carbon dioxide has played a major role in the creation of oxygen. It is the food for the plants, which release oxygen. It is also an envelope that blankets the earth and keeps it warm. Even when the sun was cooler than it is at present, the earth remained warm for life in its primitive forms to survive. But too much of it would make the earth hot, not warm and nothing living would survive.

The rate and the extent of the rise of carbon dioxide now under way as a result of our actions is comparable with that of the natural rise that terminated the last ice age. The urbanisation and industrialisation processes we have set in motion, unless halted in time, would bring the dooms day nearer. Many of our great coastal cities will be submerged in the sea. The ozone layer depletion would kill millions, not only humans but all life forms. The earth would not be inhabitable any more.

What we do to our planet is not offensive so long it is on a minor scale. When the people are few and their technology human size, then dangers are within the threshold limits of Mother Earth's power to manage through negative feedback mechanism. Had there been only 500 million people on the earth and technology were governed by the laws of biology, the ecological problems we face today would have never emerged. Further, had we appreciated that the earth is a unified living whole and adjusted our activities to the requirements of its homeostatis, looming crisis would have been warded off. We need a general physician of the planetary medicine, says Lovelock.

As part of their graduation, physicians must take the Hippocratic Oath. It includes the injunction to do nothing that would harm the patient. A similar oath is needed for putative planetary doctors if they are to avoid introgenic error: an oath to prevent the over-jealous from applying a cure that would do more harm than good.

The last section of the book deals with religion and the concept of God. In real life, one cannot separate the religious from the secular, unless one separates the intellect from intuition. Virgin Mary, to Lovelock, represents Gaia. The Pope kisses the ground he lands from the airplane; Hindus do it daily when they get up in the morning. "Any living organism, a quarter as old as the Universe itself and still full of vigour, is as near immortal as we ever need to know. She is of this Universe and, conceivably, a part of God. On Earth she is the source of life everlasting and is alive now; she gave birth to humankind and we are a part of her."

"The myth of the great Mother is part of most early religions. The Mother is a compassionate feminine figure, spring of all life, of fecundity, of gentleness. She is also the stern and unforgiving bringer of death. As Aldous Huxley reminds in Human Experience: *In Hinduism, Kali is at once the infinitely kind and loving mother and the terrifying goddess of destruction, who has a necklace of skulls and drinks the blood of human beings from a skull. This picture is profoundly realistic; if you give life, you must necessarily give death, because life always ends in death and must be renewed through death."*

There is a self-organising tendency in the Gaia as it is perhaps in the universe as a whole. Life thus is not a chance event but an inevitable consequence. Gaia is a scientific as well as spiritual phenomenon; it can be understood by a combination of the tools of both science and spirituality. To understand it, we needs analytical as well as synergic approaches. "As a scientist, I believe that Nature is objective but also recognise that Nature is not predetermined....Life and Gaia are to all intents immortal, even though composed of entities that at least include dissipative structures." tells Lovelock.

"The heartlands of the great religions are now in the last bastions of rural existence, in the Third World of the tropics. Elsewhere God and Gaia that once were joined and respected are now divorced and of no account. We have, as a species almost resigned from the membership in Gaia and given to our cities and nations the right and responsibilities of environmental regulation. We struggle to enjoy the human intervention of city life yet still yearn to possess the natural world as well." We want to have the cake and eat it also. "Poverty and suffering are not sent, they are the consequences of what we do." These are the fruits of our *Karma*. Mother Earth is on the move. She is watchful of her own fate; she must remain fit for life. "If humans stand in the way of this, we shall be eliminated with as little pity as would be shown by micro-brain of an intercontinental ballistic nuclear missile in full flight to its target."

In Lovelock's view "God and Gaia, theology and science, even physics and biology are not separate but a single way of thought." Our scientific approach, however, is reductionist, objective and analytical. True knowledge of phenomena cannot be gained by attributing purpose to it. By implication, a scientist believes that a system is the assemblage of its parts. A great many scientist realised this predicament for there was no way they could explain the beginning and end of the universe on the basis of the second law of thermodynamics. When Darwin dismissed the thought about the origin of life, he was aware of the limitations of this law.

Erich Jantsch in his book *The Self-Organising Universe* made a strong argument for omnipresence of a self-organising tendency; so that life, instead of being a chance event, was an inevitable consequence. He based his thoughts on the theory of 'thermodynamics of the unsteady state'. Thus the scientists have already hinted at the presence of God. Earth can be both material and spiritual at the same time. This is what the Vedic civilisation of India proclaimed from times immemorial.

True, nature is objective, but it is not predetermined. The famous uncertainty principle that the great physicist "Werner Heisenberg discovered was the first crack in the crystalline structure of determinism. Now chaos is revealed to have an orderly mathematical prescription.... True chaos is there as a counterpart of order." Let us therefore end this review by quoting philosopher Gregory Bateson:

> "The individual mind is immanent but not only in the body. It is immanent also in the pathways and messages outside the body; and there is a larger mind of which the individual mind is only a sub-system. This larger mind is comparable to God and perhaps what some people mean by God, but it is still immanent in the total interconnected social systems and planetary ecology."

THE TURNING POINT BY FRITJOF CAPRA

His book starts with a quotation from the Chinese philosopher I-ching. It is being reproduced here because it sums up the process of change. It tells that forcing changes is not advisable; it is enough to show the way. Each generation of men and women see the reality in its own way but in the ultimate analysis things that accord with time do take place on their own. Man's role is to endeavour:

> After a time of decay comes the turning point. The powerful light that was banished returns. Here is movement, but it is not brought about by force. The movement is natural, arising spontaneously. For this reason the transformation of the old becomes easy. The old is discarded and the new is introduced that measures accord with the time; therefore no harm results.
>
> —I-ching

According to Capra, the new concepts in physics have brought about a profound change in our worldview, from the mechanistic conception of Descartes and Newton to a holistic and ecological view, quite similar to the views of the mystics of all ages and traditions. "The exploration of the atomic and sub-atomic world brought scientists in contact with a strange and unexpected reality that seemed to defy any coherent description. ... their basic concepts, their language and their whole way of thinking were inadequate to describe atomic phenomena. I have come to believe that today our society as a whole finds itself in a similar crisis." What appears to be a discrete problem emanates from something that cannot be understood by the available tools of scientific and social analysis.

"We live today in a globally interconnected world, in which biological, psychological, social and environmental phenomena are all interdependent. To describe this world appropriately, we need an ecological perspective, which the Cartesian worldview does not offer. ... What we need, then is a new paradigm, a new vision of reality; a fundamental change in our thoughts, perceptions and values. The beginnings of this change, the shifts from mechanistic to the holistic conception of reality, are already visible in all fields and are likely to dominate the present decade," said Fritjof Capra in the preface to his book.

The book is presented in four parts. "The first part introduces the main themes; the second part describes the history of Cartesian world view; the third part discusses the impact of Newtonian thought on biology, medicine, psychology and economics; and the fourth part tells in detail the new vision of the reality that includes the emerging systems view of life, mind, consciousness and evolution – a vision that gives a holistic approach to health and healing; that integrates Western and Eastern approaches to psychology and psychotherapy and that presents a new conceptual framework for economics and technology and that explains an ecological perspective which is spiritual in its ultimate nature.... " The survival of our whole civilisation may depend on whether we can bring about such a change.

Presented below is the summary of chapter 1 of the book entitled 'The Turning of the Tide'.

We are living today in a highly complex world, not very safe for survival and development. There is crisis in all walks of life: from economics to ethics; science to humanities; and fine arts to technology. We try to find the causes and remedies but more we look for farther away we are from solution. In fact, each solution we arrive at leads us to far deeper crises.

The nuclear catastrophe apart, "the global ecosystem and further evolution are seriously endangered and may well end in a large-scale ecological disaster.... our health and well-being are seriously endangered." Environmental deterioration has been accompanied by unhealthy style of life leading to increase in systemic and mental diseases, which have no cures. Social disintegration leading to both personal and group violence has become a serious challenge. The rise in violent crimes and suicides by young people has acquired epidemic proportions. As if all these problems are not enough, mal-distribution of income and productive resources; poverty and deprivation; growing unemployment and depleting natural resources especially the energy resources have made human existence precarious.

"It is a striking sign of our time that the people who are supposed to be experts in various fields cannot deal with the urgent problems that have arisen in their areas of expertise.... To understand our multifaceted cultural crisis, we need to adopt an extremely broad view and see our problems in the context of human cultural evolution." We should shift our perspective from short to long terms – from decades to millennia. Each crisis not only point to a danger but also an opportunity.

History of cultures reveals that each historic cultural transformation was preceded by crises whose symptoms were similar to ones we face today. They include a sense of alienation, violent crimes, social disruption as well as an increased interest in religious cultism. According to Toynbee, the genesis of a civilisation consists of a transformation of a static condition to dynamic activity. The transition may occur spontaneously, through the influence of another civilisation or through the disintegration of one or more civilisations. As such what is happening in our society today is not necessarily dangerous; it may be indicative of something good in the offing, provided we are able to perceive the forces transforming our civilisation and manage them well enough to benefit from the opportunities they offer.

Tracing the rise and fall of Egyptian, Sumerian, Aegean, Hellenic, Syrian, Islamic, Orthodox Christian and Western civilisations (3000 BC – 2000AD), the author suggests that the changes have been cyclic and the time for Western civilisation for dynamic change has come. All ancient civilisation identified two main forces that made such changes universal: Chinese identified *yin* and *yang*; the Greek, love and hate and Hindus, *prakriti* and *purush*. Once a civilisation reaches a peak of vitality, it loses its cultural steam and declines. According to Toynbee, when the behaviour patterns of a society become rigid, its downfall is imminent for hard things tend to break down.

All is, however, not lost. As the painful process of disintegration sets in, society's creativity – its ability to respond to the challenges is not completely lost. A creative minority emerges to find new pathways to integrate elements of the old with the new and move forward. There is tussle between the two but the minority may succeed and the civilisation continues without a break. This is what happened to Indian and Chinese civilisations and to some extent even Iranian civilisation.

The Western civilisation likewise is passing through a series of transitions: ecological, cultural, sociological, economic, etc. The change from fossil fuels to more enduring fuels, the change from over dominance of males to equal rights for females, the change from thoughts, perceptions, values and visions of reality of an age described as industrial, scientific, competitive, technological etc. According to sociologist Pitirim Sorokin, they are derived from changes in the value systems from sensate to ideational with idealistic in between. "The sensate value system holds that matter alone is the ultimate reality (sensory perception is the only source of knowledge). Ideational value system is profoundly different." It holds that true reality lies beyond the sensory perceptions and material objects and that true knowledge can be obtained through inner experience alone. In its scheme of things super human standards of justice, truth, beauty, nonviolence, compassion, sacrifice, charity override the sensate standards. In between the sensate and ideational is the idealistic, which marks a transition wherein both sensory and supersensory values coexist. It is the stage when man attains the highest and noblest experiences in both sensate and spiritual fields. Examples of such ideational periods are flowering of Greek culture in 500 BC and European Renaissance.

According to Sorokin, the present period of decline of the Industrial civilisation marks another shift from sensate to ideation culture; but with a difference. Its sweep is global and of a magnitude never witnessed before. It cannot be prevented; it should rather be welcomed. Sorokin looks at Marxism as alternative model of change but finds it unworkable because of the inbuilt violence, competition and struggle. It is Darwinism applied to social field. He has used the Chinese way of looking at the reality (Tao) as interplay between *yin* and *yang*; a process of continuous changes. Had he been equally conversant with Indian philosophy, he would have perhaps used both Indian and Chinese ways of seeing the reality for they are similar to each other.

The characteristics of yin and yang as recognised by Capra and relevant to the situation we witness today are:

Yin	*Yang*
Feminine	Masculine
Contractive	Demanding
Responsive	Aggressive
Cooperative	Competitive
Intuitive	Rational
Synthesising	Analytic
Religion	Science

It is clear that the western society has favoured the yang during the last three centuries or so. Capra in his book has tried to prove the above. He calls for idealistic transition to make the changes smooth and less painful. In this transition both yin and yang should be combined and systems approach evolved to solve our problems. The living systems are not dominated by either *yin* or *yang*. They form multi-levelled structures. Each level forms a system, which consists of a number of sub-systems, themselves having sub-sub-systems. Arthur Koestler has called such live subsystems 'holons' for they are both wholes and parts; they have the characteristics of both yin and yang.

Toynbee has rightly said "During the disintegration of a civilisation, two separate plays with different plots are being performed simultaneously side by side. While an unchanging dominant minority is perpetually rehearsing it own defeat, fresh challenges are perpetually evoking fresh creative responses from newly recruited minorities, which proclaim their own creative power by rising from time to time, to the occasion. The drama of challenge-and-response continues to be performed, but in new circumstances and by new actors."

ENTROPY: A NEW WORLDVIEW BY JEREMY RIFKIN

The author of *Entropy: A New Worldview* book says: "Hope is the feeling that what is desired is possible of attainment. This book is about hope; the hope that comes from shattering false illusions and replacing them with new truths.

"To a civilisation nurtured on the modernist notion of future without physical constraints and a world without material boundaries, the truths of the Entropy Law will at first appear sobering, even somber. That is because this law defines the ultimate physical boundaries within which we are constrained to act.

"If we continue to ignore the truth of Entropy Law and its role in defining the broad context in which our physical world unfolds, then we shall do so at the risk of our own extinction.

"After finishing this book some will remain unconvinced that there are physical limits that place restraints on human action in the world. Others will be convinced but will conclude with despair that Entropy Law is a giant cosmic prison from which there is no escape. Finally, there will be those who will see the Entropy Law as the truth that can set us free. The first group will continue to uphold the existing world paradigm. The second group will be without a worldview. The third group will be the harbingers of a new age."

In the introductory chapter of the book, Rifkin warns: "Each day we awake to a world that appears more confused and disordered than the one we left the night before. Nothing seems to work any more....

Things around us continue to accelerate, yet nothing seems to be getting anywhere. We are bogged down, the society is bogged down; and all of a sudden we get this urge to trample over everything in our path, leaving the world behind us in disarray."

"When the whole world begins to break down and fall apart, then we must look to the way the whole world has been organised, because that is where the problem lies. For it is foolish to continue to blame individual leaders and individual ideologies for a universal problem. Of course some leaders and some ideologies are better than others." But they cannot solve our problems "because all are committed to the existing world view, one that is diseased and dying and is contaminating everything it gave birth to."

"The Entropy Law deals with physical world where everything is finite and where all living things must run their course and eventually cease to be. It is a law governing horizontal world of time and space.... The spiritual plane is not governed by *it.* The spirit is nonmaterial dimension where there are no boundaries and no fixed limits to attend to. The relationship of the physical to the spiritual world is the relationship of a small part to the larger unbound whole within which it unfolds. While the Entropy Law governs the world of time and space and matter, it is, in turn governed by the primordial spiritual force that conceived it."

"The way a civilisation organises its physical reality and the importance it attaches to the material plane of existence determines how favourable the conditions are for seeking spiritual enlightenment. The more steeped a worldview is in material side of life, the less conducive it is to the human quest for spiritual transcendence. The less attached a civilisation is to the physical world, the freer the human collectivity is to transcend the confines of the material plane and become one with the profound spiritual essence that encompasses all."

"Of one thing there can be no doubt. The entropy worldview will triumph. Everything we now hold familiar will eventually give way to its truths. As each of us becomes initiated into the inner workings of those truths, we will take up the small space reserved for using the great adventure that lies just ahead."

HUMAN DESTINY BY LECOMTE DU NOUY

This book was published soon after the Second World War in 1947. It was a time of great disillusionment for millions of innocent human being died because man could not find a way to live in peace. It appeared that there would be no end to conflicts and wars. Earlier, the wars were confined to localities and nations. Seventeenth and eighteenth centuries were marked with mass scale massacres in Africa, Australia and Americas all in the name of spread of 'modern civilisation'. The twentieth century heralded global wars. In fact they were global only in literal sense; they were wars between two opposing groups of 'civilised nations' of Europe. The rest of the world was drawn into it, not by choice, but by proxy and force of circumstances.

Two such wars had already taken place. There was disillusionment all around. This book by Lecomte du Nouy was perhaps a response to the growing cult of violence. The author has reminded us of our destiny and how we have strayed away from the path, which would take us to a stage where man would become real human.

"The rapid development of the material side of civilisation had aroused the interests of men and kept them in a kind of breathless expectation of the next day's miracle. Little time was left for the solving of the true problems; the human problems. Men were hypnotized by the incredibly brilliant display of new inventions following one another almost without interruption from 1860s onwards like children who are so fascinated by their first view of a three-ring circus that they even forget to eat or drink."

"This prodigious spectacle became the symbol of reality, and true values, dimmed by the glitter of the new star, were relegated to second place. The shift was easy and painless because philosophers and scientists of the nineteenth century had already prepared the minds of the thinking public by setting up question marks without answers." Many people could sense the dangers ahead; they tried to warn but they remained unheeded. Modern education diverted people's attention from synergy to analysis. Without becoming more intelligent they were trained to employ the tricks of rational thought. It opened up new opportunities for material advancement and body welfare. Science was used to sap the base of religion. To be religious became degrading. People feel proud in declaring themselves secular or even agnostic or a theist.

The author asserts that the aim of human life is the realisation of a superior conscience and the perfection of self by a harmonious fusion of all the specifically human qualities. The trend set during the last two hundred years, has made human survival and development precarious. This trend, however, cannot be reversed by the means, which are no longer credible; the same logic, which has given rise to the present situation, will have to be used to demolish it too. "The aim of the author is specifically human. He is convinced that intelligence has deprived man of all reason for existence by destroying, in the name of science still in the cradle, the doctrines which up till now gave a meaning to individual life, a reason for effort, a transcendent end to attain: namely the religions."

"Now, what characterizes man, as *Man*, is precisely the presence in him of abstract ideas, of moral ideas, of spiritual ideas, and it is only of these that he can be proud of. They are as real as his body and confer to his body a value and an importance, which it would be far from possessing without them. ... If, therefore, we want to give meaning to life, a reason for effort, we must try to revalorize these ideas scientifically and rationally, and it seems to us that this can only be achieved by tying to incorporate them into evolution, by considering them as manifestations of evolution, in the same way as the eyes, the hands, and articulate speech.

"It must be demonstrated that every man has a part to play and that he is free to play it or not; that he is a link in a chain and not a wisp of straw swept along by a torrent; that, in brief, human dignity is not a vain word, and that when man is not convinced of this and does not try to attain this dignity, he lowers himself to the level of the beast." These and other related ideas have been convincingly propounded by the author using the rational approaches and scientific methods we are familiar with.

"Two different paths", says the author, "may eventually lead to the comprehension of man. The first, revelation, is a direct road, but is closed to a great many people and independent of rational thought. The second, on the contrary, is strictly rational and scientific. It leads us to consider man as one of the elements of the whole, the universe and to study this element as a function of the external world." This study has, however, to be done through the faculty of the mind and hence it must remain dependent on the structure of the brain.

We know the external world through our senses; but the senses do not give the reality as it is. Different people see and feel things differently. Much depends on who sees and feels and from what distance. We see the earth flat as we walk on it. But if we see it from the Jupiter, it would be just another luminous point in the sky. The very reasoning, based on observations from different perspectives, is thus false and hence the conclusions derived there from must also be false. "As we have no other means of knowing and describing nature but those given us by our senses and our reasoning faculties – we must be extremely cautious and never forget the relativity of the picture which we construct – a relativity with respect to the recording instrument, man."

REFERENCES

Fritjof Capra (1982), *The Turning Point: Science, Society and the Rising Culture,* New York: Simon & Schuster.

Jeremy Rifkin (1980), *Entropy: A New World View,* New York: Viking Press.

James Lovelock (1989), *The Ages of Gaia*, Oxford: Oxford University Press.

Lecompte du Nouy (1947), *Human Destiny,* New York: Longmans.

14

Hind Swaraj in the Light of Recent Futures Studies

This chapter examines the theses proposed by four recent social scientists on models of a new post-modern world order or post-industrial civilisation. The authors of these theses did not have Gandhi's *Hind Swaraj* in view while arriving at their conclusions; some of them might have not even read Gandhi. They do, however, corroborate the conclusions Gandhi arrived at in Hindi Swaraj even if only broadly.

Gandhi presented framework of a Whole Theory of Life; his point of departure was moral and ethical bases of human progress. Rarely do modern thinkers look at human destiny from Gandhian perspectives. What we see in the books reviewed here is only a compartmentalized picture of reality as observed by Gandhi. Yet, these books are important because they do take us a step forward, at least mentally, in what Gandhi thought, said and did.

The books touch on Gandhi's views on religions, nature, ecology, education, technology, social organisation, politics and a variety of other related issues. These are:

(1) *The Clash of Civilisation and the Remaking of World Order* by S.P. Huntington;
(2) *The Third Wave* by Elvin and Heidi Toffler;
(3) *De-schooling Society* by Evan Ellich; and
(4) *Mega Trends* by Naisbitt.

THE CLASH OF CIVILISATIONS BY SAMUEL HUNTINGTON

'The Clash of Civilisations and Remaking of World Order' has been one of the most widely discussed books during the 1990s. It centres on an issue, which has become highly germane in recent years, *i.e.*

Islamic terrorism. Incidentally, it also forms one of the main concerns of *Hind Swaraj*, *i.e.* violence free society. Written with a view to finding the pathways for modern industrial civilisation, otherwise known as Western civilisation, to survive and continue to play a leading role in reshaping the future of the world, some of its conclusions are at odds with those of *Hind Swaraj*. The book does, however, point out that Western civilisation cannot become a universal civilisation and the future lies in multi-civilisational world order each living in symbiotic relationship with others.

Huntington's main concern is the dangers posed to western civilisation by other civilisations specially the Islamic civilisation. Islam combines religion and politics and hence no Islamic country is progressive; nor is it in peace. Moslems cannot live as a minority. This is proved from the fact that no Moslem country has peaceful relations with its neighbours. Huntington has tried to prove that there is no possibility of Islam and other religions living in peace. Gandhi, however, thought otherwise. He tried to look for religion of religions and thus to unite all religions. All religions are noble, said he. He made inter-religious amity one his main missions.

There are some similarities also. Like Gandhi, Huntington too considers modern industrial civilisation a special case, outside the main currents of world civilisations, even if for different reasons. He finally suggests that Western civilisation should go back to its roots, cultivate its strong points and be well prepared to defend itself. Surprisingly, Gandhi does not find a place in the references cited by Huntington either because he was not aware of Gandhian literature or because he considered Gandhian views contrary to what he wanted to advance.

The book has twelve chapters grouped in five parts. A gist of each part as presented in chapter 1 is given below:

"Part I: For the first time in history, global politics is both multi-polar and multi-civilisational; modernisation is distinct from Westernisation and is producing neither a universal civilisation in any meaningful sense, nor the Westernisation of non-Western societies.

Part II: The balance of power among civilisations is shifting: the West is declining in relative influence; Asian civilisations are expanding their economic, military and political strength; Islam is exploding demographically with destabilizing consequences for Muslim countries and their neighbours; and non-Western civilisations generally are reaffirming the value of their own cultures.

Part III: A civilisation-based world order is emerging: societies sharing cultural affinities cooperate with each other; effort to shift societies from one civilisation to another are unsuccessful and countries group themselves around the lead or core states of their civilisation.

Part IV: The West's universalist pretensions increasingly bring it into conflict with other civilisations, most seriously with Islam and China; at the local level fault-line wars, largely between Muslims and non-Muslims, generate 'kin-country rallying,' the threat of broader escalation, and hence efforts by core states to halt these wars.

Part V: The survival of West depends on Americans reaffirming their Western identity and Westerners accepting their civilisation as unique not universal and uniting to renew and preserve it against challenges from non-Western societies. Avoidance of a global war of civilisations depends on world leaders cooperating to maintain the multi-civilisational character of global politics.

According to Huntington, in the post-Cold War world and for the first time, global politics has become multipolar and multicivilisational. Nation states are still the principal actors in world affairs but their behaviour is shaped not only by the pursuit of power and wealth but also by cultural preferences, commonalities, and differences. The revitalisation of religions is reinforcing this trend. Cultural conflicts among civilisations are becoming more common today than ever before. And if there is chance of another world war, it would be among the civilisationally divided groups of nations.

He traces the present turmoil in the Islamic world particularly the terrorism, which has become a major threat to world peace, to the weakening of the nation states and the emergence of civilisation as the rallying point for the grouping of the nation states. And if what is happening in Europe (banding of nations into European Union) is any indicator, one cannot rule out the coalescing of the world into seven or eight civilisation groups: the Sinic, Japanese, Islamic, Hindu, Western, Latin American, and African. Four of these are based on four major religions of the world: Christianity, Islam, Hinduism and Confusianism.

"Every civilisation sees itself as the center of the world and writes its history as the central drama of world history. This has been even more true of the West than of other cultures. Such mono-civilisational viewpoints, however, have decreasing relevance and usefulness in a multi-civilisational world. Scholars of civilisation have long recognised this truism. In 1918 Spengler denounced the myopic view of history prevailing in the West with its neat division into ancient, medieval and modern phases relevant only to the West. ...A few decades later Toynbee castigated the 'parochialism and impertinence' of the West manifested in the 'egocentric illusions' that the world revolved around it, that there was an 'unchanging East' and that 'progress' was inevitable....Fifty years after Toynbee, Braudel similarly urged the need to strive for a broader perspective and to understand 'the great cultural conflicts in the world, and the multiplicity of its civilisations'. The illusions and prejudices of which these scholars warned, however, live on and in the late twentieth century have blossomed forth in the widespread and parochial conceit that the European civilisation of the West is now the universal civilisation of the world." Let me remind the reader that much before all these scholars, Gandhi in *Hind Swaraj* (1909) asked Indians to reject the satanic Western Civilisation and fall back on Indian civilisation, which was older, richer, and closer to the image of a true civilisation.

Huntington then debunks the theory of Western civilisation as universal and suggests religion and language as the two main defining factors in human relations and they both differ from one civilisation to the other. Modern civilisation is not the same as Western civilisation; nor is Western civilisation modern. Each civilisation has its own form of and route to modernity. Examples are Japan, which rejected the West in fifteenth century and then modernised itself. Kemalist Turkey presents another model. It Westernised and modernised with a bang but has remained Islamic in its detail contours. China followed another path. It rejected Westernisation and Modernisation to begin with but after the Cultural Revolution opted for Western style modernisation without rejecting the basic Confucius values. Modern societies have much in common; they are, however, not homogenous.

The West according to Huntington is fading in power but still powerful enough to turn around. Other cultures have found new identities and consider themselves superior to West in some if not in all spheres. The success of Asian societies in economic development has made them proud of their achievement; they ascribe their economic miracle to Asian cultural values rather than Western influence and Protestant ethic. On the other hand the Muslims try to look for their identity in Islam and the civilisation associated with it. Today practically all demographically Muslim majority countries of the world are more Islamists culturally, socially and politically than they were two decades back. While in other civilisations secularization and democratization made major *inroads*, in Muslim countries it was Islamisation.

By 1975 population in the West tended to be stabilized. In other cultures too efforts are afoot to control population. But the trend in Africa and Islamic countries was just the reverse. The demographic explosion and implosion in Islamic countries speeded up and the population of the young concentrated more and more in cities. It is these young men especially who became the targets and tools of Islamic movement. Larger population need more resources and hence Islamic societies are volatile and push outward to occupy new territory or to become majority where they constitute a minority using the very institutions which they try to supplant.

The trend that is set is this: people of same cultural background try to band together. Westerners ally with the Western countries, Islamic with Islamic, Sinic with Chinese and so on. Nationalism is weakening as a rallying point. Organisation of Islamic countries supports Pakistan on Kashmir not because Pakistan's stand is right or wrong, but because it is an Islamic country. Each of the cultures has a core area to which other countries of the same culture subscribe as supporters. Sinic culture has China as its core; Hindu has India; Orthodox has Russia. The West is tending to rally around USA and Africa South of Sahara around South Africa. Brazil is emerging as the rallying point in Latin America. As far as Muslim countries are concerned, there is no core area. This naturally poses a major problems for both Muslim and non-Muslim societies. The transition zones dividing the zones of major civilisations, which Huntington calls fault lines, are highly volatiles and violence prone. Today most of the conflict zones are along the fault lines.

Finally, Huntington comes to the main purpose of the book: to assess the prospects of Western civilisation. He cites history to prove that being dynamic, civilisations too rise and fall; merge and divide; and also disappear. He quotes Quigley who has charted seven stages in the evolution of civilisation: mixture, gestation, expansion; age of conflict, universal empire; decay and invasion. After they reach their pinnacles, they start going down. Would the Western civilisation too go down?

The above analysis of the past need not be repeated in the future. History does not always repeat itself. Man has now acquired sufficient information, knowledge and physical means to check the demise of any civilisation. West too need not decline to become irrelevant. But the real problem lies not in economic and political power of the west but in its moral decay. No society can stop its decay if it declines morally. Moral decline means:

(1) increase in antisocial behaviour, such as crime, drug use, and violence generally;
(2) family decay, including increased rates of divorce, illegitimacy, teen-age pregnancy, and single parent family;
(3) decline in social capital, that is membership in voluntary associations and interpersonal trust associated with such membership;
(4) general weakening of work ethics and rise of the cult of personal indulgence; and
(5) decreasing commitment to learning and intellectual activity.

The future health of the West and its influence on other societies depends in considerable measure on its success in coping with those trends, which give rise to the assertions of moral superiority and universality by Muslims and Asians. "All civilisations go through similar processes of emergence, rise and decline. The West differs from other civilisations not in the way it has developed, but in the distinctive character of its values and institutions. These include most notably Christianity, pluralism, individualism, and rule of law, which made it possible for West to invent modernity, expand throughout the world, and become the envy of other societies. ...They make Western civilisation unique, and Western civilisation is valuable not because it is universal but because it is unique."

Among the various steps the United States must take to compensate for the decline of its power, it must stop imposing its own values on others and interfering with other civilisations, says Huntington. And this applies to all core states of the major civilisations. "West requires the renewal of Western identity. The security of the world requires acceptance of global multiculturalism." Fortunately each culture has almost common principles of morality. Minimal moral concepts of truth and justice are found in all cultures. There are also minimal moral negative injunctions, most likely, rules against murder, deceit, torture, oppression and tyranny, What people have in common is more the sense of a common enemy (evil) than the commitment to common culture?" Human society is universal because it is human, particularly because it is a society. At times we march with others but mostly we march alone. Yet a 'thin' minimal morality does derive from the common human condition and universal dispositions are found in all cultures. Let each civilisation adhere to its own values

Instead of promoting the supposedly universal features of one civilisation, the requisites for coexistence demand a search for what is common to most civilisations. In a multi-civilisational world, the constructive course is to renounce universalism, accept diversity, and seek commonalities.

Huntington cites the example of Singapore, which defines its shared values in following terms:

- Nation before ethnic community and society above self;
- Family as the basic unit of the society;
- Regard and community support for the individual;
- Consensus instead of contention;
- Racial and religious harmony.

Singapore is committed to parliamentary democracy and clean government but the above shared cultural values exclude political values. Singapore is an Asian country and it must remain Asian where the rights of the community are more important than the rights of individuals. None of these values would however be rejected by any other civilisation. The above example applies to all civilisations and countries.

Huntington asks: "Modernization has generally enhanced the material level of Civilisation through out the world. But has it also enhanced the moral and cultural dimensions of Civilisation? To some extent, it has. Slavery, torture, vicious abuse of the individual have become less common. But if the present scenario is any indicator, a global breakdown of law and order, failed states and increasing anarchy in many parts of the world, a global crime wave, transnational mafias and drug cartels, increasing drug addiction in many societies, a general weakening of the family, a decline in trust and social solidarity in many countries, ethnic, religious and civilisational violence and rule by the gun is omnipresent in much of the world. In country after country and city after city crime appears to be soaring and morality at a discount.

Law and order is the first prerequisite of Civilisation, but it is fading almost everywhere." Civilisation seems to giving place to barbarism and heading towards the Dark Age or Kaliyug as Gandhi would say.

Why these Satanic tendencies all over the world? So far, the West ruled over the world and imposed its civilisation in its most uncivilized way. As its hold weakens, the pent up feelings and energies of the people against the imposed values and elimination of their own civilisational values are on the rise. "In the 1950s Lester Pearson warned that humans were moving into 'an age when different civilisations would have to learn to live side by side in peaceful interchange learning from each other, studying each other's history and ideals, and art and culture, mutually enriching each others' lives. The alternative in this overcrowded little world is misunderstanding, tension, clash, and catastrophe.' The futures of both peace and Civilisation depend upon understanding and cooperation among the political, spiritual and intellectual leaders of the world's major civilisations. ...In the emerging era, clashes of civilisations are the greatest threat to world peace, and an international order based on civilisations is the surest safeguard against world war."

Humanity can return to sanity only by recognizing that there are certain moral principles that cut across all civilisations, which must be adhered to and vigorously promoted. People must return to their own cultural roots and recapture the values, which do not injure the values of others as Singapore has done. This is what Gandhi too said as early as 1908 in *Hind Swaraj*.

THE THIRD WAVE BY ELWIN AND HEIDI TOFFLER

Tofflers' *The Third Wave* is path-breaking in many ways. The Future Shock they brought out in 1970s warned the world of the ecological crisis it was entering. It had it impact on the thinking of the people all over the world. Environment became a pet theme of seminars and conferences and many studies and reports followed suggesting policies and programmes designed to change the course of economic development. It ultimately culminated in what is now popularly known as Sustainable Development.

The Third Wave was published in 1980s. It takes a systemic view of the problems humanity faces today and gives pointers to the direction in which it is likely to move in the future. The conclusions of the book are quarter or half way to what Gandhi suggested in *Hind Swaraj*. Gandhi's point of departure was moral as the basis for human progress; Tofflers still believe that the Industrial Civilisation, in its next incarnation, would become humanistic. They consider human progress in stages and come to the conclusion that the world was entering the post-industrial civilisation, which would be based on information technology.

According to Tofflers, we started as hunter-gathers; we were nomads. We chased our food and moved as food moved, following water and seasons. The sick, old and weak were left behind and died. Our tools were the blade and the club, mimicking the weapons of animals. The valued commodity was physical strength. We were in the stone age; some of us in the bronze age; some others is semi-iron age. Then, a new style of life and living began, which the Tofflers call the First Wave or First Cultural transformation.

Domestication of animals and crops heralded the first wave. Permanent settlements began and as crops changed with season round the year the concept of cyclical time emerged. Everyone worked the farm. It was the age of extended family. People were generalists and there, was practically no waste. Every thing was custom made, by hand, among the family. Work was done at home or in the farm; barter was the medium of exchange. The most valued commodity was land and that was the only source of revenue for whatever government was there. Knowledge was experiential; people with more experience had more knowledge. Age was valued and respected.

There were conflicts among the farmers and hunter gathers and among the farmers themselves. But they were settled without much bloodshed. Three innovations appear to set the stage for the Second Wave:

(1) Accurate clocks enabled people to work on schedule;
(2) The printing press enabled them to transmit information across space and time; and
(3) New developments in metallurgy (iron and steel) for farm implements.

As the tools improved, the powers of nature were harnessed and new sources of energy were discovered to operate the tools. Steam engine was invented; it revolutionized the mode of production of goods. The primacy of agriculture came down rather drastically at least in the West.

The Second Wave work involved capital investment in better tools, labour force and factories where all the means of production could be assembled. And thus were born Capitalists, Managers, Labour Unions, Corporations, etc. As work moved from home to factory, people moved from village to city leaving wives back home to look after first wave activities. Workers became specialists in just one little part of the total activity. And thus gender gap widened. And soon the nuclear family became a norm. The era of mass production set in and hierarchic organisations came up to manage the big factories and corporations.

The natural resources were exploited beyond the nature's capacity to recoup. The time changed from being cyclical to linear.

There were teething troubles in changing over from first to second wave civilisation. Factories were burnt by Luddites, the enraged peasants. American Civil War according to some was the reflection of the conflict between First Wave South and Second Wave North.

The two world wars of the twentieth century changed the scene again. This time the change resulted from the requirements of the armed forces. Ballistic computations drove the development of the first wave computer. Radar sensor systems extended the visibility, and code breakers needed information processing system. In fact the Cold War was the major force behind all these changes. And thus ensued the Third Wave.

The Information Revolution commenced when the Industrial Revolution peaked in the same way as the Industrial Revolution commenced when the Agricultural Revolution had peaked in the West. "The huge companies and military organisations needed to track what they had, what they were doing, and what they were spending." The new tools amplified their senses and memories. Among these tools the telephone played a major role. The classical factory system is on the way out; work is being outsourced to distant places. With easy access to information, the respect which older people commanded is declining. Even money is being replaced by credit card.

Thus the Third Wave civilisation is marked with six major characteristics:

(1) Work is not tied to any place; it can be done even at home.
(2) Education must be continuous and life long.
(3) Size does not matter; even small companies can compete with giants.

(4) Location, space and mass do not matter.
(5) Time matters a lot.
(6) Women have a far better role to play.

Tofflers consider energy as the basis of civilisation. First Wave civilisations drew their energy from 'living batteries' – human and animal muscle-power – or from sun, wind and water. Forests provided the domestic fuel for cooking and heating. Millstones turned the waterwheels and windmills pulled the underground water up. Horses and bullocks pulled the plow and carts. As late as the French Revolution, Europe had 14 million horses and 20 million oxen. All these sources were renewable. As against this, the Second Wave societies drew their energy from coal, gas and oil, which are non-renewable fossil fuels.

The above shift consumed nature's capital to subsidize industrial civilisation, and to accelerate economic growth. Wherever the Second Wave went, nations built towering technological and economic structures assuming that cheap fossil fuels would be endlessly available. Political ideologies did not matter, nor did the religion and level of development, the shift from dispersal to concentrated, from renewable to non-renewable, from many different sources to a few was apparent. Fossil fuels formed the energy base of all Second Wave societies.

How did it all happen? On August 8, 1960, the Oil giant Exxon Corporation decided to drastically cut down the royalty it paid to the oil-producing countries; other Oil companies followed suit. The oil producing countries retaliated and formed OPEC. In 1973 when the Yom Kipper war broke out, the OPEC reduced the supply of crude oil forcing the world economy to spin down. OPEC's revenues increased four fold and chain reaction set in practically all walks of life. The Third Wave had come to the surface and death of industrialism and the rise of new civilisation had commenced. We try to find answers to many of our puzzles in the past like a ship's crew, trapped in a storm and trying to navigate between dangerous reefs without compass or chart.

The world that is fast emerging from the clash of new values and technologies, new geopolitical relationships, new life styles, and modes of communication, demands wholly new ideas and analogies, classifications and concepts. We cannot depend on the past, nor can we 'cram the embryonic world of tomorrow into yesterday's conventional cubbyholes.' We have to develop a synergic view, move away from specialization and then and then only can we see in the midst of destruction and decay, striking evidences of birth and life, of an emergent civilisation more sane, sensible, and sustainable, more decent, and more democratic that any we have ever known.

When we look at *Hind Swaraj*, we realize that Gandhi could foresee the birth of a new civilisation over a century before Tofflers wrote their book. But he did not stop at a new version of industrial civilisation, which Tofflers have presented in The Third Wave. Gandhi's saw a different scenario far beyond the Information Age. The Third Wave is mainly concerned with economy, business and work. Gandhi's *Hind Swaraj* is concerned with the future of man.

DESCHOOLING SOCIETY BY EVAN ELLICH

Born in Vienna in 1926, Evan Ellich studied theology and philosophy at Gregariam University, Rome. After acquiring Ph.D. in history at the university of Salsburg, he went to the USA as assistant Pasteur in Irish-Puerto Rircan Parish, New York City. He was Vice Rector of Catholic University of Puerto Rico during 1956-60 where he organised intensive training for American priests in Latin American culture. Cofounder of International Documental Centre (CIDOC) in Guevara, Mexico, he directed a research seminar on International Alternative in Technological Society with focus on Latin America. Ellich has written widely on themes related to alternative futures. He was Gandhian not only in thought but also life, living and work. I had the privilege of having him in the Institute of Development Studies, University of Mysore for a day in 1975 and having detailed discussion on the book reviewed here. He passed away in 2001.

Referring to the theme of the book the author says that "I owe my interest in public education to Everett Reiner. Until we first met in Puerto Rico in 1958, I had never questioned the value of extending obligatory schooling to all people. Together we have come to realize that for most men the right to learn is curtailed by the obligation to attend school. The Essays given at SIDOC and gathered in this book grew out of the memoranda which I submitted to him, and which we discussed during 1970, the thirteenth year of our dialogue. The last chapter contains my afterthoughts on a conversation with Erich Fromm on Bachofen's Mutterrecht."

"Universal education through schooling is not feasible. It would be no more feasible if it were attempted by means of alternative institutions built on the style of present schools. Neither new attitudes of teachers towards their pupils nor the proliferation of educational hardware or software (in classroom and bedroom), nor finally the attempt to expand the pedagogue's responsibility until it engulfs his pupils' lifetimes will deliver universal education. The current search for new educational funnels must be reversed into the search for their education inverse: educational webs which heighten the opportunity for each on to transform each moment of his living into one of his learning, sharing and caring. We hope to contribute concepts needed by those who conduct such counterfoil research on education – and also to those who seek alternatives to other established service industries."

"Many students especially those who are poor, intuitively know what the schools do for them to continue the process and substance. Once these become blurred, a new logic is assumed: the more treatment there is, the better are the results; or, escalation leads to success. The pupil is thereby 'schooled' to confuse teaching with learning, grade advance with education, a diploma with competence, and fluency with the ability to say something new. His imagination is 'schooled' to accept service in place of value. Medical treatment is mistaken for healthcare, military poise for national security, the rat race for productive work; health, learning, dignity, independence, and creative endeavour are defined as little more than the performance of the institutions which claim to serve these ends, and their improvement is made to depend on allocating more resources to the management of hospitals, schools and other agencies in question."

Ellich has shown that "the institutionalization of values leads inevitably to physical pollution, social polarization and psychological impotence, three dimensions in the process of global degradation and modernized misery." He has explained how this process of degradation is accelerated "when nonmaterial needs are transformed into demands for commodities; when health, education, personal mobility, welfare, or psychological healing are defined as the result of services or treatments. I do this because I believe that most of the research now going on about the future tends to advocate further increases in the institutionalization of values, that we must define conditions which would permit precisely the contrary to happen. We need research on the possible use of technology to create institutions, which serve personal, creative and autonomous interaction and the emergence of values, which cannot be substantially controlled by technocrats. We need counterfoil research to current futurology."

Ellich's objective is to define man's nature and the nature of modern institutions, which characterize the prevailing worldview and language. He has chosen school as his paradigm. The conclusion he has drawn, apply to other agencies of the modern state: the consumer, family, the army, the police, the media and the church. "Not only education but social reality itself has become schooled. It costs roughly the same to school both rich and poor in the same dependency. The yearly expenditure per pupil in the slums and in the rich suburbs of anyone of twenty US cities lies in the same range – and sometimes is favourable to the poor. Rich and poor alike depend on schools and hospitals, which guide their lives, form their worldview, and define for them what is legitimate and what is not. Both view doctoring oneself as irresponsible, learning on one's own as unreliable, and community organisation, when not paid for by those in authority, as a form....For both groups the reliance on institutional treatment renders independent accomplishment suspect. The progressive underdevelopment of self-and the community-reliance is even more typical in Westchester than it is in the northeast of Brazil. Everywhere, not only education but society as a whole needs 'deschooling'."

Poverty has been modernized by the bureaucracies, which claim "a professional, political and financial monopoly over the social imagination, setting standards for what is valuable and what is feasible. This monopoly is at the root of the modernization of poverty. Every simple need to which an institutional answer is found permits the invention of a new class of poor and a new definition of poverty. Ten years ago in Mexico it was the normal thing to be born and to die in one's own home and to be buried by one's friends. Only the soul's needs were taken care of by the institutional church. Now to begin and end life at home become signs either of poverty or special privilege. Dying and death have come under the institutional management of doctors and undertakers,"

"Once basic needs have been translated by a society into demands for scientifically produced commodities, poverty is defined by standards, which the technocrats change at will. Poverty then refers to those who have fallen behind an advertised ideal of consumption in some important respect. In Mexico the poor are those who lack three years of schooling, and in New York they are those who lack twelve."

The poor have always been socially powerless; now they are dependent on political bosses and are disabled by lack of schooling. Modernization of poverty combines the lack of power over circumstances with a loss of personal potency. Modernization of poverty is now a global phenomenon even if it appears in different guises in poor and rich countries.

The United States spent around three billion dollars between 1965-68 to help six million children of poor families. Nothing changed thereafter. The disadvantaged children continue to be far behind their counterparts from middle class families. The money so allocated did not produce desired effects. "School appropriate the money, men and goodwill available for education and in addition discourages other institutions from assuming educational tasks. Work leisure, politics, city living, and even family life depends on the schools for habits and knowledge they presuppose, instead of becoming themselves the means of education. Simultaneously, both schools and the other institutions, which depend on them are priced out of the market. It would be almost impossible to provide equal opportunities for education and health.

Equal education is both feasible and desirable goal but this could not be achieved by obligatory schooling. Ellich, therefore, proposes the state to de-link itself from education. Neither learning nor justice is promoted by education. This could be done by detatching competence from curriculum, "... inquiries into a man's learning history must be made taboo like inquiries into his political affiliation, church attendance, lineage, sex habits, or racial background. Laws forbidding discrimination on the basis of prior schooling must be enacted.

"The second major illusion on which the school system rests is that most learning is because of teaching. ...Most learning happens casually, and even most intentional learning is not the result of programmed instruction. Normal children learn their language casually, although faster if their parents pay attention to them....yet there are many skills which a motivated student with normal aptitude can master in a matter of a few months if taught in this traditional way."

Ellich asks for skill training that can be given by anyone possessing skill; one need not go to school. "But at present those using skills which are in demand and do require a human teacher are discouraged from sharing these skills with others. This is done either by teachers who monopolize the licences or by unions which protect their trade interests. Skill centres which will be judged by customers on their results, and not on the personnel they employ, or the process they use, would open unsuspected working opportunities, frequently even for those who are now considered unemployable. Indeed there is no reason why such skill centre should not be started."

"Opportunities for skill learning can be vastly multiplied if we open the 'market'. This depends on matching the right teacher with the right student when he is highly motivated in an intelligent programme, without the constraint of curriculum."

"The deschooling society implies a recognition of two-faced nature of learning. A insistence on skill-drill alone could be a disaster; equal emphasis must be placed on other kinds of learning. But if schools are the wrong places for learning a skill they are even the worst places for getting an education....Schools are even less efficient in the arrangement of the circumstances which encourage the open-ended, exploratory use of acquired skills (liberal education). The main reason for this is that school is obligatory and becomes schooling for schooling's sake: an enforced stay in the company of teachers, which pays off in the doubtful privilege of more such company. Just as skill instruction must be freed from curricular restraint, so much liberal education for inventive and creative behaviour can be aided by institutional arrangement, but they are different, frequently opposite nature."

"Only the mobilization of the whole population can lead to popular culture. The equal right of each man to exercise his competence to learn and to instruct is now pre-empted by certified teachers. The teacher's competence in turn is restricted to do what he may be done in school. And, further, work and leisure are alienated from each other.... A radical alternative to a schooled society requires not only new formal mechanisms for the formal acquisition of skills and their educational use. A deschooled society implies a new approach to incidental or formal education."

Education in the villages of the medieval times was highly synergic. "Traditional society was more like a set of concentric circles of meaningful structures. ...In the village language, and architecture and work and religion and family customs were consistent with one another, mutually explanatory and reinforcing. To grow into one implied the growth into the others. Even specialized apprenticeship was a byproduct of specialized activities, such as shoemaking or the singing of the psalms. If an apprentice never became a master or a scholar, he still contributed to making shoes or to making church services solemn. Education did not compete for time with either work or leisure. Almost all education was complex, life long and unplanned.

The above model may not fit the contemporary society, which is the result of conscious designs and hence the educational opportunities must be integrated into them. "Our reliance on specialized, full-time instruction through school will now decrease, and we must find more ways to learn and teach: the educational quality of all institutions must increase again."

Those who are aware of Gandhi's concept of Basic Education would agree that Evan was so very close to Gandhi. In fact, he elaborated Gandhian concept of work based education accessible to all.

THE MEGA TRENDS: BY JOHN NAISBITT

Here is a book that detects from American newspapers and magazines ten major trends likely to shape the future of the world. He studied newspaper reports of the past few decades prior to the publication of the book and tried to find the changes in themes on which articles and news were published. His objective was to warn the business and industry of the emerging world order and what they ought to do to remain competitive in the future too. Apparently, its conclusions have to be taken with a bit of caution. The trends detected may change in the future. Further, they may be temporary and may not sustain for long because they are based on the information reported in newspapers and magazines published during a given period, which was selected arbitrarily. The author does not use his intuition, nor does he base his conclusions on any theoretical construct. Yet he does give some insight into the future, which is built on the past at least partly and is not separated from the present.

The trends noted suffer from another weakness. They are based on the study of American newspapers and magazines and hence they would be more relevant to the USA. We cannot take them as global trends although we cannot deny the fact that in the post-Second World War scenario, the world is getting so closely integrated that what is relevant for one country is not irrelevant for the rest of the world. In the words of the author "These trends will affect your life and your business. Trends tell you the direction the country is moving in. The decisions are up to you. But trends, like horses, are easier to ride in the direction they are already going. When you make a decision that is compatible with the overarching trend, the trend helps you along. You may decide to buck the trend, but it is still helpful to know it is there.

"This book describes the environment in which to consider the decisions of life; what to study; the right job to start a business; join a union; or run for public office.

"My purpose is to offer the readers a new context within which to sort out and assess today's events."

The book was first published in 1882 but it continues to be relevant even today. Further, it touches some of the aspects which *Hind Swaraj* touches. It gives an impression that some of the changes which Gandhi envisaged are already in offing. This proves the seminal character of *Hind Swaraj*.

The Ten Mega Trends Naisbitt has discussed are:

(1) Industrial Society to Information Society;
(2) Forced Technology to High Tech/ High Touch;
(3) National Economy to World Economy;
(4) Short Term to Long Term;
(5) Centralization to Decentralization;
(6) Institutional Help to Self Help;
(7) Representative Democracy to Participatory Democracy;
(8) Hierarchies to Networking;
(9) North to South;
(10) Either/Or to Multiple Option.

Industrial to Information Society

The information age has already arrived. Old industrial structure has given way to knowledge based occupational structure. The distances have narrowed beyond imagination and, to use Marshall McLuhan's terminology, the world has become a global village. The professional workers of the USA even in the 1950s had become information workers: lawyers, teachers, engineers, doctors, architects, librarians, accountants, computer operators, etc. just to name a few. Know how has become a new source of wealth; nay, it is the wealth. Unlike the natural resources or brain power, it is brain intensive resource, which cannot be concentrated in a few hands. "Unlike other forces in the universe, however, knowledge is not subject to the law of conservation: It can be created, it can be destroyed, and most importantly it is synergetic – that is whole is usually greater than the sum of its parts."

"The restructuring of America from an Industrial to an Information society will easily be as profound as the shift from an agricultural society to an Industrial society" says Naisbitt. He quotes Daniel Bell that it is the interaction among people cutting across space that marks the

Information age. "During our agricultural period, the game was man against nature. An industrial society pits man against fabricated nature. In an Information Society – for the first time in civilisation – the game is people interacting with other people even if remotely."

This is not to suggest that agriculture and industry would disappear. It is only to suggest that even these activities will be information run and information based. Industrial production would be computer operated and so would the agricultural system be. All departments of life would have to change their style of working to suit the requirements of the information age.

But there is a catch. Information is not knowledge, nor is it wisdom. There is already an overload of information cluttering the decision-making processes. Synergy of information produces knowledge and when knowledge is intermixed with spirituality, one gets the wisdom to discriminate right from wrong. It is unfortunate that in the Era of Information what is lacking most is wisdom.

One may also question the thesis that Information Age is different from the Industrial Age in its essences. For all practical purposes it is nothing but a special case or even a continuation of the Industrial Age. The Agricultural Age was dominated by nature, and manual power of Asia; the industrial age by manual power and brain power of Europe; the next age it appears be based on brain power and Soul Force (to use Gandhi's terminology) of the whole world. The vibrations of its undercurrents are being felt all over the world.

Forced Technology to High Tech/ High Touch

Naisbitt asserts that technology has its own implications for human life. It can disorient man from himself and his community and society. Technological explosion must be backed by group-therapy movements, which speed up inner growth of individuals. Further, there is need for skill upgradation to make the best use of advanced technology. One need not be fearful of technology, if one knows himself and does not allow technology to disrupt his family and community. Thus, computer can become liberator in many ways provided that it is accompanied by high touch that is opportunity to get together, to see 'smell' and feel each other and by skills to use it to the best advantage of the self and society.

Technological advances must be backed by cultural and social advances, and by new educational policies and programmes so that the distance that technology creates among people is reduced and participation in work and other social activities is enhanced, "the more the technology around, the more the need for human touch."

It would be pertinent to compare this concept with Gandhi's views on technology. Gandhi was not against technology, he wanted technology to serve the people; it should be under the control of the people; it should not throw the people out of job and if it must, those displaced must be enabled to get their minimum needs met. Thus Gandhi in a way suggested negative income tax for those who become victims of advanced technology.

National Economy to World Economy

Another trend that became visible in the second half of the twentieth century is the globalization of the economy. The industrial supremacy of the West particularly of the USA waned. The reasons were clear. The advantages that the USA had of early start in communication technology were no longer there. The new technology was mastered by many other countries particularly Japan. As time passed, the Third World countries moved forward and challenged American supremacy. To day India, a country known for slow economic growth marched forward and became a major global player in information technology. Economic growth of the ASEAN countries too increased as did that of China, South Korea, Hong Kong, Taiwan etc. And thus the hold of the USA on world market declined within just a few decades.

The globalization of industry was accompanied by production sharing. Final products involved many countries contributing resources, technology, skilled manpower etc. In many cases even capital sharing through joint ventures were common features. Competition thus became world-wide, no longer limited to a particular firm or even national firms. This gave two types of economies in the USA: sunrise and sunset.

Global interdependence has increased and no country can now stand alone. "The more economically interdependent we become, the more we will do the human thing, in my opinion, and become more assertive about our distinctiveness, especially our languages" says Naisbitt. Gandhi too promoted globalization but with a difference. The base of his globalization was a self-reliant local community. Gandhi's global society would have lesser linkages as one moved from village to state and from state to nation and finally from nation to the world.

Short Term to Long Term

Yet another feature of the post-Second World War economy is long term planning. Earlier, American businessmen had only short-term perspectives. With increasing competition and destabilizing role of information technology, long-term thinking has now come to rule the business and industry. Some excerpts from the relevant chapter of the book will illustrate the point. "Our commercial history is filled with examples that failed to change with a changing world, and became tombstones in the corporate graveyard. ...If you don't know what business you are in, conceptualize what business it would be useful for you to think you are in. ...Money is information in moving. ...The shift from money to electronics is as important as the earlier shift from barter to money. ...Strategic planning is worthless—unless there is first a strategic vision.... there are cities and companies, unions and political parties, in this country (USA) that are like dinosaurs waiting for the weather to change. The weather is not going to change. The very ground is shifting beneath us. And what is called for is nothing less than all of us re-conceptualizing our roles."

Centralization to Decentralization

The Agricultural system was decentralized because agriculture is land extensive activity. "Early America was a community of farmers, and agricultural society lends itself to decentralized government. The Industrial Revolution changed this pattern and centralization became the norm: it pervaded all walks of life: economic, social, political and technological until about 1950s. With the advent of Information Revolution, the centralized structures started crumbling and the rebuilding of the society from the bottom up began. Power started shifting from Centre to the lower level territorial units like states, city corporations and counties in USA. These trends became clear in India too particularly in the 1990s.

Gandhi was the votary of decentralization. In his scheme of things village was the basic unit of polity. He advanced the oceanic circle theory of socio-economic organisation wherein the lowest level unit, *i.e.* village, is considered to be self-governing republic. Thomas Jefferson's 'the less government, the better' is in fashion all over the world. In fact Gandhi looked forward to a day when the government would wither away.

Institutional Help to Self-Help

One of the major thrusts of Gandhi was self-reliance through Swadeshi. In fact he wanted the government's role in day-today life of the people to be limited to support when so required. People should develop their own institutions and manage their own affairs. This means that the local resources should be transferred to the local units: village panchayats and city municipalities.

Self-help has always been a part of American life. It again took the form of a movement in 1970s "that cut across institutions, disciplines, geographic areas and political ideologies. Self-help means community groups acting to prevent crime, to strengthen neighbourhoods, to salvage food for the elderly, and to rebuild homes, without government assistance or at least with local control over government help"

According to Naisbitt, fifteen million Americans had joined over 500,000 self help groups which bypass the traditional avenues of institutional assistance in favour of dealing with people like themselves who have solved or trying to solve the same problem. There are self help groups for almost every conceivable problems.

Representative Democracy to Participatory Democracy

Naisbitt saw a secular move to opt for participatory democracy. People started asking questions about decisions taken by governments They wanted to be consulted on issues that concerned them. This trend was visible not only in government circles but also in corporations and business enterprises.

Gandhi wanted decentralization of governmental and other functions, down to the village level. He wanted the villages to take decisions by consensus so that the opinion of a minority is not ignored. He advanced the oceanic circle theory of socio-economic Organisation wherein the lowest level unit, *i.e.* village, is considered to be self-governing republic. According to him majority is not always right. In fact, more often than not many important changes in society have been brought about not by the majority but by the minority.

Hierarchies to Networking

For centuries, the pyramid structure was the way we organized and managed ourselves. From the Roman army to the Catholic Church, to the organisation chart of the General Motors and IBM, power and communication have flowed in an orderly manner from the pyramid's top, down to its base, from the high priest, the general, the CEO perched at the very top, down through the wider ranks of lieutenants and departmental managers clustered in the middle, to the workers, foot soldiers, and true believers at the bottom." A major change began in the nineteen sixties and seventies which made hierarchic systems inefficient. New movements began to smash it and move on networking mode.

Networks are interlinking of the people for direct communication using phones, conferences, visits, photocopying, books, pamphlets, parties, grape vines, newspapers and mutual friends, just to mention a few. Networks offer horizontal links, which hierarchically organized bureaucratic systems can never offer. Networks were there in the past too but they were limited to elites. In the new dispensation they are egalitarian penetrating the common people. As such rewards come by empowering others, not by trampling over others.

Let us recall Gandhi's views about hierarchies. He stood for decentralization, horizontal solidarity, and human brotherhood. What Gandhi said in this connection in 1909 was practically repeated even in the context of business and economics by many of the Western authors like Naisbitt.

North to South

In this chapter Naisbitt gives the shift of population and economic activities from Northern states of the USA to the southern states. There was a time when Northeast was the core area of the USA; core area in all respects. North was the guide post for the South. Whatever happened in the North became a norm to be followed in the South. From 1980s the things changed and many of the industrial and service activities centered in the north started gaining prominence in the south and southwest. The new opportunities in the field of petrochemicals, oil, and space age technologies located themselves in the south. The great cities like New York, Chicago and Detroit lost not only the industries that gave them economic base but also population, especially quality population.

In India too the south has surged ahead of the once rich north. The states which once formed the economic core of the country (UP, Bihar, MP, Rajasthan) now constitute the region of sick (BIMARU) states. It has happened because the northern states were too sluggish to face the new challenges.

Either/or to Multiple Options

And finally Naisbitt discusses the widening opportunities for people in the West. Earlier, the choices were limited; in the new age they have become multiple. This applies to all aspects of life. The market is full of consumer goods of great variety, people have choices in politics, entertainment, and jobs. Individualism has triumphed. Joint family is no longer the basic unit of society; community has become a formal organisation. Women who were not in the job market, now compete with men and have taken up jobs which once belonged to the masculine gender.

The multiple choices have crept in such very personal affairs like religion. People are no longer wedded to one religion; they are trying to take what is good in all. Same is the case with arts and aesthetics. People are becoming more religious but perhaps less spiritual.

Naisbitt wrote Mega Trends for the western audience. But he considered it relevant to other parts of the world too because the trends he noted were global in nature and hence sooner or later they will set in all countries and regions of the world. Although he published the book in 1882, his conclusions are still more or less relevant. The changes he noted are sweeping the whole world even if their impacts are variable from civilisation to civilisation and country to county.

The book is important to us because his conclusions, even though addressed and relevant to business and industry, are pertinent to all facets of life. He paid greater attention to business and industry because that was the audience he had in mind. The reader can easily note that Naisbitt's conclusions are in line with what Gandhi has advocated in *Hind Swaraj* in many respects. That is the reason why the book has been reviewed here.

CONCLUDE REMARKS

The reader, if he had not been familiar with the above books, would be wonderstruck at what Gandhi said more simply and illustratively in *Hind Swaraj* several decades earlier. Yet, he was ignored, may be because time was not ripe for what he conveyed. The purpose in juxtaposing these books with *Hind Swaraj* is to bring home the fact that Gandhi was not just a visionary, a person who was looking for utopia. His worldview was not based on unrealistic idealism; it was rooted in the emerging future as seen by him—a future hidden behind and underneath the apparently roaring successes of European science and technology. Gandhi could feel the death agonies of decadent industrialism and birth pangs of a new humane, and truly modern civilisation as early as 1908, if not earlier, as did the four authors referred to above in 1980s.

Gandhi lived in an era of Industrial Revolution at its peak. No one dared to challenge its superiority, rationality, and potentiality as prime means of state power and emancipator of suffering humanity particularly the labour class. It had helped colonization of the world; it had taken toll of millions of lives in Americas and Australia and maimed many more; it was marching fast to destroy a number of great civilisations. It was so 'successful' that only a few brave souls like Gandhi had the guts to challenge it. He could perceive its ephemeral nature more clearly because of his Indian background but he was not alone. He was in good company of many of the late 19th and 20th century thinkers like Rouseau in the USA, Tolstoy in Russia, Prince Kropatkin in France, P.A. Sorokin in the USA.

Hind Swaraj is an indictment of industrial civilisation, and the mentality underlying it. There are missing links in his thoughts as presented in the book because he capsuled all that he wanted to say in just 60 pages and in a language within the reach of the common man. After Tulsidas, Gandhi was the first great Indian to communicate with the people of India in their language and style; to bring himself down to the level of the people; to think with them, to feel with them, and to live with them. Tulsidas produced a great epic: Ramcharit Manas; Gandhi translated the epic into practical wisdom to set off a movement that aimed at bringing Ramraj in India. *Hind Swaraj* gives the outline and rationale of the Ramraj he was fighting for.

Gandhi was not an academic, nor it was his purpose to write a thesis. He was trying to communicate with those who, even without knowing him, shared his thoughts. They were the potential collaborators and followers in his struggle for the emancipation of the 'oppressed' humanity. He wanted to tell them that the stakes were bigger, larger and more far reaching than they appeared to be; that the cause they were fighting for was a right one and in the direction of transforming the sensate world into an idealistic one. [Sorokin, Pitirin A., 1937-41 *Social and Cultural Dynamism* (4 volumes), New York: American Book Co.]

Capra took advances in physics as his point of departure and extended his scientific analysis to human field. Rifkin looked at the laws of thermodynamics to trace the root cause of the multifaceted and complex problems humanity faces today. Naisbitt took recourse to content analysis of relevant newspapers and magazines to arrive at the emerging counter currents. Toffler has put a general and larger question before us: Where are we heading to? And he answers thus: Whether we know it or not, most of us are already engaged in either resisting or creating the new civilisation" in offing. The Third Wave gives the form and shape of this new emerging civilisation, which Gandhi called 'truly modern'. Gandhi presented in *Hind Swaraj* his own model of 'modern civilisation', a model closer to that of Sorokin's 'Ideational Stage'.

Capra-Rifkin-Naisbitt-Toffler model of New Civilisation is presented from the vantage point of post-industrial developments and confusions in the West pointing to the way out of the morass in which the west finds itself today. Gandhi in *Hind Swaraj* and elsewhere, looked at industrial civilisation from the vantage point of what was fundamental and everlasting in Indian civilisation. He tried to convey the message that oppression was built in industrialism and that the salvation of the oppressed lay in the rejection of the very source of it.

For Capra, Rifkin, Naisbitt and Toffler the new civilisation will emerge from the debris of modern industrial civilisation; from the obsolescence of Newtonian scientific paradigm and from the twists and turns in human destiny. Civilisation changes in waves; now is the turn for a new civilisation, different from what we have consciously or otherwise created and experienced during the last couple of centuries. For Gandhi, it heralds a new assertion of what Indian civilisation has stood for from ancient most times to the present and a fresh manifestation of human consciousness. If we remove dead load of industrialism piled upon Indian civilisation, and throw out the incongruities and impurities, which have blackened its face, we will have a truly modern civilisation, said Gandhi. What these incongruities and impurities are and how can they be removed without violence, forms the sum total of *Hind Swaraj*.

REFERENCES

Elvin and Heidi Toffler (1984); *The Third Wave,* New York: Bentam Books.

Evan Ellich, *De-schooling Society.*

John Naisbitt (1984), *Mega Trends: Ten New Directions Transforming Our Lives,* New York: Waener Books.

S.P. Huntington (1997); *The Clash of Civilisation and the Remaking of World Order,* New Delhi: Penguin Books, India.

15

The Message of Hind Swaraj

It is now over 95 years since Gandhi wrote *Hind Swaraj*. Despite its age, the book has remained relevant to this day because the problems and issues, which inspired him to write it have not disappeared: the crisis which gripped the society then has rather deepened. Violence is more pervading today than it was in 1909; the role of doctors, lawyers and other professionals in nation building has deteriorated further; the parliamentary democratic structure has failed to deliver goods; the living conditions of the poor have not improved to the extent they ought to; and the quality of the political leadership of the country, with some exceptions notwithstanding, no longer commands the respect and confidence of the people. We are one of the most corrupt countries of the world; we are not a very peace loving country either—religious and caste conflicts continue unabated and even on small matters we tend to come to blows; and we stand very low even in conventional human development index. In fact we continue to be gripped by all those maladies that Gandhi wanted free India to be free from.

Let me hasten to add that India does not stand alone in this respect. As Gandhi pointed out in *Hind Swaraj*, sensual and undesirable things spread fast and spiritual and desirable things move at snail's pace. Given the speed of modern communication system much that is undesirable becomes a global phenomenon within no time. Violence has spread everywhere; no one is out of reach of Osama-bin-Laden and his likes. The conflicts among peoples and nations have claimed more lives since 1950, than the Second World War. Indirect violence in form of hunger, exploitation and denial of human rights has maimed millions of people. Environmental destruction, poverty, social inequity, ignorance and immorality continue to plague the world, the 'heroic' efforts to root them out notwithstanding. We have done well in science and technology, in national economic growth and diversification; and to some extent in social infrastructure. Our failure lies in the absence of very slow progress on the human front, *i.e.* moral and ethical front. We have failed to make man a better man so that our economic and technological achievements could percolate down to all those who need them most. Gandhi wished India to move forwards on the spiritual front while not neglecting the economic and social fronts. He wanted *sarvodaya*, the *udaya* (rise) of all; he wanted India to follow the path laid by its own civilisation, the middle path. India, in spite of Gandhi, has yet to make a choice.

Fifty years is not a long enough time to assess achievements of an ancient civilisation that India is but it is good enough time to discern stirrings and convulsions, which set the trends and tendencies. Even a cursory look at the post-independence history of India shows that its main preoccupation has been material progress often at the cost of moral advancement. May be, the circumstances prevailing in 1947, when the country became independent and which Gandhi did not foresee, made us continue on the beaten path unmindful of its pitfalls. We were inspired by the 'great achievements' of the Soviet Union and encouraged by global acceptance of Western civilisation as the only route to development. We were in hurry to show some results but we got caught in the whirlpool of the declining phase of industrial civilisation. Even otherwise, one doubts if the followers of Gandhi really were committed to his paradigm of development. They accepted Gandhi as the leader of the freedom struggle; they also accepted, even if hesitatingly, the means he adopted in fighting the British rule. But very few of them really knew, leave aside believed, in his grand design of a new world order. This was clearly reflected in Nehru's reply to Gandhi's last letter to him. Nehru was Fabian socialist highly impressed by the economic progress USSR made in a short time even at a great human cost. Gandhi's village did not appeal him for it represented the dead past. For him the big dams, big cities, huge factories and sprawling scientific laboratories were the modern temples of India. He was right, but he was wrong too.

In between the two images of India, one sketched by Gandhi and the other by Nehru, stood millions of people who worshiped Gandhi as a Mahatma but admired Nehru as the builder of modern India. People had faith in Gandhi but hope in Nehru. Questions about Gandhi's image of India of the future were not articulated and raised earlier because the priority lay in winning freedom and Gandhi was the torchbearer for this onerous task.

Gandhi could foresee the problems ahead for he did know that western civilisation and all that it meant was highly attractive to senses and would be able to maintain its hold on India and overshadow the grand panorama he painted for India of the future. In his last days he felt quite powerless. The Congress leadership was not willing to go along with him. It was not possible to create an alternative leadership. He had to do with whatever was available. Nehru was the best bet; he was sincere, honest and liked by the people. Gandhi, therefore, pinned his hopes on him and declared him as his political heir apparently for a transition period during which he hoped India would move from turmoil to peace and opt for its own path of development and change.

Several factors combined to force India to retrace its steps from the Gandhian path. One of them was the misgiving Gandhi created by tracing his ideas back to the ancient civilisation of India. It gave the impression that he was trying to take the country back to the 'golden past'. The fault however did not lay with him. None of his ideas could be understood if it were seen in isolation. What he said on one subject had to be correlated with what he had said on the other subjects. Modern reductionism blurs holistic visions. It sees only in parts. Gandhian thought became a victim of this weakness of modern scientific approach. Second, India was already a part of the industrial civilisation, even if as a subaltern. It was difficult for it to move away from this path partly because one just cannot reverse the gear of development instantly without inflicting damage to existing pace and style of progress; and partly because people were too impatient to see some change soon after the freedom dawned. It was easier to speed up progress in conventional sense by pushing the economy harder than to reverse the gear and change the meaning of development.

In political field, Gandhi's immediate goal was parliamentary democracy, but in economic and social fields, he never set short-term goals. His concept of *Swaraj*, Swadeshi, villagization, appropriate technology, moral economy, and development from below and within did not mesh with the exigencies of the then prevailing situations and the value systems of the Congress leaders. He did make Indians sit-up and think about their great past but the new model of Indian civilisation he presented was faint and often misunderstood by the people. Lakhs of people died in the aftermath of partition of India; nonviolence failed to stop it, not because it had inherent weaknesses but because the society was not yet prepared for it. There was a large gray area between nonviolence and violence. Gandhi was not explicit about it partly because he had no time to work on details, and partly because he was convinced that his followers would further work on the model and find their own solutions as they apply his ideas in varying situations.

Gandhi knew that no development trajectory could be changed in the short run because it involved changes in all aspects of life. He worked for parliamentary democracy even while condemning it, because he thought that it would become the stepping stone for the goal of real grass roots level democracy. Gandhi did not suggest a similar transitional model for economic development. He did not have time to elaborate on all the things he said on various issues. We are not sure what modifications he would have made if he were alive today. Being a pragmatic, he would have certainly revised his views. He had been experimenting with truth all through his life and had always changed his views once they were proved wrong or impractical. But I doubt, he would have changed any of his basic postulates for they emanated from a vision of human evolution which was unique and which is now being proved right. I have selected ten areas on which questions have always been raised and are being raised even today. Gandhi is revered in India; not many people would dare to criticize him openly partly because his ideas are based on eternal values, which incidentally are now considered to be idealistic and peripheral and partly because the critics have nothing better to offer.

The purpose of this chapter is not to suggest that Gandhi's critique of modern industrial civilisation was flawed. It is to suggest that in the light of the developments of the last 50 years, both positive and negative, it requires a fresh look and assessment even if to restate that he was right. What happened since his assassination in 1948 was in line with what happened all over the world. Those happenings have now become factors, which influence the decisions successive generations have to make. Naturally then, the path he suggested to transform the modern mechanical civilisation into a truely humane civilisation with a strong moral foundation must be different and perhaps far more difficult too.

We have now reached a stage to summarize the message we get from *Hind Swaraj*. As mentioned earlier, *Hind Swaraj* contains all that Gandhi said and did during his life-time in nutshell. And the Mahatma stood by the essence of everything he wrote in this little book. In some other context he said that he could not be consistent because he was growing spiritually. Each day he discoveral new things and hence he changed his views in response to new knowledge gained by him. But in the case of *Hind Swaraj* he refused to make any change barring some words because a lady friend objected to their use. Here lies the importance of the book.

The message that one gets from *Hind Swaraj* can be put in two categories: eternal and time and space specific. Eternal messages are those, which are ever relevant and pertinent and which are valued by all societies and cultures. For example, truth, nonviolence, love, and compassion are valued by all cultures and religions; it is quite another thing that most of them fail to adopt them in real life situation. Within the framework of the above eternal messages, there exist a number of time and space specific messages and practices, which are related to a given set of problems a society faces at different times and places. This applies to *Hind Swaraj* too.

This chapter is devoted to a discussion on messages *Hind Swaraj* conveys – both eternal and time and space specific.

ETERNAL AND UNIVERSAL MESSAGES

Human Destiny Lies in Spiritual Development

Gandhi considered life to be sacred and human life to be more sacred. Man as a species evolved from animal existence. Thus far, Gandhi was with Darwin. But unlike Darwin, Gandhi did not consider evolution to have stopped. His physical evolution stopped with the evolution of large enough brain to think, remember and recall events and ideas. The evolutionary process then moved to the soul of conscience. Man became civilized and is moving towards superhuman state. The movement from human to superhuman state may take as much time as from animal to human state. Thus in Gandhi's theoretical formulation, evolution of the Homo sapiens has not ended. It passed through various animal species and is currently in progress through various 'species' of Homo sapiens. Some of these humans are very close to animals; they act in response to their senses. Some are highly evolved and act in response to their inner call, *i.e.* the call of the soul.

Human body is matter and so is the brain. Both are time and space specific and destructible. Beyond the body and brain is the soul, which is part of the larger soul, otherwise known as God or

Truth. The soul is limitless: it is all pervading and never ending. It unites everything: organic and inorganic; living and nonliving. It unites everything into a single whole. A highly evolved super-conscious human being transcends the body and mind and sees and feels himself as a part of the whole. He has empathy for everything; he is compassionate and loving.

It took billions of years for Homo sapiens to emerge from animal state; and it must take centuries at least for Homo sapiens to get to the state of super-consciousness. What can man become is vividly demonstrated by freaks like Rama, Krishna, Buddha, Christ, Mahavira, Zoroaster, Mohammad, Gandhi and many others. But in real life situation majority of people still conform to animal urges for the animals are closer to them than super-conscious individuals of their own species. Gandhi demonstrated the potentialities of man for self-realization and thus to achieve the state of super-consciousness. An ordinary M.K. Gandhi became Mahatma Gandhi, not by renouncing the world but by living in it, being part of it, and reforming it from within.

Goal of Human Life is Self-Realisation

Self-realization is the goal of human life. Animals do not seek self-realization for they are not aware of their Self. Their Self is limited to sensual urges. Man is in the conscious stage seeking self-realization in sensual satisfaction like his ancestor animals did or in mental gymnastics to penetrate the depth of matter. Rarely are born the likes of Gandhi who try to penetrate the depth of the inner self and realize the potentials, which separate man from the animal as also from himself.

Gandhi advocated self-realization through self-sacrifice and service of others; through self-denial and freedom of all; through truth and nonviolence, love and compassion; and through *Swaraj*, *Swadeshi*, *Swadharma*, and *Sarvodaya*. All these terms in Gandhian praxis conveyed a single integrated meaning; they are aspects of the same reality. A Self-seeker sees them as different doors to enter the *Samadhi*.

Gandhi thus raised human life far above the matter of which the physical universe is made; it takes to the Ultimate Reality and Sublimity. He gave meaning, purpose and dignity to human life not by working outside the hum drum of the world in the caves and forests but being, living and working within it.

Man-Nature Relationship is Symbiotic

Gandhi was a deep ecologist. He has repeatedly mentioned Cosmic Law that keeps the universe in balance. This law is synergic, all pervading and symbiotic. For Gandhi, earth is not the home of man alone, as geographers tend to believe; it is the home of life. Life is the product of the symbiosis that pervades nature, the earth and the whole universe. Changes in nature take place within a given threshold limit. On a grand scale of the planet, even major changes like ice age are within the threshold limits. But such changes take place at the interval of thousands and lakhs of years. At the human scale, the small, medium and large eco-systems that constitute the larger planetary ecosystem, maintain the necessary conditions for life to prosper. Any tempering with the elements of these ecosystems is fraught with dangerous consequences.

Modern civilisation has never been mindful of the harm it could inflict to the ecosystems. We have now reached a stage where we face water famine because of overuse of the water resources and warming of the global climate to melt the polar ice and thereby to inundate their coastal plains all over the world driving millions of people from their hearth and home. We have created social and economic conditions, which take millions of innocent human lives and many more millions of animal lives. Loss of human life negates the very purpose of civilisation and that of animal life negates the principles of ecology and symbiosis.

Our ancient civilisations were far more eco-friendly than the modern industrial civilisation. Earth, in India, was treated as Mother Earth; the goddesses Kali and Durga. It was not just the Home of Man, it was the Home of All Life Forms giving limited rights to man to interfere with it and assigning unlimited duties to keep the ecological balance intact. It is time to reconsider our attitude towards nature and adhere to the injuctions of the Cosmic Law.

True Meaning of Freedom is Swaraj

Hind Swaraj is a Magna Carta of freedom – freedom for humanity and each individual human being from fear – fear of hunger, of other human beings, of government, of even death. Fearlessness is the essence of freedom. Those who are gripped by fear cannot be free to think, to speak and to act. Fearlessness comes from self-realization, which is a long process of dedicated practice of truth and non-violence.

Freedom is not something that can be given and taken; it is not something that can be bought and sold in the market. It is not a thing; it is a feeling that comes from self-realization – from knowing oneself as a part and parcel of the one omnipresent and omnipotent Soul. A free man is fearless and fearless man is free. A free man follows the dictates of his conscience; not of exigencies of the situation; nor what his senses demand. A free man follows his duties; his *Dharma*.

A free man is *anasakta*; he does not care for the consequences of his action for his welfare. Whatever is right must be done, *karmanevadhikaraste ma faleshukadachana.* One has to perform his duties without caring for results, says *Gita*. Gandhi was a true follower of *Gita*; he called *Gita* the mother who nourished him and guided him on a righteous path.

Development Means Sarvodaya

Gandhi questioned the meaning progress as conceived in his time as illusory and inimical to the real progress, which could be none other than moral progress. Economic progress based on mechanical devices on the one hand and exploitation of nature and fellow human beings on the other takes man closer to the animal in him.He loses his soul and works aimlessly for body welfare alone.

Gandhi presented a new model of progress and called it *Sarvodaya, i.e.* rise of all. By rise he meant, the spiritual progress toward human destiny through continuous efforts at self-realization. Man need not discard the world to move towards his destiny; he can do that while being a part of the human society. *Sarvodaya* means multi-faceted development of the individuals, families, groups, societies and humanity as a whole. All must have access to the material goods and services – food, clothing, housing, education, health, security and self-respect – necessary for a decent living. All must be equal in these respects. What constitutes the need has to be determined from time to time keeping in mind the number of people, ecological .constraints and the level of material development. All these basic needs must be fulfilled to create necessary conditions for spiritual development. For the hungry, bread is God, said Gandhi. Gandhi, therefore, set his goal on creating a social order in which basic human needs of all are met satisfactorily.

There is no way to meet the basic needs of all satisfactorily, so long as human progress is built on the foundation of increase in the number of wants. There must be a limit to the size and number of wants each individual and society should aspire to satisfy for each time a want is satisfied, it gives rise to new wants. Man thus gets enmeshed in wants and more wants and has no inclination and time for self-realisation. In fact, he regresses morally; as he progresses materially especially when the later is based on competition that tries to outdistance others. There is a mad race for material advancement; a few achieve success, many hope to achieve success and many others are caught in poverty syndrome; success remains a dream.

Realizing that man can never become wantless by satisfying his wants as and when they come, Gandhi suggested *Sarvodaya*, which minimizes wants and thus makes man wantless. Gandhi was almost wantless. He left behind just five material objects: a piece of loin cloth, a watch, a pain of spectacle, a pair of slippers, and a stick for support while walking. He did not envisage a society of hermits but he did envisage a society where everyone enjoyed equality in basic needs, in human rights, in self-respect and human dignity. Those who earned more, must use the surplus for the welfare of the society; they should treat the additional wealth as trust property with themselves becoming its trustees.

Technology is the Means Not the End

Would Gandhi still stand with what he said on science and technology and its product, the machine? I think he would. He was critical of science and technology because they were misused to destroy nature and man both. He was not so much opposed to machinery as to machine mentality. Science and technology enabled man to produce weapons of mass destruction. Mechanization has thrown millions of people out of jobs; they were deserting villages and migrating to cities. Even today that process has remained unchecked.

Let us take science first. Gandhiji was critical of science because it analyzed but did not synergize. As such its findings were not always beneficial. The ecological and environmental problems we face today are the products of truncated scientific achievements. And so are the urban and industrial problems. The problem of violence is acerbated because of the weapons of mass destruction in the hands of people who are morally poor.

In a society where wants are unlimited science and technology go together; one depends on the other. He was perturbed by the back sliding of India in the industrial field due to import of cloth manufactured in Manchester in the eighteenth and nineteenth centuries. And he proclaimed in *Hind Swaraj* that a machinery, great symbol of modern civilisation represented a great sin.'

We have to look at his attack on machinery from his Whole Theory of Life. First, machinery changes the mentality of the people; they start thinking that they can master the nature and the world. Second, machinery helps them produce goods on a mass scale and out-compete the household products for which India was known from times immemorial. Third, machine production rendered millions of people unemployed particularly in rural areas. Fourth, mass production by large industries gave rise to large cities and equally large slums where mill workers lived. And fifth, machinery increased locomotion and reduced manual work to the minimum, which in turn reduced human touch in day-to-day life and adversely effected in the health of the people.

All the five points Gandhi raised are valid. Today even our vocabulary has changed to conform to machine language: the terms like engine of growth, fine tuning, social engineering, oiling the social system, kick start, etc. were not heard just a century back. There is no doubt that the technology has robbed man of humility; of his sense of belonging to the cosmos on the one hand and life on the earth on the other. Life is mechanized and the universe is conceived as a huge machine so fine-tuned that it just does not collapse.

Prior to the machine age, people were perhaps worse of materially but better of morally. They were more sensitive to rights of others and their own duties towards them. Mass production has its deleterious effects on self-sufficiency. Things are produced for the market, not for consumption. It is also true that mass production has rendered the rural artisans jobless. World had witnessed several waves of urbanization but the industrial age gave rise to an altogether different type of cities with large factories, sprawling slums, degraded environment and fractured human relations.

Gandhiji was very forthright in condemning machinery. "Machinery is like a snake-hole, which may contain from one to a hundred snakes. Where there is machinery there are large cities; and where there are large cities, there are tram-cars and railways, and there only does see electric light.... I cannot recall a single good point in connection with machinery." Of course he later clarified his statement by saying that he was not against machines as such. Even human body is a machine. He was against machine mentality. "Nature has not provided any way whereby we may reach a desired goal all of a sudden. If, instead of welcoming machinery as a boon, we should look upon it as an evil, it would ultimately go."

It is true that machine-mentality is not good for human progress. To do away with this mentality, man must minimize his over dependence on it. But that does not mean that technology, which Gandhi calls machinery, is evil. Its use can be evil. Human civilisation even if it is based on moral principles cannot be without machinery. After all, as Gandhi himself has said, our own body is a machine; it is a live machine, is another matter. A plough is a machine; a needle is a machine; and even a pen is a machine. A machine should be considered good so long as it is under the control of man; it is bad, when it starts controlling man. So let us use machine without developing machine mentality.

The twentieth century saw the culmination of the mechanical era and the introduction of the era of information technology. In the mechanical era the distance was reduced to such an extent that it came to be measured in terms of time. Instead of asking how far a place was, people asked how many hour drive or flight it was. In the information technology era, even that concept of distance has been thrown overboard. Messages reach from one place to another instantaneously. As such it would be possible to have greater interaction with friends, relatives and professionals.

Another major change of interest in this regard is the divisibility of technology and its miniaturization so that it can be taken to the place where people are. A computer for example can be operated at home whether in a city or a village. The software to operate machines and to get certain data processed can be produced sitting at home even in a village; the need for large cities for this purpose would no longer be there, if not immediately, in not too distant a future. People do not have to move from villages to cities. In fact the possibility of people and offices moving from large cities to suburbs and surrounding villages has already begun. So some of the drawbacks of modern technology, which rightly prompted Gandhi to oppose it may not remain in future. In fact information technology may become the force of decentralization rather than centralization.

Then we must get back to the issue of protecting our culture from the satanic forces. Even to think of using the atomic power for destructive purposes, is sinful. How can we think of killing millions of innocent humans? After all what for do we exist here on this earth?

Not to kill each other. But we cannot deny the fact there is some merit in balance in mutual destructive power. The satans are mad caps but they are cowards too. They like to destroy others so that they can rule over the world. As such it would be unethical for a democratic government not to be prepared for the worst. And hence while the craze for machines must come down, the governments must advance the frontiers of technology for scientific research and possible use in national defense.

I am quite aware that the distinction between what is offensive and defensive is never clear. No one has ever fought a war for 'offensive' purposes. But let us hope that the very forces, which bring down the craze for machines would also guide at least the democratic governments to be judicious in the use of such weapons.

In view of the above developments, Gandhiji's opposition to machinery would have to be tempered down but his basic premise that technology which did not make man a better human being and which forces him to act immorally has stood the test of time and must guide our technology policy in future. I doubt that Gandhi would have opposed the use of radio, television and other devices for educating the people but he would have certainly condemned its current use.

Economy should be Human Centred

In this connection the reader should appreciate that Gandhi, while referring to western civilization, really meant industrial civilization. Gandhi aimed at a society based on the principle of 'from all according to ability to all according to need.' He advocated equality of professions in matters of wages. And felt that the distinction between manual and mental work should go and everyone should perform manual labour for this purpose as well as to keep him self healthy. Copying the west will be destructive, said he. It has so proved now.

Development in essence means human development, which in turn means multifaceted development of human personality. To confine development to economic activities is a dangerous proposition and this is what the world has been engaged in for the last two centuries with the consequences we have suffered and are still reaping. Development is measured in terms of GDP. In this development scenario economy grows but man decays. And this situation would not only continue but also escalate so long as we continue to define development in money terms.

Politics should not be Divorced from Ethics

India was lost to the British not because British were cleverer and more powerful than Indians but because we invited them, said Gandhi. "English had not taken India. We have given it to them. They are not in India because of their strength, but because we keep them. …They came to our country originally for trade. Recall the Company Bahadur; who made it Bahadur? They had not the slightest intension at the time of establishing a kingdom. Who assisted the company's officers? Who was temped at the sight of their silver? Who bought their goods? History testifies that we did all this. In order to become rich all at once, we welcomed the company's officers with open arms. We assisted them. If I am in the habit of drinking *Bhang* and seller thereof sells it to me, am I to blame him or myself? By blaming the seller shall I be able to avoid the habit? And if a particular retailer is driven away, will not another take his place?"

"When our princes fought among themselves, they sought the assistance of Company Bahadur. The corporation was versed alike in commerce and war. Its object was to increase commerce and make money. It accepted our assistance and increased the number of its warehouses. To protect the latter, it employed an army, which was utilized by us also. Is it not then useless to blame the English for what we did at that time? … Hence it is truer to say that we gave India to the English than that India was lost."

It is clear that Gandhi came to the above conclusion after a deep contemplation. On the surface, it appeared that India was lost because of British intrigues, their superior arms, and organisational capacity. Gandhi did not agree with this explanation. He asserted that the British did not come with a huge army; they came as traders. We chose to ally ourselves with them. In fact the Indian Rajas and Nawabs were only too eager to help the British control India. The British used their quarrels to defeat them all and ultimately sat on the throne of Delhi.

What happened in India was just the opposite of what happened in Japan. When India was being colonized, Japan kept foreigners away from the country. In fact a large number of foreigners were killed because they were considered to be a threat to Japanese culture and nation. Japan was divided into so many Shogunates; each fighting the other. But when the question of foreigners occupying Japan arose, they all joined hands and kept them out. Japan functions as a single corporate body even today. They take new ideas and technologies from outside; adapt them to their own requirements and use the adaptations to innovate something new. Japanese are proud of their cultural heritage and they are not apologetic about it only because foreigners do not like it. The courtesy and honesty at the popular level that one witnesses in Japan even today is because of the fact that they have been able to retain their cultural heritage.

Gandhi visualized a new India proud of its culture and heritage; an India, which will not consider itself inferior to others; and an India, which will show to the world the path of non-violence.

Revolutionaries Changes are Short Lived

We do not have to look to others for the avenues to solve our problems. Each culture provides avenues for problem solving, progress, improvement, development, and self-realization. It is particularly so with Indian culture which has an unbroken record of integrated development for over 5000 years. Indians did not have much to learn from outside. They should be proud of their heritage and not try to imitate the West, said Gandhi.

And he added, there were no short cuts to progress. Those who wanted to use weapons to win freedom were mistaken. They might be able to free India from colonial rule but they would not be able to build a nation far different from England. England relied on violence to subjugate others. By using the same means, Indians would be following the British. And thus the potentials of Indian culture in bringing peace and harmony in the world will be lost for ever. This potential could be realized only if Indians understand their own culture. Once they came to know it, they would be able to rebuild India within no time. It is however difficult for people bitten by the bug of western civilisation to do this.

Gandhi was not in favour of revolutionary changes for such changes were not lasting. In this connection he gave the example of Italy, which failed to become free as Mazzini envisaged. One can add the cases of French Revolution and Bolshevik revolution. He likened a nation to a tree. As a tree does not grow in a day, a nation also cannot be built in a day. Nation building follows a biological process; it takes its own time. "Nature has not provided anyway whereby we may reach a desired goal all of a sudden." It was easy to change a government by violence and replace one ruler by another but it was very difficult to bring about a government of the people, by the people and for the people without first preparing the people to take responsibilities. Nation meant people;

national independence meant people's independence; and nation progress meant people's progress.

INDIA'S SPECIFIC MESSAGES

India Became a Nation much Before the British Came

Gandhi asserted that "we were one nation before they (the English) came to India. One thought inspired us. Our mode of life was the same. It was because we were one nation that they were able to establish one kingdom. Subsequently, they divided us." Why did our ancestors establish "Setubandhu (Rameshwaram) in South, Jagannath in the East and Haridwar in the North as places of pilgrimage. ...You will admit that they were no fools. They knew that worship of god could have been performed just as well at home. But they saw that India was but one undivided land so made by nature. They, therefore, argued that it must be one nation. Arguing thus, they established holy places in various parts of India and fired the people with an idea of nationality in a manner unknown in other parts of the world." It is unfortunate that we the so-called civilized people consider India a geographical entity with many nations.

"India cannot cease to be one nation because people belonging to different religions live in it. The introduction of foreigners does not necessarily destroy a nation; they merge in it. A country is one nation only when such a condition obtains in it. That country must have faculty for assimilation. India has ever been such a country. ...In reality, there are as many religions are individuals, but those who are conscious of the spirit of nationality do not interfere with one another's religion. If they do, they are not fit to be considered a nation. If the Hindus believe that India should be peopled only by Hindus they are living in dreamland. The Hindus, the Mohamedans, the Parsees, and the Christians who have made India their country are fellow countrymen, and they will have to live in unity, if only for their own interest. In no part of the world, are one nationality and one religion synonymous terms; nor has it ever been so in India.

Religions should Unite, Not Divide

"Religion is dear to me and my first complaint is that India is becoming irreligious. Here I am not thinking of the Hindu or the

Mohamedan or the Zoroastrian religion but of that religion which underlies all religions. We are turning away from God." And he added" "Hinduism, Islam, Zoroastrianism, Christianity and all other religions teach that we should remain passive about worldly pursuits and active about Godly pursuits; that we should set a limit to our worldly ambition and that our religious ambition should be unlimited. Our activity should be directed into the latter channel... True there is lot that is humbug in all religions. Such things are in other spheres of life too. But the humbug of modern civilisation, to which we are trying to adhere is far worse than that of religions. It is also true that lot of cruelties have been done in the name of religion. But we cannot say that these cruelties are part of the religion. They will also happen so long as there are to be found ignorant and credulous people."

Legal System Should Reduce Litigation

Gandhi came down very heavily on the legal profession as it was practiced in his time. Unfortunately, nothing has changed since then. According to Gandhi, the lawyers should help resolve conflicts; in stead they make people quarrel and go to the court of law. Lawyers like doctors take up that profession not "in order to help others out of miseries, but to enrich themselves. It is one of the avenues of becoming wealthy and their interest exists in multiplying disputes. It is within my knowledge that they are glad when men have disputes."

"But the greatest injury they have done to the country is that they have tightened the English grip.... It is wrong to think that courts are established for the benefit of the people. Those who want to perpetuate their power do so through the courts. If people were to settle their own quarrels, a third party would not be able to exercise any authority over them. ...Without lawyers courts could not have been established or conducted and without the latter the English could not rule."

Seeing these remarks in the present context, they do seem to be highly pertinent and prophetic. India did not held Gandhi and adopted British institutions and modes of governance. If we see the quality of our politicians who get into parliament, state legislatures, and local bodies, we realize how right was the Mahatma. If the current trends continue, very soon most of our elected representatives will be murderers and goons. Their number is already alarming.

Gandhi came down heavily on the legal system introduced in India by the British. He knew the inside story because he too began his career as a lawyer. He was not a very successful attorney. By a queer chance, he had to go to South Africa to plead a case. Here he underwent several indignities, which many others must have experienced before him. The way Indians and other coloured people were treated aroused in him an urge to fight against injustice. And thus began his epic journey on the road that Indian civilisation had laid and re-laid for centuries.

Gandhi felt that an honest lawyer would try to reduce conflicts, to bring the opposite parties together for compromise and honest settlement of disputes. He would not encourage people to go the court. This "profession teaches immorality; it is exposed to temptation from which few are saved....My firm opinion is that lawyers have enslaved India, have accentuated ... dissentions and have confirmed English authority."

When two persons or groups quarrel, an "ordinary man will advise them ...that both of them must be more or less at fault and would advise them no longer to quarrel. But they go to the lawyers. The latter's duty is to side with their clients and to find out ways and arguments in favour of the clients to which they (clients) are often strangers. If they do not do so, they will be considered to have degraded their profession. The lawyers, therefore, will, as a rule advance quarrels instead of repressing them. Moreover, men take up that profession, not in order to help others out of their miseries, but to enrich themselves. It is one of the avenues of becoming wealthy and their interest exists in multiplying disputes. It is within my knowledge that they are glad when men have disputes. Their touts, like so many leaches, suck the blood of the poor people."

"Lawyers are men who have little to do. Lazy people, in order to indulge in luxuries take up such professions. This is a true statement. Any other argument is a mere pretension. It is the lawyers who have discovered that theirs is a noble profession. This is a true statement. They frame laws as they frame their own praises. They decide what fees they will charge and they put on so much side that poor people almost consider them to be heaven-born."

"Why do they want more fees than common labourers? Why are their requirements greater? In what way they are more profitable to the country than the labourers? Are those who do good entitled to greater payment? And if they have done anything to the country for the sake of money, how shall it be counted as good?"

"Some families have been ruined through them (lawyers); they have made brothers enemies. Principalities, having come under the lawyer's power, have become loaded with debt. Many have been robbed of their all. Such instances can be multiplied.... But the greatest injury they have done to the country is that they have tightened the English grip....It is wrong to consider that courts are established for the benefit of the people. Those who want to perpetuate their power do so through the courts. If people were to settle their own quarrels, a third party would not be able to exercise any authority over them. Truly, men were less unmanly when they settled their disputes either by fighting or asking their relatives to decide for them. They became more unmanly and cowardly when they resorted to the courts of law. It was certainly a sign of savagery when they settled disputes by fighting. Is it any the less so, if I ask a third party to decide between you and me? Surely, the decision of the third party is not always right. The parties alone know who is right. We, in our simplicity and ignorance imagine that a stranger, by taking our money, gives us justice."

"...without lawyers courts could not have been established or conducted and without the latter the English could not rule.... If pleaders were to abandon their profession and consider it just as degrading as prostitution, English rule would break up in a day."

Health Care Should Care for Health, Not Diseases

"Doctors have almost unhinged us. Sometimes I think that quacks are better than highly qualified doctors. Let us consider: the business of a doctor is to take care of the body or properly speaking, not even that. Their business is really to rid the body of diseases that may afflict it. How do these diseases arise? Surely, by our negligence, or indulgence. I overeat. I have indigestion. I go to a doctor; he gives me medicine. I am cured. I overeat again. I take the pills again. Had I not taken the pills in the first instance, I would have suffered the punishment deserved by me and would not have overeaten again. The doctor intervened and helped me to indulge myself. My body thereby certainly felt more at ease; but my mind became weakened. A continuance of the course of medicine must, therefore, result in loss of control over the mind."

"Why we take up the profession of medicine? It is certainly not taken up for the purpose of serving humanity. We become doctors so that we may obtain honours and riches. Doctors make a show of their knowledge and charge exorbitant fees. Their preparations, which are intrinsically worth a few pence, cost shillings."

Health is defined as a state in which man is bodily, mentally, and spiritually sound. A person with sound health is devoid of diseases; his mind is alert, sharp, critical, analytical synergic, and his attitude towards others is positive, compassionate and loving. Health depends on many factors but the two of them are most crucial: style of life and external environment. The style of life covers food habits, care of the body, schedule of work, nature of work, the mind set and thought processes. External environment includes housing, work place, social setting, and natural environment.

Health is largely the responsibility of individuals. A healthy style of life produces healthy body, mind, and attitude. Even if the external environment is unhealthy, one can ward off its ill effects by a healthy style of life. Modern medicine, however, has a different approach to health. It does not aim at healthy life; it aims at disease free life. As noted earlier, a disease free life is not necessarily a health life.

Gandhi felt that by introducing the modern medicine in India, "English have certainly effectively used the medical profession for holding us. English physicians are known to have used their profession with several Asiatic potentates for political gain. Doctors have almost unhinged us. Sometimes I think that quakes are better than highly qualified doctors."

Gandhi also objected to use of animals in medical research. "All religions say that it is not necessary to take so many lives for the sake of our bodies." He was right in saying that people do not take up the profession of medicine for the service of the people. They do it so that they become rich. He could see how people were cheated. Medical preparations, he said, "are intrinsically worth a few pence, cost shillings. The populace, in its credibility and in the hope of ridding itself of some diseases, allows itself to be cheated."

"It is worth considering why we take up the profession of medicine. It is certainly not taken up for serving humanity. We become doctors so that we may obtain honours and riches. I have endeavoured to show that there is no real service of humanity in the profession, and that it is injurious to mankind. Doctors make a show of their knowledge and charge exorbitant fees.... The populace, in its credibility and in the hope of ridding itself of some disease, allows itself to be cheated. Are not the quacks then whom we know, better than the doctors who put on an air of humaneness."

Material and Moral Developments Must Go Together

"I believe that the civilisation India has evolved is not to be beaten in the world. Nothing can equal the seeds sown by our ancestors. Rome went, Greece shared the same fate; the might of pharaohs was broken; Japan has become westernized; of China nothing can be said; but India is still, somehow or the other, sound at the foundation. ...It is a charge against India that the people are so uncivilized, ignorant, and stolid that it is not possible to induce them to any changes. It is a charge really against our merit. What we have tested and found true on the anvil of experience, we dare not change. Many thrust their advice against India, and she remains steady. This is her beauty; it is the sheet-anchor of our hope."

"The tendency of the Indian civilization is to elevate the moral being; that of the western civilization to propagate immortality. The latter is godless, the former is based on a belief in God. So understanding and so believing, it behoves every lover of India to cling to the old Indian civilization even as a child clings to the mother's breast." In this connection, the reader should appreciate that Gandhi, while referring to western civilization, really meant industrial civilization.

Our ancestors "saw that kings and swords were inferior to the sword of ethics, and they, therefore, held the sovereigns of the earth to be inferior to the Rishis and the Fakirs. A nation with a constitution like this is better to teach others than to learn from others. In the education system of free India "Religion that is ethical education will occupy the first place."

GANDHI IS PROVED RIGHT

Gandhi has described modern civilisation a disease. It needed cure. It is a disease of mind. Once the mind is gripped by it, it is difficult if not impossible to come out of it. It is like psychological AIDS. Man sees no meaning in life except bodily comfort at whatever cost he can secure it. What is most tragic is that those afflicted by the disease call the healthy ones sick. They consider themselves developed, modern and progressive. Unfortunately, the disease has gripped the world more profoundly than ever before; it is spreading like a pandemic.

"Ever since the late 1940s" says Toffler "a single dominant strategy has governed most efforts to reduce the gap between the world's rich and poor.... This approach starts with the premise that second wave societies are the apex of evolutionary progress and that, to solve their problems all societies must replay the industrial revolution essentially as it happened in the West, Soviet Union and Japan. Progress consists of moving millions of people out of agriculture into mass production. It requires urbanization, standardization, and all the rest of the second wave package. Development, in brief, involves the faithful imitation of an already successful model."

"Scores of governments in country after country have, in fact, tried to carry out this game plan. A few like south Korea or Taiwan, where special conditions prevail, appear to be succeeding in establishing a second wave society. But most such efforts have met with disaster." And even these Asian tigers have now come down to the ground realities. Their industrial production has tapered off and their currencies stand devaluated. Toffler asks 'Is classical industrialization the only path to progress? And does it make any sense to imitate the industrial model at a time when industrial civilisation itself is caught in its terminal agonies?" This is exactly the question that Gandhi raised. And he raised it at a time when Industrial Revolution was not on its last leg of journey, but at a time when it reigned supreme. He could see the end of industrialism clear 75 years ahead of Toffler.

Commending the movement for village and cottage industries in India, Toffler says, "It confronts the need to slow down the massive migration to the cities. It aims to make the villages – where the bulk of the world's poor dwell – more livable, it is sensitive to ecological factors. It stresses the use of cheap local resources rather than expensive imports. It challenges conventional all too narrow definition of efficiency. It suggests a less technocratic approach to development, taking local custom and culture into account. It emphasizes improving the conditions of the poor rather than passing capital through the hands of the rich in the hopes that some will trickle down."

The post-Gandhian decades now confront a new wave – the Information Wave. Gandhi predicted the death of Industrialism and it has come sooner than later. It is however natural for all those who were born in this era or who are part of it, politicians, scientists, technologists or even common people to forget it; they feel like fish out of water and cling to it. "It is now possible ... for a society to attain a high standard of material living without obsessively focusing all its energies on production for exchange. Given the wider range of options brought by the Third Wave, cannot a people reduce infant mortality and improve life span, literacy, nutrition, and the general quality of life without surrendering its religion, values, and necessarily embracing the western materialism that accompanies the spread of second wave civilisation."

Tomorrow's development strategies will not come from Washington or Moscow, or Paris or Geneva but from Africa, Asia and Latin America. They will be indigenous matched to actual local needs. They would not overemphasize economics at the expense of ecology, culture, religion or family structure and the psychological dimensions of existence. They will not imitate outside models.

Gandhi considered the industrial civilisation to be unnatural; inherent in it were the seeds of its own destruction. By the end of the twentieth century, its destruction became imminent; but there are still people both in the industrialized and the industrializing worlds who cannot see the writings on the wall. They cling to the dying path in the hope that the wind will change its direction sooner than later. The opportunities have started unfolding in practically all walks of life; but they are blind folded.

One has to agree with Jagadish Kapoor that 'a new balance has now to be struck between' the most advanced science and technology available to human race and 'Gandhian vision of the idyllic green pastures, the village resembles.' One wonders if Gandhi would have rejected gobar gas plants, solar cookers and lights, telecommunications, remote sensing, improved agriculture, water saving irrigation techniques, bio-fertilizers, etc. True, many of these can be misused, but the harm they inflict would be minimal. So along with the information technologies making it possible to decentralize product and leave the industrial era behind, and in some cases even by-passed, we must strive to build the Gandhian model of development.

The western thinkers we have discussed in this chapter are very close to Gandhi but they are still away from him. Main thrust of Gandhi is truth, ethics and morality. All that Gandhi has to say emerges from these. Gandhi refuses to treat human beings as mere biological phenomenon. Evolution of species was not biological alone. It was spiritual too. The biological evolution was completed over a million years ago. Neither the body nor the brain is going to change. The spiritual evolution is continuing. All *avatars* and messengers of God, despite cultural differences, point to the direction in which man must move. They suffered and died so that others can live in peace. They were full of love and compassion, tolerance and forgiveness, self- respecting and respecting others.

The microchip can only create conditions for new civilisation; it can be a good tool to chisel the future. But it would not outline the kind of future we must chisel. Morality alone can provide the outline. The latest technology we have added to our arsenal can destroy all life on the earth within no time. Only a truly modern civilisation as envisioned by Gandhi can save the world from destruction and annihilation.

CONCLUDING REMARKS

Uniqueness of Indian civilisation lies in its continuity, dynamics and openness. To begin with all civilisations were akin to Indian civilisation. They too measured progress using moral and ethical standards. While India and China continued to retain their basics without any major break, other ancient civilisations succumbed to the violence unleashed by wars, natural calamities and human avarice. The greatest interruption was brought about by industrialization in Europe during the last few centuries. Jesus Christ who sacrificed his life so that the others could live in peace, would never have approved of the mass killing and subjugation of innocent people by his followers, felt Gandhi.

Gandhi saw a silver line in the prevailing darkness. Realizing that in spite of the attractions of the Industrial civilisation, India was not so thoroughly corrupted. Majority of its people were still untouched by it; they were however steeped in poverty and ignorance. He found the ground still favourable and decided to revive the time-honoured values of Indian civilisation and create a society, which would not only free Indians from political bondage but also free the whole humanity from mental and cultural bondage.

How did he achieve such a feat? There was no readymade approach and methodology. He devoted his entire life in finding the answer to this question. Starting in South Africa, he led the freedom struggle in India. He called his autobiography "My Experiments with Truth". He was poised to undo the harm inflicted on the people of India by unnatural partition of India in 1947; his assassination on 30th January 1948 cut short his mission which has remained unfulfilled. Gandhi's assassination was perhaps the most spectacular, even if most tragic, by-product of his incessant search for peace. Gandhi was another and perhaps the latest, but hopefully not the last link in the chain of the great men who tried to steer humanity towards its moral destiny. The reverberations of his life continue to challenge us and will continue to challenge humanity for ever for his goal was not a point but journey to eternity.

Each generation produces Gandhi of its own to experiment with Truth; each experiment is different and is governed by a different set of circumstances but the goal remains the same: peace through moral development. And thus humanity moves on its undulating and at times tortuous evolutionary path towards a civilisation that allocates all its material and intellectual resources for the moral upliftment of humans. In his little but seminal book (*Hind Swaraj*), Gandhi has drawn the broad contours of the new civilisation he worked for. His greatest contribution lay in devising a means by which not only individuals but also groups and societies, nay the whole humanity could seek its evolutionary goal.

More than ninety years have elapsed since Gandhi wrote the *Hind Swaraj* (centenary should be celebrated in 2008-09). When we survey the world events since then, we realize that the questions that Gandhi asked still remain unanswered and mission that he undertook still remains unfulfilled. Take the case of India: the colonial rule is gone but the colonial mode of exploitation continues unabated. Globally speaking peace is still a dream and a large section of humanity is still in bondage of one form or the other. Violence that took away Gandhi's life continues to spread its tentacles all over the world. More people have died in mini-wars since 1945 than the ones who died in Second World War.

This is not the time to sit idle with diffidence but to redouble our efforts to experiment with Truth and Nonviolence as Gandhi did in his lifetime and some of his followers followed suit both in India and elsewhere. I am confident that the volume will set the reader thinking and help him find a way to solve his own problems peacefully and to join hands with others to solve the larger problems of violence world faces today. And if we all can solve our problems peacefully, then the national and global problems will find their own peaceful solution. We are the building blocks of the local, national, and global societies. We individually and jointly determine the behaviour of the society at large. Hopefully, the book will also help put the meaning of development in its right perspectives.

Let us now develop a set of shared Gandhian values, which should distinguish us from other nations and societies and make us once again a people worth emulation.

Moral Progress Is Real Progress

Violence Breads Violence: Ahimsa is Therefore Our Parmodharamah

Duties Are More Important Than Rights

Treat Society Above Self

Consider Village/City Neighbourhood as Basic Unit of Society

All Religions Are Great: Have Respect for Them

Consensus Instead of Contention Is the Essence of True Democracy

Respect the Dignity of Individual and His Basic Human Rights

Nature Is Sacred: It Sustains Us: Do Not Interfere with It Thoughtlessly

The skeptics will always have doubts about the practicability of Gandhian thoughts. Human nature cannot be changed, they say. No arguments would convince them. The following quotation from I-Ching, the famous Chinese philosopher, may help them think again.

> *"After a time of decay comes the turning point. The powerful light that has been banished returns. There is movement, but it is not brought about by force.... The movement is natural, arising spontaneously. For this reason the transformation of the old becomes easy. The old is discarded and the new is introduced. Both measures accord with the time, therefore, no harm results."*
>
> —I. Ching

PART IV

REALIZING HIND SWARAJ

16

Global Agenda for Action

We saw in the previous chapter, the basic theses of *Hind Swaraj* and came to the conclusion that the India of Gandhi's dream has yet to emerge as a viable socio-political alternative. The only major legacy of Gandhi that continues to persist in India is democracy. Gandhi's immediate goal was parliamentary democracy but his concept of democracy was not the one that prevails in the country today. He wanted to gain parliamentary democracy and then work for the real democracy.

If we think that the ideals of *Hind Swaraj* are worth pursuing then India must show to the world that science and spirituality must meet on a common ground to ensure continuity of the evolutionary process, which the man started millions of years ago. Let there be no catastrophic end to this process. We must introspect and reassess the policies we have been pursuing ever since we acquired political freedom from the British. We have lost track of India of Gandhi's dream. We have flowed with the current; we have not tried to take in the direction Gandhi suggested and which has now been endorsed by many a thinker even in the west.

This chapter offers a framework for action, which with suitable modifications can help achieve the goals of *Hind Swaraj* during the twenty first century. Action to usher in Gandhian world order cannot be sectional and partial. His model was holistic and hence the action must reflect holism. We are so much used to dividing life into disciplinary compartments that we find it rather difficult to come out of the analytical grove. Whatever we do is departmentalized and partial as if the problems we try to solve are compartmentalized. We have specialists on even minutest phenomenon but not on the whole life; on integrated man with different manifestation of personality depending on the time and space.

GLOBAL PROBLEMS WE FACE TODAY

We live today in a global village. The terminology is significant because Gandhi wished that the day was not far off when the world would live in villages (small communities) not in cities. Low and behold! We too have realized that the earth is a village. Why are we enamored with the concept of village? Why in this era of information technology we have thought of villages, which even in 2005 AD symbolize backwardness and retrogression? It is craving in us to reach out to something that we have lost in our race for progress. It is the Human Touch that we have lost and that we want to get back but we are reluctant to recognize the follies we committed; nor are we willing to reverse the gear or even turn steering wheel.

Gandhi, using his hindsight, saw what was going on and why? He used the scientific logic to understand what was wrong with the world and why? He experimented with remedies that could cure the disease of 'modern civilisation' and what is palliative and what is curative. And using his foresight he could go beyond his times in the distant future to suggest what was preventive and lasting. Only after looking at the realities from all the above perspectives and holistically, he presented his theses, which in nutshell, are given in *Hind Swaraj*.

Modern science and technology have reduced the world into a global village. There is nothing that is left on the earth that needs to be explored. Man has ascended the highest mountain peak and descended to the ocean bottom. He has reached the frozen poles. His exploratory curiosities and urges have, however, not stopped. He has turned his attention to outer space: to the moon, and then to mars and now to the Jupiter. But he has not even ventured on the exploration of the inner self: the divine in him. He has failed to feel human and be free and blissful. He has failed to peep into the future of man: where is he heading to and where he should head for? He has crossed the physical distance but failed to cross the spiritual distance that separates man from man, people from people, and nation from nation. There is chaos in the world that is otherwise well ordered.

Bridging the Great Divides

The world is divided into several compartments: rich and poor, developed and undeveloped, North and South, G-7 and G-15, agricultural and industrial, scientific and spiritual, and so on. Seeing from the moon, the astronauts realized that the earth was one single living planet: it has oceans and continents but they exist because they are interdependent and need each other. Land without water and water without land has no meaning. The global village is interconnected yet it is divided and partitioned. Modern communication enables man to communicate with any part of the world in seconds, yet the world we live in is non-communicating. Each racial, ethnic, linguistic, political and economic group tries to fend for itself often at the cost of the rest of humanity and if there is communication it is more for division and competition than for unity and cooperation

Each country and each block of countries tries to safeguard its own interests – legitimate or illegitimate. To cite an example, the recent (2003) Cancun (Mexico) meeting of the WTO to sort out the trade differences among the developed and developing countries ended in failure because the developed countries did not want to give up the privileges they had enjoyed so far *vis-à-vis* the developing countries. There was a time (18th and 19th centuries) when England did not allow the transfer of technology to the USA lest it caught up with her and challenged her political and economic supremacy in the world. Now the USA does not allow the transfer of technology to developing countries for the same reasons. Apparently, we have not made any progress during last three centuries in this regard.

It is difficult to bridge the gaps so long as our attitude to human relations remains what it has been and is. The globe has become a village but only superficially. It is interconnected and interdependent but only mechanically. A village forms a community of humans who cooperate with each other and help each other. The pains and pleasures are shared jointly. It is the human touch that matters not the mechanical and electronic touch. Our global village is a village only in name; it has yet to become a village in substance. The tragedy is that even our villages have come under the grips of modern civilisation to such an extent that they too are losing their village culture and acquiring the culture of the global village.

Making Progress Progressive

We have made great progress during the last few centuries in fields, which were neglected earlier. But we have regressed in fields, which make Homo sapiens human beings and which, ensure the survival and further development of our species. Let us examine in some details the regression we have been subjected to.

Loss of Spirituality

By spirituality I mean the faith in the dictum that all life is one united and hence each species has a right to live on this earth and use its resources. If all life is united then all humans must be more united as a species; and they must coexist and share each other's pains and pleasures. Earlier, it was believed that we are all the children of one and the same God. If God is Truth and it resides in each and every life form, then all humans are a part of the God, which is the soul of all souls. This sense of unity is now lost. Humans are killing other humans. There are terrorists who kill innocent people thinking that they are serving their religion and culture. This growing feeing of 'We and They' has made this world a hazardous place to live.

I do not mean to suggest that the people in days bygone were all spiritual and there was no war or conflict. I do, however, mean to say that there is vast difference between the wars of the past and the wars of the present. In the past (prior to 17th century) the capacity of man to destroy was limited. How many people one could kill in a war using hands and sticks? Today, one individual is enough to destroy the whole human race. As the destructive power of man has increased, his spiritual power too ought to have gone up so that he could control his senses and the weapons he wielded. Unfortunately, this has not happened. In fact man today has no *Swaraj* (self-control); his greed has no limits and, therefore, his destructive power too has no limits. The great divides pointed out earlier are just the reflection of and coterminous with his loss of *Swaraj*.

Loss of Ecological Balance

The ecological problems we face today have resulted from the retrogressive steps we have taken especially during the last century. Our over-emphasis on material advancement and short-term perspectives has given rise to an alarming situation. Climatic change, azone layer depletion, pollution of food, water, and air and a host of social problems have put our life in jeopardy. So while on the spiritual front we have lost the human touch, on the physical front we have lost confidence in our abilities and perceptions.

As stated else where in this volume the earth system functions so smoothly that there have been no upheavals in it for the last several millennia. It is not to say that there were no disturbances; it is to suggest that such disturbances did not change the condition in which life can exist and prosper. Now man has started changing the earth system in a fashion that may render the earth inhabitable. The food, the water, the air and the other ingredients of the environment, which sustain life are getting polluted or exhausted. While old traditional diseases are being eradicated, new and incurable diseases are emerging each year.

All Pervading Violence

Added to the problems discussed above, there is a growing fear that human race may become the victim of its own violent behaviour. It refuses to halt further spread and development of atomic weapons. The stockpile of conventional weapons is enough to wipe out humanity and all that it has created during the last 5000 years. The new and more deadly weapons being added every year to the existing arsenal would make the world more vulnerable to the human follies.

It was hoped that the United Nations, despite its limitations, would provide enough checks and balances to obviate unilateral action by nation states but what has happened recently with respect of Iraq has belied the this hope. Just one militarily strong nation decided to attack Iraq and the United Nations could not stop it. Let me hasten to add, that I personally do not consider Saddam Hussain to be a ruler of merit to be defended. But the question is not what type of ruler he was: the question is whether a country has the right to attack any country on the basis of the quality of its leadership.

Such actions unfortunately take us back to the medieval times and remind us of gun boat diplomacy of the colonial era. United Nations represents the collective wish of the whole humanity. To go against the collective will is regressive and unethical. Let there be no unilateral action to resolve a problem without the formal sanction of the United Nations.

GANDHIAN SOLUTION

How relevant is *Hind Swaraj* and all that Gandhi has conveyed through it almost a century ago? A century is a long period but the twentieth century had witnessed a series of upheavals—social, political and economic in the world. It is during this century that the Industrial Revolution matured and entered the era of decay; it is during this century that the Information Revolution was set in; it is during this century that two World Wars were fought; it is also a century which ushered in and heralded the end of the Cold War, which shaped international relations for over seven decades; it was during this century that colonialism ended and the last bastion of it in South Africa collapsed like a pack of cards.

There were positive developments too. It was a century that produced leaders like Mahatma Gandhi, Mao-tse-Tung, Ho Chi Minh, Nelson Mandela, Roosevelt, Churchill and many others discussed in this volume at appropriate places. These great leaders were uncommon people who responded to the challenges of their time and brought about major changes in human relations. Gandhi among them stands apart for he not only had something that all these leaders had but also something that they did not have. Gandhi was not a statesman as such; nor he was a political leader. He was not a saint either. He was a peculiar mix of spirituality and politics. He responded not only to the challenges that humanity faced in the twentieth century but also to those it faced ever since its emergence into a cultural entity. He was concerned as much with the external world in which life persisted but also the internal world, which gave man a distinct identity. For him tending a goat suffering from pain was as important or even more important than attending a meeting to decide the future of India. No questions were unimportant to him especially the question related to human welfare. While dealing with questions of eternal values, he did not forget to seek answers to the mundane questions that will make the life of some one more bearable.

Gandhi went to the roots of human evolution. Unlike Darwin, he looked at the whole process of evolution not as mere response of the species to the changing environment but as nature's design to have species, which were less and less dependent on the environment. The ultimate purpose of this design was to produce a species, which would be responsible for its own evolution. In Gandhian praxis then, the very evolution of the earth was designed to evolve this ultimate life form, *i.e.* man. The future man, Gandhi perceived, would be guided by his consciousness (*atman*), not by the sense organs. Such a man would come into being only if humanity learns from nature and moves in the direction of love and compassion.

Gandhi was not the first to chart out a path that he treaded. Many a great men and women had descended on the earth before him: Mahavira, Gautama Buddha, Zoroaster, Christ, Mohammad and many others still to be excavated from prehistoric debris. It so happened that India was fortunate to have larger share of these great men of wisdom. Practically every century had its own self-realized great men like Kabir, Tulsidas, Ramkrishna etc. to re-enforce the tendencies that take humanity a step forward on the road to its destiny. Each one enriched humanity in one's own way. Gandhi was the latest link in the chain.

AGENDA FOR ACTION

Whither humanity? This is a question that has been repeatedly asked by all civilisations and all generations of people. We got an inkling of it in the aforesaid paragraphs. We can now set the agenda for action.

Making Global Village a Reality

Despite its limitations, the United Nations is the only global institution, which can stop the world from anarchy. It was created for avoiding wars and nothing should be done to weaken it. Unfortunately, the UN is so structured that five countries which constituted the main Allied Powers in the Second World War were made permanent members of the United Nations Security Council and given veto power to restrain warring parties from going to war or to impose peace where war has broken out. Sixty years have elapsed and several new countries have emerged as major powers but the five permanent members of the Security Council refuse to give in. They do not want the permanent membership of the Council expanded, nor do they want the veto powers of the permanent members withdrawn. They want their supremacy to be maintained.

Renewed efforts are needed to restructure the United Nations so that the number of permanent members is increased and the veto power of such members is scrapped. The countries, which qualify as new permanent members are: Japan and Germany (developed countries) and India, Nigeria, and Brazil (developing countries). To make the change acceptable to the present permanent members, the veto power could be retained in a modified form. Only one-third of members can veto a decision of the Council. This could be provided for a period of ten years or upto 2015.

Gandhi envisaged a world government, which may one day emerge after the national states become less relevant and local governments take their roots. He wanted local governments (Panchayats) to be pillars that would constitute the higher-level governments. In his scheme of things higher the level lesser the power and lower the level more the power. And thus the Panchayats at the village or micropolitan level become the strongest units. Such a state of governance would not come in the immediate future. We would have to work for it. In the mean time, and so long as the nation states remain the fulcrum of governance, he envisaged a strong United Nations. Gandhi pleaded the United Nations to support India's nonviolent struggle for independence. He also wanted them to support the cause of South African Indians.

Launching Inter-faith Dialogue

Religion plays a very important role in society; it influences the conduct of man and his culture. It has been and can become a very forceful vehicle for spreading the message of peace and teaching people to adopt love and compassion in place of hatred and cruelty. Unfortunately, the type of unity needed among various faiths to launch such a movement is not there. Although all religions are different paths of reaching the God or Truth, they fight among themselves to prove that a particular path is better than others. If all religions have produced *avatars*, prophets and saints following their own paths, no one path can be said to be superior to others. If the religious leaders who are supposed to spread the message of truth and promote love and compassion cannot settle their own meaningless differences amicably, how can they guide the humanity to move towards peace and harmony?

It is necessary, therefore, for all faiths to come together; get rid of the ill feeling and hatred they have against each other; and jointly lead the humanity to righteous path. They should stop converting people having faith in other religions to their own, for all the religions being equally great conversion, from one to the other is a meaningless exercise. One can and should find salvation within one's own religion. If God is one, how can one convert a person from one God to the same God another? Gandhiji branded conversion a sin. If all the religious leaders agree not to indulge in converting people from other religions to their own, the interfaith unity would become a reality.

It is interesting to note that the religions of Indian origin have no concept of conversion. We find Hinduism, Buddhism, Jainism,

Sikhism and other religions co-existing without any difficulty. One can find adherents of more than one religion in the same family. It is the religions that took their birth in West Asia, which indulge in conversion from other religions. I think that the leading figures of all religions should get together and discuss how to reduce conflicts among them and if conversion is not a part of the core of the religion, it should be done away with.

Another step they must take is to start a regular inter-religious dialogue with a view to uniting all the religions to spread human values. It would help if the leading figures of various religions visit the places of worship of other religions separately or jointly. Several Hindu pontiffs and saints have started this practice. They have visited Christian and Muslim places of worship. There is no reason why Christian and Muslim religious leaders cannot visit Hindu places of worship or congregation. This practice would certainly go a long way in improving inter-religious understanding.

Yet another step that would be highly conducive to inter-religious understanding is the declaration of certain common minimum programme by all religions. Let me propose a five-point programme:

(1) God is one and only one. Different religions identify Him by different names. Names are just names; people should not fight in the name of His name;
(2) People should learn about all religions and respect all religious places;
(3) Nonviolence is the creed of all religions; violence should not be resorted to irrespective of the cause or provocation;
(4) Love and compassion are the essence of all religions and hence people should practice them irrespective of the religion they follow; and
(5) Service to humanity especially the poor is equivalent to worshipping the God. People should be therefore, to charitable to others.

Strengthening the United Nation's

What is needed immediately is the strengthening of the United Nations as the global agency for peace and human development.

We have already discussed the need to adopt nonviolence as a creed to improve inter-religious understanding. Here I would like to emphasize that nonviolence is more powerful a weapon to fight the evil than violence and hence it deserves to be promoted by all sections of the society. If there is anything that is brought out so forcefully by Gandhi in *Hind Swaraj*, it is nonviolence. He distinguishes Indian civilisation from European civilisation very clearly by applying the measuring rod of nonviolence. While the Indian civilisation in general adheres to non-violence or soul force, the European civilisation has specialized in violence or brute force.

The United Nations has adopted non-violence as its method of resolving conflicts among nations. But many member nations qualify it by the exigencies of the situation *i.e.* there are situations when violence becomes necessary. But they do not define the situation. Countries use violence rather frequently because they think the situation so demands. I think, violence should be used in the rarest of the rare cases and that too under the supervision of the United Nations. No cause can justify violence. This applies to nations as well as to the individuals.

Equitable Access to Earth's Resources

Earth has enough to meet everyone's need but not everyone's greed, said Gandhi. Any possession beyond one's needs must deny someone his basic needs. If the earth is now recognized as a global village then all the resources this village has must be distributed as equitably among its inhabitant as possible. No one should go hungry and no one should be drowned in luxury. We have to find a middle path.

The above formula should apply to the world as much as to the nations and cities and villages. Many countries apply this formula at the international level but they do not practice it within their own territories. I think the principle of equity in matters of natural resources should be applied at all levels, from local to international. Special efforts should be made to divest those having more and to transfer to those who have less than what they require to meet their basic needs.

Human Dignity as Global Concern

Human dignity must become a global concern. No country should be allowed to temper with it. The UNDP now publishes annual report on Human Development. It is certainly a step forward. But this report suffers from several limitations. The core of human development or for that matter even economic development has to be the enhancement of human dignity and this is possible only when there is no poverty in the world; there is no exploitation of nations by nations, individual by individuals and all religions learn to live together as different paths to reach the same summit.

17

National Agenda for Action

Gandhi considered Indian civilisation superior to modern industrial civilisation for it goes beyond body welfare to promote those human values, which lead man to super-consciousness. Indians, therefore, need not copy the West; they should adhere to the principles of their own civilisation and take inspiration from it. While saying so, Gandhi did not mean any disrespect for the western civilisation for, in his view, the modern civilisation might have originated in the West, but it is not Western. Modern civilisation has proved as injurious to the East as it has to the West.

Let us examine first the contents and perspectives of Indian civilisation, which, if revived and strengthened, could make India great and help the world live in peace and harmony. Gandhi wrote *Hind Swaraj* in 1909 in response to the problems of the day. Some of the problems were related to human values and human destiny. They continue to exist to this day. In fact, they have become more serious requiring urgent attention. Some others were time specific even if with wider and long term ramifications. Here we propose to stress on the first category of problems.

BASIC PRINCIPLES UNDERLYING ACTION

Non-violence Alone Can Bring Peace

Gandhi was deeply concerned about the violent activities of Indian anarchists for he considered violence to be counterproductive and against the basic tenets of Indian civilisation. Gandhi considered violence to be the main feature of modern civilisation; he did not, therefore, want India to be a camp follower of the West. "I believe that the civilisation India has evolved is not to be beaten in the world. Nothing can equal the seeds sown by our ancestors. Rome went;

Greece shared the same fate; the might of pharaohs was broken; Japan has become westernized; of China nothing can be said; but India is still somehow or the other, sound at the foundation....The people of Europe learn their lessons from the writings of the men of Greece or Rome, which exist no longer in their former glory.... In the midst of all this, India remains immovable and that is her glory. It is a charge against India that her people are so uncivilized, ignorant and stolid, that it is not possible to induce them to adopt any changes. It is a charge really against our merit. What we have tested and found true on the anvil of experience, we dare not change. Many thrust their advice on India, and she remains steady. This is her beauty; it is the sheet anchor of our hope."

Gandhi then gives his own definition of civilisation and says: "civilisation is that mode of conduct, which points out to man the path of duty. Performance of duty and observance of morality are convertible terms. To observe morality is to attain mastery over our mind and our passions. So doing, we know ourselves. The Gujarati equivalent for civilisation means good conduct. If this definition be correct, then India, as so many writers have shown, has nothing to learn from anybody else, and this is as it should be. We notice that mind is a restless bird; the more it gets, the more it wants; and still remains unsatisfied. The more we indulge our passions, the more unbridled they become. Our ancestors, therefore, set a limit to our indulgence. They saw that happiness was largely a mental condition. A man is not necessarily happy because he is rich, or unhappy because he is poor. The rich are often seen to be unhappy."

And he concluded that nothing would make India free so long as it remained callous to its own culture and tried to ape the West.

He laid five cardinal principles for civilised behaviour:

(1) Morality is the essence;
(2) Nonviolence is the creed;
(3) Duties are more important than rights;
(4) All religions are noble; and
(5) Self-realization is goal of human life.

Gandhi believed that moral, not material progress will make man a perfect human being, different from animal not only physically but also behaviourally and spiritually. The only way to cultivate morality was to adhere to non-violence in thought, words and deeds.

A non-violent person would perform his duties (*dharma*) unmindful of his rights for he knows that the rights of all would remain preserved if everyone performed his duties. All religions took man to a common point, *i.e.* Truth or God or self-realization. The paths are different but the destination is the same. All quarrels among religions are related to the paths, not to the destination. Let each one pursue his religion truthfully without interfering with other religions; without making uncharitable remarks. Gandhi did not consider any religion or religious book to be final. The religious books were written by human beings (who by nature are imperfect), they can only tell the relative truth, not the whole truth, which is almost impossible to comprehend, for Truth is God.

Indian civilisation aims at unity in diversity, which allows individuals and groups to follow their own time honoured code of conduct while at the same time adhering to the ethical and moral principles of a larger society. As long as the outsiders coming to the Indian cultural realm tried to adjust themselves to its principles and values and tried to live peacefully with the indigenous people even if maintaining their own way of life, there was no problem. Problem arose with Moslems who came with a religion, which they considered to be final and beyond any progress. Despite frontal attack on indigenous faiths and values associated therewith, the indigenous religions tried to coexist and avoid bloodshed. They lived under very adverse conditions. During the reign of Akbar, the Great, the situation improved but the policy of reconciliation initiated by Akbar was reversed by Aurangzeb, his great grandson. When the British came, Hindus did not have the will and desire to counter them for they found no difference between the Moslem rulers and the British rulers while the Muslims had incompetent leadership in the descendents of Aurangzeb. The establishment of British rule further widened the chasm between Hindus and Moslems. Gandhi, during the struggle for independence, tried to rekindle the light of reconciliation between Hindus and Muslims but he failed. India was divided in 1947; and then Pakistan in 1971. The process of reunification has just begun in the form of SAARC and may culminate into a South Asian Union on lines of European Union.

Gandhi summed up his concept of true religion in following words: "The poet Tulsidas has said, 'Of religion, pity, or love is the root, as egotism of the body. Therefore, we should not abandon pity so long as we are alive.' This appears to me to be a scientific truth. I believe in it as I believe in two and two being four. The force of love is the same as the force of soul or truth. We have evidence of its working at every step. The universe would disappear without the existence of that force."

"Brute force is not natural to India soil." Indians would, therefore, have to rely solely on soul-force. We must not consider that violence is necessary at any stage for reaching our goal. Then and then alone we would be true Indians and would become an example for the rest of the world."

Voluntary Poverty Alone Can Ensure Equity and Ecological Balance

'There is enough on the earth to meet everyone's need but not every one's greed', said Gandhi. This sums up his philosophy for the new world order. We cannot live in luxury without making some people poor; without destroying the ecology; and without making ourselves unhealthy. In a quick survey of housing situation in Allahabad city, the author came to the conclusion that if all the people lived in houses, which are decent and adequate enough to lead a comfortable life, there will be no slums in the city, nor unhygienic living. That is the reason why Gandhi felt distressed when he saw a palace. Such edifices were decent architecturally but indecent humanly. They deprive many a people of the basic housing needs.

Linked to this concept is the idea of 'human size', which Shoemacher popularized as 'Small Is Beautiful'. This principle applies to different aspects of life. By small, Gandhi meant human size. On speed, he remarks, God had given man two feet to walk and run. Had He wanted him to fly, he would have given him wings. This is not to suggest that there should be no railways, aeroplanes, etc. It does, however, mean that man should not forget his primary responsibility, *i.e.* to give priority to his neighbourhood. Further, as his speed increases, he should develop institutions, which would compensate for the loss of face to face contact and interaction.

Human size has its other implications Machines, when they become too big, start controlling the humans. They have their imperatives to be met in order to be efficient. Man becomes a tool in the hands of the machine, not the other way round. Let their be machines but machines should not be allowed to control man and force him to do things which are essentially inhuman.

But we should not be enamoured of all that is small. A small atom bomb was used to kill millions of people just in one stroke. A small dose of poison is enough to kill a person. A small step in wrong direction can take man away from human dignity and divinity. It is not so much the issue of small or big as that of human size, *i.e.* natural in-built capacity of man to perceive and live with maximum autonomy and maximum interdependence. Anything huge is hugely complicated with hundreds, nay millions of interlinks; it needs huge infrastructure to manage it. Man looses his identity in the maze of machines and complex socio-economic systems.

Gandhi, therefore, advocated smallness in all walks of life. Small houses, small human settlements, small machines, etc., which can be better tuned to ecological needs on the one hand and management efficiencies on the other. The small could grow into a bigger system if so many people get together into a cooperative venture to manage it. So the problem is not small or big; problem is human size and the protection of human freedom and dignity.

Equality and Human Dignity Go Together

Gandhi was a votary of complete equality among human beings in so far as the basic human needs were concerned. In his ideal society, the doctor will receive the same wages as a scavenger. But he did not extend his idea of equality to the absurd level of everyone living the same way and doing the same thing. No two human beings were the same or even similar in many aspects of life. Their mental equipment is not the same; their capacity to do manual work is not the same; their training is not the same nor is their family background. He, therefore, suggested that let there be a variety, different people doing different things but all engaged in doing some manual labour so that they are not divorced from nature.

Gandhi brought the issue of human dignity to the forefront. All human beings have a right to get food, shelter, clothing, education, medical help, freedom, security and self-respect. This equality should have nothing to do with parentage, place of birth, occupation and other accidental happenings over which man has no control. He was of the view that nothing should be done that would injure human dignity. It is on this ground that he condemned colonialism for it deprived man of his fundamental right to choose his own government, colonialism injured human dignity with vanity and without remorse.

Real Democracy is Bottom Up

Our democratic system stands derailed. The type of people getting elected to parliament, state legislature, and Panchayati Raj institutions is not the one the founding fathers of Indian republic had envisaged. Recent constitutional changes giving more powers to Panchayati Raj institutions have not halted the deteriorating situation. In fact, these changes have made no difference even to these institutions. Panchayat, for all practical purposes, has become dysfunctional.

Gandhi had given enough indications in *Hind Swaraj* about his views on western style democracy. He did work for parliamentary democracy, but only as an interim measure. He aimed at participatory democracy from below. And the below in his scheme of things of corporate life was the village with a population of about 1000 persons, which in the present context of population growth and density and rapid means of transportation and communication amounts to 5000 adults. The following quotation from *Hind Swaraj* would remind us of Gandhi's views in this regard:

About British Parliament, he said "the best men are supposed to be elected by the people. The members serve without pay and, therefore, it must be assumed, only for the public weal. The electors are considered to be educated and therefore we should assume that they would not generally make mistakes in their choice. Such a Parliament should not need the spur of petitions or any other pressure. Its work should be so smooth that its effects would be more apparent day by day. But, as a matter of fact, it is generally acknowledged that the members are hypocritical and selfish. Each thinks of his own little interest. It is fear that is the guiding motive. What is done today may be undone tomorrow. It is not possible to recall a single instance in which finality can be predicted for its work. When the greatest questions are debated, its members have been seen to stretch themselves and to doze. Sometimes, the members talk away until the listeners are disgusted. Carlyle has called it the 'talking shop of the world'. Members vote or their party without a thought. Their so-called discipline binds them to it. If any member, by way of exception, gives an independent vote, he is considered a renegade. If the money and the time wasted by Parliament were entrusted to a few good men the English nation would be occupying today a much higher platform. Parliament is simply a costly toy of the nation. These views are by no means peculiar to me. Some great English thinkers have expressed them. One of the members of that Parliament recently said that a true Christian could not become a member of it. Another said that it was baby. And it has remained a baby after an existence of seven hundred years, when will it outgrow its babyhood?

Looking at the way our Parliament functions today, we realize how right the Mahatma was. Gandhi, therefore, asked his countrymen to promote grassroots level democracy by setting Village Panchayats all over the country. He identified village as the basic unit because India was, and still is, a country of villages. A deeper analysis of his views, however, indicates that he would have liked to include the city governments based on mohallas or neighbourhood councils as basic units. And thus it was not only the rural village, which was to be self-governing, but also each urban village and neighbourhood.

Gandhi's village was, however, not the same as villages as we see in India today. He conceived of highly developed villages all over the country producing almost all their basic needs locally and within a group of villages and exchanging goods and services they could not produce with adjoining villages. Gandhi's village will have its own school, health facility, cooperative, non-farm functions, etc. Gandhi was against ostentatious living for the obvious reasons. And, therefore, he did not want human settlements all the way from villages to cities being ostentatious. He was not against the creation of wealth provided that the wealth so created was used for public welfare. His theory of trustiship was the antidote for both capitalism and communism and his gram *swaraj* was the antidote for national level Parliament going astray.

ACTION FROM ABOVE

In a fast changing world, there is no programme of action, which remains relevant forever. What is, however, eternal is the Cosmic Law and Law of Species. It is within the framework of these laws that humans live and act to meet their objectives and goals. Transgression of these laws brings disasters and frustrates human endeavours. The national agenda we propose are relevant to the situation as it prevails in India in the first decade of the twenty-first century; not to the first decade of the twentieth century when Gandhi wrote *Hind Swaraj*.

Today India is passing through a very difficult phase in its cultural and socio-economic journey. Economic inequality despite respectable economic growth, political degeneration despite the legacy bequeathed by Gandhi, ecological problems despite a civilisation that has special regard for nature, and social disintegration despite cultural unity which can be traced to thousands of years. Until 15 August 1947, India hoped to blaze a new trail and show to the world that there was another paradigm of development quite different from the western paradigm that produced Industrial Revolution. That hope was blunted for the very people who fought for *Swaraj*; they opted for political institutions that denied power to the masses, and those who wanted to wipe out tears from each and every face of India opted for economic growth and human development. Now after half a century of mal-development, we find ourselves in great confusion. Poverty, unemployment, illiteracy, ill health, and environmental hazards continue to plague our motherland. And there is no prospect of these problems being resolved even in the distant future.

We propose below a few essential steps that must be taken sooner than later to make the country moving again. These steps are practically the same which Gandhiji would have suggested in the revised edition of *Hind Swaraj*.

Electoral Reforms

The distortions that have crept in our electoral system are well known. The situation has come to such a pass that democracy in India is on the verge of derailment. The major defects that have entered the system are:

(1) fraudulent electoral practices and entry of anti-social elements as candidates;
(2) ever increasing role of money and muscle power, instead of service to people, in elections;
(3) derailment of democratic processes by increasing cases of defections; and
(4) deteriorating moral standards of elected representatives.

Electoral system in India is so deeply corrupted that there is hardly a member of parliament or state legislature or even Panchayati Raj institutions who has not used fraudulent means to get himself elected. The nature of fraud varies from candidate to candidate and constituency to constituency. There are cases of candidates with criminal background having so much frightened the voters that no other candidate dares to contest against them. And then there are candidates, who indulge in booth capturing in connivance with government officials managing the elections or by frightening the people away from the polling booths.

There is no law to debar criminals from seeking election and the possibility of such laws being enacted in the near future are dim. How can criminals legislate against themselves? To add to the problem, the government machinery that manages elections has also turned corrupt to a great extent. Without their tacit and some times even active support of one or the other candidate, electoral fraud is just not possible. There can be no booth capturing or miscarriage of counting without the connivance of the officials managing the booths and counting of votes.

I (author) had a practical experience of it. I was a candidate for parliamentary seat from Pratapgarh district of Uttar Pradesh in 1989. Being an educationist and erstwhile Vice-Chancellor of Allahabad University, I was quite popular among the people of the region especially among the people of the constituency. I was the first in the district to go abroad on scholarship for higher studies, first from the district to become university professor and first indeed to become the Vice-Chancellor of the prestigious University of Allahabad. I was known for my administrative qualities and also a friend of the common people. Seeing the response of the people, I was confident of winning the seat. While inspecting the booths on the polling day, I came across a convoy of nine jeeps and cars rushing along a minor road of the constituency. I was in a jeep and unarmed for I had no fear. I was told that the convoy belonged to the my rival and it was organized by the erstwhile member of the state legislature. He carried out this nefarious activity with the connivance of the government officials managing the election. In fact, even the district magistrate who was chief election officer was supervising not the election but the booth capturing on behalf of an influential candidate of a particular party. The rigging of the election was so massive that I could get only one vote at my home booth; even my wife 'voted against me'. Most of ballot boxes were filled by not ballot papers but ballot paper books. The local MLA who had organized the fraud had declared a week in advance that I would not get more than one vote at my home booth. Incidentally, he was friendly to me that I could not even suspect that he could indulge in such a heinous crime.

The booth capturers moved in convoys of 4 to 7 jeeps. There were four such parties. They went from booth to booth and took away all the ballot papers and stamped them in favour of the candidate who had hired them. I was amazed to see that the policemen and election officials managing the booths fully cooperated with the booth capturers. They filled the ballot boxes with ballot papers stamping the name of their favourite candidate who belonged to a Zamindar family of the district and had held very important position in Mrs. Indira Gandhi's cabinet. He won the seat; I lost it. And to see that he won with thumping majority, on the day of counting the whole affair was so managed that the author's counting agents were threatened and even beaten. When ballot boxes were opened, we found hundred of books of ballot papers just stamped in favour of the Zamindar candidate. We objected but of no avail for the District magistrate who was the returning officer himself worked for that candidate. We caught the district magistrate with some ballot boxes being brought from outside while the counting was on. How many ballot boxes were thus replaced, we could never know.

Had there been a fair election, I would have won. I was the first candidate with strong academic and moral background to contest election from that constituency for quite a long time. There was wide support for me from all sections of the society. Further, I fought the election honestly spending only Rs. 1,75,000, which was the legal limit at that time. But there was no way I could match the opponent in money and muscle power. I lost. I appealed for recounting, but failed to get any relief. It so happened that the candidate who indulged in malpractice against me could never get elected again and died a few years later. But the MLA who organized the show for him continues to win elections with thumping majority. He has specialized in booth capturing with the help of government officials whom he keeps in good humour. He has booth capturers in every village of the constituency.

This type of electoral practice has led to emergence of more dreaded criminal politicians in the district. The district, which was known for great political leaders like Raja Ram Pal Singh (one the founders of the Indian National Congress), Raja Awadhesh Pratap Singh, Rai Bajrang Bahadur Singh, and Pt. Munishwar Dutt Upadhyaya and, which provided the base for Pandit Nehru and several other leaders for political action under the leadership of Gandhiji in the pre-independence days, has become a den of booth capturers and criminals posing as politicians. It may be that the situation is not so disturbing in all the constituencies of India but disease is spreading fast.

It was hoped that the Election Commission of India would be able to stem the electoral rot and keep the system clean but despite its commendable work within the existing laws, it has failed on many fronts. The introduction of electronic voting machine has improved the situation to some extent but where the people who manage the system and the machines are themselves corrupt, it cannot make any major difference. In fact, the electoral fraud has now become easier for just one person can do all the voting on behalf of hundreds of people standing in the queue. When a booth is captured, the voting machine also stands captured. The election commission can do precious little. It is being increasingly realized that unless the parliament empowers the Commission to curb the electoral malpractices, Indian democracy has every chance of being hijacked by the criminals and anti-social elements.

India needs a law, which debars criminals from participating in elections. If need be, let there be an independent judicial commission to scrutinize the background of candidates seeking election as MP, MLA, or even Mayor or Pradhan of Panchayat. The founding fathers never thought that criminals would ever become MPs, MLAs, etc., and therefore, they did not make provisions in the constitution to this effect. It is the time to legislate what the founding fathers considered as given.

Another thing that is urgently needed is enhanced service motivation in those elected as peoples' representatives. It is sad but true that this motivation is weak, if not absent altogether, in most of our representatives. A good number of people seek election not to serve the people but to make money and wield power. The corruption cases against ministers, chief ministers and even prime ministers that come to light from time to time reflect very adversely on Indian democracy. And the degree to which the civil service both at the higher and lower levels has deteriorated is unimaginable. There is a growing nexus between mafias, politicians and civil servants. The common man is helpless. This is not the picture of democracy that Gandhi has drawn in *Hind Swaraj*.

Transparancy in Governance

As part of the colonial tradition of administration, we have retained even those practices, which the British themselves abandoned long back. I would like to discuss two of these traditions:

(1) Secrecy and confidentiality; and
(2) Distance between the government and the governed.

The first principle of Indian bureaucracy is confidentiality; people are not supposed to know what the government is doing, under what provisions, and for what purpose? The government is the master; people are the obedient servants. Government is supposed to know what people want, what they should get and when and in what quantity. People are at the receiving end. They are not expected to question the government; they cannot demand; they can only appeal. It may sound strange but it is so even in the first decade of the third millennium. In the name of development, the politicians and bureaucrats enrich themselves. Very little trickles down to the common people.

In this land of Mahatma Gandhi, the Members of Parliament and state legislatures are allocated funds for the development of their own constituencies. The way these funds are utilized is highly questionable. The separation of the three wings of government – legislature, judiciary and executive – is tending to disappear, especially between the legislature and the executive in conformity with the mutual convenience of both elected representatives and government officials. It is particularly so in rural areas where a great majority of the people live. We have yet to realize that development is the task of the people and not of the government. All that the government can do and should do is to support and assist the people in their own development – physical, intellectual or spiritual. The situation that prevails in India today is just the other way round. Governments generate 'development' and the people are supposed to cooperate with it without knowing the details of the programmes and projects.

This being the case, the secrecy that the government maintains in its activities is thus understandable. Secrecy gives opportunity to fool the people; the distance between the people and the government remains wide. It also enables the government officials to utilize the resources in the way they consider desirable and beneficial to the people. Thus instead of the separation of powers between the three wings of the government; there is separation between the government and people.

Let me cite an example from Bangladesh. I was at the Rural Development Academy, Bogra under the joint auspices of the UNCRD and UNICEF for about a month to train local officials and elected representatives of the Thana in preparing micro-level village plans. It was the year 1982. After the training course was over, we gave an exercise to prepare a plan for a village using the knowledge and tools provided by the experts. The trainees who ranged in age from 25 to 55 years sat together for two days but nothing emerged. On enquiry we found that the government officials and people's representatives had different perception of needs of the village and hence they were unable to agree on a joint action plan. I tried to reconcile the differences but without any success.

The third day I suggested that the two groups meet separately and prepare separate plans. This clicked and on the fourth day we had two sets of project portfolios. When both the groups presented their reports, the official plan was found to be highly inflated and defective. But it was better prepared. Our intervention brought the two groups together. But in the ultimate analysis the people's plan was by and large accepted. We funded the plan and it was successfully implemented.

The lessons we learnt were threefold:

(1) Participation of the people means people's initiative and leadership;
(2) Nothing should be kept secret; people should know how much resources are available and for what purpose; and
(3) Governmental agencies should give full and wholehearted support—managerial as well as technical—to enable the people to help themselves.

Since then I had the opportunity to work in many developing countries of Asia and Africa and of course India. The Bangladesh experience is tellingly repeated almost everywhere. In India the situation, as I find in 2005, is highly disturbing. The country has the means to eradicate poverty within a decade. More than five decades have elapsed since the independence, but the poverty syndrome remains unchallenged in real terms. I would suggest that the first step that ought to be taken to tone up the government to make it more responsive is to do away with the secrecy that separates the people and government forthwith. Right to Information should be accepted as a fundamental right of the people. I am told a law has been enacted this year (2005).

At this stage it would be pertinent to emphasize the role that information technology can play in opening the system to the people. In my view the ICT can reduce corruption in India by anywhere between 50 to 80 per cent. One of the reasons why the government officials oppose the introduction of ICT in their respective departments is this. Let people know from internet the budget of their nation, state, district, block, town, village etc. and get online information on how much money is being used for what purposes, at what time and by whom.

Urgent Educational Reforms

Education is key to real *Swaraj*: education in its true senses. And if one has to identify one reason that made the country what it is today, it is faulty education system. True education according to Gandhi has following characteristics: it is one that liberates, it changes with time to retain relevance, it develops the mind, body and soul at the same time; it is accessible to all; it is learnt from the Book of Life; it moulds the character of the pupils.

The state of education especially primary education in India is pitiable. At least one-third of the children of school going age do not go to school or if they go they discontinue their studies too early to retain their literacy competency. Only a small section of the total number of children (15-20 per cent) have access to good schooling. They are located in cities. The remaining 50 to 55 per cent have very poor schooling facilities; they live in villages and urban slums. This is the state of affairs after 55 years of independence. It is sad indeed that we still tend to blame the colonial administration for the educational mess in the country. We do not want to blame ourselves for our own poor performance in the post-independence era.

There is no doubt that we have been able to expand the educational facilities all over the country. To day practically each village has a primary school. Children do not have to walk long distances except in some remote and really undeveloped areas. But the quality of education has abysmally deteriorated. Schools do not have proper infrastructure: buildings, teaching aid and above all teachers. The teachers do not teach; they leave the students to fend for themselves.

Why this lamentable situation? Shortage of funds is quoted as the common reason. The facts, however, tell a different story. It is the rampant corruption in the education department of the government; lack of motivation in the teachers and unwillingness of the poorer sections of the society to send their children to school. But the most important factor that has hindered progress on this front is the irrelevance of the education imparted to children in government schools, which form the bulwark of primary education in India.

Gandhi made a special contribution on the theory and practice of education. The ideas he propounded had their germs in *Hind Swaraj*. "What is the meaning of education? It simply means a knowledge of letters. It is merely an instrument and an instrument may be well used or abused. The same instrument that may be used to cure a patient may be used to take his life, and so may a knowledge of letters. We daily observe that many men abuse it and very few of them make good use of it; and if this is the correct statement, we have proved that more harm has been done by it than good.

"...a peasant earns his bread honestly. He has ordinary knowledge of the world. He knows fairly well how he should behave towards his parents, his wife, his children and his fellow villagers. He understands and observes the rules of morality. But he cannot write his own name. What do you propose to do by giving him a knowledge of letters? Would you add an inch to his happiness? Do you wish to make him discontented with his cottage or his lot? And even if you want to do that he would not need such an education. Carried away by the flood of western thought we came to the conclusion, without weighing pros and cons, that we should give this kind of education.

"I do not for one moment believe that my life would have been wasted, had I not received higher or lower education. Nor do I consider that I necessarily serve because I speak. But I do desire to serve and endeavouring to fulfil that desire, I make use of the education I have received. And, if I am making good use of it, even then it is not for the millions, but I can use it only for such as you, and this supports my contention. Both you and I have come under the bane of what is mainly false education. I claim to have become free from its ill effects, and I am trying to give you the benefit of my experience and in doing so, I am demonstrating the rottenness of this education.

"Moreover, I have not run down the knowledge of letter in all circumstances. All I have now shown is that we must not make of it a fetish. It is not our *kamadhuk*. In its place it can be of use and it has its place when we have brought our senses under subjection and put our ethics on a firm foundation. And then, if we feel inclined to receive that education, we may make good use of it. As an ornament it is likely to sit well on us. It now follows that it is not necessary to make this education compulsory. Our ancient school system is enough. Character building has the first place in it and that is primary education. A building erected on that foundation will last." These views are corroborated by Elich reviewed in earlier chapter.

It is the time for India to restructure its education especially at the primary level. A Commission should be appointed to suggest the measures necessary for implementing Gandhian concept of Basic Education with whatever modifications may be necessary to bring in concepts, ideas, and activities which were not considered useful or necessary in Gandhiji's time. But irrespective of the model to be implemented, India must move forward in improving the educational infrastructure.

I suggest that a multi-purpose primary school with buildings and other facilities, which India deserves as the largest democracy of the world, should be developed at a central place to serve ten Village Panchayats to begin with. The scheme should be completed in five years. And then it should be expanded to cover only five villages per school. In the following ten years, such schools should be in each Panchayat or within a radius of one kilometre.

In the next 10 years all schools should have at least four teachers each. Along with these measures, a special teachers training programme should be developed to sensitize teachers about the need for value education through personal demonstration more than teaching. This would require a fresh look at the text books too.

The multipurpose schools would have facilities for training in agriculture, forestry, carpentry, painting, carpet making, bee-keeping and several other local trades. In fact such a school was functioning in Mysore in the sixties and seventies. Somehow it lost its ethos and became yet another school of the country without identity.

Higher education in India is passing through a very critical stage. With its privatization and increasing cost, the problems have multiplied. Universities act as baby sitters more than as providers of knowledge and skill. What the society needs and what they offer are poles apart.

Most universities have lost their relevance; they are not universities in the real sense. As a university professor at Mysore and Delhi Universities and a Vice Chancellor at Allahabad University, I could see the pitiable condition of higher education from close quarters. If we consider universities to be the centres where knowledge is created and disseminated, then I can confidently say that they have lost their moorings and gone astray. Further, universities are the centers where information is converted into knowledge and knowledge into wisdom. Indian Uiversities no longer play the first two roles; they do disseminate second hand information in its raw form. As I sit in my room preparing the manuscript of this book, I can hear the noise of the young men and women of Allahabad University parading the streets of the city in support of one or the other candidate for student's union election. The scene is at times worst than the parliamentary election. For a month the university would remain closed as far as learning is concerned for no classes would be allowed until the elections are over. It is quite another matter that most of the students do not attend classes either because the teachers are busy teaching in coaching dhabas outside the university or the students do not find lecture relevant either for their life or even for their examination which takes place at the end of the year, if at all.

Higher education in India needs surgical changes. Our universities must become centres where information is converted into knowledge and knowledge into wisdom. In other words, research must become the backbone of the university education. A teacher who teaches from the books is a thief. Unfortunately many a university teacher do not teach at all; he coaches candidates for various government services. And what about the university administration? The other day some employees assaulted the Registrar of Allahabad University. The vice-chancellors have become political appointees and hence they would not take any stand against the government. So the mess continues unabated. The picture I have drawn is true and applies in particular to all state universities in the country.

Commenting on higher education, Gandhi says in *Hind Swaraj*: "I have learned Geography, Astronomy, Algebra, Geometry, etc. What of that? In what way I have benefited myself or those around me? Why have I learned these things? Professor Huxley has thus defined education: 'That man I think have had liberal education who has been so trained in youth that his body is the ready servant of his will and does with ease and pleasure all the work that as a mechanism it is capable of; whose intellect is a clear, cold logic engine with all its parts of equal strength and in smooth working order… whose mind is stored with the knowledge of the fundamental truth of nature…whose passions retrained to come to heel by a vigorous will, the servant of a tender conscience...who has learnt to hate all vileness and to respect others as himself. Such a one and no other, I conceive, has had a liberal education, for he is in harmony with nature. He will make the best of her and she of him."

If we take the clue from *Hind Swaraj* and apply the concept of higher education to the university system, universities in India should:

(1) mould the minds of the youth for creativity, self-reliance and value based life;
(2) be free from government control both financially and administratively; they should be endowed with adequate resources to stand on their own feet;
(3) become centers of excellence in knowledge creation and dissemination *i.e.* be research oriented, and
(4) have a crash plan of action to move from the state of irrelevance to relevance.

The test of the success of universities in India should lie in their ability to prepare the young men and women who come through its doors for higher education to become creative and help solve the problems humanity faces today. Let me relate here the changes that could be brought about in Allahabad University during my three-year stint as its Vice-Chancellor. This would give an inkling of what can be done if we make a long term plan and honestly implement it to make our universities serve the purpose outlined above.

During a short period of just three yeas, it was possible to weed out the antisocial elements and over-aged hangovers from the Students Union of the university. The Union became active in promoting and organizing cultural and social activities such as music concerts, sports, games, and other creative activities never witnessed before. It joined hands with the university administration in making the campus peaceful and conducive to learning.

The university cleaned the system of fraudulent admissions by introducing admission tests. It was challenged in the court unfortunately by a section of the teachers of the university who ought to have been happy with the move. It was cleared by the Supreme Court of India as a right and legally sound step. The university planned to start eleven new departments, 21 Centres of Research and six new Faculty Boards for Management Sciences, Information Technology, Interdisciplinary Studies, Earth Sciences, Literature and Mass Communication in the next five years. The University expanded the physical infrastructure by investing over Rs. 10 crores. A dozen industrial and commercial houses were approached to invest in the university infrastructure and to open new centres of research relevant to the fields of their interest. Five of these houses requested the university to constitute joint committees to chalk out the programmes of action.

After my retirement, the new vice-chancellor reverted back to the old rut. The roads built were dismantled; the foundation stones for new building laid by eminent people were shifted, and the except for the new departments (Computer Science, Fine Arts, Geology, Journalism, Anthropology and Sociology) which were already in place, the plan for the rest were scrapped. The plans of the buildings were altered and some of them remained incomplete and many others never saw the light. Interestingly, the people who came in the way of University moving forward were teachers. I received full support from the student and for they knew that their and university's futures were one and the same. Teachers opposed any change for they had developed terrific vested interest in the university. Most of them tried to get their own children, brothers, sisters and other relatives as teachers. As in 1985 about 40 per cent of faculty members were relatives of former teachers and administrators. The educational records of these teachers revealed that a great number of them were just ordinary students up to the 12th standard. They became bright students in bachelor degree and topped the at the Masters level, only because of tutelage of this relatives which were ensconced there.

University teachers were divided into two camps on caste basis: one headed by the Brahmins and the other by the Kayasthas. It is strange that so highly qualified intellectuals of India were so caste ridden. If the Vice-Chancellor was a Brahmin, the Kayastha group would oppose him as matter of principle; and similar was the case if the Vice-Chancellor belongs to Kayastha community. I found the Kayastha group highly skilful and united while the Brahmin group highly disparate and easily swayed by allurements. This is not to suggest that all Brahmins and Kayastha belonged to these groups. I came across that wonderful teachers who were academicians through and through. In fact at least 25 per cent of the teachers of Allahabad University belonged to this category. Another set of 25 per cent performed its duties but had no interest in the university. The remaining 50 per cent did not deserve to be university teachers; they indulged in caste politics, incited and misguided the students, and vitiated the academic environment day in and day out.

A few teachers created trouble in the university and then came forward to help solve the problems. The group was highly skilful in fomenting trouble through politically motivated student leaders. They change their roles when a new vice chancellor comes; they always work in unison and thus remain notoriously relevant.

I have related this experience to tell that unless a majority of teachers are loyal to the university, nothing substantial can be achieved. And for this reason the universities should reconsider their current recruitment policy and move away from local to national, if not international, market. No university can be great if it recruits its own students as teachers and no university can survive in the modern era unless it is relevant and caters to needs of the society. Too many changes are taking place in India today. Unfortunately, universities have no interest in them. Should Allahabad University not have Centres for research in ecology and environment, transport, rural development, urban management, Panchayati Raj, molecular biology, land resources, water resources, biotic resources, population studies and host of other sciences and social sciences? Why is it that the University of Allahabad has no field laboratory in social sciences, sciences and other fields? It does not concern itself with its surroundings apparently because it has no interest in it. How can it then be a relevant institution of learning?

Universities should be close to the people they serve; they should be relevant to region they are located in and they should produce student who do not seek jobs but jobs seek them. This is what Gandhi wanted the universities to be.

Towards Sarvodaya

One of the major concerns of Gandhi as expressed in *Hind Swaraj* was ecology. He felt that the whole universe particularly the earth functioned following certain laws to remain in perpetual balance. It is this balance, which made the earth alive with all the ingredients that support various life forms including the Homo sapiens. Once this balance is disturbed, all that is live would die. In the past there have been occasions when species unable to live in harmony with the laws of nature disappeared. Man should do nothing that would disturb that balance because once the earth's threshold of tolerance is crossed the species not able to live within the norms would have to die. Man may be the next in line if he ignores the Cosmic Law.

Gandhi was highly critical of modern industrial civilisation because it tried to transcend the Cosmic Law and diverted man from the path of his destiny, *i.e.* to evolve spiritually as a super-conscious human being. He commended Indian civilisation, despite its several weaknesses, because it had self-corrective measures to temper both these weaknesses. The concept of 'simple living and high thinking,' which he advocated took care of both ecological balance and spiritual growth. In *Hind Swaraj*, Gandhi gives only an inkling of his views on ecological balance but was very elaborate on spiritual growth for the obvious reason that the latter took care of the former too.

India has now reached a stage of development when it can change over from pure material to spiritual-cum-material development. Material development is necessary to enable each individual to have access to all those material and social needs, which constitute the essential prerequisites of a civilized society. All must get adequate and good quality food, housing, clothing, education, health services, security and dignity. Spiritual development leads man to his destiny: super-consciousness. This means inculcation in the development process of all those values, which make man a better man, *i.e.* imbued with truth, love, compassion, and sacrifice for others.

"I do not believe in the doctrine of the greatest good of the greatest number. It means in its nakedness that in order to achieve the supposed good of the fifty-one per cent, the interests of the forty-nine per cent may be, or rather, should be sacrificed. It is a heartless doctrine and has done harm to the humanity. The only real, dignified, human doctrine is the greatest good of all, and this can only be achieved by uttermost sacrifice." (*The Diary of Mahadev Desai* – I, 1950, p.19).

Some critics feel that Gandhian thinking on development is 'other worldly'. This is however not so. Bread is God for the hungry, said Gandhi. To a common man God comes into the picture only when his basic needs are fully satisfied. So, for a poor man material development is the first propriety. But once the basic needs are satisfied, more material development is not likely to improve his quality of life. Then there is need for spiritual development more than the material development lest he starts accumulating material goods to the extent that others are deprived of their basic needs and natural system is imbalanced to endanger the life.

For those who are well off materially and are engaged in acquiring more to live comfortably and luxuriously, Gandhi prescribed spiritual development. They must be educated to consider the whole world to be a single family; they must part with their excess wealth for those who have less. They must develop love and compassion as the essential elements of their life and living.

Gandhi thus felt that all human beings need development but some need more material development while others more spiritual development. At this stage, let me emphasize that in Gandhian praxis there is no separation between material and spiritual development. They are two sides of the same coin. Even a poor man needs spiritual development. Otherwise, when he becomes rich, he would behave the same way as the rich he hated earlier behave. We notice this phenomenon in modern India quite frequently. Once the son of poor man becomes rich because he got good government job with lot of opportunities for amassing money or he becomes a people's representative serves himself well to become rich, his behaviour does not change, In fact he becomes a part of the rich men's league and does not recognize his poor brethren as his. This is because the poor vie to become rich to do the same things, which the rich do. That is why Gandhiji coined the term Sarvodaya (development of all and every respect).

I think India should now initiate a 'Sarvodaya Model of Development'. At present the emphasis on material development need not be down graded but it must be shifted to upgrade the quality of life of the poor. India has all the resources to banish poverty within 10 years but somehow the way we try to achieve the targets take us nowhere. We appear to be busy digging holes and filling them up; we feel tired due to over work but do not see light across the tunnel. We have neglected the spiritual development because we have failed to make a distinction between religion and spirituality; we have misinterpreted secularism; we have lost interest in futures—we live in the present and dance around a lamp which burns and then leaves us in agony or death bed.

The time has come for India to move towards Sarvodaya—Holistic Development – a judicious mix of economic, social and spiritual development. In other words the current paradigm of economic development must change and a massive programme to regenerate India economically, socially and spiritually must be launched. In order to do this, India must redefine 'secularism' which has come to mean state disdain for religions. The word was imported from Europe and incorporated in our constitution. According to an editorial of *Times of India* (Sept. 22, 2003): "Secularism is a word that in Indian context is like a red rag to a (saffron) bull. It has been so abused and misunderstood that perhaps it is time to think of an alternative." And it suggests interfaith harmony, which every state must promote. India is a religious country; there are no two opinions on this issue. But it is perhaps the only country in the world where the state has tried for the last fifty five years to brand religion as a product of antiquity having no relevance in modern paradigm of development. The state prides itself in being irreligious.

Secularism as a policy tool should mean working with all religions to propagate truth, nonviolence, compassion, morality, and human brotherhood. Was Asoka the Great a communal emperor? According to our constitution, yes, he was. Was Gandhi a communal person? According to our Constitution, yes he was. He was talking of Ram Raj, Ram Nama, Dharma, God, and host other things, which do not find a place in the dictionary of secularism. We have seen the result of the neglect of religion.

Religion in its spiritual and non-sectarian avatar can put this country on a very high pedestal both economically and culturally. We have great spiritual leaders like Satya Sai Baba, Sri Guru Ravishankar, Maulana Wahiduddhin Khan and many others who preach inter-faith harmony and have followers from all religious groups. They preach religious harmony and lay emphasis on 'development of the individual' (*Vyakti Vikas*). While promoting material progress, the state should support these non-sectarian religious leaders to propagate spirituality at the individual and community levels. It should not be against these activities, nor even be indifferent. Unless we have strong movements to strengthen the moral fabric of the country, the task of *Sarvodaya, i.e.* holistic development would remain incomplete; and we, as a nation, would be ruled by anti-social elements of the society, the goons and the mafias.

If we claim to be a civilized people, we must be morally strong; and since source of morality is religion, we cannot afford to be irreligious or antireligious. Indian civilisation elevates moral being, says Gandhi (HS p. 55). Should then we not be prepared to rethink about the meaning of secularism and bring it in the fold of spiritualism?

Planning for Gram Swaraj

Some forty years ago in 1960s I suggested a new rural development policy which divested then policy of over-centralization and over decentralization at the same time. It was the Growth Centre Policy. It called for a five-tier spatial framework for rural development:

(1) Growth Pole
(2) Growth Centre
(3) Growth Point
(4) Service Centre
(5) Central Village

According to the scheme of things suggested, four to five villages should be served by a Central Village which would have all the necessary facilities for economic, social, cultural and spiritual development of the people. The Central Village would also be the headquarters of the Village Panchayat. Each of the villages under the jurisdiction of the Central Village would function as the self-governing wards of the Village Panchayat.

Five Central Villages would be served by a centrally located Service Centre, which would have higher-level functions for rural reconstruction. The Service Centre would be a mini town with all necessary facilities for rural, industrial and commercial development. And five Service Centres would be served by a Growth Point which in essence would be a Development Centre or market town with necessary manufacturing and commercial functions. A growth point would have anywhere between 50,000 to 25,000 population; a Service Centre between 10,000 to 15,000 population and a Central Village around 5,000. The service area of a Central Village would have approximately 25,000 population. The two higher-level cities (growth pole and growth centre) would be developed out of the existing cities by making them environmentally clean, economically balanced, politically well managed and spatially integrated with lower level growth foci.

I would like to reiterate that the approach suggested is Gandhian in details. This proves the point that Gandhian thinking on development is both theoretically and logically sound.

It appears a similar but less elaborate approach has just been suggested by His Excellency the President of India, Sri APJ Abdul Kalam as part of his India: Vision 2020.

ACTION FROM BELOW

Having discussed the national agenda, let us see what needs to be done at the local and individual level. *Hind Swaraj* laid great emphasis on moral development of man to make economic development meaningful, equitable, and ecologically sustainable. But no society can become morally strong if persons who constitute it are not moral. That is why Gandhi laid lot of emphasis on *Swaraj* (self-control) through moral development.

In this section of the chapter we would look at the sectors, which need attention at the local and individual level to promote Sarvodaya, *i.e.* development of all so that each individual and group in India enjoys the fruits of natural resources and human ingenuity equitably and leads a blissful life. Let it be our Aim.

Re-structuring of the Panchayati Raj Institutions

India has a long history of local self-government. Even the colonial administration could not ignore this long tradition. After independence Panchayats and municipalities were given added importance but the real effort at making them a constitutionally guaranteed bodies with powers and resources came after the 73rd Constitutional Amendment conceived originally by Sri Rajiv Gandhi.

Despite the progress made on the constitutional and legal fronts, local self-government in India has yet to take deep roots. The state governments have been reluctant to transfer power to the local authorities and hence India has failed so far to move in the direction of *Swaraj*, which in Gandhian frame of reference means our capacity to 'rule ourselves... such *Swaraj* has to be experienced by each one him self.' These ideas were later translated into the concept of gram panchayats. In Gandhi's own words:

> "Independence must begin at the bottom. Thus every village will be a republic or Panchayat having full powers. It follows, therefore, that every village has to be self-sustained and capable of managing its affairs even to the extent of defending itself against the whole world. It will be trained and prepared to perish

in the attempt to defend itself against any onslaught from without. Thus ultimately it is the individual who is the unit. This does not exclude dependence on and willing help from neighbours or from the world. It will be free and voluntary play of mutual forces. Such a society is necessarily highly cultured in which every man and woman knows what he or she wants and, what is more, knows that no one should want anything that others cannot have with equal labour." (*Harijan*, 28-7-46)

"Distinguished travellers from the world came to India in the days of the yore from China and other countries. They came in quest of knowledge and put up with great hardships in travelling. They had reported that in India there was no theft; people were honest and industrious. They needed no locks for their doors. In those days, there was no multiplicity of castes as at present. It is the function of the Panchayat to revive honesty and industry. It is the function of the Panchayats to teach the villagers to avoid disputes, if they have to settle them that would ensure speedy justice without any expenditure.... "the Panchayats should see to cattle improvement. They should show steady increase in the milk yield."

"The Panchayats should also see to an increase in the quantity of foodstuffs grown in their village. That is to be accomplished by properly manuring the soil.... Then, they must see to the cleanliness of their village and its inhabitants. They must be clean and healthy in body and mind. I hope that they would have no cinema house. People say that cinema can be a potent means of education that might come true some day, but at the moment I can see how much harm cinema is doing. They have their indigenous games. They should banish intoxicating drinks and drugs from their midst. I hope they will eradicate untouchability if there is any trace of it still left in their village. The Hindus, the Muslims, the Sikhs, the Parsis and the Christians should all live as brothers and sisters." (*Harijan* 4-1-48. pp. 499-500)

I think the stage has now come when India should empower the people in real terms and make panchayats autonomous in resources and decision-making. When we are talking of panchayats, we are not excluding the cities. Cities should be divided into neighbourhoods of 5,000 to 10,000 people and the neighbourhood welfare associations should function as Panchayat to handle day-to-day local problems of the community. Such a move would take the community closer to *Swaraj*.

Reviving the Cooperative Movement

Gandhiji laid great emphasis on cooperation, which acquires special attention in a country like India, which is known for cooperation, instead of competition. He drew inspiration from ancient India in this regard. "We have had no system of life corroding competition. Each followed his own occupation or trade and charged a regulation wages." He further elaborated these points in his subsequent writings. "Individual liberty and inter-dependence are both essential for life in society. Only a Robinson Crusoe can afford to be all self-sufficient. When a man has done all he can for the satisfaction of his essential requirements he will seek the cooperation of his neighbours for the rest. That will be true cooperation." (*Harijan*, 31-3-46, pp. 59).

One of the weakest links in local development in India is lack of cooperative action, which was the hallmark of Indian civilisation once upon a time. During the colonial era, institutionalized cooperative movement following the European model was launched in India. It did make some progress, and much of rural India was covered by the movement. It provided loans, seeds, fertilizers and variety of other facilities to the farmers. But as time passed and especially after independence, the movement came under the control of the governmental agencies and voluntarism that made it unique practically disappeared. It now stands discredited as a governmental programme headed by a minister and secretary in each state.

Gandhiji's vision of *Swaraj* had a strong element of cooperation. In fact *Swaraj* would have no meaning without cooperation. The time has now come for India to have fresh look at the way cooperative movement is being managed by the country. The first step in this direction would be to get rid of government control over it. The movement needs government support but not control. The second step that is needed is integration of the movement with the Panchayati Raj institutions. The third step needed is its professionalization to put in place appropriate checks and balances and specialization. And the fourth step that would set the movement on right path is voluntarism.

India has successful cooperative ventures. The brightest example of it is Amul (Anand Milk Union Ltd.) in Anand, Gujarat. It is a cooperative venture of hundreds of mini cooperatives spread over the countryside producing and contributing milk. There is no reason why such ventures cannot succeed elsewhere in the country. In order to make *Hind Swaraj* a reality urgent step are needed to remove the weaknesses this movement suffers from and to set them right.

From Wage Employment to Self-Employment

Agro-industrialization was the strongest point of ancient Indian economic system. Villages were not only the producers of agricultural commodities but also of industrial products. When the links and interdependence between agriculture and industry was lost, India became a poor country. This happened during the colonial period. Industry became the activity of cities; villages were left with agriculture. Unsupported by industry, agriculture became a helpless activity struggling to survive rather than prosper. And then a time came when industry located thousands of kilometres away made it its handmaid and forced it to supply raw materials it needed at a price too low for it to even survive.

Indian agriculture at the time of Independence in 1947 was not even hand to mouth. It was ship to mouth. The danger of famine loomed large on the country. But for the American food aid at the right time and in appropriate quantity, India like China would have lost millions of human lives. No steps were, however, taken to rethink about the relationship between agriculture and industry. Fortunately, the Green Revolution came to India in the 1960s and agricultural production based on high yielding seeds, chemical fertilizers, and irrigation increased. By the time American food aid stopped, food production had gone up to meet the food requirements of the country. Today, India produces more food than it can consume.

Green revolution, however, was a mixed blessing. While it made India self-sufficient in food, it had serious negative impacts on ecology and environment. Further, it benefited only the high rainfall and irrigated regions of the country leaving the rain fed dry regions untouched. The ecological problems have now gripped the whole country; the rain fed dry regions have doubly suffered: they suffer the spill over of environmental pollution on the one hand and low crop productivity on the other.

While environmental issues are being tackled at the national as well as local levels, the issue of unequal development resulting from unequal impact of green revolution can be mitigated by reverting to the old system of agro-industrial development and integration of agriculture and non-farm activities. Our target should be to produce at least half of the industrial (including agricultural processing) goods in the countryside in the next 20 years or so.

One of the strategies to promote industrialization of rural areas is what I call Micropolitan development. There must be a micropolis, *i.e.* growth point linking let us say 100 villages around it with all necessary infrastructure for non-farm activities. This process has already begun but in such a haphazard way that it would produce not micropolises but rural slums.

The micropolices should be developed keeping in view what a village of India ought to be, let us say by 2025. In this regard the picture of Indian villages of the future drawn by Mahatma Gandhi are highly relevant.

"My ideal village will contain intelligent human beings. They will not live in dirt and darkness as animals. Men and women will be free and able to hold their own against anyone in the world. There will be neither plague, nor cholera, nor smallpox; no one will be idle, no one will wallow in luxury. Everyone will have to contribute his quota of manual labour.... It is possible to envisage railways, post and telegraph... and the like." A Bunch of Letters (1958), pp. 505-06.

Vyakti Vikas (Development of the Self)

The centre piece in Gandhi's scheme of things was the individual. Unless the individual human beings are so brought up and trained to be truthful and nonviolent, nothing could be achieved. So there is a need for programmes and activities, which would aim at *Vyakti Vikas* or development of the individuals. Gandhi envisaged a situation in which *Vyakti Vikas* would be automatic. The whole system should operate in such a way that no effort was needed to achieve this goal. But in the initial stages and unless the system is geared to that goal, sustained efforts would be necessary.

Vyakti Vikas is not something that could be left to schools alone. It has to begin from the day a baby is conceived. According to recent findings, babies in the womb have feelings; they even smile and open their eyes to see in darkness surrounding them. The way the mother leads her life, has its impact on what the baby's character would be. The training of motherhood is the beginning of *Vyakti Vikas*. After the child is born, begins his care in the world he would spend 75+ years. What type of home and its surrounding he/she lives? Who are the people who take care of him/her and how they live? Quantity and quality of mother's milk and then foods determine the baby's health as do the environment in which it breathes, moves and plays.

School is the next great institution, which impact *Vyakti Vikas*. And then after the school one may go for higher education. All these mould the character of the child. The process of *Vyakti Vikas* however does not stop here. The whole life is an opportunity for *Vikas*. There are great teachers, Saints and Sufis in all religions who are engaged in *Vyakti Vikas*. I have already mentioned the names of Sri Sri Guru Ravishankar, Mata Anandmai, Satya Sai Baba, Wahiduddin Khan, Nirankari Guru and several other spiritual leaders who can arouse the people spiritually. They try to lead humanity from darkness to light. Mahatma Gandhi is the most shining example of twentieth century who changed the whole course of freedom movement from violence to non-violence.

A great future awaits humanity. And this future lies in *Vyakti Vikas* or Human Development through spiritual awakening and new style of economic progress. It is easy to get people who are highly qualified in science, engineering, technology and humanities but not easy to get people who have character. Much of what is wrong in the society to day is because of lack of character. The time has come for a new movement that makes man a better human being, not only economically but also and more importantly, spiritually too. This movement has to begin from India, the India of Buddha, Mahavira and Gandhi.

Gandhi was indeed right when in 1945 he suggested that the then Indian National Congress should be disbanded and converted into Lok Sevak Sangh, which could act as check on the government going astray and ensure that the basic tenets of Indian civilisation were adhered to both by the government and the people.

Appendices

APPENDIX-A

NOTABLE EVENTS IN GANDHI'S LIFE DURING 1869-1914

October 2, 1869

Mohandas Karamchand Gandhi was born at Porbandar, Gujarat; his mother Putlibai and father Karamchand belonged to a middle class business (*bania*) community.

1876 – 1881

Gandhi got his early education at home; later he attended primary school at Rajkot.

1881

Gandhi joined Kathiawar High School; was married to Kasturbai Nakanji the same year. It was a child marriage.

1887

Passed high school examination and joined the Sanwaldas College but did not fair well. Apparently he was a dull and pensive child.

1888

His father and grandfather were prime ministers (*diwans*) of one or the other of the several little princely states of Kathiawar. Gandhi was advised to go to England for Law degree so that he could also step in the shoes of his father. But his mother Putlibai thought otherwise. Fearing that her son would indulge in meat eating and other vices in

England, she objected to the proposal. Gandhi took an vow to abstain from wine, women and meat. The mother gave in then. His caste elders however were not convinced; they tried to dissuade him from going abroad. Ignoring their objections, he left Bombay on September 4 reaching London on October 28. Soon after he joined the Inner Temple for Law degree.

1889

While in England, Gandhi first tried to become a perfect English gentleman and emulated English dress, speech and mannerism. He learned French and dancing too. But soon he realized that the British ways did not suit him. He came to know Madame Blavatsky and Annie Besant, the two ladies who later proved to be a great help to Gandhi. He was introduced to theosophy and the literature related thereto including Arnold's *Song Celestial* and *The Light of Asia*, *Bhagavadgita* and *Bible.*

1890

Gandhi became interested in vegetarianism. He read periodicals on vegetarianism, started experimenting with vegetarian food, and attended international vegetarian meeting. Edwin Arnold was the president of the Vegetarian Club of which Gandhi was the vice president. He joined the Vegetarian Society of England.

1891

It was the last year of his studies. He came closer to the Vegetarian Society and wrote an article in the *Vegetarian* (a magazine) against alcohol; attended lectures by Dadabhai Naoroji; and appears to have developed a firm faith in honesty and hard work. In June, he was called to the Bar and enrolled in the High Court.

Gandhi sailed for India on June 12. On reaching Bombay, he learnt about his mother's death. Soon he met Raichandbhai, a jeweller, a poet and an ascetic whom he considered a person of great religious perception. To satisfy his caste elders, he went to Nasik to expiate the impurities he might have acquired while abroad. He stayed at Rajkot with his brother Laxmidas. Rajkot being a small place, he applied for enrolment as a lawyer in Bombay High Court.

1892

He was allowed to practice at Kathiawad Agency court but found practice there rather difficult. He proceeded to Bombay but in his first appearance in Bombay High Court, he became so nervous that he just slumped down without uttering a word. Perhaps he lost confidence in himself and decided to return to Rajkot where he helped his brother in the preparation of petitions etc.

1893

As the luck would have it, Dada Abdulla & Co, South Africa, asked Gandhi to help in their court cases. He immediately accepted the offer and left for Durban leaving his wife and child back at Rajkot. On reaching Durban he found himself an unwelcome visitor, as most black Asiatics were. Gandhi attended the Durban court after a couple of days of arrival; the judge asked him to remove the turban. Gandhi felt insulted. He refused to take the turban off and left the court. The event was well publicized through the press and news of the defiance spread around in all sections of the society through the words of mouth at times in an exaggerated manner.

After a week, he left for Pretoria by train to attend to his client's work. The journey proved to be a turning point in Gandhi's life. He was thrown out of the first class railway compartment because a White passenger refused to travel with a coolie. He was humiliated by a coachman and was denied a place in a hotel. He was kicked off on the footpath prohibited for the coloured by a White man near President Kruger's residence. Gandhi resolved to fight the evil of discrimination tooth and nail but not by resorting to court cases, which a lawyer would generally think to do but by creating a moral force against an immoral system of governance. He called a meeting of Indian Memon merchants with the help of Sheth Tyeb Haji Khan and discussed the conditions in which Indians were forced to live and work in Transvaal and Orange Free State. The meeting decided to form an association to fight for justice and help redress the grievances the Indians had.

He was introduced to Christian literature by his friends; did not consider it moral to get converted to Christianity but he did realize that all that the White men were practicing in South Africa was unchristian.

1894

Gandhi put into practice his idea of peaceful conflict resolution by arranging an out of court settlement of a case between his client and his adversary. This gave Gandhi lot of publicity and of course tremendous self-confidence. His stature went up both as a man and as a lawyer.

Gandhi decided to return to India and settle down ther.. A farewell was arranged by the Indian settlers. Gandhi was informed that a new Bill was likely to be introduced in the Natal Legislature to disfranchise Indians. The parting meeting was turned into a forum to pressurize Gandhi to postpone his return to India. Gandhi was in quandary; he was sure how to fight against the injustice being perpetrated. He happened to lay his hand on Tolstoy's *Kingdom of God is Within You*. He also corresponded with his Christian friends in England and religious leaders like Raychandbhai in India. He saw light at the end of the tunnel. And Gandhi was all set to make experiments with Truth.

A committee was constituted to agitate against the Bill. Representations were sent to various authorities requesting them to postpone the consideration of the Bill. 500 Indians signed a petition presented to the Natal Legislative Assembly and waited in deputation to the Premier and Governor. Gandhi wrote to Dadabhai Naoroji at that time in England requesting him to intervene on behalf of Indians. The Bill was passed and sent to London for Royal assent. The representations, however, did not stop.A petition addressed to Lord Rippon, Secretary of State for Colonies was signed by 10,000 Indians and sent through the Governor. It requested Rippon not to send the Bill for Royal approval.

Gandhi formed the Natal Indian Congress on the lines of Indian National Congress back home in India for sustained agitation. He was its first Secretary. He applied for enrolment as a member of Natal Bar. Despite opposition from the White controlled Bar, the Supreme Court permitted Gandhi to practice in Natal Courts. This time he obeyed the court order to remove his turban because he did not want to waste his time on minor issues.

Gandhi broadened his sphere and appealed to the White residents for sympathetic approach towards Indian cause. He always reminded them that Christianity stood for justice and fair play and so did the British government.

1895

Gandhi appealed to Natal Assembly again for reconsideration of the Bill; sought intervention of Lord Elgin, Viceroy of India and sent a lengthy petition to Chamberlain requesting for stay of Royal Assent to the Bill. The Royal assent was denied but it did not give much relief to Indians. A fresh Bill was sent by Natal Government for Royal approval. So the fight did not stop. By this time, some Europeans too realized the injustice being done to Indians; they too supported the Indian stand.

1896

Gandhi spent much of this year writing and sending petitions and protests against the new Township Regulation Franchise Bill introduced in the Natal Legislature in a modified form. Gandhi represented to the Legislative Assembly and also to Chamberlain to stop the Bill from being passed. It was, however, passed on May 13. He was requested to go to India and acquaint the people, the Indian National Congress leaders and the Indian government, with the provisions of the Bill and the problems faced by Indians in South Africa.

Gandhi reached Calcutta on his way to Rajkot. Due to some delay in the departure of the train, he stopped over at Allahabad and met the editor of the Pioneer. The Pioneer building is located in front of the Senate Hall of Allahabad University (it is a read brick structure known as FCI building; it has been purchased by the university and is likely to be demolished soon). Gandhi sent a slip to the editor asking for an interview. The latter was busy; he just kept the slip on the table and continued his work. Gandhi had to wait for one and half hours. He sat down on the platform of a well, which still exists and I hope it would be retained as a monument later, when the editor saw the slip, he rushed out and took Gandhiji inside. He profusely apologized for what had happened and interviewed Gandhi. When the South African Whites read the interview they decided to stop Gandhi from re-entering South Africa.

On reaching Rajkot, he published a Green Pamphlet, which detailed the conditions in which, Indians were living in South Africa. The Reuters at Bombay gave a very good even if misleading coverage on the pamphlet. Reading this, the South African Whites were further infuriated. They formed an European Protesting Association and decided to stop Gandhi from entering South Africa.

From Rajkot, Gandhi went to Bombay and met Ranade, Badruddin Tyabji and Pherozshah Mehta and then visited Poona, Madras, Calcutta, and Nagpur to meet important leaders. He returned to Bombay and sent telegram to the Viceroy at Calcutta drawing his attention to the new regulations under which Indians would have to live only in specified localities. He left Bombay by SS Courtland with Kasturbai and two children. In the mean time, the Indian National Congress in its Calcutta meeting on December 31 adopted a resolution condemning the treatment meted out to Indians in South Africa and appealing to the British government to take remedial measures.

1898

The Natal Government declared Bombay as plague infested zone; the ship carrying Gandhi and his family was not allowed to dock until January 11. Gandhi took the opportunity to address the passengers of the ship on the Christmas day. The Europeans held a meeting on January 4 to protest against 'Indian invasion' of Natal.

Much of this year also went in drafting and sending petitions against the Location Policy of the Transvaal Government and fighting test cases in the court. Gandhi cabled the Viceroy of India with a copy to the Secretary of State for India to intervene. He sent representation to Indian National Congress and pleaded for pressuring the Indian Government to take up the case of Indians with the Secretary of State. No success was in sight but Gandhi continued his efforts relentlessly to exhaust all legal and peaceful avenues before using force, even if only moral and to enlist the support of all communities specially Indians.

1899

The major event of the year was the Boer War. Gandhi asked for the facilities for Indians to leave Transvaal and volunteer for ambulance service. He volunteered to render service to the government. The Colonial Secretary, was informed of the readiness of Indian volunteers to leave to the front and to work as stretcher-bearers. Gandhi organized a very successful ambulance corps to take care of the wounded.

Another major activity of the year was the use of the press by Gandhi to ventilate Indian grievances. He sent copies of the petitions to all newspapers, wrote a special article for the *Times of India* on plague panic in Natal and refugee situation and gave an interview to the *Star of Johannesburg* about the Indians Location Order.

1900

The Boer war over, the service rendered by the ambulance corps was lauded. Gandhi gave detailed account of the work of the corps to *Times of India* for publicity in India. Indians joined the English in celebrating victory of the British in the Boer war. He appealed the people to donate liberally for Durban Indian Hospital and famine relief in India.

Gandhi wrote to the town clerk against a rule, which did not allow coloured to sit in rickshaws drawn by Indians but marked for whites only. Also presented a petition to the Governor of Natal in this regard. He also forwarded a resolution on South African Indians to Dadabhai Naoroji for the consideration of the Indian National Congress in its next session.

1901

It was year of varied activities. Apart from drafting petitions and meeting people, he also visited India to lobby with Congress leaders.

Gandhi condoled the death of Queen Victoria and asked Indians in general to pay tribute to the Queen for being sympathetic to Indian causes. He sent petitions against the denial of refugee Indians to return to Transvaal to the Colonial Secretary, Bombay government, military governor of Johannesburg, and the High Commissioner for India. He wrote to friends in England about the disabilities being imposed on Indians. He suggested to the British Committee to appoint a joint committee with East Indian Association to suggest measures to do away with anti-Indian laws in South Africa.

Gandhi was terribly grieved to hear of Raichandbhai's death. He decided to visit India for lobbying. The Natal Indian Congress arranged a farewell for him. People gave several costly gifts to him and his family members. But he returned them all and asked for the formation of a Trust for the purpose. He sailed for India on November 13 with a promise to return within a year. His ship passed through Port Louis, Mauritius where Indian community accorded him reception. He reached Rajkot on December 14 and left for Calcutta via Bombay to attend the Indian National Congress meet. On December 27, he moved a resolution on South Africa.

1902

Gandhi stayed in India for much of this year. His mission was to acquaint the people with the problems of Indians in South Africa, to enlist their support and to arouse a feeling of patriotism in them. Apparently, Gandhi started feeling rather intensely that unless India was free, Indians would not receive the kind of treatment they deserved.

From Calcutta, he went to Rangoon, Burma. On return from there in the first week of February, he stayed with Gokhale at Calcutta for several days. From Calcutta he went to Benares (to meet Annie Besant), Agra, Jaipur, Palanpur, and finally to Rajkot where he started practicing law. Wrote notes to several important persons and a special article to the *Times of India* and urged the paper to raise its voice against the anti-Indian Natal Bill prohibiting Indians from certain areas settled by the Whites.

Gandhi acted as Secretary to the State Volunteer Plague Committee in Rajkot. On July 19, he left Rajkot to set up legal practice in Bombay but on an urgent call from South Africa, he left Bombay on November 14. On reaching Durban, he decided to go to England as head of a Natal Indian deputation to wait on Chamberlain, the Secretary of State for Colonies, to urge him to end the indentured labour system.

1903

It was quite a busy year for Gandhi. He settled down in Johannesburg and wrote to Dadabhai Naoroji and Gokhale almost every week about the situation unfolding in South Africa with particular reference to the fight he had launched. A mass meeting was held in Johannesburg on May 6 to protest against the intention of the colonial government to confine Indians to bazars. He requested Dadabhai Naoroji and Gokhale to take up the issues of registration tax, Asiatic Immigration and relocation of Indians in selected areas (Bazars).

Gandhi led an Indian delegation to the governor of Transvaal against compulsory registration act. Petitions were submitted to British Committee for India; Transvaal Governor; Natal Legislature;

and Natal Council against all discriminatory laws especially the Location and Bazar laws to be imposed on Indians in Natal Colony. He informed Dadabhai Naoroji that despite opposition, the municipal ordinance (Bazar Act) was passed and notified. He cabled the British Committee, India and the *Times of India* about the refugee problem created by the Bazar Act and cabled Chamberlain to withhold royal assent to Immigration Restriction Bill passed by the Natal Assembly. He also informed the Indian National Congress meeting in Madras of the seriousness of the problem created for the Indians and also appealed to the Associated Chambers of Commerce, India to exert pressure for the amendment in the discriminatory laws.

Indian Opinion commenced publication under the editorship of Mansukhlal Nazar. By this time Gandhi had a fairly good and intimate contact with Indian National Congress and its leaders like Dadabhai Naoroji and Gokhale.

1904

Once the relocation of Indians became a *fait accompli*, Gandhi involved himself in minimizing the problems they faced. He approached the Health Officer, Johannesburg about the unsanitary conditions and overcrowding in Indian locations. Since the Town Council refused to take responsibility he improvised a hospital and arranged for naturopathy treatment of plague victims.

Gandhi wrote to Johannesburg Press and *Rand Daily Mail* about the plague epidemics in the city. He also informed Indian leaders about it. A new ruling of the Supreme Court that the term 'residence' in Law 3 of 1885 did not include place of business gave some relief to Indians. Gandhi read Ruskin's *Unto This Last* while travelling to Durban by train. Addressing Indian at Durban he said that success of Indians depended on self-sacrifice. In the mean time, an Anti-Asiatic Convention was held by the Europeans in Pretoria; it called for drastic steps to eliminate Indians from the Colony. Gandhi protested against the venomous and intemperate language used at the Anti-Asiatic Convention.

A new phase in Gandhi's struggles started this year. He founded the Phoenix Settlement and the office of the *Indian Opinion* also was shifted there. He took over its editorial.

1905

Gandhi opened the year with letter to Gokhale about *Indian Opinion* and the role it was playing in arousing the people against the injustices perpetrated on Indians. He delivered four lectures on Hindu religion at the Johannesburg Theosophical Society and sent a memorial to Natal Legislative Assembly regarding the Bills to amend the Municipal Corporations Act. He addressed the Natal Indian Congress at Durban; criticized the Bills concerning licences for firearms; private locations; unoccupied rural lands; and occupied dwelling houses for they all affected Indians adversely.

Gandhi kept in touch with the situation developing in India. He demanded abolition of salt tax in India; criticized the Cape Immigration Act and Challenged the *Daily Express* on disparaging remarks against Indian traders. In July, he called upon South African politicians to reconsider their stand on Indian issues in the light of the contributions of Indians to the defence of the Empire and the development of the colonies.

Protest by Indians notwithstanding the Poll Tax Bill was passed by the Natal Legislative Council. The Council, however, rejected the Locations and Land Tax Bills. The British Indian Association protested the application to Indians of the new municipal laws for coloured people. Gandhi condemned the maltreatment of Chinese miners. Lord Selbourne's pronouncement that administrative in justice to natives was a blot and a disgrace, was serialized in the *Indian Opinion*.

Lord Curzon partitioned Bengal. Gandhi called for united opposition to the partition and backed Gokhale for the next president of the Indian National Congress. Gandhi commended *Bande Matram* as India's National Anthem. Gandhi also took up the cause of the Japanese workers. He led a deputation to Lord Selborne to protest against the treatment to British Indians in Transvaal. The Asiatic National Convention requested the Lt. Governor to appoint a Board of Control to process applications for entry into the Colonies.

The efforts made by Gandhi borne some fruits; the Cape Colony Supreme Court ruled that Indians had the right of domicile on the basis of long residence even if unaccompanied by their families. He appealed to the Indians to be vigilant and to continue the struggle 'with reasonableness ... with patience and with persistence.' Gandhi commended the cause of education and asked Indian to arrange for the best possible education for their children.

1906

With the passage of time, Gandhi's activities increased and his area of concern and action broadened to cover all Asians and all such subjects who were discriminated against. Gandhi proved to be a law-abiding citizen. He would not obey a law or authority, which was based on brute force, injustice and discriminatory treatment. He did not ask for anything more than what British citizens under the British constitution and law should get on the basis of equality. This stand of Gandhi brought many a British also on his side. They supported Gandhi in his struggle to secure rights for the Indians.

The Poll Tax (1 Pound per head) was imposed on Indians aged 18 and above. The Early Closing Act was also enforced. The protest meetings were held against discrimination in tramcars, poll tax, early closing rules, etc through the British Indian Association. Two tragic events forced Gandhi to divert his attention. San Francisco experienced a devastating earthquake on January 2 and Zulu Rebillion broke out in February. Gandhi exhorted Indians to volunteer their services to the Government. He wrote to Dadabhai Naoroji to use his good offices to safeguard the interests of Indians in Orange River and Transvaal Bill that proposed to amend the Cape Immigration Restriction Act, 1902. In March he addressed a coloured peoples meeting at Johannesburg in this regard.

On March 31, the Imperial Government set up a Commission on Transvaal Constitution. Gandhi deprecated import of Indian labour for mining and represented to various authorities in Transvaal, England and India to redress Indian grievances.

On April 14, the Natal Indian Congress decided to send a delegation to England under the leadership of Gandhi to apprise the government and others about the situation in Natal and Transvaal. Gandhi met the railway authorities regarding restrictions on Indians to travel in certain trains between Johannesburg and Pretoria. On May 12, he supported Home Rule for India on the ground of justice and for sake of humanity.

The representation of the British Indian Association against the law requiring Indians to secure residential permit before entering the colonies was rejected by Lord Selbourne; Indians, however, won the court case against discrimination in tramcars.

Gandhi by this time had reached a stage of self-realisation where he was prepared to abjure all worldly possessions. He wrote to his brother Laxmidas to this effect.

Gandhi offered to organise an Ambulance Corps to take care of the victims of Zulu war. The Natal Committee accepted the offer. Gandhi was given the rank of Sergeant Major by the government. By July 19, the Corps was disbanded as the war was over. Gandhi suggested the constitution of a permanent Corps but it never became a reality. Later the Natal Governor thanked Gandhi for services rendered by the stretcher-bearer corps.

The proposal of the Colonial Secretary to introduce a Bill to register Asiatics in the Transvaal was opposed by the British Indian Association. Gandhi kept Dada Bhai Naoroji informed of the proposed Bill and the hardships Indians would have to undergo. He used the forum of Indian opinion to demand full liberty for Indians and to exhort Indians to organise protests against the Colonial Secretary's statement on re-registration Ordinance.

Despite protest the Ordinance was approved and introduced in Transvaal Assembly. Gandhi described the move as a crime against humanity. He branded it a Black Act and called upon people to resist it. He advised people not to register and offered himself to court imprisonment first. On September 11, a mass meeting of the British Indian association was held at Johannesburg wherein it was decided to resist the ordinance if it became a law.

On September 14, an Indian woman Punia, travelling by train was arrested, because she did not have re-registration permit. She was tried and rearrested for defying orders to leave the colony. Gandhi wrote to press criticizing the Transvaal government's war on women and children. He criticized the *Transvaal Leader* for its charge that Indians were importing women of dubious character to the colony. The statement was however retracted after some time.

It was decided to send a two-men delegation (M.K. Gandhi and H.O. Ally) to England. In the mean time Lord Selbourne informed Gandhi that the ordinance would not get royal assent until the deputation had visited England and presented its case to him. The deputation reached Cape Town from Johannesburg on October 3. It was given a grand reception by Indians.

The Deputation reached London on October 21. Gandhi was met by Polak and Professor Parmananda. Among the persons who were met by Gandhi were: Pandit Shyamji Krishnavarma, Sir Muncherji Bhownaggaree, Dada Bhai Naoroji, Sir William Wedderburn, Sir George Birdwood, Sir Richard Soloman, F.H. Brown, Sir Curzon Wyllie, Ameer Ali, Sir Lapel Griffin, Lord George Hamilton, Winston

Churchill, Bernard Holland, Mrs. W.C. Banerjee, Secretary British Committee of Indian National Congress, Mrs. Spencer Walton, W.T. Stead, Miss Winterbottom, Theodore Morison, John Morley, Secretary of State for India, A.J. Balfour, A. Little, and Sir Raymond West. In most cases Ally accompanied Gandhi. The above list is not complete. It is given to indicate how busy was Gandhi in convincing almost every one who mattered of the case of Indians in South African colonies.

Gandhi submitted a representation to Lord Elgin, Secretary of State for Colonies, and John Morley, Secretary of State for India. He participated in the meetings of National Indian Association, London Indian Society, Pan-Islamic Society. The Liberal MPs of House of Commons requested the Prime Minister to meet the Delegation led by Gandhi. Gandhi left London on December 1. In the mean time Churchill informed the House of Commons that the controversial Ordinance would not be proceeded with for the time being. The deputation reached Johannesburg via Cape Town on December 21. The deputation was accorded reception at many places. Gandhi asked people not is relax they must continue their struggle till complete inter-racial equality is achieved.

1907

Gandhi gave an account of the activities of the delegation to British Indian Association. In a letter to *Outlook*, he demanded full civil rights and share in governance of the colonies for Indians. The imperial government refused to approve the bill to exclude Asiatics from trading licences, and those who have been deprived of their rights would be compensated.

The Asiatic Registration Bill was passed by the Transvaal Parliament in March. In a mass meeting of Indians it was decided not to abide by the Registration Act. The resolution passed in the meeting was presented to General Smuts at Pretoria. He spoke at the meeting of the Natal Indian Congress in Durban.

Some Members of Parliament under the leadership of Lord Ampthill met General Botha and Mr. Morley in regard to the problems of Transvaal Indians. Another group led by Sir Henry Cotton met Mr. Morley. They both promised to do whatever they could to mollify the feelings of Indians.

Gandhi launched a press blitzkrieg against the Act through *Rand Daily* and *The Star* and prepared all Asians for a big and novel fight he had already shaped in his mind. On July 1, the Act was enforced in Pretoria and a permit office opened. Gandhi addressed meeting of Indians at Pretoria, Folksrust, Hamidia Islamic Society at Johannesburg, Transvaal Football Association, and several other places.

As the preparations for an new fight began in South Africa, in India over 20,000 persons gathered to observe the anniversary of the Swadeshi movement. Gandhi wrote to General Smuts suggesting some modifications in the Act. The British Indian Association submitted a giant petition signed by 4522 Indians against the Act. Protest meetings were held all over South Africa where Asians lived and hartal was observed in Transvaal. Gandhi defended Sundarlal Pandit, the first Indian arrested under the new Law and met him in Pretoria jail. By the last date of the registration (November 30) only 500 of the 13,000 Indians had opted for registration.

In India, the first anniversary of Bengal Partition was observed as a day of mourning. Lala Lajpat Rai was released from jail. Gandhi wrote to Gokhale to form a 'Hindu-Muslim Compact' during the ensuing session of the Congress.

The struggle that Gandhi launched was for the first time called *Satyagraha*.

1908

The Transvaal Immigrations' Restriction Act, 1907 (TIRA) and Transvaal Asiatic Registration Act, 1907 (TARA) came into force on January 1. A mass meeting was held in Surti Mosque, Fordsburg against the Acts. Gandhi appeared in Johannesburg court to defend Nawab Khan prosecuted under TARA.

Meetings were held in India and England urging the British government to intervene. At a meeting in the New Reform Club, London, Sir W. Wedderburn wanted the Imperial government to intervene and ensure that the Indians in Transvaal got the treatment keeping with imperial tradition because it spent three million pounds each year on the defence of Transvaal. M.A. Jinnah was sent by Anjuman Islam, Bombay to England to create public opinion against the ill-treatment of Indians.

Gandhi, in order to exhaust all other peaceful means offered to get all Indians voluntarily registered if the Act was withdrawn.

Cartwright brought the compromise letter to General Smuts. General Smuts agreed to the formula. On January 30, the Assistant Colonial Secretary also accepted the compromise. Gandhi was taken out of jail to Pretoria to meet General Smuts and sign the compromise document. Asiatics were permitted to trade in restricted areas pending the formalisation of the agreement.

Gokhale raised the issue in the Central Legislative Council at Delhi. Lord Ampthill introduced a call-attention motion in the House of Lords. The *Times of London* blamed the colonial office for 'lack of imagination'. It called for an agreed imperial attitude towards self-governing colonies.

To explain the rationale and the procedure for voluntary registration, Gandhi addressed a number of meetings of Indian. In one of the meetings a Pathan (Mir Alam Khan) assaulted Gandhi for going back on his words and betraying the community. He was arrested and jailed. Later apologized to Gandhi for the wrong he did. On March 6, he left for Phoenix Settlement.

Soon it was decided to discontinue the practice of indentured labour system. But new problems were in store for Indians. The Transvaal Municipal Association passed a resolution to deny franchise to Africans and Asiatics. It was proposed to move all the Asiatics to Bazars but Natal Agricultural Union opposed the move because Indian labour was essential for cultivation. The British Indian Association wrote to General Smuts protesting against the draft amendment to Transvaal Municipal Law. Gandhi was back in Johannesburg to give a lead in the new fight against indignities.

Back home in India a bomb was exploded on April 30 at Muzaffarpur. A bomb factory was discovered and Aurobindo with 50 others was arrested. Several Indians were unable to voluntarily register as they were out in India or due to some other reasons. Gandhi wanted the last date to be extended. Despite several appeals to General Smuts and imperial government, it was not agreed to. This amounted to breach of trust and Gandhi decided to launch yet another *Satyagraha* to burn all registration cards. On June 2 eminent whites met and reaffirmed their support to Indian cause.

Gandhi was invited to meet General Smuts on June 6. Gandhi asked for immediate withdrawal of Transvaal Asiatic Registration Act (TARA) else he would appeal to the Supreme Court for return of applications for voluntary registration. At the instance of the Imperial government, it was decided to modify TARA. Gandhi did not consider the amendments adequate enough to be accepted. Gandhi gave a press statement blaming General Smuts for breach of compromise. In a mass meeting on June 24 at Johannesburg, it was resolved to withdraw the applications. Shorabji Shapurji entered Transvaal as a test case. Gandhi defended Shapurji but the Johannesburg court ordered him (Shapurji) to leave the Colony within a week.

The British Indian Association decided to do unlicensed hawking as a means of protest and penance. Ebrahim Ismail and Suliman Bagas were jailed for hawking without licence. Shapurji was also jailed with hard labour. Several Indian leaders were deported from Pretoria. Gandhi along with others squatted at the railway station. He addressed Indians at Hamidia mosque. Much of September was spent in sending petitions and appealing the people in England to help settle the matter. The BIA also took up the question of diet given to Indian prisoners. They demanded ghee instead of animal fat.

In October Gandhi asked Natal Indians to agitate for ending indentured labour system. Gandhi was arrested at Volksrust on October 7 along with 15 other Indians for entering Transvaal without registration certificates. He was produced before the magistrate but refused to avail of bail. He appealed to Indians from jail to continue the agitation and to face jail-going for the sake of the motherland. Gandhi was given the work of road making. Indian leaders like Lajpatrai, Sir M. Bhownaggaree and Bipin Chandra Pal protested against mass arrest of Indians particularly the treatment meted out to Gandhi in the prison. Sir Ferozshah Mehta cabled Lord Ampthill from India that people in India were very much exercised over maltreatment of Indians in jail and asked for British government's intervention. The Viceroy of India also conveyed to the Colonial Office the resentment brewing in India.

On October 22, Gandhi was removed from Volksrust jail to Johannesburg jail in convict's garb. In Daya Lala's case he refused to use cab and walked to the court with prisoner's cap. Muslims telegraphed protest against General Botha's statement that Muslims did not join the passive resistance movement. BIA complained to the Attorney General about ill treatment of Indian's in jail and warned the government to continue the agitation till Indians demands were acceded to. Mrs. Annie Beasant sent a message of hope and cooperation to Gandhi. Lord Selbourne conveyed to General Botha imperial government's view that Indians should get considerate treatment and that limited number of educated Indians should be permitted to get in.

On December 12, Gandhi was released from Volksrust jail. He was interviewed on the way to Johannesburg about the ill-treatment in prison. The Hamidia Islamia Society held a meeting to honour Gandhi. He addressed meeting of Tamil community in Johannesburg. General Botha refused to amend the law. Gandhi received rousing reception at Durban. The movement continued and more Indians courted arrest.

1909

Gandhi, in his New Year message, exhorted the people to adopt Swadeshi. He also said that jail going was the most effective means of fighting political disabilities. Several Indians were arrested for refusing to give thumb impression and producing registration certificates at Volskrust, Durban, Johannesburg, Cape Town, and several other places. In an interview to *Natal Mercury* Gandhi stated that Indians were fighting with 'cleanest weapons possible.'

Ritch protested to Colonial Office against Natal Government Notice banning admission of Indian students above 14 to higher grade schools. Kasturba was operated. Gandhi was arrested at Volksrust while on his way to Johannesburg for failing to produce registration certificate. He was deported and escorted to border but he returned immediately to court re-arrest. He was released on his own recognizance: returned to Johannesburg.

On January 19, the supreme court ruled deportation of registered citizens illegal. Gandhi announced through the press that Indians had entered the third and final phase of their struggle. Gandhi asked Indian merchants to place all their assets at creditors' disposal as a mark of sacrifice. There was a wide speculation in government and White men's circles that the Indian merchants would not fall in Gandhi's 'trap'. *Daily Mail* termed passive resistance as an act of coercion. Naidoo's appeal against Asiatic Registration Law was dismissed by the Natal Supreme Court. *The Star* welcomed the judgment and commented that only a few 'deluded faddists will consent to sacrifice their business and credit at the dictation of Messrs Gandhi and Cachalia.'

Gandhi requested Lord Curzon to intervene. The movement spread and many more Indian traders followed Cachalia and refused to take licences. Cachalia, Naidoo, Rustamji and many others were arrested and sentenced to three months jail term and 50 pounds fine. Kasturba's condition improved.

During February the Imperial Government withheld the assent to Asiatic Act of Rhodesia. Many more passive resisters were awarded prison terms ranging from 3 to 6 months. On March 2, Gandhi was transferred from Volksrust to Pretoria jail where he was given the work of polishing prison doors and floor. Wives of the Indian traders also courted arrest. The proposed Act of Union of South Africa was discussed at the meeting of the coloured peoples and demanded representation for them. The British Indian meeting at Hamidia Islamic Society was addressed among others by Coovadia, Kallenbach and Polak.

On March 8, Gandhi was taken to the court handcuffed as a witness. Chinese passive resisters congratulated Gandhi. In a letter to Johannesburg press, Doke wrote 'the great majority of our Colonists' feel ashamed that a man of the character and position of Mr. Gandhi should be needlessly insulted in this manner (handcuffing). Natal Indian Congress and British Indian Association passed resolutions to continue the passive resistance until all the demands of Indians regarding registration are met.

Many Indians and Chinese were deported. Transvaal Supreme Court ruled that Asiatics were not disabled from securing licences in mining areas. A mass meeting of Indians at Johannesburg repudiated Botha's contention that Indians were satisfied with their status in the colony. On May 24, Gandhi was released from Pretoria Central Jail; it was his third imprisonment. He addressed a meeting in Mohammedan Mosque Hall and said that he held no pleasure at being released and that the methods the colonial governments have used would not break spirit of Indians. He received a rousing reception at Park Station. He exhorted Indians to resist unjust law.

Gandhi wrote in *Indian Opinion* his experiences in jail and meaning and implications of *Satyagraha*. Thus Gandhi moved from passive resistance to *Satyagraha*. He addressed several meetings. Gandhi defended the arrested people. The British Indian Association decided to send yet another delegation to England. The BIC asked the Colonial Secretary not to arrest the members of the delegation. The Colonial Secretary feigned ignorance about the delegation; Gandhi repudiated his claim.

Gandhi and Habib left Johannesburg for Cape Town en route to England. In the mean time all attempts to a reasonable settlement were dashed against the obdurate stance of the colonial administration. Polak left Natal en route to India.

On June 2, Sir Curzon Wyllie was assassinated by Madan Lal Dhingra in London. In a meeting of Indian students held in London under the presidentship of Surendranath Banerjee Gandhi condemned Wyllie's murder. Nagappan discharged from Johannesburg jail died within a week. Nagappan was given public funeral by Indians. BIA requested the Government of India to intervene and help remove the offending laws from the statute books of Natal and Transvaal colonies.

Gandhi had become a popular name in India. Bengal Provincial Congress Committee proposed his name for the next president of the Indian National Congress. Gandhi and Hajee Habib reached London on July 10; they were interviewed by South African Associated Press Agency. They met Ritch, Abdul Caadir, Sir Muncherjee Bhownaggaree, Lord Ampthill. Back in South Africa, six Indians were deported from Transvaal, and ghee was no longer given to prisoners. Natal Indians addressed petition to Secretary of State for Colonies regarding the grievances related to indenture, franchise, trade, etc. Habib Muslim Society held a mass meeting to express sympathy with Transvaal deputation. British Indian League Cape Town also adopted a resolution urging government to give sympathetic consideration to Transvaal deputation. A similar meeting was held by Indians in Johannesburg at the Hamidia Mosque.

On July 14 Gandhi met Ameer Ali and H.E.A. Cotton, editor of *India*, Sir Richard Soloman and Lord Ampthill. Among those who called on Gandhi during the week was Sir William Lee-Warner. Public meeting was held in Pretoria urging the imperial Government to give sympathetic hearing; 14 Indians were deported from Transvaal to India. In the mean time a public enquiry into circumstances leading to Nagappan's death commenced.

Gandhi wrote to Gokhale to help Polak do his work as scheduled on July 23. Gandhi and Habib met Lord Morley. House of Lords debated and passed second reading of Union Bill. Gandhi attended the Suffragette meeting at St. James Hall. Natal delegation arrived in London on July 31. Gandhi wrote a letter to Lord Ampthill repudiating the charge that the Transvaal movement was instigated and financed from India and that it had anything to do with violence.

On August 10, a deputation on behalf of the Coloured Peoples and Natives under the leadership of Scheiner met member of the House of Commons who assured support for the amendments proposed by Gandhi. In the mean time Gandhi sought Lord Crewe's intervention to prevent any further deportation of Indians. Gandhi formula was sent to General Smuts. The inquiry into the circumstances of Nagappan's death did not satisfy the Indians. No settlement was visible by September 10. 80 Chinese passive resisters were arrested. Back home in India a large number of meetings were addressed by Polak acquainting the people about the *satyagraha* in South Africa and its successes. Gandhi and Habib promised to Lord Crewe that if theoretical right of entry were acceded to, the *satyagraha* would be called off. On September 22, a meeting of the Chinese passive resisters held at Johannesburg decided to continue the movement and sympathized with the deputation.

In India Polak went around the country, met opinion leaders and apprised the people through meetings and discussions the work being done by Gandhi and his associates in South Africa and England. Gandhi wrote to Tolstoy about the passive resistance movement. He got the reply through a 'Letter to a Hindoo.' In a letter to Polak, Gandhi advised Indians to carefully observe the passive resistance movement he had launched and try to launch a similar movement in India. Gandhi decided to educate people about the Transvaal situation and published 2000 copies of 'Statement of Transvaal Case.' The Whites opposed the abolition of indentured labour as that would adversely affect them.

On October 14 Gandhi wrote to Polak expressing his views on 'Modern Civilisation' which were later elaborated in Hind *Swaraj*. The *satyagraha* continued unabated in South Africa and several of the leaders and commoners were arrested and rearrested. On November 13, the Transvaal Indian deputation (Gandhi and Habib) decided to return to South Africa. The same day an attempt was made at Ahmedabad to assassinate Lord Minto, Viceroy of India.

While on board S.S. Kildonan Castle, Gandhi wrote *Hind Swaraj* on ship stationery between November 13 and 22. He also wrote prefaces to the Gujarati and English versions of 'Letter to a Hindoo. 'In the House of Lords, the Colonial Secretary announced the efforts being made to resolve the Transvaal entry issue. Arrived at Cape Town on November 30, cabled Gokhale to thank Ratanji Tata for donating Rs. 25,00,000 for Transvaal struggle. The Colonial Secretary admitted in the House of Commons that a more stringent law than the one existing in Transvaal was there in Orange River Colony. He arrived at Johannesburg, gave an interview to the Reuter at Park Station. And told *The Star* that the theory of equality before law must be restored forthwith.

Thus far Gandhi was successful in creating public opinion in England as well as South Africa, India and America in favour of the Indian cause. He was not able to convince the governments to change the laws. But he kept the pressure on. The *satyagraha* continued in more intensified form. Success came in 1914. And then Gandhi left for India never to return again in flesh and blood.

1910

Churchill informed the House of Commons that instructions were issued to treat the passive resisters in jail humanly. Leo Tolstoy died on November 20. Indian National Congress meeting at Allahabad passed resolution on December 15 supporting the cause of Transvaal Indians. The *Satyagraha* continued.

1911

In Viceroy's Legislative Council in Calcutta, Indian government announced to prohibit further emigration of indentured Indians to Natal. The Chief Justice Lord de Velliers of the Supreme Court declared the expulsion order of Mahmud Chhotabhai as null and void and ordered the registered Asiatic right to get registration certificates. In London Duke of Connaught hoped for the early settlement of Indian question.

On April 22, Gandhi informed that passive resistance could be suspended if General Smuts gave some assurances. General Smuts in repay gave assurance to repeal Act 2 of 1907 (TARA) and that passive resisters would be released. Gandhi accepted the Provisional Settlement. Italy invaded Turkish territory.

1912

The African Political Organisation was inaugurated by Dr. Abdur Rehman. Gokhale arrived in Cape Town on October 22. He was received very warmly both by the official and unofficial circles. He returned to India via Mozambique and Zanzibar. Gandhi and Polak accompanied him up to Zanzibar and then returned to Cape Town via Dar-Es-Salaam. Wherever they went, they were warmly and respectfully received. There were serious differences of opinion between Botha and Hertzog during Gokhale's visit. Gandhi condemned terrorist attack on Lord Hardinge in Delhi.

1913

Harassment of Dayal Brothers and Gujjar, a Cape Indian by Cousins, a custom officer was severely criticized by Polak, A.M. Chachalia, *The Natal Mercury*, and many others. Cousins was replaced by Harry Smith. BIA was informed of the proposed withdrawal of prosecution against Dayal brothers.

Agitation against restrictions on the movement of Indians continued and many individual cases were taken to the court. Despite the promise to change the laws, nothing could be done because of the differences among the cabinet members. Gandhi agreed to suspend the passive resistance if General Smuts gave certain assurances. Smuts in reply reiterated his desire to bring forward amendments to the existing law removing restriction on the people of Asian origin. Gandhi decided to retire from public life after the announcement of the Provisional Settlement.

Smuts clarified the points raised by Gandhi and reiterated that: he would introduce a legislation during the following session which would repeal TARA; give right to minor children to enter with parents; give legal equality to all immigrants; passive resisters with valid claims to register but deported under TARA could apply for registration by December 31, 1911; Asiatics with valid cliaims to registration who left South Africa owing to passive resistance, though not deported, could apply for registration up to a limit of 30. About 180 Chinese and Indians who refused registration under voluntary system could apply by December 31, 1911; the seven Indians Gandhi had referred to would get permission to stay. Smuts requested Gandhi to accept the settlement. Gandhi agreed and gave a list of passive resisters to be released. Individual cases of harassment, however, continued.

1914

This was the last year of Gandhi in South Africa. Gandhi and C.F. Andrews left for Pretoria to meet General Smuts. Gandhi wrote to Gokhale expressing his desire to return to India and learn from him. He also wrote about the poor health of Kasturba and doubted her survival for too long. The Indian Relief Bill was passed. Gandhi addressed valedictory letters to Indians and paid tributes to all those who suffered and died for the noble cause of securing for coloured people the basic human rights.

On July 4, he took leave of Phoenix Settlement and left for Johannesburg en rout to India via London. At Cape Town he was taken in a huge procession. Left for England. Second World War broke out on August 4. Gandhi was given reception in hotel Cecil, London by English and Indian friends. Lala Lajpat Rai and Sarojini Naidu were among those present. Gandhi offered unconditional service to the Empire. Indian Volunteer Corps was formed and it started working near Southampton. He sailed for India on December 19 with Kasturba Gandhi.

APPENDIX-B

GLOSSARY OF TERMS USED IN *HIND SWARAJ*

Home Rule

Hind Swaraj has an alternate title, *i.e.* Indian Home Rule. In the first decade of the twentieth century, Indians wanted to get dominion status for India in the same way as Canada or South Africa had. Gandhi was involved in the struggle to get some basic rights for Indians in South Africa. He felt that one of the reasons why Indians were not respected in South Africa was the status of India in the British Empire as a colony. He, therefore, supported the demand for Home Rule or Self-Government, which the Congress Party was spearheading. There must have been an idea of total independence leading to the formation of a sovereign India, but the immediate goal was fixed as Home Rule.

Swaraj

Swaraj in political sense means self-government but Gandhi gave a far more comprehensive meaning to this term. First, even politically *Swaraj* means something more than just self-government; it means self-government that is in tune with Indian culture and tradition. Governance by indigenous people using foreign means and methods is not *Swaraj*. Second, *Swaraj* also means self-control. Each individual has to be a *Swaraj*ist, *i.e.* a person who is trained to have control over his senses, animal passions and instincts. Real *Swaraj* is possible only if people become Swarajists; then alone they can evolve real *Swaraj*.

To illustrate his point Gandhi has given the example of Italy, which after gaining independence from Austria remained the same. It did not change as Mazzini had desired; it remained Austrian in governance with Italian rulers. If India too got her Home Rule and continued with British methods and values of governance, it would not amount to *Swaraj*.

History

Real history is the record of the progress humanity makes to reach its destiny. And the destiny is moral superiority. Man must get over the animal instincts and sensual urges to become superhuman morally (not physically). He must replace brute force with soul force or force of love. History must tell the story of this journey: the victories and failures; the causes and consequences; and the factors and forces involved.

The history as we have today suffers from two flaws. First, it is a record of wars and conflicts, which are really interruptions in the flow of the main currents of true history. Second it lays so much emphasis on emperors and kings and other political leaders and their deeds that interrupted historical flow that what the masses did and suffered remained neglected.

According to Gandhi, one of the reasons for the above flaws is the writing of history of the world by the Europeans. They looked at the history of other nations in the light of their own civilisation and whatever did not fit their scheme of things and thinking was branded as backward and primitive. So moral values were branded as primitive values. Wars were justified and so were industrialization, colonization, and even mass murders. Millions of people were shot dead and all this was justified in the name of religion, self-defence, progress, and politics.

Modern Civilisation

Gandhi considered Modern civilisation as the fountainhead of all evils. Modern civilisation should not be equated with Western civilisation although Gandhi uses the words interchangeably. Gandhi was all appreciative of Greek and Roman civilisations and he considered Christianity to be a great religion and Christ an embodiment of love, compassion, charity and sacrifice. Any civilisation based on these civilisations and religions could not be treated as Satanic or a representative of Black Age (*Kaliyuga*).

By modern civilisation Gandhi meant the modern Industrial Civilisation which in his view had no affinity to older civilisations of

Europe. Modern civilisation was an interruption in the man's progress towards *Swaraj*; towards a true civilisation based on truth and nonviolence. As such modern civilisation has yet to come; it is still in the womb of time. Gandhi considered this civilisation to a nine days wonder. He agreed with an English writer who called modern civilisation a disease.

True Civilisation

Gandhi considered Indian civilisation a true civilisation because as far as its tendencies are concerned it still aims at moral uplift of man and has all those characteristics, which inspire man to return to the path of sanity. Indian civilisation is marked by continuity and hence its original values have remained intact even if blurred. The mind has not changed even if the mind set has changed.

A true civilisation would carry man towards peace and harmony; towards love and compassion; and towards *Vasudhaiva kutumbakam*. In a true civilisation human dignity would never be trampled and therefore the nacked inequality that prevails in modern society would be a thing of the past.

By giving a new definition to civilisation, Gandhi gave a new meaning to progress, which in modern terminology is called development. Development does not mean economic progress, nor does it mean improvements in body welfare. Progress means moral progress and hence economic development can only be a supporting means of true development. It cannot be called development.

Patriotism

Patriotism in common parlance means love of one's country and readiness to sacrifice for it. The patriotic people would never harm the interests of their nation. Gandhi however gave a different meaning to patriotism. The first charge for any individual or group of people is to serve all that is living, specially the human beings. Nothing should be done that would harm the people no matter who they are. A patriotic person would thus love the nature and all that constitutes the nature including all human beings.

Brute Force

Brute force is equivalent to violence. Animals use their brute force to settle their quarrels. Human being use their muscle power or brainpower to settle scores. They invent weapons of various kinds to kill each other and now have in their possession the weapons of mass destruction. They are now in a position to destroy all life on planet earth.

The physical force used to defeat the opponent or to take revenge against an adversary is called brute force. This force could be of three types: first, to think of hurting someone; two, to say something that hurts someone; and three, to physically hurt someone with the intention of giving him pain.

Use of brute force is one of the main characteristics of modern civilisation. It is civilisation, which is full of conflicts of various kinds and the means used to resolve the conflicts is brute force. War is the extreme case of brute force and of course the use of atomic power the penultimate.

Soul Force/Force of Love

Soul force is the opposite of brute force. Soul is full of love for it unites all living things into a common Great Soul (*Parmatma*) and therefore it cannot hate anything. Soul force wins over brute force by self-sacrifice rather than by hurting or killing the opponent. Modern civilisation, according to Gandhi, is one, which is imbued with soul force or love force.

Gandhi used passive resistance, which later developed into *Satyagraha* as a means to resolve conflicts. The best example of soul force was the sufferings Jesus Christ underwent to save the perpetrators of injustice from hell. Lord Ram's abdication of the thrown of Ayodhya in favour of his younger brother respecting the desire of his parents and all the sufferings he went through is also an example of soul force.

Duty

Duties indicate what one owes to the community or society in which one lives. No one would be what he is, but for the contribution that the family, community and larger society makes. It is the responsibility of each and every individual to return the debt he or she owes to the society. Unfortunately, there is tendency to forget one's duties and insist on securing one's rights. This is more so in modern times.

In a civilised world, duties would be more important than rights. There is competition among the people in securing rights. Force is also used to secure rights. But competition is the performance of once duties can only produce positive results. If all perform their duties the rights of all would be fully secured.

Means and Ends

While exhorting people to follow the path of nonviolence, he said "The means may be likened to a seed of a tree; and there is just the same inviolable connection between the means and the end as there is between the seed and the tree." Gandhi has repeatedly said that violence breeds violence and so long as man uses violence as a means to settle his disputes, he would continue to suffer violence.

Gandhi also said that means and ends are not discrete; they constitute a continuum and hence they are interdependent. What is means for one becomes the end for others and *vice versa* is also true. For example, killing a person may be an end for one but it can also be a means to secure wealth. That is the reason why Gandhi said that both means and ends must be pure. One cannot achieve pure ends by impure means.

Voluntary Poverty

'Simple living and high thinking' is the hallmark of Indian civilisation. It does not mean that man should live in poverty; it means that man should not lead a luxurious life because it would have adverse effects on his health, would deprive others of their basic needs, and would adversely affect ecology and environment. Man should try to develop his economy but he should limit his consumption level so that he neither deprives others of their rights nor adversely affects the ecology and environment. A well developed person is one who is full of love and compassion for others yet at the same time he has all that is needed to keep his body and mind in good health and good care; not the one who has all the wealth and luxury but is greedy and self-centred.

Competition

One of the main traits of modern civilisation is competition. Everyone is in competition against everyone else. It is presumed that competition ensures efficiency and makes people work hard. Gandhi was not against competition as such but he wanted it to be limited to higher values of life such as love, affection, compassion, sacrifice, charity etc. In mundane matters related to production and consumption of goods and services, cut-throat competition is harmful to one's own progress and the progress of the society as a whole. Instead, people should opt for cooperation for it engenders fellow feeling and a sense of participation.

Equality

There is lot of misconception about Gandhi's concept of equality. He has used this concept in two different ways in *Hind Swaraj*. First, he says that all should get the same wages irrespective of the work they do. So the job of a scavenger is in no way inferior to the job of a doctor or a lawyer. A lawyer has become a lawyer because the society gave him the opportunity to study law. In fact his studies were subsidized by the society and the scavenger too had to contribute to his study.

But this was Gandhi's long-term objective. His immediate objective was to bring equality among all people in matters of basic needs: food, clothing, shelter, education, health, security and self-esteem. All these needs must be met at a level a society can afford. Let the people have more wealth than they need but excess wealth should be treated as trust property; that should not be used for luxury and anti-culture.

Bread Labour

Gandhi developed the concept of *bread labour* to indicate the need for each and every individual to participate in both production and consumption of the basic needs. Modern civilisation encouraged or rather forced specialization. Some people like farmers produced the food grains; part of it was consumed by the farmers themselves but the bulk of it was consumed by the non-agriculturalists such as professionals, industrial labour and so. This tendency produced the feeing of low and high on the one hand and distanced the consumers from producers and the production processes on the other.

Gandhi therefore suggested that in a ideal situation all should be prosumers, to use Elvin Toffler's term, and then alone a semblance of equality, fellow feeling, and respect for work irrespective of its nature would emerge. Gandhi, in his Ashrams, made people do the job they considered to be lowly such as scavenging.

True Knowledge

Knowledge is the synthesis of information to derive certain general principles. It also comes from intuition. Gandhi distinguished ordinary knowledge from true knowledge. True knowledge is one that makes Homo sapiens superhuman morally. Ordinary knowledge helps man take care of his body needs and to manage himself and his environment. In Gandhian praxis true knowledge leads man to know his Maker, Beyond the ordinary and true knowledge is false knowledge which parades itself as knowledge but takes man down physiologically, psychologically and morally.

Referring to the communal clashes between Hindus and Muslims, Gandhi tells in *Hind Swaraj* that God of both the communities is the same. "Hindus and Mohammedens in India own the same ancestors and the same blood runs through their veins. Do people become enemies because they change their religion?" ...religions are different roads converging to the same point. What does it matter that we take different roads so long as all roads lead to the same destination? "...the more we advance in true knowledge, the better we shall understand that we need not be at war with those whose religion we may not follow."

India as a Nation

Gandhi did not agree with the modern concept of a nation. He subscribed to cultural, not political, foundation of nationhood. India according to him was a nation from times immemorial. Its boundaries were fixed by physical geography: from Kashmir in the North to Kanyakumari in the South and from Afghanistan in the West to Arakan Mountains in the East. Any change in this naturally carved nation has not lasted for too long. Coalescing is the general tendency.

Within this nation several religions and peoples carved out their own niche without any conflict. India has always been a multi-ethnic, multi-religious and multi-cultural nation. The beauty of India lies in its broadmindedness; its capacity to assimilate and absorb while giving enough freedom for each individual and group to maintain its identity. Variety, not disparity, is the essence of Indian civilisation.

Swadeshi

Swadeshi means use of one's own ideas, ideals and products. One should not go after foreign things, *i.e.* things which are not our own. One should adhere to one's own religion. If there are some defects in it, one should try to remove those defects. He considered conversion to some other religion as sin. Similarly, one should not discard one's own culture and civilisation. Any defect in it should be eradicated. Extending further, one should use things made at home and produced locally. The idea is to be as self-reliant as possible. More a person is dependent on others, less free he is.

Having said this Gandhi did not want to make a fetish of Swadeshi. It would be foolish to try to produce everything everywhere. Only such things should be produced which can be produced in a given geographical setting. Those things, which cannot be produced, should be bartered from neighbourhood. It is important that the neighbours should also prosper and hence first priority should go to the neighbours. What cannot be produced locally, and in the neighbourhood, should be imported from other parts of the country and the things that cannot be produced within the country should be imported from abroad.

We should not reject a thing only because it has been imported from foreign countries because the foreigners too are our brothers and sisters. So Gandhi wanted a very different kind of globalization. His globalization had the individual and the locality in the centre and the globe in the periphery whereas the modern concept of globalization has globe in the center and the individual, family and locality in the periphery.

Machinery

Gandhi appears to be totally against machinery, another name for technology, in *Hind Swaraj* because "Machinery has begun to desolate Europe. Ruination is now knocking at the English gates. Machinery is the chief symbol of modern civilisation; it represents a great sin.... It is machinery that has impoverished India. It is difficult to measure the harm that Manchester has done to us. It is due to Manchester that Indian handicraft has all but disappeared." Machinery is like a snake-hole which may contain from one to a hundred snakes.

The above statements do not however fully represent Gandhi's views on machinery. He was against machine mentality more than against machinery and blamed its misuse to the detriment of human welfare. In 1921, he remarked that he was not trying to destroy all machines and mills. He was only trying to contain its use so that the sufferings of the people is minimized. People would have to be converted to true civilisation only then the mechanical mentality would go. And once the mentality is off, the use of machinery would remain limited to only where it was needed most. "It is not to be conceived that all men will do all these things at one time or that some men will give up all machine made things at once. But if the thought is sound, we shall always find out what we can give up and gradually cease to use it. What a few may do, others will copy; and the movement will grow like the coconut of the mathematical problem. What the leaders do, the populace will gladly do in turns.

The first priority of Gandhi was the satisfaction of basic human needs. Machinery that displaced people from work, that could be used to destroy human dignity and freedom and that generated mechanical mentality and made humans less human was rejected by Gandhi. The machine that lightened human drudgery and enabled man to serve others better was however welcomed by him. It was not the machine that Gandhi rejected, it was the ulterior motive behind its construction and use that he rejected.

Railways

Gandhi was critical of railways for a number of reasons but the most fundamental reason was speed, which hindered face-to-face communication and kept human mind disturbed. Railways along with doctors and lawyers had impoverished India for the foreign goods would have not reached the masses but for the rapid movement of goods by the railways, nor would have the Indian natural resources gone out of the country. According to him, railways were responsible for the spread of bubonic plague in the country; they had increased the frequency of famines; and they enabled evil persons to move from place to place.

In this connection one has to see Gandhi's views on railways in the context of his total philosophy with respect to human habitat. ".... Man is so made by nature as to require him to restrict his movements as far as his hands and feet will take him. If we did not rush about from place to place by means of railways and such other maddening conveniences, much of the confusion that arises would be obviated.

Our difficulties are of our own creation. God set a limit to man's locomotive ambition in the construction of his body. Man immediately proceeded to discover means of overriding the limit.... I am so constructed that I can only serve my immediate neighbours, but in my conceit I pretend to have discovered that I must with my body serve every individual in the universe. In thus attempting the impossible, man comes in contact with different natures, different religions, and is utterly confounded." Railways help man break this natural barrier.

Gandhi was a votary of small communities composed of families engaged in self-employing creative activities: agricultural and non-agricultural. Such communities would be marked with stability more than with fast movement. Anything that disturbs the stability of communities beyond a given limit must be considered undesirable, overred Gandhi.

Doctors

Gandhi was very critical of modern medicine and its practitioners. Gandhi's views in this respect have proved right. Despite great strides medical science has made, it has failed to serve the common man. It is so costly and inaccessible that its benefits generally go to only those who are economically better off. Moreover, it has not succeeded in making people more healthy than what they were before this system was introduced in India. Modern medicine is curative. It does have preventive aspects too but the objective is to administer medicines in the body to develop artificial immunity from a given disease. Thus the main concern of modern medicine is curing diseases. Gandhi decried this tendency and suggested that the job of the doctor is to help people maintain good health and to develop natural immunity against diseases.

"Doctors have almost unhinged us. Sometimes I think that quacks are better than highly qualified doctors." They have made people unconcerned about their health and lead a patently unhealthy style of life.

Lawyers

While criticizing the lawyers for promoting litigation, Gandhi was critical of the whole judicial system. "My firm opinion is that lawyers have enslaved India, have accentuated Hind-Mohammedan dissensions and have confirmed English authority." If they had done any good service to the nation, it was not because they were lawyers but because they were patriots. They side with their clients irrespective of what the client has done. If they do not do so, they would not be considered good lawyers. And thus they advance quarrels instead of repressing them. "Moreover, men take up that profession, not in order to help others out of their miseries but to enrich themselves. It is one of the avenues of becoming wealthy and their interest exists in multiplying disputes.... The chief thing to be remembered is that without lawyers courts could not have been established or conducted and without the latter the English could not rule.... What I have said with reference to the pleaders necessarily applies to the judges; they are first cousins; and the one gives strength to the other."

Education

"The ordinary meaning of education is knowledge of letters. To teach boys reading, writing and arithmetic is called primary education.... Carried away by the flood of western thought we came to the conclusion, without weighing pros and cons that we should give this kind of education to the people." And then he says that he did not intend to run down the knowledge of letters in all circumstances, what is important to realise that such an education is only a tool. In the hands of a good person, it will do good while in the hands of bad person it will be prove dangerous. Thus the first charge of education must be character building.

Once the character is built, even higher education will conform to what Professor Huxley has said: "That man I think has liberal education who has been so trained in youth that his body is the ready servant of his will and does with ease and pleasure all the work that as a mechanism it is capable of; whose intellect is a clear, cold, logic engine with all its parts of equal strength and in smooth working order.... whose mind is stored with a knowledge of the fundamental truths of nature ...whose passions are trained to come to heel by a vigorous will, the servant of tender conscience ...Who has learnt to hate all vileness and to respect others as himself. Such a one and no other, I conceive, has had liberal education, for he is in harmony with nature. He will make the best of her and she of him."

Gandhi pleaded for religious, that is, ethical education as the first and necessary component of education. To this then should be added various kinds of scientific and other knowledge; and the two should be backed by the training of the hand to create and produce things to earn one's livelihood.

Religion

Gandhi was a religious man. He lamented that India under the shadow of modern civilisation was becoming irreligious. He, however, equated religion with ethics, which were common to all institutionalized religions. In this respect, Gandhi could be compared to Kabir who drew from all religions to advocate a life full of faith in God and full adherence to reason. In fact Gandhi believed in the religion of all religions. He considered various institutionalized religions as different paths to arrive at a common point *i.e.* God or self-realization.

Gandhi called himself a *Sanatani* Hindu but he never visited temples. Yet at the same time he never asked anyone to visit or not to visit a temple. Man was free to see God in the way his inner voice dictated. He did not distinguish between temples, churches, mosques and other places of worship. And thus Gandhi believed in a universal religion. He had equal respect for all religions and all religious books. He did not consider religious books to be the works of God; they are the works of inspired men and women and hence they cannot be considered infallible. They are time and place specific and hence their rituals differ but the core ethical principles common to all religions are eternal. Gandhi believed in those principles

Gandhi considered religious conversion unethical and sinful. Religion being only a way to reach God, various cultures carved out different routes, which later took the form of institutionalized religion. All religions are therefore true. Anyone who calls his religion to be more true than other religions or the name he has given to his God superior to the names given by others, then he must be an irreligious person. If God is common to all religions, how can a person adhering to a particular religion be converted to another? A truly religious person would have the respect for other religions as he has for his own and help his co-religionists to find the path of salvation within his own religion.

He quoted saint poet Tulsidas to bring home his point of view in this regard. " 'Of religion, pity, or love, is the root...Therefore, we should not abandon pity so long as we are alive.' I believe in it as much as I believe in two and two being four. The force of love is the same as the force of the soul or truth. We have evidence of its working every step. The universe would disappear without the existence of that force."

Passive Resistance

Gandhi borrowed the term 'Passive Resistance' from Count Tolstoy. It means opposing whatever is evil without use of physical force, *i.e.* by soul force; self-suffering. "Everybody admits that sacrifice of self is infinitely superior to sacrifice of others. Moreover, if this kind of force is used in a cause that is unjust, only the person using it suffers. He does not make others suffer for his mistake. It implies that one should break the laws, which are unjust and be prepared to undergo the punishment for breaking the law.

Gandhiji later used *Satyagraha* in place of passive resistance as the latter did not express the philosophy behind the use of soul force or love force fully. *Satyagraha* has an element of force applied to the soul of the opponent; brute force is applied to the body of the opponent. *Satyagraha* has the element of pro-activeness, not passiveness. By *Satyagraha* one wants to win over the opponent; to bring him to one's side by self-suffering or sacrifice.

Passive resistance is not the weapon of the weak; it needs far more training, will power and self-control than the use of physical force. Its great quality lies in the fact that it can be used by men as well as and women, children as well as adults, rich as well as poor, and strong as well as weak with same effectiveness; it is accessible to one and all. It "is an all-sided sword; it can be used anyhow; it blesses him who uses it and him against whom it is used. Without drawing a drop of blood it produces far reaching results. It never rusts and cannot be stolen. Competition between passive resisters does not exhaust. The sword of passive resistance does not require a scabbard."

"After a great deal of experience it seems to me that those who want to become passive resisters for the service of the country have to observe perfect chastity, adopt poverty, follow truth and cultivate fearlessness."

Parliamentary Democracy

Gandhi's ultimate goal was *Swaraj* but he knew that the Swaraj of his concept was not easy to achieve. Even Gandhi was not able to achieve Swaraj in full. His immediate and short-term goal was Home Rule through parliamentary democracy on Canadian pattern, which later was converted into full independence. Gandhi was not enamoured by parliamentary democracy as practiced in England. He had some choicest words to use against the British Parliament. Further, he did not consider the decision of the majority to be necessarily right. "It is a superstition and ungodly thing to believe that an act of a majority binds a minority. Many examples can be given in which acts of majorities will be found to have been wrong and those of minorities to have been right. All reforms owe their origin to the initiation of minorities in opposition to majorities. If among a band of robbers a knowledge of robbing is obligatory, is a pious man to accept the obligation?"

Gandhi equated the British Parliament with sterile women and prostitute (later he withdrew these words when a lady friend protested to him) because it neither produced anything worth reckoning nor could it function freely. He agreed with Carlyle's remark that it was 'the talking shop of the world.' He therefore warned that "If India copies England, it is my firm conviction that she will be ruined." He worked for parliamentary democracy because he gave priority to freeing India from the British rule and thus to create appropriate opportunities to work for real democracy based on consensus rather majority and minority rule with village community as the basic organisational unit.

Human Dignity

Gandhi believed in the principle of *Vasudhaiva Kutumbakam* but considered man to be a very special case in the evolutionary process still on. While other species of life depended on the environment for evolution, man depended on himself. He decides his evolutionary course. He has the intelligence and power to destroy all life on planet earth; he also has the Soul or Love Force to transform the earth into a heavenly abode.

He believed in the Universal Soul, which could be called God, which pervaded all that is living and non-living. All living things therefore deserved respect, care and attention. Human beings the most evolved of the species possess a higher form of dignity, which must be recognized and respected. Violation of human dignity, in his view, is a sin for it comes in the way of self-realization.

The modern civilisation fails to respect human dignity. Man becomes a tool, a means to achieve 'progress'. In a society where there are poor and rich, low and high, weak and powerful, human dignity is trampled at every step. Gandhi wanted a new society based on moral values to ensure human dignity and universal brotherhood.

Village

Hind Swaraj and subsequent writings of Gandhi call for a village based society. Simple living and high thinking and ethical life can be better ensured in villages. Gandhi's village was not however the villages as India had at Gandhi's time or it has today. He considered a good village to have about a thousand persons, which in current situation would amount to about 5,000 persons. The village will be self-governing and based on Swadeshi spirit. It will have its own architect, engineer, teacher, doctor and what not. It would be a most modern community. Gandhi's village is yet to come into being. It is an idea, a practical idea; an idea, which can bring real *Swaraj*.

City

Gandhi was not against cities; he was against city life. All that is undesirable, Gandhi thought, was there in the city. City was a product of the modern civilisation and since modern civilisation was Kalyugi or Satanic, its product could not be humanistic. He did not, however, want the cities to be destroyed. City means people and their activities. Destruction of cities means the destruction of the people who lived there and their livelihood.

He has hinted at a solution. The cities can be decentralized and organically linked to villages. Each neighbourhood could function as a village; thus cities could become collection of villages organically linked horizontally and vertically.

Index

Abdulla, Dada 104, 106
Acclimatization 224
Acidification of Rain 220
Adam Smith 57, 59, 97–98
Adulteration 62
Advaita Philosophy 263
Agricultural
 Age 307
 Revolution 298
Agro-Industrial Development 383
Ahimsa 65
Ahimsa Parmodharmah, Culture of 135
AIDS 335
Akbar 145
All-India Political Conference 158
Amazon Basin Forests 219
Ambedkar, Bhimrao 155, 171
American Attack on Iraq 96
Anand Milk Union Ltd. (Amul) 382
Anti-Asiatic Legislative Acts 114
Aristotle 192
Arrival of Shankaracharya 142
Arunachala Holy Hill 185
Arundel Society 195
Arya Samaj 148, 176, 187
Aryan
 Invasion 130
 Path Symposium 240
ASEAN Countries 308
Ashramite Schools 40
Asian Societies 292
Asiatic
 Act 117
 Circles 108
Asoka's Kalinga War 14
Astronomers 214
Atom Bomb 39
Aurangzeb 146

Banaras Hindu University 63, 96
Bande Matram 160, 164, 176
Banerjee, Surendranath 110, 158
Basic Education 370
Bateson, Gregory 279
Bell, Daniel 306
Besant, Annie 4, 103, 183–84, 260
BHU Foundation Day Speech 63
BIMARU States 311
Bio-Cybernetic Laws 217–18, 225
Biological
 Principles 79
 Weapons 40
Bio-Safety 59
Black Age 27, 409
Blavatsky, Helena P. 206
Boer War 110–11, 113
Bolshevik Revolution 47, 329
Bombay Municipal Corporation 155
Bose Vigyan Mandir 179
Bose, Mrinalini 163
Bose, Sir Jagadish Chandra 179
Bose, Subhas Chandra 97, 155, 177, 268
Brahmin Widows 171
Brahmo Samaj 148, 158, 160, 176
Bread Labour 413
Bribery 62
British
 Commonwealth 157
 Raj 95, 126
 Settlement 147

Brute Force 410
Buddhism 136, 142–43
Burning of Registration Certificates 117

Capra, F. 222
Central Village 378
Centralization to Decentralization 309
Chandravarkar, Sir Narayan 156
Chapman, J. 198
Character Building 370
Charkha 76
Chatterjee, Bankim Chandra 175
Chattopadhyay, V. 168
Chauhan, Prithviraj 141, 143
Chemical Weapons 39
Chinese Boycott of American Goods 149
Christ, Jesus 338
Christian
- Civilisation 23, 195
- Socialism 195
- Theology 190

Christianity 62, 120, 294
Civil
- Disobedience 173, 200
- Rights Movement 22
- War 298

Civilisations of Rome 60
Civilised Nations 286
Classical
- Age 139
- Factory 298

Clive, Robert 147
Cofounder of International Documental Centre 300
Cold War 298
Colonial Government 238
Columbus 94
Company Bahadur 328
Company of Merchants 146
Company Raj to British Raj 146
Concept of Alternative Development 81
Conflict Resolution 65
Confusianism 291
Congress Party 96
Constitutional Amendment 379
Cooperative Movement 381
Cosmic Law 3, 33, 92, 122, 133–34, 214–15, 272, 275, 322, 361, 374
Count Tolstoy 193
Crusoe, Robinson 381
Cultural Revolution 292

D.A.V. College Movement 161
Dark Age 296
Darwin's Theory of Evolution 27, 71, 80, 270, 283
Das Kapital 254
Das, Taraknath 168
Deccan College 159
De-Emphasising Luxuries 82
Deen-E-Ilahi 94, 145
Deschooling Society 300
Destroying Trades 62
Development Centre 378
Dhingra, Shaheed Madanlal 119
Divide and Rule 173
Downfall of Capitalism 97
Dutt, R.C. 126, 153

East India Company 126, 147, 174
Ecological
- Crisis 44
- Disturbances 232
- Hazard 226
- Problems 277

Economic Equality 75
Edward Carpenter 200
Egyptian Civilisations 130
Election Commission 365
Electoral Reforms 362
Elphinstone College 155, 169–70
Emerson, Ralph Waldo 197
Energy Conservation 228
English Settlement 147
Entropy Law 284–85

Environmental
Destruction 281, 316
Pollution 231
Equality and Human Dignity 359, 413
Eternal and Universal Messages 320
European
Civilisation 30, 292, 353
Mills 9
Renaissance 48, 283

Ferguson College 157
First Cultural Transformation 297
Food Corporation of India 109
Forced Technology 307
Frederick Soddy 242
French Revolution 299, 329
Furgusson College 159

Gambling 62
Gandhara School of Art 139
Gandhi Peace Foundation 258
Gandhi, Rajiv 379
Gandhi, Mahatama
Post-Modernism of 52
Life, Events in 385
Gandhian Economics 57
Gandhian Institute of Studies 259
Gandhian Model of Development 258
Gandhian Modernism 27
Gandhian Solution 348
Gandhi-Bose Controversy 264, 269
Gandhigram Model, 77
Ganga Valley 133
Geetanjali 176
General Smuts 118
General Theory of Human Progress 216
Ghosh, Arobindo 149
Ghosh, Sri Aurobindo 162
Giuseppe Mazzini 204
Global
Agenda for Action 344
Swaraj 22
Thinking 78
Village 346
Wars 286
Globalization 54
God of Materialism 61
Gokhale, Gopal Krishna 112, 152, 157
Gram Swaraj 78
Planning for 378
Grand Trunk Road 145
Great Divides 345
Green Revolution 159, 382
Growth without Development 45
Gulamgiri (Slavery) 171
Gupta, Sugata Sen 258

Harappan Civilisation 131
Hierarchies to Networking 310
Hind Swaraj 96, 121, 130, 158, 188
Contemporary Relevance of 21
Objectives of Writing 13
Themes of 80
Understanding 4
Writing of 101
Hinduism 142, 331
Agility of 143
Hobhouse, Emily 207
Holistic Development 376
Home League Society 161
Home Rule 253, 408
Homo Sapiens 65, 84, 275
House of Commons 21, 115, 156
Human Dignity 66, 421
Human Rights 82, 218
Hunter, William Wilson 60
Hussain, Saddam 348
Hutton, James 274
Hydrogen Bomb 39

Imperial
Government 118
Legislative Council 173
Independent Labour Party 103
Indian Ambulance Corps 110
Indian Association 158
Indian Civil Service 158, 175, 180, 202
Indian Home Rule 121, 240
Indian Legislative Council 159

Indian National Army 268
Indian National Congress 11, 107–08, 110, 115, 149–50, 155, 158–59, 161, 177, 240, 258, 364, 384
Indian National Movement 249
Individualism 294
Indus Valley 132
Indus-Saraswati Civilisation 130
Industrial
  Civilisation 51, 92, 121–22, 195, 217, 297
  Revolution 2, 27, 190, 231, 298, 309, 336, 349, 362
  to Information Society 306
Industrialism 43, 336
Information
  Age 300
  Revolution 298, 349
  Technology 43, 54, 77
Inner Temple (Law School) 103
Institute of
  Conflict Research 268
  Development Studies 300
Institutional Help to Self Help 306, 310
Institutionalization of Religion 34–36
International Food Policy Research Institute (IFPRI) 58
Iqbal, Mohammad Allamah 178
Ishopnishad 73

Jainism 136, 143

Kabir 212
Kalam, A.P.J. Abdul 379
Kapoor, Jagadish 337
Karma 137
Kashi Vishwanath Temple 63
Khan, Jenghij 145
Khan, Sir Syed Ahmed 174
Khilji, Allauddin 144
Kildonan, S.S. 5, 120

Laden, Osama Bin 47
Lahore Congress 239
Lahore Session 107
Law of
  Biology 277
  Life 92
  Love 92, 250, 272
  Nature 134
  Species 218
  Species 272, 275, 361
  Spiritual Evolution 251
  Truth 92, 213
League of Rich Nations 43
Liberal Constitutionalists 155
Lobbying Mission to England 114
Lodi Dynasty 145
Lodi, Ibrahim 145
Lok Sevak Sangh 384
London 147
London Vegetarian Society 103
Lord Ampthill 120, 201
Lord Curzon 112
Lord Ripon 106–07
Loss of
  Ecological Balance 347
  Spirituality 347

Macintyre, William 56
Madame Blavatskey 103, 241
Madras Presidency 171
Magna Carta 4, 46, 270
Maine, Henry James Sumner 198
Malaviya, Madan Mohan 172
Mal-Distribution of Natural Resources 233
Man-Nature Relationship 231
Marshall Mcluhan 277
Material
  Developments 335, 375
  Progress 124
  Prosperity 88
  Welfare 41
Maurya, Chandragupta 137, 139
Max Muller 103
Max Nordau 204
Mazumdar, H.T. 240
Mechanical Mentality 36

Mechanization 38, 324
Medieval India 140
Mehta, Ferozshah 152, 157
Mesolithic 131
Message of
    Charkha 177
    Hind Swaraj 89
Mexican War 200
Micropolitan Development 383
Mill, J.S. 126, 200, 261
Minto-Morley Reforms 150
Mir Alam 117
Mir Jafar 147
Mir Kasim 147
Model of New Civilisation 314
Modern Civilisation 42, 71, 73, 82, 215, 409
    Characteristics of 32
Modern Communication System 316
Modern Industrial Civilisation 12, 24, 290
Modernisation 292
Modernization of Poverty 303
Moghul Empire 145
Mohammad of Ghazni 143
Mohammad-Bin-Tughlaq 144
Mohammedan Anglo Oriental College 174
Molteno, Elizabeth M. 208
Money Crops 76
Montegu-Chemsford Reform 159, 203
Moral Development 216
Muir Central College 60, 63, 96
Muslim League 150, 178

Nai Talim (Basic Education) 41
Naidu, Sarojini 208
Naoroji, Dadabhai 107, 115, 152, 155, 157
Natal Law Society 106
Natal Supreme Court 106
National Agenda for Action 355
National Economy to World Economy 306, 308
National Social Conference 170
Nationalism 293
Native Education Society 155
Natural Law 133
Nawab Siraj-Ud-Daula 147
Nazi Germany 244
Nehru, Jawaharlal 155, 177, 364
Neolithic Peoples 131
Non-Cooperation Movement 161, 173
Non-violence 67, 190, 355
    Weapon of 95
    Movement 70, 206
Nur Jehan 146

Oommen, T.K. 262
OPEC 299
Organisation of Indian Students 162

Pal, Bipin Chandra 160
Paleolithic 131
Panchayati Raj Institutions 360, 362, 379
Parliament of Religions 181
Parliamentary Democracy 421
Passive Resistance 420
Path of Self-Realization 35
Patriotism 53, 410
Period of Great Confusion in India 144
Phoenix Settlement 111, 118, 194, 268
Phule, Mahatma Jyotiba 171, 187
Plato 191
Pluralism 294
Political
    Swaraj 16
    Thinkers 152
Post-Cold War 291
Post-Gandhian 336
Post-Industrial Civilisation 289
Post-Modern Third Wave 1
Post-modernism 48, 50, 53
    Vision of 51
Post-Second World War 305
Presidency College 179
Pretoria Jail 118
Prince of Wales 173
Principles of Morality 294

Rai, Lala Lajpat 160
Raman Maharshi 184
Raman, Sir C.V. 180
Ramaswamy, Periyar E.V. 171
Ramayana and Mahabharata Culture 135
Ramcharit Manas 146, 313
Ramkrishna Paramhansa 148, 180
Ranade, Mahadev Govind 152, 169–70
Real Western Civilisation 22
Reformation in Nineteenth Century 48
Registration Act 116
 Fight against 113
Registration Boycott 116
Renaissance and Reformation 261
Representative Democracy to Participatory Democracy 310
Resources for Industrialization 94
Revolutionaries 329
Rig Veda 132
Roe, Sir Thomas 147
Rolland, Romain 205
Roosevelt 349
Rousseau 254
Rowlatt Act 161
Roy, Raja Ram Mohun 160, 176
Royal Commission 156
Royal Society of Edinburgh 274
Rural Development Academy 367
Ruskin, John 195
Russian Revolution 162

SAARC 357
Sanatani Hindu 419
Saraswati, Dayanand 148, 176, 186
Sarvodaya 20, 323, 374, 376
 Concept of 73
Satanic Tendencies 296
Satyagraha 70, 90, 116, 264
 of South Africa 10
 Technique of 77
Satyagrahi 113
Schneider, Olive 207
Scottish Mission 171
Second Wave
 Revolution 3
 Societies 299
Second World War 50, 264, 285, 316, 339, 350
Self-Corroding Competition 20
Self-Employment 382
Self-Improvement 105
Self-Preservation 4
Self-Realization 4, 41–42, 66, 81, 88, 221, 323, 357
Self-Rule 12, 156
Sen, Keshab Chandra 160
Sensual and Spiritual Forces 86
Sepoy Mutiny 127, 166
Servants of India Society 111, 157
Shah Alam 147
Sheth Habib 119
Shraddhananda, Swami 148, 176, 180, 187
Shramic Ideology 136
Shyamji Krishnavarma 162
Sikh Gurdwara Pabandhak Committee (SGPC) 167
Simon Commission 161
Sindh-Saraswati Civilisation 130
Singh, Raja Ram Pal 364
Social Reformers 169
Socialism 43, 73
Socio-Economic
 Development 218
 Economic Systems 359
Socrates 190
Somnath Temple 143
Sorokin, Pitirim 282
Soul Force 19, 411
Spencer, Herbert 205
Spiritual Development 84, 320, 375
Spirituality 88
Stuttgart International Socialist Congress 167
Sumerian Civilisation 129
Super Law 122
Super-Consciousness 88
Surendranath College 158

Sustainable Development 297
Swadeshi 19, 415
Swaraj 15, 88, 216, 412
Symbiotic Relationship 229

Tagore, Rabindranath 153, 176
Taimur Lane 145
Teachings of Mohammad 55
Technology Policy 327
Tejpal, Gokuldas 155
Theory of
  Life 216, 221, 289
  Oceanic Circle 71
  Progress 46
  Trusteeship 74
Theosophical Society 184
Third Wave Civilisation 298, 300
Thoreau, Henry David 199
Tilak, Bal Gangadhar 149, 159, 160
Toffler, Elvin 1
Transition Zones 293
Transparency in Governance 365
Transvaal Indian Association 116
True
  Civilisation 410
  Knowledge 414
Tulsidas 146
Two-Nation Theory 174–75
Tyabji, Badruddin 258

UNDP 353
UNICEF 367
Uniqueness of Indian Civilisation 338
United Nations 43, 127, 348, 352–53
United Nations Security Council 350
Urban Management 374
Urgent Educational Reforms 368

Vaishnava Philosophy of Sri Chaitanya 160
Varnashrama System 128, 134
Vasudhaiva Kutumbakam 16, 34, 92, 136, 267
  Values of 123
Vedantic Literature 272
Vedic
  Civilisation 130–33
  Period 134
  Philosophy 137
  Religion 142
Veer Savarkar 166
Vegetarianism 190
Vegetation 65
Vidyasagar, Pandit Ishwar Chandra 176
Villagization 318
Virginia Woolf 256
Voluntary Poverty 80, 412
Vyakti Vikas 383

Wage Employment 382
War of Independence of 1857 166
Warren Hastings 147
Webb, Alfred 108
Wedderburn, Sir William 202
Western
  Civilisation 247–49, 282, 292–93, 327
  Democracies 244
  Model of Development 258
  Thought 189
Westernisation 292
WMD's 126
World Bank 42
WTO 346

Zoroastrian Nation 181
Zoroastrianism 331
Zulu Rebellion 113